FAUST

THE LIBRARY OF LIBERAL ARTS

Oskar Piest, *Founder*

Rembrandt, "Faust"   ("Night," ll. 354–807)

Johann Wolfgang von Goethe

FAUST

PART ONE & PART TWO

TRANSLATED, WITH AN INTRODUCTION AND NOTES

by Charles E. Passage

ASSOCIATE PROFESSOR OF COMPARATIVE LITERATURE,
BROOKLYN COLLEGE OF THE CITY UNIVERSITY OF NEW YORK

THE LIBRARY OF LIBERAL ARTS

published by

THE BOBBS-MERRILL COMPANY, INC.
INDIANAPOLIS

The Bobbs-Merrill Company, Inc.
4300 West 62nd Street
Indianapolis, Indiana 46268

First Edition
Fifth Printing 1975
Designed by Stefan Salter Associates

Library of Congress Catalog Card Number 65-16931
ISBN 0-672-60414-0 (pbk.)
ISBN 0-672-51078-2

Preface

To the furthest degree that the translator controlled poetic resources of the English language, the present version of Goethe's *Faust* faithfully reproduces the patterns of rhyme and versification, as well as the spirit, of the original. Long admiration for the great poem prompted the undertaking; how far success has been achieved will be for readers to judge.

The total work is here presented in one volume. This was a point of prime consideration, for the poem is an inseparable unity, and its division into two parts was an accident in the course of its sixty years of composition. At several stages Goethe put the work aside as beyond his powers of fulfillment, only to resume his efforts each time after years of postponement. The separate publication of Part One in 1808 was only one of these resting points. By no means did it betoken a finished work to which a self-contained sequel might be added later. The gist of the story is a bet and the successive attempts by Mephistopheles to win it. By the end of Part One only the first of these attempts has been made, and the reader who stops there will be in a position to divine approximately as much of the poem's scope and nature as Columbus divined of the scope and nature of the American continents after his voyages about the West Indies.

The second part of *Faust* has a reputation for difficulty, and though there is some foundation for that notion, it is greatly exaggerated. A reading public that has surmounted and enjoyed the complexities of Joyce's *Ulysses* will hardly be daunted by *Faust*. The chief difficulty is presented neither by abstruseness nor by excess of erudition, but rather by a compositional method "in blocks," the precise analogy for which is Beethoven's method of "blocking out" a symphony or sonata by themes and developments of themes. English literary works, both dramatic and narrative, tend, by contrast, to move in arithmetical progression and to be "linear" in design. To

v

meet this difficulty the translator has provided an Introduction.

Perhaps only the opening section of the Introduction properly fits that title. There the reader will find a quick summary of information regarding the actual sixteenth-century personage known as Faust, the evolution of his legend, and the principal literary treatments of that legend up to Goethe's time. Section Two traces Goethe's steps in evolving his work from the first unfinished draft, the *Urfaust* of 1773–75, through the first published *Fragment* of 1790, to the completed Part One of 1808. This evolution is interesting for its own sake; but, more importantly, many a "problem" of the final work is automatically resolved by knowledge of this developmental process. Beginning with Section Three, the Introduction assumes the form of a scene-by-scene guide to the poem, which, it is to be hoped, makes coherent reading by itself, but which may prove more useful if read piecemeal, taking each subdivision either as a preparation for the relevant portion of text or as a review.

The entire Introduction is intended to present a standard, not a particular or personal, interpretation of the work. It is essentially a condensation of the very extensive commentary given in Witkowski's edition of the German text (Leipzig: Hesse & Becker Verlag, 1929), upon which the translation was based, plus material acquired by the writer in courses taken under the late Professors Ewald Eiserhardt of the University of Rochester and Karl Viëtor of Harvard University. Occasionally a detail has been given an original interpretation, for example, the explanation of "the Mothers" in Act Two of Part Two, or the stronger insistence than usual on large portions of *Faust* as transmuted autobiography.

Much of the material in the footnotes is likewise condensed from Witkowski, although there too an occasional detail may be original, as in the case of the interpretation of the final scene in terms of Baroque ceiling paintings and apotheoses. References and allusions have been identified where regular dictionaries would not suffice. The map of Greece, in the Introduction, is a valuable graphic footnote to Acts Two and Three of Part Two.

The pictures have been adapted from Witkowski's edition. They should not be considered as illustrations in the usual sense of the term; rather, they are the pictures which, in Witkowski's opinion, were in Goethe's mind when one passage or another of *Faust* was conceived and written. Some are Goethe's own drawings; others were contained, in the form of prints or engravings, in his private collection; all could have been known by him. Limitations of space required a reduction from Witkowski's total of forty-eight, and within our limitations we have added a drawing by Goethe and substituted the painting from the ceiling of Saint Ignatius' Church for Witkowski's concluding items. Each choice was dictated by the thought of how helpful the picture would be in clarifying the poem.

In preparing the English text, the translator avoided all previous English versions except that by Anna Swanwick (1849), which was consulted for subjective reasons of *pietas*. More than once that cherished old book counseled wisely and well.

Charles E. Passage

Dansville, New York

Contents

Illustrations

Introduction

I. BACKGROUND

The Historical Faust

Shadowy but unmistakable among the lesser figures of the age of Martin Luther is the actual personage known to his contemporaries and to posterity as Faust. His given name was George (Georg or Jörg), though subsequent accounts rechristened him, for reasons unknown, as John (Johann, Johannes), and though Goethe, for reasons that may have been entirely subjective, calls him Henry (Heinrich). His last name was usually given as "Faustus," which may have been nothing more than the fairly common name "Faust" with a Latin ending, or, again, it may have been the hand-picked Latin pseudonym *faustus* or *favustus*, past participle of the verb *faveo*, and meaning "the favored one," "the lucky one." He was born around 1480 in a hamlet called Knittlingen in the southwestern corner of Germany, and died in Staufen, another town of the same region, perhaps in 1539.

At age twenty-six or thereabouts he had attracted sufficient attention as a practitioner of magic to be sought out by a cleric named Johannes Trithemius in the town of Gelnhausen. But in that month of May, 1506, Faust chose to avoid the interview. At the approach of his visitor he made haste to withdraw, sending to Trithemius only the following card:

> Magister Georgius Sabellicus, Faustus junior, fons necromanticorum, astrologus, magus secundus, chiromanticus, aeromanticus, pyromanticus, in hydra arte secundus.

Which may be translated:

> Master George Sabellicus, the younger Faustus, fountainhead of conjurers of the dead, reader in the stars, second mage, seer of the future, conjurer of air, conjurer of fire, and skilled in the art of water.

The final term refers to the medical examination of urine. The "Sabellicus" is unexplained, and it is unclear precisely who was "first" to his "second" in magic. More commonly his title is given as "Doctor" (teacher, professor), and no less a person than Luther's associate, Philipp Melanchthon, states that Faust studied magic—which *was* a university subject—at Cracow in Poland.

Ascertainable facts place Faust at different times in a long series of towns across the German-speaking territory. Early in 1507 he was in Kreuznach, boasting that he knew more alchemy than all previous alchemists put together. Later in the same year he came to the University of Heidelberg where he probably stayed for a prolonged period and whence he adopted the designation of "the Heidelberg demigod." In 1513, when next reported, he was lecturing on Homer at the University of Erfurt and enlivening his classes by producing the Homeric heroes alive before his students' eyes. Incredulous moderns have suggested the use of a magic lantern or the practice of some sort of hypnotic suggestion. He also volunteered to conjure up the lost comedies of Plautus and Terence long enough to have them copied, but, so far as is known, this opportunity was missed by his contemporaries.

Crowds flocked to him at Erfurt, not only because of his fame but because of his picturesquely riotous living. On one occasion a monk from the Franciscan monastery that adjoined the inn where he lived called on him and made an earnest effort to reform his life. To his remonstrances Faust solemnly declared that he had made a compact with the Devil, forswearing God and making himself over, body and soul, to the Evil One. The monk assured him that God's mercy was infinite and that the Franciscans could perform a Mass of purification over him. "Mass this, Mass that," Doctor Faustus replied, "the Devil has fairly kept what he promised me and therefore I intend to keep fairly what I have promised and signed away to him." Such compacts were widely credited in that epoch, but moderns puzzle as to whether this reply was tongue-in-cheek badgering of the well-meaning monk by a frank unbeliever, or whether Faustus was self-deceived. The latter is not at all impossible. Certainly Faustus made serious claims for the protection of a special supernatural guardian, his *spiritus familiaris*.

During the 1520's he seems to have resided at Wittenberg, the city which legend most commonly associates with him. This was the very center of the Protestant movement, and it was here that Luther had posted his ninety-nine theses on the cathedral door in 1517. Faustus, though known to have been in the employ of the Catholic Bishop of Bamberg as late as 1520, seems to have swum easily with the Protestant current in Wittenberg. Melanchthon, half impressed, half contemptuous of him, was fairly often in his company during these years and soberly chronicled his feats of magic. Nearby Leipzig claimed, apparently as early as 1525, that Faustus made his famous exit from one of its taverns by riding through the air on a wine cask.

During the years 1525–27 when the Imperial troops were doing battle in Italy, Faust maintained that he had effected all their victories by remote control. On the other hand, minutes of the city council of Ingolstadt for June 17, 1528 indicate that the seer was ejected from that town—after the council had cautiously exacted from him a solemn promise not to take revenge on them. Again in 1534 he drew up a list of prognostics for Philipp von Hutten on the eve of the latter's voyage of exploration to Venezuela, all of which came true, according to a letter Hutten wrote his brother in 1540. But by the time that letter was written, the "philosopher," as Hutten termed him in awe, had returned to his native region and died. His corpse, it was said, was found face down, a sure sign of his infernal associations. Nothing is known of the fate of his black dog, which, as everyone knew, was a spirit that alternated between canine form and the form of a human butler.

The Faust Legend and the *Faust Book*

Braggart and charlatan that he was, Faust nevertheless awed his contemporaries. After his death, legend, like a tireless spider, wove over him web after web of illusion that caught every stray moth of wizardry from traditional and current lore, until fact and fancy were hopelessly entangled. Within twenty-five to thirty years some unknown but enterprising individual, most likely at Wittenberg, wrote out the fabulous doings of Dr. Faustus in students' Latin and put the work into circulation. Though lost, this Latin version is mentioned in the German translation made of it in the late 1570's. A manuscript copy of the latter, dating from about 1580, is still in existence. More important, however, was the reduction of this German version to print under the following title, published by Johann Spies at Frankfurt-on-the-Main, Goethe's native city, in 1587:

> History of D[octor]. John Faust, the notorious magician and necromancer. How he sold himself to the devil for an appointed time, what strange adventures he saw in that interval, himself inventing some and living through others, until he received at last his well-deserved requital.
>
> For the greater part collected from his own posthumous writings, by way of a horrible precedent, abominable example, and sincere warning to all arrogant, inquisitive, and godless persons, and set in print.
>
> James 4:7–8. Submit yourselves therefore to God: resist the devil and he will flee from you.
>
> Cum gratia et privilegio.

This is the *Faust Book* from which all subsequent Faust stories emanate. Its popularity was enormous. After the initial printing, dated Setpember 4, four additional printings were required before the year's end, not to mention a sixth printing augmented by eight new chapters. By 1589, two years later, sixteen different printings were in circulation.

The transition from written to printed form was not made without significant changes in the matter itself. Spies, the first publisher, went to great pains to explain that his pious purpose was to offer all Christians a "frightful example" of the consequences of sin. To the hero were assigned Falstaffian gluttony, intemperate drinking, and gross lust, and it was to satisfy these appetites that he greedily compacted with the infernal spirit Mephostophiles (*sic*) for twenty-four years of self-indulgence at the price of his immortal soul.

The opening chapter presents the hero as a poor peasant's son who has been unexpectedly declared heir of a wealthy cousin in Wittenberg and brought by him to that city to study theology. At the university he displays remarkable talents but also acquires the reputation of being a bizarre character. Presently he abandons theology and devotes himself to magic and medicine. Indeed, with time, he becomes a physician skilled in the use of herbs and drugs, but the narrator hurries over this point as though embarrassed to have his subject engaged in beneficent activities. Faust's initial conjuring of devils comes early in the narrative and leads in ascending sequence to the horrendous signing of the pact with Mephostophiles. Faust demands, in exchange for his immortal soul, first food and drink which must be filched for him by the spirit from royal tables, then fine garments and shoes which must be stolen from merchants, and finally a regular weekly stipend of twenty-five Kronen for the duration of the twenty-four years. On the other hand, he does display a stalwart interest in the organization of hell and, later, in the movements of the physical universe and the creation of mankind. In one scene the hellish spirits are brought before him to satisfy his curiosity. They appear in the forms of insect vermin and torment him till he is obliged to flee his house. Three copious chapters chronicle his travels back and forth across Europe, with particular attention to the pranks played upon the Pope in Rome and upon the Sultan in Constantinople. (The *Faust Book* is fiercely anti-Catholic.) India and Cairo are also visited, as well as "the island of Caucasus," from whence Faustus glimpses Eden with its four streams.

Roughly the last third of the book is devoted to the hero's feats of magic and to his amours. On Mardi Gras, by way of a diversion for his student guests, he summons up the form of Helen of Troy. Some time later, after having spent the nineteenth and twentieth years of his contract in gross debauchery, and after having spent the twenty-second year with a merry mistress, he summons Helen anew, lives with her through the twenty-third year and begets of her a son named Justus Faustus, who is possessed of vision into the future. When Faustus subsequently dies, mother and son vanish without a trace.

The final year of the pact allows the shadow of remorse to fall upon Faustus. He lamely protests to the evil spirit that he should never have entered into the bargain, but his complainings are met only with pitiless mockery. The last night is spent at a farewell supper with his student friends, to whom he delivers a lengthy adjuration to follow Christ and live holily. Then he withdraws to his room. Between midnight and one a harrowing tempest rages, then suddenly subsides. Over its din the voice of Faustus is heard screaming in anguish for help, but the students dare not venture in until the coming of dawn. In the morning they discover the room spattered with gore. Faustus' brains are sticking to the wall. His eyes and a few teeth lie upon the floor. The corpse proper is found outside on the dunghill. The book concludes with a fresh warning to the reader to avoid the steps that conduct to such a fate.

Marlowe's *Faustus*

While popular demand for the *Faust Book* in Germany was exhausting edition after edition, the saga was making its way to England through international student channels. As early as February 28, 1588 the Stationer's Register in London recorded the printing of a ballad in the English language on the theme of Dr. Faustus, though no copy of the piece survives. On December 18, 1592, the same Stationer's Register recorded the publication of the English *Faust Book* "newly imprinted, and in convenient places imperfect matter amended." This work has survived in the printing of this date, but there is no trace of its previous edition implied by the words "newly imprinted."

Between the lost ballad of 1588 and the English free translation of the *Faust Book* in 1592, the brilliant poet-pioneer of the Elizabethan drama, Christopher Marlowe, had composed, as his second major work, the play called *The Tragicall History of the Life and Death of Doctor Faustus*. His precise source or sources cannot be identified past doubt, but the most plausible possibility is that he worked from the manuscript of the book which saw its second printing in 1592, and that he composed his play in 1589 or 1590. Nor can his exact text be determined. Of a printing announced for 1601, there is no trace. The earliest extant printing was made in 1604, eleven years after the young poet's untimely death, and this text is patently corrupted by interpolations and deletions. Longer by six hundred lines is the version published in 1616, but scholars are divided as to whether the new parts are restorations from Marlowe's manuscripts or the composition of writers known to have been hired to rework the play for a stage revival in 1602.

The crucial point of Marlowe's conception and portrayal of his hero, however, can be observed with certainty from the authentic portions of the text. By and large the poet followed the outlines of the *Faust Book* with few and inconsequential changes, making his play a loose succession of scenes that chronicle some twenty-five years. Yet from this dramatic chronicle Faustus emerges a nobler figure and more imposing by far than he ever did from the pages of the *Faust Book*. The sheer exaltation of Marlowe's poetry contributes much to this effect, yet the process involves more than fine language. A sense of grandeur now marks Faustus' purposes. There is about them the Renaissance man's avidity of interest in vast projects of exploration, construction, and invention. As Faustus contemplates *the uses to which he can put the invoked spirits*, he says:

> I'll have them read me strange philosophy
> And tell the secrets of all foreign kings;
> I'll have them wall all Germany with brass,
> And make swift Rhine circle fair Wittenberg;
> I'll have them fill the public schools with silk,
> Wherewith the students shall be bravely clad;

> I'll levy soldiers with the coin they bring,
> And chase the Prince of Parma from our land,
> And reign sole king of all our provinces;
> Yea, stranger engines for the brunt of war
> Than was the fiery keel at Antwerp's bridge,
> I'll make my servile spirits to invent.

In short, he anticipates a Napoleonic vision of empire and power and couples it furthermore with a passion for unlimited knowledge. Egocentric these desires may be, just as the desires of the German prototype were egocentric, but their scope and range put to shame the paltry demands of the hero in the German folk book. At the close of his first interview with Mephistophilis (*sic*) he states the terms on which he will make the compact and bids the spirit carry his terms forthwith to great Lucifer:

> Seeing Faustus hath incurr'd eternal death
> By desperate thoughts against Jove's deity,
> Say he surrenders up to him his soul,
> So he will spare him four-and-twenty years,
> Letting him live in all voluptuousness;
> Having thee ever to attend on me;
> To give me whatsoever I shall ask,
> To tell me whatsoever I demand,
> To slay mine enemies, and aid my friends,
> And always be obedient to my will.

And when the devil has departed on the errand to great Lucifer, Faust exclaims:

> Had I as many souls as there be stars,
> I'd give them all for Mephistophilis.
> By him I'll be great Emperor of the world,
> And make a bridge through the moving air,
> And pass the ocean with a band of men;
> I'll join the hills that bind the Afric shore,
> And make that country continent to Spain,
> And both contributory to my crown.
> The Emperor shall not live but by my leave,
> Nor any potentate in Germany.

Thus Marlowe's Faustus sells his soul for pleasure, knowledge, and power, where the hero of the popular German tale sought chiefly pleasure, and perhaps the gratification of idle curiosity. Yet both are damned. The English audiences that flocked to the original performances and to the revivals in the successive reigns of Elizabeth I, James I, and Charles I, almost to the closing of the theaters in 1642, apparently felt the retribution to be just.

Faust in the Seventeenth and Eighteenth Centuries

Of Marlowe's drama Goethe was totally unaware until middle life, long after his own *Faust* was begun, and any direct literary influence from it is out of the question. Indeed, after 1642 the play, along with the great mass of Elizabethan-Jacobean drama, was relegated to the libraries of scholars. In England it did have revivals, it is true, well into the eighteenth century, but only in the form of comic "harlequinades." Meanwhile it had been transplanted to Germany, the land of its origin, by the "English Comedians."

Troops of actors so designated, trained in London, were accustomed to travel on the continent, largely in Protestant regions, and to perform their repertories in the original English. The history of their tours is imperfectly known, but they began as early as 1585 and continued for well over a century. Before long the practice developed to translate the texts into German, or, more exactly, to make wretched German adaptations of them. In Germany it was the era of the wars of religion. Society was disorganized and audiences were crude. No permanent theater buildings had yet been erected on German soil and performances were given under improvised conditions to market-day crowds. Gross buffoonery was demanded in larger and larger doses by such spectators until it was justifiable to say that the true hero of every play, regardless of subject, was almost inevitably the stock clown, Hans Wurst. One of the plays imported by the English Comedians and adapted to fit these circumstances was Marlowe's *Faustus*, which, now in junction with elements of the native tradition,

produced the variant texts of the German Faust play. Mention
of the latter, with no reference to Marlowe, is made at various
dates throughout the seventeenth century in Germany from
1608 onward, while collateral information indicates that the
subject was a perennial favorite everywhere. Ultimately these
texts descended to the puppet theaters and came to be considered as children's fare along with Punch and Judy.

Parallel with the dramatic form, the narrative form continued its own line of development. In 1599 one Georg Rudolf
Widmann published a new *Faust Book*, vastly expanded from
the original of 1587, a veritable compendium of magician's adventures underlined by stark moralizing. A new version appeared in 1674 from the hand of J. N. Pfitzer, and still another,
by an anonymous writer, in 1725. Faust ballads were also common among the populace.

With the beginning of the eighteenth century the intellectuals of Germany began to be acutely conscious of the in-
feriority of their native literature and in particular of their
native drama. The self-appointed arbiter of such matters was
the erudite and earnest Professor Gottsched of the University
of Leipzig, from whom proceeded both the diagnosis and the
recommended remedy. The pretentious court drama which
had developed in Germany in the seventeenth century he condemned as deplorable, while the popular drama, with its everlasting intrusions by Hans Wurst, he considered beneath
contempt. The Faust farces he singled out for special condem-
nation (1730). As for the remedy, it was simply, he claimed, a
matter of ever more scrupulous imitation of the French classical models set by Corneille, Racine, Molière, and their suc-
cessors. Gottsched himself, together with his wife, labored
long and arduously at translations of works from abroad and
at some independent works, without, however, achieving a
single durably successful play.

It was the versatile and able Lessing in the next generation
who was to found the German drama, and for him the French
classics were decidedly *not* the models to be followed. Cautiously groping his way from his first small plays of 1748 and
constantly testing the dramatic theories and practices of all

nations insofar as they were accessible to him, he arrived at the conclusion, which he voiced in the famous *17th Literary Letter* of February 16, 1759, that Gottsched's "reforms" of the German theater were downright mischievous, that the spirit of Versailles drama was wholly alien to the German mentality, and that the proper model for young German playwrights should be the Englishman Shakespeare. In the face of the living Voltaire, the acknowledged dean of European letters, and in a day when the court at Versailles still established the taste for the whole continent, this was startling enough, but to cap the climax Lessing concluded the *Letter* with a dramatic scene of his own composition, in the Shakespearean manner and on a native German theme, identified as Act Two, Scene Three of his *serious* play called *Faust*.

Lessing's *Faust*

It is doubtful that Act One and the first two scenes of Act Two of this play ever existed, or any subsequent scenes or acts: the fragment presented in the *17th Literary Letter* was a trial balloon. Yet Lessing had been contemplating a serious drama on the Faust theme for three or four years and he genuinely intended to complete the work. Perhaps it is well that he did not do so and that the subject was left free and open to Goethe, for, to judge from this isolated scene and from secondhand reports of the projected work from Lessing's friends, the supreme rationalist of Germany's Age of Enlightenment was not the man to handle a theme like the Faust story. The Prologue, as reported by the friends, seems strikingly conceived in setting: a ruined cathedral at midnight with devils swarming over the desecrated sanctuary. The boastful vying of these devils to outdo each other's day's achievements in deviltry sounds less promising. The play proper, still according to the reports of the deceased author's friends, was to have begun with Faust in his study in the act of conjuring an evil spirit to explain to him the mysteries of existence. Puzzling, and quite unclear from the reports, is the

notion that the action, initiated by the real Faust, was in some
fashion to be carried through by his phantom double while
he slept. At the end of the whole work a celestial voice was
to cry:

> Exult not! Ye have not triumphed over Man and Knowl-
> edge. The deity has not given Man the noblest of im-
> pulses only to make him eternally miserable. What ye saw
> and now fancy ye possess, was nothing but a phantom!

Thus Lessing's projected work was to have been another of
his many "rescues," polemical pieces in defense of unjustly
maligned men and of lost causes—in this case a "rescue" of
Faust, whom a superstitious age had represented as damned
because he dared the quest for higher knowledge. Such a
concept of a *saved* Faust was a protest against the dark
medieval age (the sixteenth century was reckoned as medieval
by Germans in Lessing's day—which, in fact, it was in Germany)
and a militant cry for the new Enlightenment of which Lessing was the principal champion in Germany. To his fellow
optimist, Goethe, the concept provided a suggestion fraught
with immense meaning.

II. EARLY DEVELOPMENT OF

Goethe's *Faust* in its completed form is a work unique in
world literature, consisting of 12,111 lines of verse unequally
divided into two parts, "The First Part of the Tragedy," 4,612
lines plus one short scene in prose, and "The Second Part of
the Tragedy, in five acts," 7,499 lines. The word "tragedy" is
used in the extended sense of a work of high seriousness and
its more common meanings are quite inappropriate, just as the
word "comedy" requires a special interpretation in Dante's
title, *The Divine Comedy*. All lines are assigned to speakers,
as in a play, though a continuous performance of the whole
from beginning to end is unthinkable. Part One has, it is true,
been a standard item in the repertories of Germany and of

other nations for more than a century and a half in one adaptation or another, but adroit condensations of Part Two have had limited success on the rare occasions when they have been attempted. Nothing, however, could be further from the truth than to imagine that the author, who was intimately associated with the practical theater through most of his long life, did not know how to frame a stage-worthy play or that he had lost the knack of it. Elaborate performances in installment form, somewhat in the manner of the Wagnerian Ring cycle of operas, are both desirable and possible, and such performances would reveal a theatrical treasure of incomparable riches. In the last analysis, however, Goethe's *Faust* is best taken as a dramatic poem for reading, one of the rare successes in that genre. The poem was a life work, begun when Goethe was in his twenties and completed when he was past eighty years of age. Not that he worked at it consistently. The significant compositional dates are 1773–75, 1788–90, 1797–1801, and 1825–31, and that simple statement of chronology provides the key to most of the "problems" of *Faust*. The work evolved with him, and in a real sense it represents the poetical distillation of his immensely full and varied life.

It will be useful to establish at the outset what Goethe's *Faust* is *not*. It is not a historical play about a picturesque sixteenth century and the actual Doctor Faustus. It is not a fanciful dramatization of the *Faust Book* of 1587. It is not a poetic drama about an ennobled character based on Doctor Faustus, as Marlowe's play had been. It is not a patriotic resuscitation of the popular Faust farces. It is not a fulfillment of Lessing's plan for a "Faust rescue," for Goethe did not come to know of that plan until after 1786. It is not a sentimental play about the unsmooth course of love between Faust and Margaret. Most emphatically, it is not a poem about sin and redemption. And finally, it is not a philosophical tract in poetic form. Just what it *is* will emerge most clearly from an account of the evolution of the work, stage by stage.

Goethe, born in 1749 of wealthy, upper-bourgeois parents in the west German city of Frankfurt on the Main, was familiar with the popular Faust stories and plays from childhood.

That this should be so was as inevitable as a modern American's awareness of the characters in the comic strips, for the old folk books were the equivalent of the comic strips, just as the puppet plays were the animated cartoons of the era. At age sixteen the handsome and gifted youth, who had written verses since he was five years old and whose education at home had been extraordinarily broad, left his native city to journey eastwards across Germany to the ultrafashionable and Francophile University of Leipzig. There he was taken aback to discover that his Frankfurt dialect made his speech sound insular, that his excellent wardrobe was not precisely what fashion required, and that salon ladies found him charming though a trifle lacking in polish. Assiduously he set about remedying these defects and was at great pains to become a dapper beau in the best Gallicizing manner. The poetry he composed in the three years of stay in this environment is largely debonair badinage deftly turned in a prescribed idiom and actually much more pleasing than Goethe, in the subsequent phases of his development, was inclined to admit. At the end of the third Leipzig year, 1768, an illness, the exact nature of which is not known, took him home in an invalid state. Two curious experiences accompanied his lengthy convalescence: first, a kind of mystical religious crisis intensified to some degree by the companionship of a lady friend of the family who was a Pietist, the continental sect parallel to the English Quakers; and second, rather extensive readings in works of cabalists and alchemists of the preceding three centuries. With the return to health came a return to his naturally robust temperament, and in 1770 he again left home to study law at the University of Strasbourg. As chance had it, there came to that very medical faculty the brilliant young philosopher, Herder, for the purpose of undergoing a delicate operation on his eyes. In the months that followed, in the enforced seclusion of Herder's darkened rooms, young Goethe made frequent visits to the convalescent, listening in wonder to the ideas which the extraordinary young man propounded. The result was that from those interviews Goethe emerged a new man and a changed artist. The ideas themselves had already found expression in print a few years previously and formed the philosophical basis for a school of literature known to historians as "Storm and Stress" (*Sturm und Drang*).

The Storm and Stress writers were young men who in the early 1770's shared certain ideas and ideals, were in most cases acquainted personally with one another, but never formed any closely cohesive or localized group. Politically they were radicals, libertarians, adhering to an ill-defined concept of "freedom" derived from readings of the eighteenth-century French *philosophes*, who were laying the ideological foundations for the American and French Revolutions. Most particularly they were adherents of Rousseau, sharing his distrust of a society which corrupted man's naturally good nature. Artistically they were also radicals, in full career of revolt against the aristocratic principles of the French classical drama. They frequently invoked the name of Shakespeare, and being themselves primarily dramatists, sought to write in the Shakespearean way. Actually they knew Shakespeare most imperfectly through the medium of a few mediocre prose translations, but fancied that they grasped his method of composition, which was to write untrammeled by any rules, passionately, at the spontaneous dictation of the heart. Their own plays were indeed defiant of such rules as the self-disciplined and selectively delimiting French classical writers had followed, and they were indeed passionate and violent. Unrestrained outbursts of emotion fill their pages. Their very language is marked by a mannered vehemence. Speeches teem with adjectives denoting intensity, verbs are selected for their intensity rather than for their precision of meaning, exclamation points hail upon their writing, and breathless haste sometimes precludes enunciation of the personal pronouns. Yet, though these plays have long since passed to scholarly limbo, these young authors were grasping for themes and procedures that would satisfy the aesthetic needs of the middle classes from which they themselves came and which were then assuming prominent position in the social order of Germany. For heroes, mature men of power attracted their attention, as well as reckless youthful idealists. They sensed the picturesqueness of historical settings. Among their heroines one type recurs with striking frequency, that of "the sinlessly sinning girl," the girl whose affections are so spontaneously pure that she yields herself to love with no thought of consequences and who comes to tragic events thereby. Their villains are cold rationalists, bigots, foes of the innocent heart. And these youthful enthusiasts sought to live like the heroes of their plays.

Both their art and their lives came to grief, and the Storm and Stress movement was of understandably short duration. Its aesthetically valid products are all works of Goethe, whose native genius transcended the anarchy of their prescriptions while giving expression to their emotional fervor. Goethe's fame was made by his Storm and Stress play *Götz von Berlichingen* (1773), a prose drama about the last of the independent knights of the sixteenth century, the fifty-six scenes of which, far from disintegrating into dramatic chaos, blend into a smoothly flowing work that anticipates the methods of the film. Some of his finest lyric poems are Storm and Stress poems. *Werther,* the short novel which swiftly expanded his fame from Germany to all of Europe and America (1774), is a combination of Storm and Stress elements with the traditions of the English and French sentimental novel. Other plays about typically Storm and Stress heroes—Prometheus, Mohammed, Julius Caesar—were planned but never realized. The highest achievement of all was the series of scenes for a Faust drama at which he worked from 1773 to 1775 without bringing them to a conclusion.

The *Urfaust*

The sequence of scenes that constitutes the original version of Goethe's *Faust,* the so-called *Urfaust,* was unquestionably conceived as a workable stage play in the idiom of the Storm and Stress writers. The period was the sixteenth century, as in *Götz von Berlichingen.* The language medium allowed a "Shakespearean" alternation between prose and verse; the prose was marked by typical Storm and Stress vehemence; the verse was an ingenious adaptation of the authentic sixteenth-century *Knittelvers* of the old Mastersinger Hans Sachs, a rugged line of four strong accents and an indeterminate number of unaccented syllables, rhymed in couplets or quatrains. The hero was a heaven-stormer who, exasperated by the insufficiency of human knowledge, conjured spirits to ascertain the meaning of life. The heroine was a "sinlessly sinning girl" who gave herself in utter love to Faust only to be abandoned by him and to bear his child in shame and desperate grief. The individual scenes were conceived as intensely lighted episodes, each complete in itself, with intermediate events left to the reader to discern by inference. The text ran to 1,441 lines of verse plus three prose scenes, something less than normal play length.

The contents of this first draft of *Faust* need now to be scrutinized in some detail.

Abruptly, without prologue of any kind, the *Urfaust* begins with a scene marked "Night," which with very slight change now stands as lines 354–605 of the completed text, just after the "Prologue in Heaven." The philosopher, alone in his study, complains bitterly of a life devoted to books which in the end have proved devoid of vital knowledge. An impulse seizes him to quit his cramped academic cell and flee to the bosom of Nature, but his eye catches the mystic tome of Nostradamus, which he opens at random to the sign of the macrocosm. Under the spell of that sign he views the physical universe, the starry sky, and is overwhelmed by its grandeur. Essentially this is a viewing in poetic form of the deistic concept of the cosmos: mathematically perfect, awesomely vast, sublimely ordered, but indifferent to, indeed unaware of, man. Sadly Faust turns away. "O what a sight!" he cries, "A sight, but nothing more!" Where will he find that which will respond to the needs of the human heart? He leafs through the mystic book, comes to the sign of the Earth Spirit—Nature—and invokes the sign. From the thickened air emerges a countenance so ghastly he has not the courage to behold it. He has invoked "Nature red in tooth and claw," the order where every living thing devours every other living thing, the jungle will that dictates the stalking of prey as the sole means of sustaining life. A startlingly unsentimental concept for a Rousseauist, but realistic, as well as anticipatory of Goethe-the-scientist of later years. In famous rhymes the Spirit identifies itself as the force that works

> in the hum of the loom of time
> Weaving the living raiment of godhead sublime.

Which is to say that Goethe has here juxtaposed the pantheistic view of Nature with the deistic view of a few lines before. Awesomely the Spirit rebuffs Faust's presumption in invoking it and declares to the philosopher,

> You are like the spirit you comprehend,
> Not me!

and disappears. But if man is alien to the cosmic order and alien to Nature as well, what *is* the spirit to which he must have recourse, the "spirit he is like"? The question is left unanswered, for just at that moment Faust is interrupted by the entrance of his pedantic little visitor, Wagner. The dialogue which ensues is a comic inversion of the scene just ended, with Wagner's wide-eyed awe of book-learning set over against Faust's rejection of books.

Without identification of any kind, the second scene announces: "Enter Mephistopheles in a dressing gown and large peruke. A Student." With moderate revision this passage now stands as lines 1868–2050 of *Faust,* Part One, where it now gives Faust time to ready himself for his journey with Mephisto. Moreover, in the later version Mephistopheles dons Faust's academic garb (not a dressing gown) and impersonates him in order to give highly ironic counsel to the bewildered Freshman about how life is to be lived at a university. In the *Urfaust* there is no mention of Faust at all, nor is there any link whatsoever with the foregoing scene. Nor is there any link whatsoever with the following scene, which introduces Faust and Mephistopheles into the famous tavern of Auerbach in Leipzig.

The "Auerbach's Tavern" scene is given in the *Urfaust* in prose, violent and powerful Storm and Stress prose, and the famous trick with the duped students drinking wines drawn from dry table wood and the exit of the visitors on a flying wine cask are both the work of Faust, as in the old *Faust Book*, not of Mephistopheles.

A scene called "Highway," only four lines in length, which follows next in the *Urfaust,* has been omitted, with no loss, from the final version.

Then, at line 457 of the *Urfaust* text there begins the sequence of episodes with Margaret. Missing are (*a*) most of the "Forest and Cavern" scene, in which Margaret does not appear anyway, (*b*) the entire "Walpurgis Night," in which Margaret appears only as a vision glimpsed from afar, and (*c*) all of Valentine's role except his initial soliloquy. The final scene in the prison is given in prose. (It is strongly reminiscent of the mad Ophelia, and Goethe read *Hamlet* in prose translation.) Otherwise the entire Margaret story is word-for-word complete in the *Urfaust,* with all its dramatic power, superb lyrics, and great beauty. The *Urfaust* ends precisely where the present Part One ends.

Had Goethe died in 1775 and left the *Urfaust* unsupported by any further lines, we should all be mightily puzzled to know what the author was driving at. Poetically the several scenes are splendid, and their brilliant originality against the background of German literature up to 1775 is breath-taking. But in what way do they hang together? And what is their relation to the Faust story? For the entire Margaret sequence, more than two-thirds of the total, is quite without foundation in the Faust tradition. Even Mephistopheles' counseling of the Freshman (Scene Two) is largely Goethe's own wry comment on education at the University of Leipzig, so that strictly speaking, only the initial spirit-conjuring scene and the prank in Auerbach's tavern are "Faust matter." The line of thought, we are compelled to deduce, must have gone something like this: Faust, having studied long only to despair of ultimate knowledge, invoked the spirits—scanned the major philosophies—only to be frustrated anew; whereupon, forswearing all contemplative thought, he plunged into the midst of living, and, as his first experience away from books, he fell in love; once involved with human beings and no longer a spectator (philosopher), he discovered that human involvements have their own dynamic, and in this instance the dynamic closed with disaster for the beloved girl.

Assuming that such *was* Goethe's line of thought, it is not at all strange that Faust's first vital experience after plunging headlong into living should be the experience of love. But why should the love end in disaster for the beloved girl? Or, if it does so because the poetic mood is a tragic one, why should the hero simply walk away at the inconclusive conclusion? The pattern of the typical Storm and Stress heroine was familiar to Goethe, and Margaret fits the pattern, but it is unthinkable that anything so profoundly moving as the Margaret story should be no more than a tale concocted to fit a current literary fashion, especially when the theme caused the author to swerve so far from the Faust subject. One scans in vain the well documented biography of Goethe for some experience of which these scenes would be the poetic transcript. There is, to be sure, the Frankfurt beloved, necessarily associated with Goethe's teen-age years, whom he names "Gretchen" in his autobiography, but her story, at least as reported by the self-biographer in his middle years, seems remote indeed from that of her famous namesake. Nor does any other known love experience of Goethe prior to 1773 parallel the events in *Faust*. Here is a "problem" more mysterious by far than the imagined difficulties of Part Two.

The age of the hero of the *Urfaust* poses a further question, to which, happily, the answer is known. The text implies that Faust the conjurer and Faust the wooer of Margaret are one and the same man. Now, a Margaret aged more than twenty is most unlikely; she is most probably to be thought of as aged sixteen or seventeen. These things being so, we are confronted with two unpleasing alternatives: either Faust is appropriately youthful as Margaret's lover, in which case he seems to have despaired of ultimate knowledge rather too soon; or he is appropriately aged for erudition and despair, but too old for

Margaret—and the text of the love scenes certainly demands equally youthful lovers.

In 1788, when next Goethe turned his attention to his neglected composition, he remedied this matter by creating the scene called "Witch's Kitchen," in which the older, conjuring Faust is magically rejuvenated to become Faust the wooer. The opening speech of that scene makes him inquire whether the witch's potions can "take thirty years off from his flesh and bone." Assuming twenty as the age best suited to the lover of Margaret, we deduce that Goethe, at least in 1788, conceived of his hero as aged approximately fifty at the play's beginning.

The tiny four-line scene marked "Highway" serves in the *Urfaust* to indicate that Faust and Mephistopheles are travelers. So far as the text shows, their destination is the (unnamed) city where Margaret lives. Only from the completed *Faust* can it be clearly seen that the pair are indeed travelers *through life,* inseparable explorers, with antithetical purposes, of the whole of man's estate. Yet the germ of this concept was present from the very start of Goethe's plan.

But under what terms do they travel thus together? Even assuming that Goethe had simply not found the time to compose a suitable entrance scene for Mephistopheles, the one indispensable component of any Faust story was the compact between the hero and the Devil, and the total absence of any hint of a compact in this case makes all else difficult of assessment.

And finally, what happened to Faust after Margaret's death? The play ends nowhere, the harmonies are all unresolved.

No one was more clearly aware than Goethe that his work lacked both a statement of purpose and a proper conclusion, and that it was far from ready for publication. *He never published it.* His manuscript, which, it is known, consisted of loose and dog-eared sheets of miscellaneous paper, is lost. But after taking up residence in Weimar in 1775, Goethe from time to time gave oral readings of his works, and on one such occasion he lent those sheets to Miss Luise von Göchhausen, a lady in waiting at the court, so that she might prepare a fair copy for

public reading. The transcript in her handwriting was discovered among the papers of a descendant by Professor Erich
Schmidt, who published it in 1886, fifty-four years after
Goethe's death and more than a century after its composition.

Faust. Ein Fragment (1790)

Following his arrival in Weimar late in 1775 and his assumption of high functions at the ducal court, a major spiritual
change came over Goethe. His social radicalism—never so
pronounced as among the lesser Storm and Stress writers—
..ed away in the fair climate of aristocracy, so that a significant segment of nineteenth-century opinion held that he
deserted the cause of the common man and sold himself to the
caste of privilege-by-birth. The accusation is unfair. After five
years of living on the keen razor's edge of emotion both as
man and as artist, an inevitable reaction set in. He craved
spiritual calm after storms of passion, and a manhood self-
possessed after an emotionally reckless youth. Socially he
found—or thought he found—these elements in a hierarchized
society under the gaze of the benevolent, intelligent young
Duke. Emotionally he found—or thought he found—them in
his devoted attachment to the serene and noble-souled Char-
lotte von Stein. Artistically he found—or thought he found—
them in the spirit of ancient Greece, which, as the critic
Winckelmann had taught, was characterized by "noble simplicity and tranquil grandeur." He came to abhor his youthful "excesses" and the literary products that had grown out of
them. For the rest of his life he was to denounce any person
or work of art which seemed to him to be marked with the
qualities of Storm and Stress. His own writing henceforth
should, he promised himself, deal with lofty themes and breathe
a timeless harmony of soul. Thus emerged Goethe the "classi-
cist." Eventually he was to discover that his "classicism," as
man and as artist, was also a phase, and not the final one, of
his complex existence. But so long as he adhered to the prin-

ciple that art *should* be characterized by "noble simplicity and tranquil grandeur," what was to become of his projected Storm and Stress play, *Faust?*

For about eleven years he simply ignored the work. Moreover, he was engulfed with official duties that sapped his creative energy, as he, with increasing alarm, observed. In 1786, just at the point when the published information about Lessing's plan for *Faust* became available, he took leave, literally overnight, of his Weimar associates and set out for Italy and the two-year sojourn which he was to term his "rebirth." The yellowed manuscript sheets of the *Urfaust* were in his luggage. In the sunny gardens of the Villa Borghese in Rome he composed the "Witch's Kitchen," the most "northern" and "Germanic" of scenes. Returning to Weimar in 1788, he felt full of creative energy and simultaneously his strict concept of classicism was beginning to undergo revision. Yet he could not bring his *Faust* to completion. With the frustrated sense that it was too good to throw away but too beset with problems to warrant further effort, he published it in the set of his collected works of 1790 under the title of *Faust. Ein Fragment,* and hoped thereby to wash his hands of it.

The *Fragment,* longer and clearer than the *Urfaust,* begins at the same point. Faust conjures from the book of Nostradamus, is rebuffed by the Earth Spirit, and is comically interrupted by Wagner. The second scene, however, as suspension points show, begins in the midst of a discussion between Faust and Mephistopheles on the matter of the compact between them (lines 1770–1867 of the completed Part One), though the compact proper is still not spelled out. It is also made clear that the two are about to start immediately upon a journey. While Faust retires to prepare for departure the Freshman comes a-knocking, and Mephisto, impersonating Faust, holds him with the sardonic colloquy which by itself had constituted Scene Two of the *Urfaust.* When the awed Freshman has withdrawn and Faust returns ready for travel, Mephistopheles speaks the all-important line: "We'll see the small world first, and then the great one too." From the newly added passages in the *Fragment* two crucial points are clarified: (1)

what Faust wants from Mephistopheles is to experience "all that is the lot of human kind" (lines 1770–71); and (2) Mephistopheles intends to begin the tour in search of such experience within the smaller circles of an individual's personal acquaintances ("the small world"), and then to continue it in the sphere of national and international affairs ("the great world").

Directly thereafter the travelers appear in "Auerbach's Tavern," where the former prose has yielded to verse and where the pranks are played by Mephistopheles now rather than by Faust. We infer that the visit to Auerbach's is an attempt by Mephisto to provide some of that universal experience which Faust craves. We also infer that the attempt is a total failure. Faust, upon entering, says, "Good evening, gentlemen," and some time later says, "I would prefer to go away." These are his only words in the course of the entire scene. Just *why* the students' cavorting and carousing at Auerbach's holds no interest for Faust—as it most certainly *had* in the *Urfaust*—is not quite clear. In the *Fragment* the isolated scene makes Faust behave like a priggish intellectual at an off-color night club.

The totally new scene which follows, "Witch's Kitchen," effects Faust's transformation from an older man into an ardent youth at the instigation of Mephistopheles, who apparently feels that only ardent youths are capable of vivid experience. The vision which Faust beholds in the magic mirror is a vision, not of Margaret, but of woman as the object of sensual desire.

Directly after his transformation Faust is seen on a city street impertinently accosting the modest Margaret, and therewith, as in the *Urfaust,* the Margaret sequence unfolds scene by scene. A curious additional piece entitled "Forest and Cavern" occurs between the conversation of the girls at the public well and the pathetic prayer of Margaret before the *Mater dolorosa.* Immediately following the latter comes the powerful "Cathedral" scene, with which the *Fragment* unexpectedly ends. Valentine does not appear at all; Faust does not writhe with remorse before Mephisto and demand his help to save the condemned Margaret; Margaret's fate is left without the tragic conclusion in the prison. Those final passages Goethe found impossible to square with any concept that declared for art's "tranquil grandeur," and he simply left them out.

Thus, in the *Fragment*, the purpose and direction of Goethe's work begin to become discernible, though by no means crystal clear. Faust, in despair, summons spirits to do his bidding and apparently makes arrangements with one of them, Mephistopheles, to gain direct experience of life instead of vicarious experience through study, to gain, as he says, direct experience of "all that is the lot of human kind"—whatever that may mean. The stipulations of the compact are still unmade. The identity of Mephistopheles is still undefined. Faust is transformed into a youth and lives through the direct experience of love with Margaret, but the fate of *both* lovers is uncertain. The harmonies are left more awkwardly unresolved than ever. Of the promised visit to "the great world" there is no mention or hint at all.

Goethe's *Faust*

AN INTERPRETIVE GUIDE

III. FIRST PART OF THE TRAGEDY (1808)

Neither the public nor Goethe's own artistic conscience would permit *Faust* to be dismissed with the 1790 *Fragment*. In 1794 a fateful chance brought him together with Schiller, the maturing author who was now Professor of History at the University of Jena. For years Goethe had avoided acquaintance with him, thinking of him always as the youthful dramatist who had had the temerity and wrong-headedness to revive the Storm and Stress movement in the early 1780's just when it was dying out naturally. He was surprised to learn that Schiller too had abandoned his Storm and Stress notions and now held views of art not too unlike his own. The friendship ripened, and of its many incalculably beneficial results, one was Schiller's successful urging of Goethe to resume work on *Faust*. Clustered about the years 1800–1801 are the dates of composition for most of the sections that round out Part One, though the serious planning for them goes back to 1797. Still Goethe delayed publication, hoping always to extend the work beyond the point of Margaret's death. But the extension resisted his efforts. Not until 1808, three years after Schiller's death, did the completed Part One appear in print.

In its final form *Faust*, Part One, opens with a DEDICATORY POEM, composed probably on June 24, 1797, in which the author recalls the vanished friends and associations that attended the undertaking of his poem twenty-five years before. It is a private poem having no direct bearing on the work itself. The PROLOGUE IN THE THEATER (composed 1802) is likewise without direct bearing on *Faust*, though it characterizes in general terms the types of ingredients that shall go into the proposed drama. The PROLOGUE IN HEAVEN (composed after 1800) affiliates the work with the old Faust plays, which often began with a prologue in which supernatural figures appeared. The three pieces together form a monumental approach to the poem proper.

For the PROLOGUE IN HEAVEN the Book of Job obviously formed the model. Dramatically it is a deliberately archaizing scene utilizing medieval morality-play techniques overlaid with fine Goethean lyric. The three archangels open the scene, Raphael speaking of the order of the cosmos, Gabriel of the alternation of order and disorder, Michael, the warrior angel, of the storms and conflicts; speaking in unison the three restate the principle of ultimate order. Before the countenance of the Lord then steps Mephistopheles, as in an old morality play, and belittles creation and mankind. Faust is mentioned, as on another occasion Job, as a model creature, and, as on the previous occasion, the Devil is given free rein to tempt this man. The Biblical setting has misled more than one reader to assume a Christian poem, whereas Goethe's purpose was the purely literary one of conferring scope and grandeur to his theme by setting the total work against a cosmic background and of announcing that Faust is to be seen as the representative of mankind.

With the scene marked NIGHT the poem proper opens and in lines essentially unchanged since 1773 the old philosopher cries execration upon the limitations of human knowledge and upon futile books. He invokes the sign of the macrocosm and contemplates the sublime order of the starry universe, only to realize that it is "a sight, but nothing more." He invokes amoral Nature, the Earth Spirit, only to be told that he has nothing in common with the spirit of growth, destruction, and regrowth that weaves infinitely at the loom of time. The pedantic Wagner interrupts with his comic awe of book-learning. Then comes new material. At line 606 the philosopher resumes his soliloquy and continues it for 201 lines. Somberly brooding now, Faust reviews his aspirations and the Earth Spirit's rebuff, and arrives at the conclusion that ultimate knowledge is to be found only beyond death. He will seek it there. He takes down an ancient phial of poison and with intense anticipation of final knowing is in the act of raising it to his lips when Easter bells and the song of angels proclaiming the miracle of vernal hope recall him to life. Their song is of resurrection, the poetic symbol for which, and only the poetic symbol, is the Resurrection.

From the night of somber brooding and frustration the poem and the "new-born" Faust emerge into the sunlit Easter day of the following scene, OUTSIDE THE CITY GATE (composed February 1801). With Goethe's typical architectonic method the scene is constructed on a fivefold pattern: (1) the "newborn" populace streams out of the dreary confines of a walled medieval town (such as Goethe had known in his youth), rejoicing in the fresh countryside; (2) Faust speaks his glorious lines about the springtime and Wagner voices his disdain of undignified merrymaking; (3) a peasant ballad is sung about a shepherd and his lass, and subtly the mood of the scene is shifted from major to minor as the ballad brings the lovers to an unhappy end; the mood is further darkened by the old peasant's recalling of the days of the plague; (4) as sunset approaches, Faust speaks the magnificent lines—symmetrical counterpart of his lines on spring—in which he would follow the sun beyond its setting; these are the poetic declaration of "the Faustian spirit"; (5) as twilight deepens around the homing travelers Faust sees the dog that circles closer and closer around him and Wagner, creating a closing spiral of fire as he runs.

An immensely long double scene, both parts of which are separately entitled STUDY ROOM, follows. Faust has brought the stray dog home and its restless growlings disturb the sweet tranquillity of the lamplit room. Before the open page of John's Gospel Faust muses over the meaning of "In the beginning was the Word." The source from which life proceeds, he feels, cannot be "Word." (To make his point, Goethe took the popular sense and ignored the wider meaning of the Greek *logos*.) Nor can the source of life be "Mind"; nor "Power." It must be "Deed." Faust, the contemporary of Luther, then translates, "In the beginning was the Deed." Goethe held that anything less than committed action was incapable of imparting life or of being life; contemplation, passive understanding without personal engagement—philosophy, in short—was sterile. At the word "Deed" the restless dog becomes obstreperous. Sensing that a spirit must be concealed there in canine form, Faust conjures it, and after some humorously horrendous evasions and Protean changes of form the spirit does indeed emerge as Mephistopheles in the guise of a traveling scholar, i.e., of a rogue-adventurer, nominally a student making the rounds of the universities.

Challenged to reveal his name, a revelation which commits a spirit to the power of the knower, he again evades his questioner. He is, he says,

> Part of that Force which would
> Do evil ever yet forever works the good.

He is also "the Spirit that constantly denies." According to the established Faust tradition Mephistopheles was a subordinate devil, one of many, in Lucifer's dominion. While adopting the story motif, Goethe goes on to make him the representative of evil as he conceived evil, that is, as the Spirit of Negation, the opposite of "Deed." Thus Mephistopheles is the sum total of all non-doing: laziness, procrastination, indifference, self-indulgence, cynicism, idle mockery, frivolity, doubt, self-doubt, disinterest, purposeless activity, wanton destructiveness of nature and beast and man. It was further Goethe's belief that all action was the effect of the juxtaposition of positive and negative poles. Around either pole standing in isolation, there was void; but set the two poles opposite each other, and there would be interaction. Faust is the representative of mankind, and, as such, wills positively to do; Mephistopheles, the Spirit of Negation, wills not to do; the two in juxtaposition produce interaction. In this sense Mephistopheles is "Part of that Force which would do evil ever [non-doing] yet forever works the good" ("doing," "Deed"). The implementation of this concept will occupy all the rest of the twelve-thousand-line poem.

But Mephistopheles is no mere philosophical allegory

foisted upon a whimsical character out of folklore. He is Goethe's most notable created figure and is highly complex. Half fancifully, it is true, the changes are rung upon his associations within Christian legend and folk belief. More significantly he is the representative of eighteenth-century Rationalism and derives more than one trait from the common notions of a satanically heartless Voltaire. He is a polished courtier, a salon gallant and a backstairs gallant, immensely intelligent, witty, ribald, on occasion appallingly obscene, devastatingly sarcastic, lascivious, a self-styled realist, a master of stratagems, pranks, and deceits, a bold-faced raconteur with a special gift for impromptu tall tales, a flatterer as insincere as he is successful; in brief, he is Voltairean mind totally devoid of Rousseauistic heart. He was originally conceived as the villain of a Storm and Stress play. He is other things still, based upon the author's subjective evaluations of living persons, and finally, as is less commonly acknowledged, he is a phase of Goethe's own personality. In his own way, Mephistopheles too is a "fragment of a great confession."

The text, which suddenly at line 1335 became dense, lightens again at line 1385, when the Devil admits he may not leave as he wishes because he is prevented by the laws of magic: a pentagram on the threshold, imperfectly drawn, hinders him. The difficulty is resolved and he goes. But before he goes he summons spirits to sing Faust to sleep. Their voluptuous melody, the syntactically difficult lines 1447–1505, is an invocation to all the senses. A modern would term it a convulsion of the libido. Faust is being sensually softened for the blow to come.

Older Faust stories had always had two meetings with Mephistopheles with an interval between them to allow the infernal agent to report to Lucifer before submitting the contract to Faust for signature. Possibly this tradition may account for the exit and immediate reentry of Mephistopheles and for the division of the scene into two parts with identical captions. Once he does return, however, the poem becomes intensely serious with the definition of the compact.

Resplendent in Spanish court costume of the sixteenth century Mephistopheles reenters, thus conveying to a German

Protestant audience intimations of the Mediterranean Latin world, of the Inquisition and Counter Reformation, and of Madrid as the capital of the German empire. He has come, he announces, to show Faust what life is. To which Faust replies, in a tone of bitter negation which can only delight the Spirit of Negation, that all costumes are indifferent to him. "I am too old," he says,

> merely to play,
> Too young to be without desire.
> What can the world give me?

And answering his own question he cries:

> Renounce,
> Renounce shalt thou, thou shalt renounce!

That is the everlasting watchword; with horror he beholds each dawn which will bring to fulfillment not one wish, not one; the god enthroned within his heart is an impotent god; existence is a misery. The Goethe who wrote these lines was himself now fifty years of age and no longer a youth of twenty imagining the thoughts of a fifty-year-old. Faust pours out his frustration and despair, then, galled by Mephisto's sly taunts, bursts forth with a curse upon all things normally prized in life. He curses aspiration, careers, fame, wife, child, wealth, wine, love, and, in mounting crescendo, hope, and faith, and above all else, patience. Mephistopheles could not do better himself, this is his very creed. He offers Faust his services for life.

In the old *Faust Book* the hero bartered his Christian soul for twenty-four years of pleasure. In Christopher Marlowe's play the same price was paid for an equal period of pleasure, knowledge, and power. In Goethe's poem the price is vague, the word "soul" does not occur, and Mephistopheles' ambiguous proposal offers service "here" in return for Faust's service to *him* when they meet again "yonder." The time span is, by implication, the duration of Faust's life. But Faust's demands are utterly unlike those of the *Faust Book* and utterly unlike Marlowe's. Specifically (lines 1678–87), he asks for food that does *not* satisfy, gold that can *not* be kept in a purse, a game at which one can *not* win, a girl who in the very moment of nestling close to him will flirt with another, honor that flashes like a meteor and is gone, fruit that rots before it is picked, and trees that leaf out anew each day. All of which is a metaphorical way of saying that he desires that which excites aspiration but, by leaving it ever unsatisfied, forces one to aspire anew. "If ever," cries Faust,

> If ever I lie down upon a bed of ease,
> Then let that be my final end!
> If you can cozen me with lies
> Into a self-complacency,
> Or can beguile with pleasures you devise,
> Let that day be the last for me!
> This bet I offer!

"Done!" says Mephistopheles, feeling that this is no challenge at all. Then Faust voices the key words of the contract:

> If I to any moment say:
> Linger on! You are so fair!

That is, if ever he will find any state of being such that he would wish it to be prolonged, then Mephistopheles may have him. To the Devil's pedantic quibbling about a contract signed in blood, Faust counters that there need be no fear of breach of promise, for all bridges have been burned behind him. At line 1750 he adds:

> Let us now sate our ardent passion
> In depths of sensuality!
> Let miracles of every fashion
> Be brought in veils of mystery!
> Let us plunge in the flood of time and chance,
> Into the tide of circumstance!
> Let grief and gratification,
> Success and frustration
> Spell one another as they can;
> Restless doing is the only way for man.

And when Mephisto replies frivolously, Faust urges further:

> But I tell you there is no talk of joy.
> I vow myself to frenzy, agonies of gratification,

> Enamored hatred, quickening frustration.
> Cured of the will to knowledge now, my mind
> And heart shall be closed to no sorrow any more.

And here in the middle of a sentence (line 1770), the text, with perfect clarity now, continues with the lines which, prefixed by suspension points, opened Scene Two of the 1790 *Fragment:*

> And all that is the lot of human kind
> I want to feel down to my senses' core,
> Grasp with my mind their worst things and their best,
> Heap all their joys and troubles on my breast,
> And thus my self to their selves' limits to extend,
> And like them perish foundering at the end.

Mephistopheles blithely consents to all of this, construing it merely as frenetic desire for diversion, for aimless adventuring and philandering, for dabbling in futile hobbies—his own cherished bustle of activity accomplishing nothing. Never does he believe that Faust means to enter body and soul into purposeful commitments for great ends. Much less does he believe that Faust, upon achieving any such great end, or nearing achievement, means to abandon the pursuit in order to throw himself into a different stream of action, and so on and on as long as life lasts. What Faust really asks is the chance to live several great lives in one lifetime, to be, as it were, in succession, the equivalents of Leonardo, Pericles, Shakespeare, and Alexander, willingly undergoing the griefs and trials of each, conceiving in ecstasy the aspirations of each, battling the foes of each, achieving the deeds of each. For his aspiration implies several *great* lives; there is no thought, for instance, of living through the life of a quiet clerk or of an Eskimo "just to see what it would be like." Nor is there any thought of repeating great lives of the past, such as Leonardo's or Alexander's; Faust means to act in the here and now, uniquely, by uncharted trails.

The reader tends to sympathize with Mephisto's incredulity at this point—but Goethe's poem is not yet done.

At line 1834 Mephistopheles announces immediate activation of the compact and the setting forth upon a journey.

Faust retires to ready himself. As the knock of the Freshman is heard, the Devil dons Faust's gown and poses as the philosopher. With the entrance of the Freshman (line 1868) there is held that old sardonic colloquy which by itself constituted Scene Two of the *Urfaust*. Truly Part One had flowered since 1775! And when the Freshman has gone and Faust, journey-ready now, comes back and asks whither they are bound, Mephistopheles says: "We'll see the small world first, and then the great one too."

By the end of this double scene marked "Study Room," Goethe has brought positive man into an alliance with negative Devil. The Yea and the Nay, inseparable until death, shall traverse the sphere of man's estate, first the intimate, then the general sphere. The man means to engage in the pursuit of great ideals, the Devil means that nothing shall be accomplished. But, unwittingly, according to Goethe's notion, the Spirit of Negation is a catalyst that precipitates "Deed," and from his constant will to work "evil" (non-doing) will inevitably come "good" (doing, "Deed.")

The travelers are next seen in AUERBACH'S TAVERN in Leipzig among the carousing students, where it is now clear from the foregoing that Faust holds aloof, not from any prudishness among low company, but because there is no positive life here. Mephistopheles, however, is quite literally in his element: noise, violent talk, political satire, wittily obscene repartee, malicious pranks, and total purposelessness. We now perceive that the miscalculating Devil has brought Faust to Auerbach's in the pathetically absurd belief that this place will offer the excited renouncer of books just the sort of existence he had been talking about when making the compact.

Once out of Auerbach's, Mephistopheles must with a comical gesture have stood and scratched his head and wondered why on earth the visit had not been a success. He must have concluded that if jolly bar friends would not satisfy his client, then recourse must be had to a lusty wench. Then he must have grimaced at the recollection of Faust's age, and then he must have hit upon the device of making his client into a youth. On precisely this errand, with precisely this purpose, he brings Faust next to the hearth of his old crony the witch, for the process of rejuvenation is a variety of creative act, and, Negative Principle that he is, Mephistopheles cannot perform the feat himself.

While ostensibly serving the story purpose of making Faust into a young man, the scene WITCH'S KITCHEN is a self-contained and wonderful poem, somewhat overly terse in expression, based on the interlocking themes of "chaos" and "sensuality." The stage directions offer a "chaotic" interior; the apelike creatures that tend the hearth talk gibberish; they play with a glass sphere, the world, which they clumsily break, and they likewise carelessly break a crown which they offer to Mephistopheles, both guarded political references to the chaos of the recent Terror in France; when the witch returns, furious at finding her hearth neglected, she scatters a chaos of flame over menials and visitors alike, whereat Mephistopheles smashes everything in sight, and then, gloating at his destructive triumph, sits enthroned in a sort of Voltairean armchair, with a brush-duster for scepter, king over chaos. All these are symbols for the chaos that antedated the formed world of the Greeks and for the tohu vabohu of Genesis—which was contemporaneous with the fall of the rebel angels who became the devils. The rejuvenation of Faust involves—and this point becomes clearer by analogy with the "Dark Gallery" scene of Part Two—a descent into Chaos, the source of life, to bring forth the new form, the new body, which is to be his. Doubtless that realm is conceived partly in terms of Lucretius' chaos of falling atoms, partly in terms of a life force, the "warm principle," the amoral drive of sensuality. Even before his transformation Faust is seized with wonder at the vision of woman as the object of desire, when he beholds her in the witch's magic mirror. The cold lust of Mephistopheles is expressed, conversely, in the startling obscenity of exposing his "coat of arms" to the witch and his brutal hilarity thereat. When the hocus-pocus is done and Faust has the hot drink in him, Mephistopheles leads him away to sweat profusely and to discover how Cupid will rise and hop about. Faust's last words before leaving the witch's establishment are a plea for one last glance into the magic mirror: his very next words, in the following scene, will be the impudent offer of his arm to Margaret as she is walking down the street.

At this point the completed Part One of 1808 recapitulates with little essential change the sixteen impressionistic scenes that constituted the Margaret story in 1775. The last three, which had been excluded from the 1790 *Fragment,* are here restored, though the final "Prison" scene has now been converted from prose to verse. One scene, fourth-last of the *Urfaust* and entitled "Night," had consisted of a single monologue for Valentine and a dialogue between a taunting Mephistopheles and a Faust torn between desire and remorse. The 1790 *Fragment,* which omitted Valentine altogether, contained this dialogue in altered form under the title of "Forest and Cavern" and placed it near the end of the sequence, between "At the Well" and Margaret's prayer to the *Mater dolorosa,* where it stood oddly as an isolated Faust-scene amid Margaret-scenes. For the completed Part One Goethe prepared another interpolation only remotely involving Margaret, the famous "Walpurgis Night." With two such half-alien scenes to deal with now, he placed them with approximate symmetry at roughly the one-third stage and the two-thirds stage of the Margaret sequence. Both scenes offer problems.

FOREST AND CAVERN presents Faust in a remote woodland retreat whither he has fled lest his passion lead him to seduce his beloved girl. With psychological improbability, Goethe assigns him a blank-verse monologue of idyllic contentment amid a kind of benevolent Wordsworthian Nature. Mephistopheles then enters to him with such keen mockery of his philosophizing that Faust is compelled to admit that passion still urges him toward consummation of desire. He returns to Margaret and the seduction ensues. Up to this point the text has consistently referred to Faust's beloved as Margaret (Margarete); henceforth she will usually, though not consistently, be called Gretchen (Margret-chen, "poor Margaret"). The scene reestablishes some connection with Faust as philosopher, but aesthetically it is problematical in its context.

With the WALPURGIS NIGHT (composed 1797; 1800–1801) the matter is quite different. Gretchen's tragedy has already come about: her mother is dead and her brother slain, both on her account, and Faust, with Valentine's murder to his charge, has been obliged to abandon her. Faust himself, in enforced absence and with desire magnified by anguish, plunges, with terrifying psychological appropriateness, into the maelstrom of debauchery of which the witches' revel on the mountaintop is the superb symbol.

The time is April 30th, eve of May Day, the spring equivalent of autumnal Hallowe'en, and by church calendar designation St. Walpurga's day. The place is the Brocken or Blocksberg, highest peak of the Harz mountains in central Germany and traditional site of the gathering of evil spirits to do homage to Satan, who thrones there on that night in the guise of a goat. Up wild paths, by the light of a dull red moon, climb Faust and Mephistopheles, arduously toiling on their way toward the unholy revel. Symbolically this is the world beyond the limits of conventional society. A will-o'-the-wisp, whose course is naturally an unstable drifting, is enlisted to be their guide. Suddenly the air is loud with the upward flight of witches (whores), some on broomsticks, some on sows' backs, screeching obscenities as they ride. Witchmasters (whoremasters), likewise riding, heckle them. A half-witch laments that she cannot reach the height. When our travelers arrive at the center of activity they find a variety of (negative) persons present: a General, a Prime Minister, a Parvenu, a thwarted Author; a Huckster Witch sells appurtenances of romance: daggers, poison, seductive gifts, dueling swords—all secondhand. Presently Faust is seen dancing with a naked young witch; Mephisto dances with an ugly old one, with whom he exchanges lines of startling obscenity. Goethe's grand poetic concept falters for a moment when, under the Greek name of Proktophantasmist (Buttocks-mage), Friedrich Nicolai, the tedious champion of outmoded Rationalism, is introduced to undergo some ribald satire. Only a small circle of readers in 1808 understood all the allusions in this passage. Strongly the poetry wells up again as Faust beholds a red mouse leap out of the mouth of his dancing partner—a fine symbol for vile language from a beautiful woman—and directly thereafter beholds a vision of Gretchen afar, the thin red line of blood from the headsman's ax encircling her throat. Affection mournfully mixed with pangs of conscience is recalled in the depths of debauchery. Mephistopheles hastily steers Faust away toward a theater where dilettantes are about to begin a play entitled THE WALPURGIS NIGHT'S DREAM, or OBERON'S AND TITANIA'S GOLDEN WEDDING.

This "play" is no play at all, but a series of forty-four satirical quatrains assigned to almost as many speakers and dealing with personal antagonisms of the author. A refrain pronounced by the accompanying orchestra of insects or its conductor marks out four major groups of speakers, and a final stanza for the same insect orchestra, *pianissimo,* indicates the wisping away of the insubstantial pageant on the breezes of dawn. An indispensable weight of footnotes keeps the airy fabric of this "Dream" from floating quite as lightly as the author must have intended it to float and from being a wholly successful attempt at creating in words the equivalent of a musical scherzo in the manner of the Romantic composers. Though the whole passage has a certain intrinsic interest about it, it was a dubious decision of the author to substitute this Intermezzo for the originally planned orgiastic finale of the "Walpurgis Night," and the first-time reader of *Faust* may well postpone its slow decipherment.

More closely integrated with the Gretchen story is the entire new scene that creates the character of Valentine, who had appeared in the *Urfaust* as the speaker of a single twenty-five-line monologue and who had not appeared at all in the 1790 *Fragment.* Not only is he a memorable figure fixed by this single scene, but his murder at the hands of Faust and Mephistopheles provides the woefully needed motivation for Faust's abandonment of Gretchen in her hour of distress. Scrutinizing readers will wonder at the absence of such motivation in the story before 1800. The presence of the twenty-five-line monologue in the *Urfaust* suggests that Goethe planned this motivating scene early, but its execution is puzzlingly late. Stylistically the new lines blend imperceptibly with their context of twenty-five years earlier.

It has been mentioned that Part One converted the prose of the final scene, DUNGEON, into verse. What is remarkable is that the scene GLOOMY DAY, which contains Faust's agony of remorse at Gretchen's fate, has been left in its original Storm and Stress prose, the only prose in the completed work. The anomaly raises the question of whether some private meaning so charged this passage with emotion that Goethe felt unable to rework it, or whether we have here only a creative artist's caprice.

The Margaret section, comprising now eighteen scenes in the final version, as opposed to sixteen in the *Urfaust* and only thirteen in the *Fragment,* forms a memorable block of writing. Its limpid lyrics have inspired composers and baffled translators for more than a century, while its simple but powerful drama has maintained it as a stage work in perennial favor. With an economy of means that compels admiration, Goethe has created living characters: Valentine, the simple soldier; Frau Martha Schwerdtlein, who, with a fascinating Mephisto as vis-à-vis, provides the best comedy scenes in comedy-poor German literature; and Gretchen, whose joy and grief unfailingly touch the heart. For so relatively short a tale, however, there seems to be an excess of catastrophe, for the conclusion involves the beheading of Gretchen for the drowning of her child after her mother and brother have already been sacrificed to her brief happiness. One arresting detail learned only in 1886 upon the discovery of the *Urfaust* indicates that the original intention had been to heighten the sorrow still further. There the stage directions for the "Cathedral" scene read: "Obsequies of Gretchen's mother. Gretchen (and) all relatives. . . ." No published version of the text retained these words, which intensify the anguish almost beyond what the poem will bear.

Yet, for all its excellence, the Gretchen sequence is not the core of Goethe's work as many people, all too many people, still imagine. Even in a cut stage version it must be apparent that the connection is tenuous between the love story and the passages that come before Gretchen's first entrance *at line 2605*. The ending is quite as apparently unresolved: the rather ineffectual hero vanishes, leaving his beloved to her fate. At best he is hapless; at worst he is a cad unworthy of so much suffering for his sake. Given the somber circumstances, he cannot be dismissed with poetic justice done, as Eugene Onegin is dismissed. As the French critic Taine remarked, Faust seems to have summoned supernatural assistance in order to seduce a poor bourgeoise, a feat rather commonly managed with merely human means. From the analysis of the compact scene it is evident that the Gretchen story must be an episode, that the mighty substructure there laid down must have been designed to support more than this fragile edifice. Moreover, the text has left its own terms unfulfilled, for the promise was to see "the small world first, and then the great one too." Thus far there has not been the slightest hint of a visit to the great world. Hence we are thrown back upon the hypothesis advanced for the *Urfaust*, which ended at the same point: the hero, forswearing books and passive knowledge, plunged into the midst of life and there fell in love. This is valid, though it remains quite as puzzling as before why the experience should lead to such profound catastrophe for the beloved girl. In short, *Faust*, Part One, like the first act of *Hamlet*, is only the impressive *beginning* of a work.

Be it said forthwith that the Gretchen story constitutes the first of the "lives" that Faust leads in fulfillment of his compact with Mephistopheles, that it is the experience within the "small world," and that further experiences in the "great world" will occupy Part Two. Goethe's poem is only fairly launched.

IV. SECOND PART OF THE TRAGEDY

It was Goethe's intention in 1797, when he began the serious planning for the completion of Part One, to carry his poem forward into Part Two, and thus in 1800 a scene-fragment entitled "Helena" was composed even before sections which have been reviewed here. Recalling that one of the major motifs of the old *Faust Book* was the hero's evocation of Helen of Troy, fairest of women, to be his paramour, Goethe was clearly harking back to the story line of the venerable source work. But inspiration faltered and other projects eclipsed his plans. In addition to his creative work—completion of *Faust,* Part One, his novel *The Elective Affinities,* and his extensive autobiography—and in addition to his official duties, he was now preoccupied with scientific experiment in various fields, particularly physics, and with the writing of his long treatise on light. The formidable combination prevented all work on *Faust,* Part Two. Vastly altered in plan, the Helena scene is next heard of in 1825, when, largely at the urging of his secretary Eckermann, Goethe turned his mind to serious planning for Part Two. It was published separately in 1827 under the misleading title of *Helena. Classic-Romantic Phantasmagoria. Interlude to Faust,* and eventually came to be part of Act Three of Part Two. Working from his seventy-sixth year to his eighty-second year, Goethe moved backwards from the *Helena* fragment to the beginning of Part Two, whence he advanced until he had filled in the gap, and then proceeded to the close, though not consistently in the order in which the scenes finally stand. The last composition was on Act Four in midsummer of 1831, and, with that last lacuna accounted for, the manuscript was sealed at the end of August and left with instructions that it be published only after the author's death. Goethe felt too old to face the aesthetic and ideological arguments which he felt sure would confront the work. Death came the following spring, and within that same year, 1832, *Faust, The Second Part of the Tragedy, in Five Acts* appeared in print.

The transition from Part One to Part Two offered difficulties to the author as it still offers difficulties to the reader, not only in the altered techniques that require a new reading approach, but in ascertaining the status of the hero. Part One with its grandiose opening and by the succession of scenes up through the signing of the compact had established Faust as a typical —though by no means average—man, a representative of the race of man, whereas in the Gretchen sequence he had become, as it were, a private individual with a specific destiny. The problem now was to bring him back to his first status. Yet, fresh from the closing lines of Part One, the reader sees Faust with four deaths on his conscience. How was such a man to continue his "lives" with so grave a burden upon him? The opening scene of Part Two, marked PLEASANT REGION, addresses itself to this question.

To Faust, lying weary but restless upon a flowery meadow, comes Ariel, Shakespeare's Ariel, who summons elfin spirits to sing him to sleep and to

> Assuage the frantic turmoil of his soul,
> Withdraw the fiery bitter arrows of remorse,
> From horror lived through, purge and make him whole.

In four stanzas corresponding to the four watches of the night, the elfin spirits perform the function of healing the wounded heart and conferring new life. Faust wakes to behold the sunrise with its mighty music (the lines paraphrase the concept of Guido Reni's painting, "Aurora"), and to sense amid awe-inspiring Alpine heights a fresh impulse of vitality. The beautifully conceived lines offer no hint as to the time lapse since the end of Part One, nor is there any reference to the specific events that occasioned those fiery bitter arrows. Weakest, probably, of all the links in the *Faust* chain, this passage is meant to stand for the healing effects of time and distance, and in a sense corresponds to the reality of Goethe's total break with his Storm and Stress past and his beginning of a completely new life in Weimar after 1775.

The autobiographical parallel is significant, for Part Two, far from being a succession of hypothetical lives imagined for his hero by a young, or even by a middle-aged poet, is a poetical distillation of the several lives that Goethe himself crowded into his own existence and viewed by him now in retrospect from his latter seventies. In more ways than one, *Faust,* Part Two, is the continuation in a new medium of the autobiography, which had chronicled only the first twenty-six years of Goethe's life and which had had for its theme the formation of an artist.

As to the concept of his poem, Goethe had now grasped the fact that he was not writing a work about an alter ego named Faust, but a work about a pair of antithetical alter egos, Faust *and* Mephistopheles, the Yea and the Nay, who must forever be together, like Don Quixote and Sancho Panza, like Don Giovanni and Leporello. As to technique, Goethe will use many of the devices and motifs, including the vastly widened range of verse forms, made current by the two generations of German Romantic writers who occupied the forefront of German letters from 1795 to about 1825, and to whom Goethe had been in the first instance friendly but distant, and in the second instance more or less hostile. Their Catholicizing and medievalizing he will use in his own fashion without relinquishing his own ideal of Hellas, which they contemned. Indeed he will transcend both the doctrines of the Romantics and his own "classicism" to make a unique work, which, under the rubric of "Acts," will present the experiences of his pair of heroes in the form of grandiose Platonic myths in pseudo-dramatic guise.

Act One

When Goethe arrived at Weimar on November 7, 1775 he was somewhat dubious about remaining there very long, but by January 22, 1776 he was writing his friend Merck that he was "involved in all the court and political affairs." By April he received Weimar citizenship. In June he was made Legation Councilor with a seat and a vote in the Privy Council of the duchy. In July he accompanied the Duke to the Ilmenau mines where he acted as overseer for their reopening. Long before the first anniversary of his arrival he felt fully established in his new home, which, indeed, except for journeys, he was never again to leave. Through the fifty-eight years of his residence there his duties and functions were to be amazingly varied. Essentially he was Prime Minister of the government, personal advisor to the Duke. In addition he was, at different times, overseer of natural resources, director of scientific and art institutions, Rector (President) of the University of Jena, supervisor of military recruitment; for long years he was director of the ducal theater. Ennobled in 1782 and henceforth Johann Wolfgang *von* Goethe, he became a member of the aristocratic society which made up the ducal court, and as such was entrusted with supervision of court festivities, especially when royalty visited from abroad. His duties on those occasions corresponded to those of the Elizabethan Master of the Revels. He was, in short, foremost citizen in a sizeable sector of the "great world."

The composite of all these experiences forms the subject matter of Act One, where Faust and Mephistopheles come to the court of a purely fictional and unnamed Emperor. Originally Goethe had intended to specify Holy Roman Emperor Maximilian I, 1493–1519, who figured in the Faust legends, but in line with his preference for generalization he determined for the mythlike court where historical fact would not hamper the exposition of his theme. The era, like that of *Faust*, Part One, is nominally the sixteenth century.

The act proper opens with the second scene, marked IMPERIAL PALACE. The archaic word *Pfalz*, rather than either of the modern German words for palace, *Palast* or *Schloss*, sets the mythical tone. The Emperor, enthroned, is hearing the complaints presented by his Privy Council, but his frivolous first action before hearing business is to name the new visitor at court, Mephistopheles, as his jester. Willingly the Devil accepts the post from which negative criticism may be leveled with impunity, where irresponsibility is expected, and from which he may easily gain the ear of the pleasure-loving monarch. The reports of the Ministers are all gloomy. In no department of the empire, not even in the Imperial household, is there order or sufficiency. Pained but ineffectual, the Em-

peror hears all of them and then turns for advice to Mephistopheles. The latter first oozes courtier's flattery, then declares
that all these problems have a single cause, the lack of money.
He suggests that the soil abounds in buried treasure and hints
that he knows how to come by it, but when questioned he
changes the subject and, through the court astrologer, pro-
poses entertainments and diversions. Impulsively the Emperor
proclaims carnival for the time remaining until Lent and dis-
misses the Council.

The long third scene, SPACIOUS HALL, is a Mardi Gras
masquerade, elaborate as some of those festivities which
Goethe supervised in his capacity of "Master of the Revels"
(for example, the great masquerade of 1818 in honor of the
Empress of Russia's visit), but it is introduced here to present
in symbolic form a panorama of society and the state. A Herald
identifies the allegorical figures as they enter, and each speaks
verses appropriate to the roles. The total scene shows four
major groups of maskers:

1. To the music of mandolins Garden Girls first appear, followed by personified aspects of feminine charm. Flowers
themselves and sellers of flowers, they set out their wares under trellised arbors. Gardeners, their masculine counterparts,
join them and sell ripe fruit alongside the flowers. A Mother
and Daughter present the tireless searchers for a suitable husband. The lower occupations are shown by fishermen, fowlers,
and a Woodcutter, while a Parasite and a Drunkard indicate
nonworkers of society.

Transition to the next group is effected by mere stage directions when a band of poet types is brought in, all too enthusiastic to let any one of their number speak. The Graveyard
Poets flirt with a freshly risen vampire with whom they immediately withdraw.

2. Figures from Greek mythology enter next, whom the
Herald welcomes after the Graveyard Poets. (Goethe's classical
preferences are felt.) The Graces, the Fates, and the Furies—
these last in a striking variation from their usual natures—
make way in turn for a charade-tableau of the State: an elephant (the State itself) and four ladies. Walking in chains at

either side of the mighty beast are Lady Fear (excessive anxiety) and Lady Hope (fatuous optimism); mounted on its neck and guiding is Lady Prudence, and on its back is Lady Victory with outspread wings.

Carping at the tableau and its significance is Mephistopheles in the double mask, one face front, one face back, of Zoilo-Thersites (Zoilus, the Greek critic who belittled Homer; Thersites, the foul-mouthed ruffian of the *Iliad*). When the Herald berates him for his carping and strikes him with his staff, Mephistopheles suddenly undergoes a startling transformation, then vanishes, one half of him escaping as a slithering adder, the other half as a swooping bat.

3. Through the masking crowd the Herald discerns the approach of a chariot that mysteriously bears its occupants, two men and a boy, through the mass of people without displacing anyone. At line 5504 the Herald confesses he cannot identify the radiant Boy Charioteer in robes of purple and gold nor the tableau as a whole. The Boy Charioteer identifies himself (line 5573) as "Lavishness and Poetry," while he names his master, who is Faust, as Plutus, god of wealth. As Faust-Plutus praises the gifts of his Charioteer, than which, he says, he owns none so precious himself, the Boy distributes jewels among the grasping crowd. The jewels, however, prove worthless in vulgar hands; pearls become crawling beetles, and gems turn into butterflies that escape. The gaunt third figure in the chariot is Mephistopheles as a personification of Greed, antithesis of Plutus and the Charioteer. A second vehicle apparently brings up an attendant chorus of dragons, traditional guardians of buried treasure, who obey Faust's directions to unload a huge treasure chest. Faust touches the chest with the Herald's wand, which in his hands is a magic wand, and the chest opens to disclose masses of gold. The Boy Charioteer is at this point dismissed. The dialogue between Faust and the Boy Charioteer takes on surprising and poignant meaning if the reader will take Faust-Plutus as Goethe the Prime Minister of Weimar and the Boy Charioteer as Goethe the poet hindered in his creative work by his official and social duties. Faust's wand glows and holds the greedy crowd at bay. In

the free moment Mephistopheles steps up to the chest and kneads the masses of gold into a phallus, which he offers to the ladies.

4. Just then choruses of Fauns and Satyrs, Gnomes from the mines, and Giants who call themselves "wild men" from the Harz Mountains, announce the arrival of Great Pan. In this last role the Emperor now comes in and is at once escorted to the chest of gold. In his eagerness to behold the treasure this money-starved monarch thrusts his face too close to the magic stuff. His beard takes fire, then his whole costume, and presently "Pan-ic" seizes the whole assembly. But the fire is only magic fire and under Faust's control. The whole episode has been devised by him, partly as a warning to the ruler, partly to impress upon him how potent a magician he has at court. The scene closes with magically induced rain descending upon the flames and confusion.

With this illusion of fire the text is brought close to the old *Faust Book* once more, for in that work Dr. Faustus produced streams of fire amid the court of the Sultan in Constantinople. As for the near burning of the Emperor, Goethe very likely had in mind a favorite history book of his youth which narrated the horrendous event of 1394 at the court of Charles VI of France (which Poe altered to make the still more gruesome tale *Hop-Frog*), when the King joined six of his courtiers in making themselves up with pitch and straw as "wild men" and mystifying the rest of the company; the Duc d'Orléans, annoyed at one of the "wild men" for too familiar teasing of the Duchesse de Berry, seized a torch and held it to the masker's face, only to discover, as the disguise burst into flame, that it was the King; the six companions rushed to save Charles and four were burned to death in the rescue.

The fourth scene, PLEASURE GARDEN, brings Faust and Mephistopheles before the Emperor next morning to crave his pardon for the illusory trick. The genial Emperor grants immediate forgiveness and goes on naively to tell how thrilling he found the whole event. Mephistopheles is skillfully exploiting the monarch's vanity and gullibility when the various Ministers enter to announce an overnight miracle. The whole country is full of joy and movement, everyone is spending the new paper money which has just appeared in circulation. To the astonished Emperor the Treasurer explains that His Majesty himself wrought this miracle, for, the night before, when he was dressed as Great Pan, he had signed a master note from which thousands of copies have been run off during the night. The notes are redeemable in the gold which lies in the Emperor's soil—as yet unmined. The delighted sovereign assures Faust and Mephistopheles of his particular favor and on the spot makes gifts to his servants of anything they desire.

In economic matters Goethe was decidedly conservative. In his own lifetime he had witnessed the collapse of paper money values from lack of support by gold both in the French First Republic and in the Germanies during the Napoleonic wars. More specifically, the device of wealth-for-all was modeled on the paper money scheme initiated (in all good faith) by John Law in Paris in 1716 just after the death of Louis XIV. In the present case Mephistopheles is, of course, the instigator, for he had nothing but scorn for that spiritual wealth of poetry dispensed by Faust-Plutus and the Boy Charioteer, and in his own "realistic" way has seen to it that "the people shall have what they want." The economic disaster that resulted from John Law's plan was postponed until 1721; the total disaster that will result from this "negative" device of Mephisto will not be revealed until Act Four. Goethe liked to hold partly elaborated themes in suspension while other matter was developed.

In the more or less regular alternation of "easy" and "difficult" scenes in this act, the next scene, DARK GALLERY, broaches the new and complex subject of the conjuring of Helen of Troy. The Emperor, now much impressed at Faust's powers, has expressed the desire that Helen and Paris be summoned from the ancient dead to appear at his court, and Faust, to Mephisto's dismay, has agreed to fetch them. Grudgingly "the Father of All Hindrances" admits there *is* a way by which the alien heathen folk of old may be approached. Faust must descend to "the Mothers" by untrodden paths into the realm of emptiness. When Faust replies that "there is a smell of witch's kitchen in the air," the clue is given that it is to Chaos, to the realm of pre-being, that he must go, thence to "re-produce" Helen and Paris from the "matrices"—"Mothers" —from which they originally proceeded. Goethe here combines the notion of Chaos with his own variant of the Platonic "forms" or "Ideas," those perfect matrices in heaven from which all earthly things are turned out in imperfect copies. In another sense Faust descends into the untrodden realms of mind toward the "idea" of Helen, who is the symbol of beauty as the Greeks conceived beauty, and his journey parallels the clarification of a concept by the human intelligence. Into Faust's hands the negative Devil entrusts a small, cold, metal key, which, immediately it is touched by the positive man, glows, grows, and flashes with light: static information becomes infused with insight. With an oblique reference to the Copernican universe, Mephistopheles bids Faust *descend*, though, as he says, he might equally well bid him *rise*, for Chaos is outward from any point on the spherical earth; mind, too, is in any direction. Faust stamps his foot as bidden, and "descends," while the Devil remarks: "I'm curious too to see if he gets back."

The interval of Faust's journey is filled by the purely comic scene, BRIGHTLY LIGHTED ROOMS, in which Mephistopheles gives one lady a recipe for removing freckles, stamps devilishness into the lame foot of a lady who longs to dance, explains a love philter to a third lady, and to a frustrated adolescent page gives the counsel that *older* women will welcome his advances.

HALL OF KNIGHTS brings the monarch and his court together in an improvised theater, with amusing quibbles about taste in stage *décors*. In priestly garments Faust emerges before the spectators' view and, following Mephisto's previously given directions, solemnly evokes the shades of Paris and of Helen of Troy. Impervious to the "Greek drama" and its spiritual wealth, the audience has eyes only for the beauty of the performers. Skittish women languish at sight of Paris, the men resent his youthful comeliness; the men ogle Helen greedily, while the women find her a hussy and are outraged at her voluptuous waking of her lover with a kiss. A scholar doubts her authenticity and prefers "the text." As for Faust, he perceives Helen's "meaning" and is ravished at the sight of her. His ravishment corresponds to Goethe's own belated ravishment at discovering the wonders of ancient Greek art and literature but it is expressed in terms of Plato's doctrine of the perception of beauty, that divine madness described in the *Phaedrus*. It can be no coincidence that the *Phaedrus* also contains a celebrated myth of a chariot, horses of good and evil, and a charioteer. Putting these facts together with the notion of "the Mothers," which derives from passages in the *Phaedo* and the *Republic,* one gets the impression that attentive readings in Plato underlie considerable portions of Act One. In his "divine madness" Faust advances upon the pair of beautiful ghosts, concepts of ancient Greek beauty, seizes Helen for himself, and turns the key against Paris. An explosion rocks the hall, the spirits vanish, Faust falls to the floor, and, as Mephistopheles loads him onto his shoulder and carries him away, the act ends.

Properly speaking, Act One is not a closed and self-contained sequence about the experience of Faust and Mephistopheles in "the great world," though that is its central assignment, but rather the initiation of two or three themes for the whole of Part Two. It has been mentioned that the effects of Mephisto's economic policies will not be known until Act Four. The last three scenes, transitional in nature, prepare the vast developments of the Helen theme in Acts Two and Three. Yet these scenes are properly placed, for Helen, as the symbol of beauty in the Greek sense, is but a more specific kind of that spiritual wealth of poetry which Faust-Plutus and his Boy Charioteer offered the Emperor's realm in the masquerade, much as Goethe the poet-missionary offered the spiritual wealth of poetry to Weimar and Germany. Not once, but twice, Faust makes "positive" gifts to this government, and each time he meets with no more than a moment of idly curious interest from the people. In the first instance they preferred Mephisto's quick and easy riches-for-everybody, and in the second instance they ignored his "Greek drama" to look, as in a vaudeville, only to the physical charms of the players.

Dramatically, the action omits Faust so frequently that he seems hardly more than a caller at this court, rather than the equivalent of Goethe in the latter's active and many-sided participation in the affairs of Weimar. Yet it is probable that Goethe at the ducal court in 1775 and long thereafter conceived of himself first and foremost as a poet on the lofty mission of spiritual elevation of a court and country. Metrically, Act One has considerable variety, but a certain uniform tone of language obscures this fact, like a long piece of music without change of key. The poetical devices seem a bit forced. The masquerade is perhaps less effective to a modern than it was to Goethe and his contemporaries, who knew such entertainments at first hand. Or perhaps it is that romantic notions of masquerade balls set us off on the wrong foot. Certain it is that there is an excess of charade-like guessing of identities and purposes in that long scene. With Mephistopheles at his versatile best throughout, and with much that is humorous and striking, a certain academic quality besets the act, and economics resists induction into poetry. Nor does Goethe's Tory attitude on this subject lend conviction to the wisdom purveyed. Thus Act One stands, interesting, resourceful, skillful, ingenious in the extreme, fascinating in parts—and cold. Act Two is quite another matter.

Act Two

It is poetically just that one of Goethe's first missions in the employ of the Duke of Weimar should have been to supervise the reopening of the mines at Ilmenau in the summer of 1776. The occasion roused his interest in geology, a subject to which he later devoted careful attention for long years. Eventually he was, after much reading of and listening to professional geologists, to write articles himself as contributions to that body of knowledge, just as he was to study, listen, and eventually to write original research papers on botany, on zoology, on comparative anatomy, and, above all, on physics. All aspects of the natural sciences concerned him, and he lived in that era before intense specialization, when intellectuals could still cope with the major works being written in the various departments of science. Indeed, the French *philosophes* had made the pursuit fashionable, as they had made laboratories respectable, which once had been dark kitchens for cranks with dubious purposes. It was the era, moreover, when the earth sciences, as opposed to mathematics, astronomy, and some aspects of physics, were just advancing beyond the combined knowledge of Greece and the Renaissance. Greek theory was still a valid basis for scientific thinking, and Goethe, steeped in the classics, was keenly aware of Greek theory. He was quite as much aware of the contemporary theories that conflicted with the Greeks and with each other. As an amateur, but a talented amateur and a participating one, he lived through the tremendous intellectual experience of the birth of modern science. The poetic distillation of that experience, combined with its implications for education—both in the usual sense and in the closer etymological sense of "evolution" ("leading forth," *educere*)—form the basis for Act Two. Overlaid upon this abstract basis will be the search for Helen, the Greek ideal of beauty; but the finding of Helen will be postponed until Act Three, and the search, meanwhile, will be for Greece, Helen's country.

Faust, still unconscious from the shock of beholding Helen, is brought at the opening of Act Two on the shoulders of Mephistopheles to that same GOTHIC ROOM in which the *Urfaust* had first presented him as a rebel against dead learning. The cobwebs have multiplied, and the ink is dry in the inkwell, but the room is unchanged; the very quill once dipped in blood to sign the compact with the Devil is still upon the desk. A frightened servant answers Mephistopheles' imperious ring, and from him we learn that Wagner, who works assiduously in the adjoining laboratory, has preserved the room intact against the day of Faust's return. When the timid fellow has retired, a second surprised inhabitant discovers the open door and enters. It is the Freshman whom once Mephisto had badgered while waiting for Faust to make ready for their journey into the world. The Freshman, now termed Bacca-laureus, recognizes his former counselor and truculently now advances upon him to denounce him and his advice of old. Erudition, he has discovered, is a garment spun over naked ignorance by fraudulent professors. The Devil readily admits the truth of this, but says that greenhorns cannot face the truth but must discover life by bitter experience; the professor, for all that he avoids speaking the truth, is still no fool. The Baccalaureus, however, is bitter at time wasted on untruth in education, and in a passionate outburst praises youth as the only commodity worth having. It was an aged Goethe now who assigned to him the lines:

While we [young people] were winning half the world, what can
You say you've done? You've nodded, drowsed, and spun
Your dreams, and weighed and pondered plan on plan.
Old age indeed is a cold fever spent
In a capricious frost of discontent.
Once past the age of thirty, men
Already are as good as dead;
It would be best to shoot you then.

That the lines are further a witty persiflage of some actual words of the philosopher Fichte—Professor at the University of Jena, of which Goethe was Rector—is indicated by the part-ing speech of the Baccalaureus, which is a devastatingly ironic summary of Fichtean philosophy.

Directly by its contents, and indirectly by its raising of thrilling echoes from the earlier half of Part One, the scene evokes anew the quest for ultimate knowledge. What is even more arresting is the poetic intensity of the lines, especially after the cool detachment that marked most of Act One.

At the beginning of the second scene, LABORATORY, patient, pedantic Wagner is discovered at his alchemist's hearth engrossed in the creation of a miniature human being, a "homunculus," in a retort. Mephistopheles in jovial mood drops in for a call and is informed of the gravity of the ex-periment in progress. The very presence of Mephisto alters the situation. Whereas Wagner's previous attempts had ended in failure, there is now a flash of light in the clouded retort, and when the glass clears, there is the homunculus alive inside it. The "little man" would be visible to an audience only as a light inside a test tube, for he is without substance, the mere "idea" of a man, though the chemicals in the retort have apparently assumed the crinkled, half-a-walnut-meat appearance of an extracted brain. Straight off the tiny creature speaks in rhymed pentameters, first to bid his daddy, Wagner, clasp him to his bosom, though not so hard as to break the containing glass, and then to greet Mephistopheles as a kind of co-father.

That the negative Devil should have assisted in a creative act seems at first out of character, but the fact is that his intellect has served as a catalyst for the plodding Wagner. As Goethe knew from alchemical readings as long ago as his convalescence of 1768, homunculi are restlessly active immediately after creation, as well as fully intelligenced and clairvoyant. Mephistopheles, who, with the knowledge of the ages, is aware of this, puts Homunculus directly to the test. Opening the door to the study where Faust lies still unconscious, he allows the newly made creature to float through the air, in his containing glass necessarily, and over to Faust. Hovering there, Homunculus reads aloud the thoughts of Faust's mind. The thoughts are a vision of glorious feminine form, of Leda, in fact, and the approach of Jupiter in the form of a swan, and the begetting of Helen. (Goethe had in mind such a painting as Correggio's "Leda.") Mephistopheles is amazed, for, as he says, *he* sees nothing at all. To which Homunculus replies:

> I believe it! Bred up north
> And from the Misty Ages issuing forth,
> From wastes of priestcraft and knight-errantry,
> How could your eye be free?
> In gloom alone you are at home.

With utter distaste he surveys the Gothic room and says that if Faust awakes here he will die on the spot. Mephistopheles, for his part, is more than ready to go elsewhere; but he is hardly prepared for the next suggestion of Homunculus, that they go to the Classical Walpurgis Night: he has never heard of such a thing. "How could you?" asks Homunculus, "Romantic ghosts are all that you would know." "Romantic" here means, of course, "post-Classical, medieval." Then he says:

> Northwestwards, Satan, lies your pleasure-ground;
> Southeasterly this time our sails are bound.

Mephistopheles' dismay increases at the prospect of journeying to *ancient* Greece, but Homunculus insists it is the only place where Faust may be cured. There are, what is more, Thessalian witches there. Mephisto pricks up his ears; he has always wondered what Thessalian witches were like. The journey shall begin at once, with Mephistopheles transporting Faust as usual on his flying cloak; Homunculus will light the way with the glow of his glass bottle. "And I?" asks Wagner plaintively, only to be brusquely bidden by Homunculus to remain among his books. The travelers set forth.

Through space *and* time, "southeasterly" to *ancient* Greece the three travelers go. Faust, still unconscious, is already there in spirit, as the dream of Leda showed. He will seek the land which classical theory of the eighteenth century claimed was the land of ideal beauty, and specifically he will search for Helen, the epitome of that classical beauty. Mephistopheles, as medieval, Western, Christian devil, goes reluctantly, knowing that he will be out of place. His task will be to find amid ancient Greece the equivalent of his own negative pole. As has been said earlier, Goethe held that life was by definition the interaction between poles. He held further that in Western European civilization the fundamental polarity, of which all other polarities were variants, was that between good and evil. As one of the first European thinkers to perceive the radical difference of classical civilization, he determined that the difference depended upon a subordination of the good-evil polarity to the supreme polarity of beautiful-ugly. Hence, if Mephistopheles is translated to ancient Greece, he will have to identify himself with ugliness. To discover this fact for himself and then to search out supreme ugliness, will be his task. As for Homunculus, the miniature man contained, without substance, in a glass, the mere "idea" of a man, *his* task will be to discover the means of acquiring substance and a form.

The CLASSICAL WALPURGIS NIGHT, Goethe's own fanciful invention and so named only to relate the two parts of his poem, is the night when all the spirits of antiquity are abroad in Greece, thus providing the travelers with a maximum opportunity to search through the components of Classical civilization. A prologue in "classical" hexameters opens the extraordinarily long scene of 1,482 lines, which will thereafter have four sub-scenes, though the action is continuous. The prologuist is the witch Erichtho, the place is the Thessalian battlefield where Caesar defeated Pompey near the town of Pharsalus in the Roman civil war of 48 B.C. Ghostly tents cover the field, lighted by ghostly campfires and the moon. As Homunculus' flashing bottle descends from the skies, the eerie pageant fades except for the fires, Erichtho strides quickly away, and the travelers alight. At the instant when Faust's foot touches Grecian soil he awakes from his unconscious state with the words, "Where is she?" Reaching a quick agreement, the three newcomers separate so that, at Mephistopheles' suggestion, each may seek his own adventure, questioning his way among the fires.

At this point (line 7079) the scene assumes the form of a great fugue in which the interlocking adventures form the three voices. Admittedly difficult on first reading, the bold device gains in power and beauty with every new "hearing," but the beginner is advised in the interests of clarity to sort out, first the sections pertaining to Faust, then those pertaining to Mephistopheles, and to leave until last the consecutive reading of the Homunculus sections. This procedure will be followed here.

FAUST: lines 7181–7213 and 7249–7494. Faust, wandering along the upper Peneus River, chances upon a group of Sirens and Sphinxes and inquires of them where Helen is to be found. The Sirens give elusive answer, but one of the Sphinxes tells him he must ask of Chiron the Centaur. Faust sets off to find the latter. He next appears among the whispering reeds, water nymphs, and swans of the moonlit lower course of the river;

the region is the celebrated Vale of Tempe. Galloping hooves are heard approaching and soon the famous Centaur comes by. Faust hails him, but the restless creature will not stay. At his bidding Faust clambers upon his back, and, as they gallop across country, plies with questions this noblest of pedagogues, tutor of heroes. For a moment they pause long enough for Faust to jump down before the shrine of the prophetess Manto. She knows, as Chiron did not, the way to Helen. With the words, "I love the cravers of the impossible," the prophetess takes him into her shrine. By a secret way down which she once smuggled Orpheus she will guide Faust to the hollow core of Olympus, to the realm of the famed dead, and to Helen.

Of Faust no more will be seen until Act Three, but we have observed him pass from wise Sphinx of fantastic form, to wiser Chiron, half horse, half man, to wisest Manto of wholly human form.

MEPHISTOPHELES: lines 7080–7180, 7214–39, 7676–7800, and 7951–8033. Comically ill at ease as he stalks about the upper Peneus, Mephistopheles finds classical characters far too full of life, and, more often than not, too wholesomely naked to be lewd. Aimlessly he quibbles with the Griffin about its name, bandies riddles with the Sphinx, and grimaces at the coloratura of the Sirens. Sourly he listens as Faust comes along and makes his eager inquiry about Helen, and when Faust has gone in search of Chiron, he scans other weird creatures with distaste. His attention is roused when the Sphinx points out a chorus of Lamiae whom he might follow.

When next we meet him (line 7676) he does come upon the Lamiae, lady vampires with painted faces and foul bodies. They flee when he pursues, return to him when he stops. He manages to catch a few of them but they are too repulsive even for him. In the chase he loses his way, and for a moment we see him encounter Homunculus.

At line 7951 he turns up in a forest region where suddenly he catches sight of the three hideous Phorkyads in their cave. In almost total darkness sit these hags, who possess among them one eye and one tooth which they pass about for alternate use. The Devil feels an irresistible impulse to borrow the costume of one of them, without, however, borrowing the eye or the tooth. He then strikes their pose and says delightedly, "And here I stand: Chaos' well-beloved son!"

Of Mephistopheles no more will be seen until Act Three, but we have observed him pass from wise Sphinx of fantastic form, to more loathsome Lamiae, to Phorkyads, ugliest of forms, to whom he now assimilates himself.

CHORUSES; the SEISMOS EPISODE. With these two blocks of action set clear, it should be mentioned before proceeding to that of the Homunculus that skillfully varied lyric passages, always assigned to water spirits, introduce the shifted settings of the sub-scenes of the "Classical Walpurgis Night." The *first* of these, presenting the river god Peneus himself and his nymphs, blends into the dialogue with Faust before the arrival of Chiron. The *last* of them, sung by divinities of the sea and seashore to begin the sub-scene at the Aegean Gulf, continues at intervals to the end of the act to become the chorus finale. The *second*, however, which comes when the setting is temporarily shifted back to the river headwaters, admits of a curious episodic development of its own, and, like an episode in a fugue, arrests the forward movement of the whole for a brief time. In this instance the Sirens' song is rudely broken by Seismos (Earthquake), who bursts forth from underground in random giant violence to cast up a hill where no hill was before. We see the hill formed, we watch it become populated with fantastic creatures—pygmies, dactyls, and the like—who fall to warring one against another, and presently, within the Homunculus action proper, we see it annihilated by a falling meteor. Ultimately the whole episode stands as a refutation of the "Vulcanist" theory of earth formation, of which we shall speak in a moment.

HOMUNCULUS: lines 7830–7950, 8082–8159, and 8219 to the end of the act. When after his pursuit of the Lamiae Mephistopheles chances upon Homunculus, the latter laments that he has been earnestly seeking a form with which he might begin existence, but that of all forms he has beheld this night he would not like to assume the shape of any. He has, however, heard of two philosophers who talk of "Nature! Nature!" and he is now trying to find them. Just as Mephistopheles leaves him, the two philosophers come along, hot in dispute about the origin of the earth. They are the historical scientific philosophers of antiquity, Anaxagoras and Thales,[1] but more particularly they are representatives of the rival geological theorists of the eighteenth century known as the "Vulcanists" and the "Neptunists." Anaxagoras speaks for the Vulcanists when he claims that all earth formations are the result of fire, volcanic eruption, and other forms of sudden and violent combustion, while Thales voices the Neptunist concept of "all life from water" by slow stages of evolution. Like an ingenuous Freshman—and all characters except the choruses in Act Two are either professors or students—Homunculus comes between the two and begs to be allowed to proceed at their sides, for he has himself a yearning to evolve into form. The two scientists tolerate his company and continue their walk and their argument. Exasperated by his opponent, Anaxagoras stops to implore the moon to bear witness to the validity of his theory. At just that moment the meteor falls upon that hill with the warring creatures. Anaxagoras throws himself to the

---

1. The historical personages could not have held this disputation, since they lived a century apart: Thales from *ca.* 640 to *ca.* 546 B.C. at Miletus in Ionia (now western Turkey), and Anaxagoras from *ca.* 500 to *ca.* 428 B.C. at various places, though his middle years were spent at Athens, where he was the friend and teacher of Pericles.

Thales, who was later reckoned among the Seven Sages, apparently wrote nothing, being, rather, a practical man who introduced Egyptian systems of land measurement and Babylonian astronomy into Greece. He is usually credited with predicting the eclipse of May 28, 585 B.C., and to him is attributed a theory that all things developed out of the proto-element, water.

Anaxagoras, on the other hand, was a writer on scientific theory, though the surviving fragments of his works are insufficient to define his ideas with certainty. He seems to have taught a modified atomic doctrine, with "mind" as a separate entity independent of matter. His astronomical concepts were said to be influenced by the fall of a meteorite in 468–67 B.C. at Aegospotami, on the European shore of the Dardanelles. He postulated a whirling mass in the cosmos, of which the heavenly bodies were portions flung out into space, and he conceived of the sun as a red-hot stone.

Pydna
(168 B.C.)
Mt.
Olympus

Act II

TEMPE

PINDUS MTS.

Peneus River

Mt. Ossa

THESSALY

Mt. Pelion

Pharsalus
(48 B.C.)

Pherae

Mt.
Parnassus

Delphi

ATTICA

ACHAIA

ELIS

PELOPON

Eleusis

Corinth

Stymphalus

Athens

NESUS

ARCADIA

ARGOLIS

Act III

Pylos
(Nestor's city)

Taygetus

Eurotas River

MESSENIA

Mts.

Sparta

GREECE
Part II, Acts II & III

ground in abject terror, but Thales is unimpressed, for, as Homunculus observes, the hill which was round before is now jagged, and the warring creatures are annihilated, but the hill is still there. The fire of the Vulcanists can modify the earth's surface in details like the shape of a hill, but water and slow evolution were the actual creative forces. Thales bids Homunculus follow him to the sea: there he shall behold remarkable things.

Leaving the upper Peneus region, where the hill was made jagged, where Mephistopheles is pursuing the horrid Lamiae, and where all the creatures are grotesque, Thales takes Homunculus past the lower waters of the Peneus (the Vale of Tempe), where already the creatures that Faust encountered (nymphs, swans) were of more gracious form, and on to the shore of the Aegean, where from the life-giving sea will come the noblest forms. Their first encounter there is with Nereus, the old man of the sea. But Nereus has no advice for Homunculus. Like Chiron, this pedagogue has been advising humans these many years and the results are just as if he had never uttered a word. Moreover he wishes not to be disturbed, for tonight is the night when his daughter Galatea, loveliest of sea-goddesses and successor to Aphrodite herself, will make her annual visit to this very bay. Thales bids Homunculus address himself next to Proteus, likewise a sea-god and master of all forms. Sirens, Nereids, and Tritons, gathered for the coming of Galatea, sing while Proteus is being sought. As of old, he changes from form to form at the approach of humans, but at last he is lured like a curious fish by the light of Homunculus' bottle to disclose himself in his genuine heroic form. Something about the tiny creature takes his fancy and he gives him true advice, the poetic version of "ontogeny recapitulates phylogeny," namely, that life must be initiated in the sea and that it must begin small and evolve by slow degrees to highest form. Amid the singing of the sea creatures Proteus leads Homunculus to the water, changes himself into a dolphin, takes the miniature man in the bottle onto his back, and swims out to "wed him to the ocean."

Just then the chorus discerns great flights of doves from

Paphos flying cloudlike about the moon, and the cantankerous
Nereus arrives in great excitement to behold the coming of
Galatea. From open ocean she comes in her rainbow-hued
shell-chariot escorted by her countless sisters. The latter have
with them their lovers, drowned sailors whom they have rescued. All the divinities of ocean are also in the procession,
which now moves landwards but which must pass without
stopping and regain the open sea. Wistfully Galatea waves
greeting to her father, who laments that she may not stop
with him. Across the moonlit waves the procession turns sea-
ward again, while Thales exults in the vision of the life-conferring water, and while Nereus mourns. Suddenly, far out, a
light flashes and the waves repeat its shining: Homunculus
has dashed his bottle against Galatea's chariot and at the feet
of the most beautiful of forms dissolves himself into the sea
whence all life began and whence he shall begin his own evolution through all forms to the highest form. Ecstatically the
chorus sings:

> What marvel of fire lights the waves as they dash
> Against one another with glittering clash?
> Such shining and waving and blazing of light,
> All forms are aglow on the path of the night
> And all things are bathed in a vastness of flame.
> Prevail then great Eros whence everything came!
>
> Hail to the sea! Hail to the waves
> Which sacred fire in brilliance laves!
> Hail to water! To fire, all hail!
> Hail, rare adventure of this tale!
>
> Hail to gently coursing airs!
> Hail to earth's mysterious lairs!
> Honor be forevermore
> To you elements all four!

With this pantheistic hymn to the living earth the extraordinary scene brings Act Two to a close.

Act Three

Beginning at the Renaissance, successive generations of Europeans have found immense inspiration in ancient Greece, but always with this odd circumstance, that each generation has felt bound to correct, with a certain degree of indignation, the erroneous views of its predecessors as to what rightly constituted "Hellas." In different eras, Erasmus, Racine, Winckelmann, Nietzsche, and Sir Gilbert Murray, to mention only a few names, have declared the ultimate nature of Greek culture. It is amazing what contradictions mark their statements. Goethe's Greece lies midway along that chain of names and is coincident with no one of them. What is more important, his was not a static concept but one which changed with the years.

After the emotional convulsions of his Storm and Stress years he had devoutly confessed that art should conform to that definition of "noble simplicity and tranquil grandeur" which Winckelmann had declared to be the essence of Greek art. From 1775 to his Italian journey of 1786-88—his "rebirth" —Goethe had earnestly striven toward that ideal. Yet, if *Iphigenie*, his classical work par excellence, be taken as representative of that period, it will strike the modern reader as distinctly un-Greek. Its heroine is mixed of Rousseauistic and Christian-Pietistic sensitivities; her course of action is predicated upon an eighteenth-century assumption of the rational nature of man; her exile place in Tauris seems like a cover-name for Germany and a modern age, and when she yearns, "seeking the land of the Greeks with her soul," one feels she speaks for the author about the ideal land where *he* never was. After the Italian journey and his "rebirth," Goethe's Hellenism became decidedly less ethereal and, as in the *Roman Elegies*, decidedly more fleshly and realistic. He had modified, but by no means renounced, his allegiance to "Hellas." The cry of the German intellectuals was still "Be a Greek!" and Goethe's voice supported that cry. The anti-Hellenism of the Romantics seemed to him rank apostasy, their medievalizing sheer retrogression. In his old age he came to perceive that Greece, while still a godlike dream, was, after all, *only* a godlike dream. The dream, as he experienced it in its splendor and in its evanescence, forms the subject for Act Three.

SCENE ONE. In full conformity with the metric and scenic usages of the ancient Athenian drama of Euripides, Act Three opens upon a sunlit scene of the return of Helen of Troy to the palace of her lawful husband Menelaus in Sparta. Himself tarrying with his warriors at the landing site, Menelaus has bidden Helen precede him home, there to inspect his trophies and also to make all preparations for a sacrifice to the gods. Gloomy premonition troubles her spirit as she leaves her Chorus Maidens in the outer sunlight and enters the bronze doors of the palace to look to this task. She comes back presently, horrified by a repulsive hag whom she has found crouching at the hearthside and taken at first for a servant. When the hag herself emerges into the sunlight, the Chorus recognizes her as one of the detestable Phorkyads. The latter counters their aversion by calling them ill-mannered, illegitimate warriors' baggage from long campaigns away from home, and when Helen takes their part, she bids her hold off her pack of cackling geese. A lively give-and-take of name-calling ensues between the Chorus and the Phorkyad until Helen asserts her authority as mistress of the household. The Phorkyad, vastly intrigued at meeting the famous lady, questions her about all the conflicting gossip associated with her name. Eventually she puts herself at Helen's command and is told to prepare the instruments of sacrifice. But the Phorkyad now reveals that Menelaus intends to make his errant wife his sacrificial victim: he will behead her and thereafter hang all her Chorus Maidens from the rafters of the house. Horror and fright seize them all. But the Phorkyad also knows a means of rescue. They shall flee to a barbarian of kindly manners who has a fortified castle to the north, established there in Helen's long absence from home. The barbarian, as yet unnamed, is Faust, and the castle is described in terms of the fortified places set up by medieval Frankish knights who conquered the kingdom of Achaia (Greece) and ruled it from 1204 until the coming of the Turks in 1446. The journey is quickly determined upon, and even as they make ready to go, mist comes over the sun and envelops them. Bewildered, they are transported in cloud, which they fear may be the darkness of death closing round them for the second time. Forbidding walls become perceptible through the mist and the terrified maidens are sure that they are being committed prisoner.

The mist clears to reveal all the characters translated to the courtyard of a medieval castle, where SCENE TWO continues without interruption.

Scarcely less bewildering to them is the spectacle of Faust dressed in full court costume of the Middle Ages and descending the donjon stairs amid the pageantry of a medieval processional. He advances toward Helen and presents her with his watchman, Lynceus, whose life she may demand or whom she may pardon, as she pleases, for the lynx-eyed sentry has failed to give warning of any approach—indeed, did not perceive the cloud-borne group at all until they were within the fortress. As spirits, they were invisible. Helen pardons the innocent culprit gladly but is puzzled by the chivalric deference paid to her by such a presentation for judgment, just as a little later she is puzzled by Faust's seating her upon his throne while he in knightly fashion kneels before her and kisses her hand. She is further puzzled by the speech of Lynceus, who has addressed her at length in rhymed stanzas unknown to Greek ears. She asks Faust how she may learn to speak in rhyme. Delighted that she is pleased with the speech of his people, he will not only teach her the art of rhyming but also the music of his nation. While the Chorus continues to speak in rhymeless lines of Greek pattern, Faust and Helen speak of their mutual love in rhymed couplets. There is a distinct possibility that Goethe wished this duet to pass over into actual song, as in opera, for opera was an invention of the latter Renaissance (1600) and was created by the union of revived ancient Greek drama with modern European music. In any event, this love duet is the symbolic wedding of Greek beauty with the spirit of Western European civilization. Meanwhile the external characteristics of Greek drama are preserved in this scene. The Chorus remains on stage throughout and the three-actor rule is observed, first with Faust-Helen-Lynceus, and presently with Faust-Helen-Phorkyad. The Phorkyad now rushes in to proclaim the approach of a vengeful Menelaus with his armies. This motif is left as a loose end and the news serves only as a pretext for Faust's enumeration of the Grecian provinces subjugated by Germanic peoples, all of which together he now offers as dedicated vassal states to Helen the Queen. Symbolically, modern nations are dedicated to the ideals of "Hellas." In complete devotion to his Queen, Faust now bids his castle yield place to lovely forests, for he would dwell with his beloved in Arcadian bliss.

It is amid the ideally beautiful landscape of ARCADIA that the third and final scene of Act Three takes place. The Chorus Maidens lie dispersed and sleeping upon the lawns as the Phorkyad wakes them to announce that Faust and Helen have been dwelling in complete isolation in the picturesque grottoes of the mountainside. Joyous to relate, a son has been born to them, and the Phorkyad waxes maternally lyrical in the description of the beautiful youth of tireless vivacity who yearns most of all to fly. Already he has terrified his parents with his graceful but reckless leaping about the mountain crags. On one occasion they were sure he had plunged to his death, but he emerged in fanciful dress, bedecked with flowers, with a golden lyre in his hands and an aura of flame about his head, a very Apollo. The Chorus are comparing the description with the legend *they* know concerning the birth of Hermes (the Homeric Hymn to Hermes), when all at once the exquisite tones of a harp arrest their attention. So moving are the wordless strains that for the first time the maidens leave off their Greek-like speech and express themselves in rhyme, as is appropriate for a modern art. The Phorkyad tells them that the legends of the old gods are useless now and that music must touch the heart. Their hearts *are* touched, and with *Romantic* "sensibilité," even to tears, as they sing:

> Let the sun's bright blaze go blind,
> If dawns in the soul arise,

which is to say that they renounce the sun-clear objectivity of Greek art for the subjective, modern intuitions of the sensitive heart.

Enter at this point Faust, Helen, and the offspring of their union, the youth Euphorion, personification of Romanticism. The text of the pages which follow resembles, even to the superficial glance, the short lines of an opera libretto, so arranged as to provide various vocal combinations with chorus support. The parents fondly watch as their graceful son sports and dances with the Chorus Maidens. A talented dancer working with a talented choreographer could make this dance a dazzling spectacle full of meaning. One of the chorus maidens rebukes Euphorion for his too ardent attentions and proves that she too is spirit by bursting in flame and vanishing in air. As the youth shakes off the last of her flames, his ear catches the sound of the distant sea. For sheer delight he goes rushing up among the cliffs, exulting in the wild exertion. Watching him, the Chorus sings:

> Sacred Poetry,
> Skyward may it climb,
> Gleam as furthest star
> Far and onward far . . . .

From a cliff top Euphorion beholds the shock of war strike Greece and he would join in the combat. Wings, real or fancied, appear at his back, he throws himself upward in flight, and a glory of flame is seen about his head. An instant later he plunges to the ground as the Chorus in horror cries, "Icarus! Icarus!" From the depths of earth his voice is heard:

> In this dark realm, Mother,
> Leave me not alone!

The lament which the Chorus now sing was originally a separate poem composed by Goethe for Lord Byron when that famous Romantic poet perished in the Greek war of liberation (1824). Its presence in this context betokens the symbolic use of Byron and his fate to represent the whole Romantic movement and *its* fate. To Goethe's mind both were wild, impetuous, unrestrained, beautiful, and by their very natures destined for premature death.

How little stable is the union of Greek beauty and Western spirit is further evidenced by the disappearance of Helen. With a cry to Persephone to unite her with her son, she embraces Faust a last time and descends to the underworld from which he had evoked her. Her garment and veil alone remain in his hands. Just so, one may by mighty magic evoke the "glory that was Greece," but in this latter age it will not come to true life. It will fade away, leaving as the only tangibles the fragments of Greek art and Greek literature, the "garments" of the spirit which has passed. Yet even these are precious: Helen's robe becomes cloud and wafts Faust far away from Arcadia. The Phorkyad gathers up the garments, together with the lyre of Euphorion—the remains of briefly glorious Romanticism.

The leader of the Chorus Maidens now summons her sisters to return with her to Hades from which they came. The maidens object that queens may live in Hades, but that underlings like themselves,

> in the background,
> Deep in meadows of asphodel,
> With the gangling poplars
> And the sterile willows for companions,

have no amusement there but are reduced to ineffectual shades that squeak like bats in darkness. Rather, they will remain amid eternally living Nature, as wind-stirred trees, as living waters, as vineyards bright with grapes. Goethe believed (like Keats) that life was a "vale of soul-making," that the purpose of existence was to achieve a distinct and durable personality. Such a personality once achieved would survive death, while other humans would pass into the eternally living pantheistic universe where the indestructible components of their selves would continue existence dispersed through Nature. As the Chorus Leader cries,

> All those who have achieved no name, nor willed great ends,
> Belong among the elements,

the transformations take place before the spectators' eyes to the accompaniment of a superb choral song. A part of the Chorus is turned into trees in leaf, in blossom, or fruited; another part becomes mountain pools or brooks that hurry toward the fertile lowlands; still others hasten to the vineyards and the Bacchic harvest to come.

When all have disappeared and been transformed and the stage is empty, the Phorkyad lays aside her mask of ugliness and her veil, to face the audience as—Mephistopheles. Transvestism and the smirkingly maternal role of a nurse pressed the ugliness to its grotesque extreme.

Act Four

After the splendors of Acts Two and Three, the fourth act, last to be completed of all of Part Two, is pitched noticeably lower in tone, though its first scene, HIGH MOUNTAINS, still carries echoes of the strong musical cadences that preceded it.

The cloud, once the robe of Helen, has traversed several days of flight to set Faust down in a bleak mountain region. He discerns it move away "eastward," assuming as it goes goddess-form: "With Juno's semblance, yet like Leda, Helen, . . ." Suddenly a seven-league-boot plants itself down; a second follows; Mephistopheles steps down from them; the boots march on of themselves. With a grimace at the dismal waste of rocks Mephistopheles explains how such wild regions of the earth's surface are testimonials of the rage of the devils when they were first cramped in hell. (Mephisto shows himself as a variety of Vulcanist.) Amid this wilderness the Devil now tempts Faust with "the kingdoms of the world and the glory in them." (The marginal gloss, Matthew 4, is one of several specifically indicated Biblical sources adduced in this act, and if their insertion was made by the hand of Dr. Riemer, Goethe's associate, rather than by the poet himself, their presence serves to indicate a good deal about the author's intentions and methods. The Biblical allusions are somber ones and they darken Acts Four and Five, in contrast to the bright mood established in the "Greek" sections of the foregoing acts.) For his own part, Mephistopheles says *he* would like to settle down in a nice little city full of people and affairs, though he would also like a fine country seat with Versailles-like gardens and fountains, big jet fountains with little fountains on the sides to "hiss and piss a thousand trivialities"— and with, of course, beautiful women, for, as he says, he always thinks of those beautiful creatures in the plural. But Faust, fresh from the fading of Greece, still yearns for deeds, and his mind now turns, he announces, to masterdom and ownership. In traversing the ocean in his recent flight, it had struck him that a mighty work could be undertaken in the reclaiming of sea wastes for human habitation. To push back the water, to create land—that is what he would like to do now. The thematic arc is already projecting itself into Act Five, where there will be question of such a project, but Faust's plan is interrupted by the clangor of trumpets of war, and therewith the central matter of Act Four is broached.

Mephistopheles, who has scanned considerable territory while walking about in his seven-league-boots, now explains the trumpet calls. The Emperor of Act One has come upon evil days. The paper money brought economic chaos to his realm, followed by social chaos. Civil war has broken out, a rival emperor heads dissident armies, and these trumpets are the signal for perhaps the last battle of the hard-pressed monarch. Let Faust enter the battle, let him be a General, let him win for the Emperor, and then let him ask the Emperor for the gift of a tract of seashore. That would be a start for the sea-reclaiming project. Faust agrees. He guesses that Mephistopheles will use more than one unfair device to win this battle, and his guess is confirmed when three ugly characters come into sight, heading, with Mephisto's approval, for the scene of action. They are "the three mighty men" of II Samuel 23:8–9, here named Bullyboy, Havequick, and Holdfast.

The second scene, ON THE PROMONTORY, presents the battle as seen from and as reported to the Emperor's tent. Mephistopheles has created a whole army of empty suits of armor into which he has conjured spirits, and these robot-like fighters find much success on the right flank. When the left flank is threatened, he further produces the illusion of mountain streams in flood in which the enemy goes through all the motions of death by drowning. Reluctantly the Emperor accedes to these stratagems and by means of them the battle is won, though the prior scene detailed a very practicable battle plan drawn with military-school skill by the Emperor's officers. Mephistopheles exults as darkness falls on a scene of total and murderous confusion.

The third scene, THE RIVAL EMPEROR'S TENT, shows the headquarters of the now routed enemy plundered by looters and then seized officially by the victorious Emperor. No sooner is the latter in possession than he discovers that he is compelled to give away almost everything he has gained in order to hold the loyalty of the men, both civil and ecclesiastical, who helped him gain it. The only mention of Faust in the entire scene is the demand made by the Archbishop in the closing lines, to the effect that any land Faust has shall be subject to all Church levies.

In assessing Act Four it is interesting to note that its contents correspond to no real events in Goethe's life. His one military experience was as a member of the Duke of Weimar's staff in the disastrous campaign of 1792–93 against the French Republic. But neither that experience, nor, more strikingly, any observed events from the career of Napoleon, relates, except in the most general way, to Act Four. The tone, like the tone of Act One, is that of a tale of long ago and far away. Its nearest analogue is the claim made by the historical Dr. Faustus to have managed the Imperial victories in Italy in 1525–27 by remote control and certain tricks associated with the Faustus of the later folk books. Technically, Act Four serves several purposes, among them, to draw to its conclusion the suspended arc of story from Act One and to acquire momentum for Act Five. Its rightful place in the scheme of the poem will be clearer in retrospect. Poetically, it may be characterized as somber and fraught with menace.

Act Five

In three terse scenes, oddly lyric in tone and entitled OPEN COUNTRY, PALACE, and DEEP NIGHT, Goethe has interwoven the classical legend of the hospitable old couple Philemon and Baucis with the Biblical story of Naboth's vineyard (I Kings 21) to indicate Faust's "experience" of empire in Act Five.

In the first of these scenes, a traveler once befriended in need by the old couple comes once again to their house and is received with their unfailing hospitality. From them, as all three are sitting over supper in the cottage garden, he learns of how one day an Imperial herald came by, proclaiming that a great project of reclaiming land from the sea was about to be undertaken. With astounding speed, which Baucis rightly suspects was more than human, the work had gone forward, so that now fields and towns flourish where once there was only watery waste. The first construction on the new land was the splendid palace where Faust now lives.

In that palace we find him in the second scene, morose and exasperated that in his fine new territory there should be one old element to mar its beauty, the cottage of Philemon and Baucis standing on a rise of ground, once a peninsula, and the adjoining chapel with its irritating bells. Into the sunset harbor sails a treasure-laden ship, from which, as it lands at the palace quay, Mephistopheles disembarks with "the Three Mighty Men." As for the treasure they bring, the Devil explains that war, business, and piracy are indistinguishable from one another. Faust evinces little interest in the treasure or in the worldwide commerce that affords it. His vast wealth, his empire itself, which Goethe has made the rough equivalent of The Netherlands at the height of its fortunes, are obscured by the nagging thought of the old couple with their ugly cottage and discordant chapel bells. His annoyance breaks forth in bitter complaint. Mephistopheles whistles up the Three Mighty Men.

In the third of these scenes, Lynceus the tower warden (as in Act Three) sounds the alarm that the old people's cottage and the chapel are burning. Faust receives Mephistopheles and the henchmen with stout reproach: his instructions had been to effect the purchase of the property, not to destroy it. Cynically Mephistopheles recounts how the old couple died quite easily of fright and only a chance visitor put up resistance and had to be killed. Faust curses the land and bids the henchmen share it as they will.

For so vast an enterprise as the founding of a worldwide commercial empire something less oblique and less tangential than these three scenes would seem to have been in order. Broader treatment, however, would surely have involved complications, particularly in view of the fact that this empire of Faust's was non-historical, and Goethe was satisfied to indicate by a few strokes the empire theme which was necessary to his plan. As with Act Four, there is no parallel with real events of Goethe's life. The opening speech of Lynceus (lines 11,288–11,303) is often cited out of context for its vigorous affirmation of life in old age.

The scene marked MIDNIGHT follows upon DEEP NIGHT without interruption or change of stage set; the rest of Act Five is to be conceived as continuous action too, though the setting will be shifted twice more. To Faust's door come four grey women named Want, Guilt, Distress, and Care. All four would assail him, but the rich man's gate bars all but one, Care, who slips through the keyhole. As the others withdraw in bafflement they see their brother Death approaching. Dame Care (Frau Sorge), a familiar figure in German folklore, normally signifies those material privations here assigned to her companions in grey, but with Goethe she is the representative of spiritual privation: self-doubt, fretful nonspontaneity, worrisome borrowing of trouble. In this instance she comes as the ally of old age to make Faust turn from deeds to a passive waiting for death and a somber preoccupation with eternity. He resists her power, and the utmost she can do is strike him blind. Most remarkable is his reply to her question of whether he has ever known Care:

> I have but raced on through the world;
> I seized on every pleasure by the hair;

What did not satisfy, I let go by,
And what eluded me, I let it be.
I have but craved, accomplished my delight,
Then wished anew, and so with main and might
Stormed through my life; first grandly and with passion,
But now more wisely, in more prudent fashion.
I know enough about the world of men,
The prospect yonder is beyond our ken;
A fool is he who that way blinks his eyes
And fancies kindred beings in the skies.
Let him stand firm here and here look around:
This world is not mute if the man is sound.
Why need he stray off to eternity!
What he knows here is certainty.
So let him walk along his earthly day:
If spirits haunt him, let him go his way,
Find joy and torment in his forward stride,
And at each moment be unsatisfied.

Thus at age one hundred, the age explicitly specified by
Goethe for his hero in this scene, Faust's avidity for experience
and his will to strive are unabated since the moment of his
compact signature, and old age is simply one more obstacle to
be faced and overcome. To man's final breath there is no moment fit for slackening of effort.

The immediately succeeding scene, GREAT FORECOURT
OF THE PALACE, contains the counterweight to the compact scene of Part One and the climax of the entire poem. This
is Goethe's optimistic transformation of the horrendous death
of Dr. Faustus, which in all previous versions of the story, except Lessing's, was the prelude to eternal damnation of the
presumptuous and foolhardy magician. The scene begins with
a grotesque "Dance of Death" by Lemurs, half-decayed
corpses with life still in them and eager to claim a new member to their company. Into the palace forecourt comes Faust,
blinded by Care but with inner vision still clear and directed
upon *this* world, advanced to extreme age at the end of that
second lifetime conferred upon him by the witch long ago.
(If he was fifty years old at the poem's beginning, and if he
was returned to age twenty in the witch's kitchen, then eighty

years have elapsed since his transformation and his total life span is 130 years.) He mistakes the sound of the Lemurs digging his grave for the work he has ordered on the dikes that contain his land from the sea. All at once, unaware that he is dying, or indifferent to the fact, his mind is caught by a great new plan for which he would strive. He will have the swamps drained and thereby

> For many millions I shall open spaces
> Where they, not safe but active-free, have dwelling places,

that is to say, not in smug and deedless security, but under conditions where they may pursue great ideals of great existences, as he has done. The protective dikes will inevitably need constant care, and the active dwellers will have to join their energies against the ever-menacing sea. The land will be a paradise, a Utopia, populated by a race of Faustlike, striving men. Indeed, says Faust in a famous quatrain of the speech in question:

> To this opinion I am given wholly
> And this is wisdom's final say:
> Freedom and life belong to that man solely
> Who must reconquer them each day.

In these terms he would like to see his Utopia a world-state of "many millions," thronging with human beings, young and old, *surrounded by danger* which shall compel them to great striving and great deeds, "On free soil standing with a people free." The passage is brief and it is couched in general terms. To press the words to make them signify a socialist state is wholly unwarranted. Goethe was thinking poetically of a race of heroes, and the slight hint of egalitarianism concerns an "equal temper of heroic hearts" with no tinge of nineteenth-century political philosophies. Politicians invoking Goethe for some local cause will cite these words at their peril.

The thought of such a *future* achievement so exhilarates Faust that he exclaims (translator's italics):

> Then to that moment I *could* say:
> *Linger on, you are so fair!*

. . . .
Foresensing all the rapture of that dream,
This present moment gives me joy supreme.

Pronouncing these words he dies. Mephisto coldly remarks
that now all Faust's striving is for naught. He is just as dead
as if he had never striven at all. And that is why *he* prefers
eternal emptiness. In his eyes the compact is now forfeit by
virtue of Faust's pronouncing of the fatal words which indicate that he has at last found something with which he is
satisfied, beyond which he would renounce all striving: the
Devil now may have him. Mephistopheles reckons too fast.

Without pause, the scene BURIAL shows the Lemurs laying Faust's body in earth while the Devil waits for his spirit
to emerge so that he may triumphantly confront it with the
evidence of the compact and its blood signature. Anxiously he
frets about escaped souls and the difficulty devils have nowadays in gaining what is rightfully theirs. The scene passes over
into the grandiosely grotesque as he summons all kinds of
devils from hell to assist him at this crucial moment. As in a
medieval morality play, hell opens on the left and devils pour
forth; some fat with short, straight horns, some thin with long,
crooked horns, more and ever more of them. But on the right,
heaven opens and choirs of angels descend. The roses falling
from their hands turn to flames as they touch the heads of
the cowering devils. Mephistopheles rages as the angels sing
that the infernal powers must give up what does not belong
to them, yet at the same time his purposes become confused
amid these hovering creatures of love as he is taken with a
sudden urge of homosexual lust toward the boy angels. He
has not yet sensed that Faust's compact is not forfeit, that the
fatal words were pronounced in the glorious and positive will-
ing of a new ideal, not in a weary or smug negativism of satisfaction with a state already achieved: "Then to that moment
I *could* say . . . ," not, "Then to that moment I *do* say." Before
this point becomes clear to him, the angels have gathered up
Faust's *immortal part* (*Unsterbliches*), that essential personality which will survive the shock of death—the word "soul" is
avoided—and are bearing it away on high.

Just as the "Burial" scene made poetic, symbolic use of naive medieval dramaturgics for Goethe's own poetic purposes, so the finale, entitled MOUNTAIN GORGES, puts to purely poetic use certain elements of Catholic legend. The scene is a waste mountain region at the various levels of which figures of ardent aspiration sing toward the infinite skies. Earthbound still are the Pater ecstaticus, the Pater profundus, and the Pater seraphicus, whose persons signify aspiration from heights, depths, and middle regions and who only remotely parallel Saints Anthony, Bernard, and Francis of Assisi. Above the earth hover angels, one group of whom bear Faust's "immortal part" and sing:

> Delivered is he now from ill,
> Whom we a spirit deemed:
> "Who strives forever with a will,
> By us can be redeemed."

The "immortal part" of Faust is then entrusted, not to "the more perfected angels" nor to "the younger angels," but to the lowest order of blessed spirits designated as a "chorus of blessed boys," souls of infants "midnight-born," i.e., born dead and therefore having lived no lives at all. With them, Faust will begin a spiritual evolution from lowest to highest degree of perfection, parallel to the corporeal evolution begun by Homunculus in the sea and proceeding from no form at all to highest form. Cosmic Love will unfailingly attract the evolving spirit onward and upward.

The finale began on earth, in "mountain gorges," with figures of intense aspiration; the scene has already shifted to the mountain peaks; in a moment earth itself will be left behind, the vision will rise into the blue sky, and all personages are spirits possessed by cosmic Love. At the last point of earth the Doctor Marianus (teacher of the mysteries of the Blessed Virgin) invokes the vision of the Virgin Mary amid the blue heavens. She appears, the distance-beckoning one, attended by three feminine personages of holiness and certain clarified sinners. One of the latter, "formerly named Gretchen," sings before the Mater gloriosa certain beautiful lines that are a conversion to bliss of the words she once addressed in anguish, when in life, to the Mater dolorosa. She perceives Faust's approach and begs to be his guide in the realm of light, just as Beatrice once led Dante through heaven. The invocation of the Doctor Marianus has already echoed Dante's famous prayer to "Virgin, Mother, Queen" in the last canto of the *Paradiso,* and the surpassing grandeur of the final passage of *The Divine Comedy* was patently the source of inspiration for the conclusion of our poem. The blue infinities of sky are now the realm of Faust's onward movement. "Rise," says the Mater gloriosa to Gretchen,

> Rise, and in higher spheres abide;
> He will sense you and find the way.

Again the Doctor Marianus echoes the Dantean "Virgin, Mother, Queen," and as the entire vision, with Faust contained within it, is closed away in limitless distances, the work concludes with the eight-line Chorus mysticus:

> All transitory
> Things represent;
> Inadequates here
> Become event,
> Ineffables here
> Accomplishment;
> The Eternal-Feminine
> Draws us onward.

The final footnote to the translation attempts a paraphrase in prose of these difficult lines, but the final couplet, which has occasioned untold shedding of ink, requires special comment. The text reads:

> Das Ewig-Weibliche
> Zieht uns hinan.

This most certainly does not mean what Peer Gynt thinks it means when he misquotes:

> "Das Ewig-Weibliche
> Zieht uns an."
> (The Eternal-Feminine
> Attracts us.)

No shallow romanticism can be tolerated here. The trouble-some couplet must be seen as the twilit intuition of something ineffable; the evanescence of the scene and the superscription "Chorus mysticus" so indicate. It is known that Goethe held that women were possessed of a higher ethical sense than men. The finale, it will be noted, placed even the visionary males on earth but placed the feminine figures on high. This concept underlies the couplet, in which the term "the Eternal-Feminine" seems to be a paraphrase for Love in the complex and exalted sense used by Dante in the final line of the *Paradiso:* "The Love that moves the sun and other stars." Under no circumstances does it mean that Gretchen has waited through five misguided acts of Part Two for her errant lover to rejoin her in heavenly marriage.

In retrospect, it now becomes clear that Goethe's Faust, unlike all other heroes of that name, compacted with the Devil for unlimited opportunity for varied human experience, and that Goethe, working largely on an autobiographical basis, has taken his hero through a series of "experiences" to which we may conveniently assign the following titles.

1. Love (the Gretchen episode, second half of Part I)
2. The life of a Prime Minister—Court Poet, "the great world" (Part II, Act I)
3. Science and Pedagogy (Act II)
4. Art (Act III)
5. Generalship (Act IV)
6. Empire (Act V)

These will be seen to constitute two orders of progression, one a descending order in terms of the number of human indi-viduals who participate in such experiences: many persons love, but few rule empires; the other an ascending order in terms of the number of human individuals affected by a single man who does participate in such experiences: only the be-loved submits to the lover, but thousands submit to their ruler. In all cases the positive man is accompanied by the negative devil, whose permutation of role through varying circumstances provides a perennially fascinating, amusing, and inexhaustibly thought-provoking subject. Throughout the work the author has insisted upon a personal conviction (rather than a philosophy) to the effect that active participation in high endeavor infinitely outweighs all passive learning or contemplation, that such "doing" is, in very fact, life itself by definition. The scene with Dame Care in Act Five caused the very aged Faust to reaffirm ardently his belief in this supremacy of action and striving, and his words of affirmation were the personal reaffirmation of the same ideal by the eighty-year-old poet who wrote the lines. Faust's dying words are the glowing thought of a new goal to strive for, a Utopian world-state. The adding of such an "experience" to the list just enumerated will show that "Utopian world-state" will appropriately extend both the descending and the ascending orders of progression. Finally, the afterlife, about which the Faust of Act Five ("Midnight") had expressed frank doubts, is represented in the finale as a realm in which the "immortal part" of Faust, his essential and achieved personality, unencumbered by mortal body, will strive further onward, by implication infinitely and forever. Both orders of progression are still further extended.

So vast a work as Goethe's *Faust* could not be undertaken, even by a genius working, as in this case, for a lifetime, without blemishes and partial failure. It is easy to pick flaws in the poem. The hesitation between genuine theater and a poem for reading is tantalizing; there are obscurities; there are disputable premises and disputable deductions made upon those premises; from the viewpoint of Anglo-Saxons, used to an arithmetical progression of elements in a play, the story line is often elusive; the Gretchen episode en bloc shifts the author's own approach to his hero and subject, necessitating a dubious procedure to regain the generalized concept of both; the erudition is sometimes taxing; devout Christians have more than once taken objection to the "philosophy" of the poem, while those to whom democratic ideals are paramount have accused both work and author of egocentrism, aristocratic aloofness, and even moral irresponsibility; the former say the poem's ideals lack humility, the latter say the poem's ideals are impractical, and both agree in saying the author left the general run of mankind out of consideration.

In reply to this last accusation it must be said that the poem is a personal poem stating one (extraordinary) man's opinion and the distilled essence of his actual life; it does not preach or harangue, it makes no pretense to being a systematic philosophy. Once accepted in this way, it presents powerful dramatic scenes, poetry of a high order sustained through a dazzling variety of forms and moods, unforgettable characterizations, intellectual content as immensely provocative now as it ever was, and, above all, the sense of a comprehensive view of life, a synthesis of mind and heart, attempted nowhere else in a single book except by Dante. With the comprehensive view one is free to agree or disagree, but it was a rare spirit that won the vision and a rare artist that commanded the means to contain its centrifugal components. For *Faust* is decidedly not a heap of beautiful fragments, but an awesome unity comprising inexhaustible variety. The twelve great gods of Olympus may scour the earth to find its equal.

FAUST

Dedication[1]

Once more, dim wavering figures from the past,
You come, who once rose to my troubled eyes.
Shall I attempt this time to hold you fast?
Does my heart tend where that illusion lies?
You crowd up. Good, then. Rule my will at last,
As from the mists around me you arise.
I feel youth's impulse grip my heart again
At the enchantment wafting from your train.

You bring along the scenes of happy days,
And many well-loved shadows rise to view;   10
And, as in olden, half-forgotten lays,
First love and early friendships rise anew;
The labyrinthine tangles of life's ways
Are with fresh lamentation threaded through,
With kind folk brought to mind who of fair light
Were robbed by Fate, and vanished from my sight.

They will not hear the now ensuing songs,
Those souls to whom the former ones I sang;
Dispersed and scattered are the friendly throngs,
Mute are the voices that responsive rang.   20
My poem [2] now to unknown crowds belongs,
Whose very plaudits cause my heart a pang,
And those who once took pleasure in my art,
If living, wander through the world, apart.

---

1. This Dedication, written probably on June 24, 1797, is more properly an "Invocation" by the author who, at the age forty-eight, is about to resume work on his poem which has lain all but untouched since he was twenty-six. The first stanza refers to the characters in the poem; the third stanza refers to Goethe's deceased father, sister, and friends of his youth. The Dedication was prefixed to the completed Part I of *Faust* in 1808 and is reckoned an integral part of the total work.
2. Reading *Lied* ("poem"), rather than *Leid* ("sorrow"), which, though it was listed by Dr. Riemer in 1809 as a misprint, was never corrected in Goethe's lifetime.

And I am seized by yearning long unknown
Unto that gravely silent spirit-land;
My murmured song strays through the range of tone
Like an Aeolian harp from strand to strand;
Tear follows tear, a tremor shakes my bone,
My strict heart feels itself made mild and bland—   30
What I possess, as though far off, I see,
And what is lost seems the reality.

Prologue in the Theater[1]

THEATER MANAGER   DRAMATIC POET

COMIC CHARACTER

MANAGER. You two who often stood by me
In times of trouble and distress,
What hopes have you for our success
With this work here in Germany?
I'd like to please the crowd that has collected,
Since they both live and let live. As we meet,
The posts are set, the stage has been erected,[2]
And everyone expects a special treat.   40
They sit there in their seats with eyebrows raised
And patiently prepare to be amazed.
I know what gets the public interest
And yet I've never been in such a spot;
True, they are not accustomed to the best,
But all the same they've read an awful lot.
What can be done to make things fresh and new
Yet have them meaningful and pleasant too?
It really pleases me, to tell the truth,
To see the crowds come streaming toward our place,   50
Wave after wave flood toward our ticket booth
To squeeze in through the narrow gate of grace.[3]
In broad daylight, before the hour of four
They fight their way with blows up to the wicket
And much like starvelings begging bread at baker's door,

---

1. Written 1802 in imitation of the prologue to Kālidāsa's *Sakuntalā* (written *ca.* A.D. 375), most famous of Sanskrit dramas, which Goethe read in translation.
2. In the late eighteenth century, acting companies run by a manager (*Theaterdirektor*) who was both producer and director still traveled about and performed in improvised quarters, but such sideshow booths or crude temporary platforms as are described here were then only quaint and rare survivals in provincial market squares.
3. Compare the "strait gate" of Matthew 7:13.

They almost break their necks to get a ticket.
The poet's miracle alone can sway
Such various minds; perform it, friend, today!
POET. O speak not of the motley multitude!
My spirit flies in horror from the sight.   60
Conceal from me that milling, jostling brood
That sucks us down the whirlpool by their might.
No, guide me to some holy solitude
Where pure joy blooms for poets' sole delight,
Where love and friendship in divine hands bear
Our hearts' true bliss and give it loving care.
    Ah, what welled up from deep within our breast,
What our lips hesitantly tried for sound,
Now badly put, now haply well expressed,
Is in the moment's frenzy lost and drowned.   70
And often only years will pass the test
In which the form's perfection can be found.
What dazzles, fills an instant and is gone;
The true will for posterity live on.
COMIC CHARACTER. Don't talk posterity to me!
What if *I* talked posterity,
Who would provide *this* world with fun?
They want it and it shall be had.
The presence of a fine and sterling lad
Means something too, I think. And one   80
Who is engaging will not ever be
Embittered by the audience's moods;
To stir them more effectively
He craves to play to multitudes.
Just have good will and show your competence,
Let Fantasy with all her choirs be heard—
Emotion, passion, reason, and good sense—
But not without some nonsense, mark my word!
MANAGER. Above all, let there be enough live action!
They like to watch, and that's the chief attraction.   90
With lots of things before their eyes displayed
For crowds to stare and gape in wonder of,
There's most of your success already made

And you're the man whom they will love.
By mass alone the masses can be won,
Each picks out something for himself. Provide
A lot, provide for many, and everyone
Will leave the house and go home satisfied.
In staging any piece, stage it in pieces!
With hash like that your chance of luck increases;   100
It's served as easily as it's invented.
Why fuss to get a perfect whole presented?
The public only pick it all to pieces.
POET. How bad such hackwork is you do not seem to feel!
How ill it fits with real artistic mind!
The trash in which these bunglers deal
You turn into a principle, I find.
MANAGER. At such reproaches I take no offense.
To make a thing and get results with it
A man must use the best of implements.   110
Remember it's soft wood you have to split.
See who they are for whom you write today!
One comes to while an hour away,
Another's overfull from dinner scenes,
And what is worst of all, I say,
So many come from reading magazines.
They come here scatterbrained, as to a masquerade,
Steps winged by curiosity alone;
The ladies treat us to themselves and gowns, unpaid,
And stage a show all of their own.   120
What are your poet's dreams up there on high?
Why does a full house put you in good mood?
Observe your patrons from close by:
Half are indifferent, half are crude.
One wants a game of cards after the show,
One wants a wild night in a wench's arms.
Why should you poor fools trouble so,
For ends like this, to court the Muses' charms?
I tell you, give them more and more and yet more still,
You won't go wrong with such a plan of action;   130
Just see you give the people some distraction,

For satisfy them, that you never will—
What ails you? Is this rapture or distress?
POET. Then find some other man to write your play!
Why should the poet lightly fling away
His highest right, the right that Nature lent
Him, just for your sake and in frivolousness?
How does he move all hearts to tenderness?
How does he conquer every element?
If not by harmony that wells forth from his heart   140
And takes the world back down into his heart?
When Nature, listless at her spinning, skeins
Around her spindle endless threads of life,
When unharmonious creatures of all strains
Clash in encounters of vexatious strife:
From that monotonous line in endless prolongation
Who singles portions out for rhythmic words?
Who summons things unique to general consecration
So that they may resound as splendid chords? [4]
Who whips the tempest's rage to passion's wrath?   150
Makes sunsets burn in high solemnity?
Who strews all springtime's blossoms winsomely
Upon the sweet beloved's path?
Who twines the green leaves of no consequence
To crowns that merit wins in every test?
Unites the gods, gives high Olympus sure defense? [5]
The might of man in poets manifest.

---

4. The metaphors are mixed. Nature, like the first of the three Fates but also
in the sense of ll. 508–9, spins the endless thread of life, monotonous in its
very variety. The poet selects portions of this listlessly spun, endless, formless
thread, and to these portions gives literary form ("rhythmic words") and
moral significance. These unique episodes take on permanent significance for
all mankind ("general consecration"), e.g., the episode of the historical Macbeth is lost in the web of history, but Shakespeare's *Macbeth* has received
poetic definition. The musical metaphor arises from the monotonous *sound*
of the spinningwheel, from which the poet gathers individual threads of tone
into full chords.
5. "Unites the gods" (*vereinet Götter*) apparently conveys the classical notion
of the poet as mythologizer, one who defines the sublimity of all gods. "Gives
high Olympus sure defense" (*sichert den Olymp*) apparently means "affirms
the ideal," though Witkowski believes it means "assures man's achievement
of the ideal," i.e., by "scaling Olympus" or achieving heaven.

COMIC CHARACTER. Then use the powers that in you lie
    And ply the trade that poets ply
    The way you carry on a love affair.   160
    By chance one meets, one feels, one lingers there,
    And step by step one is involved;
    Joy grows, and then by trouble is resolved;
    One is enraptured, then along comes grief,
    Before you know it there's a novel sketched in brief.
    O let us also give just such a play!
    You need but reach into life's full array!
    All men lead lives, and though few realize it,
    Their lives hold interest, anywhere one tries it.
    In bright-hued pictures little clarity,   170
    Much error and a glint of verity,
    That is the way to make the best of brew
    To cheer the world and edify it too.
    Then to your play will come youth's fairest bloom
    Harkening as to an oracle that speaks,
    And from your work all tender souls consume
    The melancholy food that each one seeks;
    Now one and now another will be roused
    And each find what in his own heart is housed.
    They can be brought to tears or laughter with great ease,   180
    They love illusion, have respect for ardent animation:
    With finished men there's nothing that will please,
    But boundless thanks will come from those still in formation.
POET. Then give me back the former times
    When I myself was still a-growing
    And when the spring of songs and rhymes
    Uninterruptedly was flowing,
    When mists concealed the world from me,
    When buds enclosed miraculous powers,
    And when I picked the thousand flowers   190
    That filled all dales abundantly.
    With nothing, I still had enough with youth,
    Joy in illusion and the urge for truth.
    Give me back the ardors of
    Deep, painful happiness that I had then,

The force of hate, the might of love,
O give me back my youth again!
COMIC CHARACTER.
    You do need youth, good friend, in any case
When enemies in battle round you press,
When pretty girls their arms enlace   200
Around your neck with fond duress,
When victors' crowns allure your glance
From hard-won goals still far away,
When after whirlings of the dance
You dine and drink the nights away.
But taking up the well-known lyre
And playing it with strength and grace,
Approaching a goal that *you* desire
With amiably digressive pace,
That, elder Sirs, should be your aim,   210
And we accord it no less reverence.
Age does not make us childish, as they claim,
But finds us children in a truer sense.
MANAGER. Sufficient speeches have been made,
    Now let me see some actions done!
While all these compliments were paid
Some useful goal could have been won.
Why talk about poetic mood?
It never goes with hesitancy.
If you are poets, well and good,   220
Then take command of Poetry.
You're well aware of what we need.
We want strong drink, it is agreed;
Then brew me some without delay!
Tomorrow will not see what is not seen today,
And not one day must go to waste;
Resolve must seize occasion fast
By forelock, and do so with haste;
Then it will hold on to the last
And move ahead because it must.   230
You know on German stages we
All try experiments today,

So do not stint in any way
On sets and stage machinery.
Use both sky-orbs, the large one and the small,
Be lavish with the stars, be free
With water, fire, and mountain wall,
Have birds and beasts in quantity.
Thus all creation will appear
Within our narrow wooden confines here,   240
Proceeding by Imagination's spell
From heaven, through the world, to hell.[6]

6. The allusion is not to any idea in *Faust*, but to the old multiple stage of medieval drama—such as Goethe uses in the second-last scene of Part II— with heaven on the right, the world in the center, and the "jaws of hell" on the left. See ll. 11,644 ff.

Prologue in Heaven

THE LORD, *the heavenly hosts;*[1] *afterwards*
MEPHISTOPHELES. *The three* ARCHANGELS
step forward.

RAPHAEL. The sun sings as it sang of old
  With brother spheres in rival sound,[2]
  In thundrous motion onward rolled
  Completing its appointed round.
  The angels draw strength from the sight,
  Though fathom it no angel may;
  The great works of surpassing might
  Are grand as on Creation day.   250
GABRIEL. And swift beyond conception flies
  The turning earth, now dark, now bright,
  With clarity of paradise
  Succeeding deep and dreadful night;
  The sea in foam from its broad source
  Against the base of cliffs is hurled,
  And down the sphere's eternal course
  Both cliff and sea are onward whirled.
MICHAEL. And storms a roaring battle wage
  From sea to land, from land to sea,   260
  And forge a chain amid their rage,
  A chain of utmost potency.
  There blazing lightning-flashes sear
  The path for bursting thunder's way—
  And yet thy heralds,[3] Lord, revere
  The mild procession of thy day.
ALL THREE. The angels draw strength from the sight,
  Though fathom it no angel may;

---

1. In the manner of a medieval sovereign at a convocation of his vassals.
2. Job 38:7 "When the morning stars sang together, and all the sons of God shouted for joy." Witkowski feels that any allusion to the classical "music of the spheres" is unlikely.
3. "Heralds" (*Boten*) literally translates Greek *aggeloi* ("angels"); compare "envoys" (*Gesandte*) in l. 11,675, which does the same.

The great works of surpassing might
Are grand as on Creation day.   270
MEPHISTOPHELES. Since you, O Lord, approach again and see
These people here and ask us how we do,
And since you used to like my company,
Behold me also here among this crew.
Excuse me, I can not be eloquent,
Not even if I'm scorned by all your staff;
My grand style would provoke your merriment
If you had not forgotten how to laugh.
Of suns and worlds there's nothing I can say;
How men torment themselves is what I see.   280
The little earth-god stays the same perpetually
And still is just as odd as on Creation day.
He would be better off at least
If you had not endowed him with the heavens' light;
He terms it Reason and exerts the right
To be more brute than any beast.
He seems like—craving pardon of Your Grace—
One of the spindle-shank grasshopper race
That flit around and as they hop
Sing out their ancient ditty where they stop.   290
He should stay in the grass where he has sung!
He sticks his nose in every pile of dung.
THE LORD. Is there no more that you could add?
Is finding fault all you can do?
Is nothing on earth ever right with you?
MEPHISTOPHELES.
No, Lord! I find things there, as always, downright bad.
The human race in all its woes I so deplore
I hate to plague the poor things any more.
THE LORD. Do you know Faust?
MEPHISTOPHELES.   The Doctor?
THE LORD.   And my servant.
MEPHISTOPHELES. He serves you in a curious way, I think.   300
Not earthly is the poor fool's food and drink.
An inner ferment drives him far
And he is half aware that he is mad;

From heaven he demands the fairest star,
From earth all peaks of pleasure to be had,
And nothing near and nothing far
Will calm his troubled heart or make it glad.
THE LORD. Though now he serves me but confusedly,
  I soon shall guide him on toward what is clear.
  The gardener knows, when green comes to the tree,   310
  That flowers and fruit will deck the coming year.
MEPHISTOPHELES. What will you bet you lose him if you give
  Me your permission now to steer
  Him gently down my path instead?
THE LORD. As long as he on earth may live,
  To you such shall not be gainsaid.
  Man errs as long as he can strive.
MEPHISTOPHELES. Thank you for that; for with the dead
  I never hankered much to be.
  It is the plump, fresh cheeks that mean the most to me.   320
  I'm out to corpses calling at my house;
  I play the way the cat does with the mouse.
THE LORD. Good, then! The matter is agreed!
  Divert this spirit from his primal source,
  And if you can ensnare him, lead
  Him with you on your downward course;
  And stand abashed when you have to confess:
  A good man harried in his dark distraction
  Can still perceive the ways of righteousness.
MEPHISTOPHELES. All right! It won't be any long transaction.   330
  I have no fears at all for my bet's sake.
  And once I've won, let it be understood
  You will admit my triumph as you should.
  Dust shall he eat, and call it good,
  Just like my aunt, the celebrated snake.
THE LORD. There too feel wholly free to try;
  Toward your kind I have borne no hate.
  Of all the spirits that deny,
  The scoffer burdens me with slightest weight.
  Man's activeness can all too easily go slack,   340
  He loves to be in ease unqualified;

Hence I set a companion at his side
To goad him like a devil from the back.
   But you, true sons of gods,[4] may you
Rejoice in beauty that is full and true!
May that which is evolving and alive
Encompass you in bonds that Love has wrought;
And what exists in wavering semblance, strive
To fix in final permanence of thought.

(*The heavens close, the* ARCHANGELS *disperse.*)

MEPHISTOPHELES. From time to time I like to see the Boss,   350
And with him like to keep things on the level.
It's really nice in one of such high class
To be so decent with the very Devil.

---

4. *Göttersöhne* literally translates the Hebrew *Bene Elohim* of Genesis 6:2.

The First Part of the Tragedy

Night

FAUST *restless in his chair at his desk in a narrow and high-vaulted Gothic room.*

FAUST. I've read, alas! through philosophy,
 Medicine and jurisprudence too,
 And, to my grief, theology
 With ardent labor studied through.
 And here I stand with all my lore,
 Poor fool, no wiser than before!
 I'm Master, I'm Doctor, and with my reading 360
 These ten years now I have been leading
 My scholars on wild-goose hunts, out
 And in, cross-lots, and round about—
 To find that nothing can be known!
 This burns my very marrow and bone.
 I'm shrewder, it's true, than all the tribes
 Of Doctors and Masters and priests and scribes;
 Neither doubts nor scruples now can daunt me,
 Neither hell nor devils now can haunt me—
 But by the same token I lose all delight. 370
 I don't pretend to know anything aright,
 I don't pretend to have in mind
 Things I could teach to improve mankind.
 Nor have I lands nor treasure hoards,
 Nor honors and splendors the world affords;
 No dog would want to live this way!
 And so I've yielded to magic's sway,
 To see if spirits' force and speech
 Might not bring many a mystery in reach;
 So I no longer need to go 380
 On saying things that I don't know;
 So I may learn the things that hold
 The world together at its core,

19

So I may potencies and seeds behold,[1]
And trade in empty words no more.
　O if, full moon, you did but shine
Your last upon this pain of mine,
Whom I have watched ascending bright
Here at my desk in mid of night;
Then over books and papers here,   390
Sad friend, you would come into view.
Ah, could I on some mountain height
Rove beneath your mellow light,
Drift on with spirits round mountain caves,
Waft over meadows your dim light laves,
And, clear of learning's fumes, renew
Myself in baths of healing dew!
　Am I still in this prison stall?
Accursed, musty hole-in-the-wall,
Where the very light of heaven strains   400
But dully through the painted panes!
　By these enormous book-piles bounded
Which dust bedecks and worms devour,
Which are by sooty charts surrounded
Up to the vaultings where they tower;
With jars shelved round me, and retorts,
With instruments packed in and jammed,
Ancestral junk together crammed—
Such is your world! A world of sorts!
　Do you still wonder why your heart   410
Is choked with fear within your breast?
Why nameless pain checks every start
Toward life and leaves you so oppressed?
Instead of Nature's living sphere
Wherein God placed mankind of old,
Brute skeletons surround you here
And dead men's bones and smoke and mold.
　Flee! Up! And out into the land!

---

1. "Potencies" (*Wirkenskraft*) and "seeds" (*Samen*) were alchemists' terms
for "energy" and "primal matter," the latter being analogous to "atoms."

Does not this mystic book indeed,
From Nostradamus' very hand,[2]   420
Give all the guidance that you need?
Then you will recognize the courses
Of stars; within you will unfold,
At Nature's prompting, your soul's forces
As spirits speech with spirits hold.[3]
In vain this arid brooding here
The sacred signs to clarify—
You spirits who are hovering near,
If you can hear me, give reply!

(*He opens the book and glimpses the sign of the
macrocosm.*) [4]

Ha! Suddenly what rapture at this view   430
Goes rushing through my senses once again!
I feel a youthful joy of life course new
And ardent through my every nerve and vein.
Was it a god who wrote these signs whereby
My inward tempest-rage is stilled
And my poor heart with joy is filled
And with a mystic impulse high
The powers of Nature all around me are revealed?
Am I a god? I feel so light!
In these pure signs I see the whole   440
Of operative Nature spread before my soul.
Now what the wise man says I understand aright:
"The spirit world is not locked off from thee;
Thy heart is dead, thy mind's bolt drawn!
Up, scholar, and bathe cheerfully
Thy earthly breast in rosy dawn!"

---

2. Michel de Notredame (1503–66) was a younger contemporary of the historical Faust, an astrologer, and the composer of a volume of rhymed prophecies of the future.

3. Emanuel Swedenborg (1688–1772) states in his *Arcana coelestia* that spirits communicate thoughts instantaneously without the medium of words or speech.

4. A mystic symbol representing the total universe.

(He contemplates the sign.)

How all things interweave to form the Whole,[5]
Each in another finds its life and goal!
How each of heaven's powers soars and descends
And each to each the golden buckets lends;   450
On fragrant-blessed wings
From heaven piercing to earth's core
Till all the cosmos sweetly rings!
    O what a sight!—A sight, but nothing more!
Where can I grasp you, Nature without end?
You breasts, where? Source of all our lives,[6]
On which both heaven and earth depend,
Toward you my withered heart so strives—
You flow, you swell, and must I thirst in vain?

*(Impatiently he turns pages of the book and glimpses the
sign of the Earth Spirit.)* [7]

How differently I am affected by this sign!   460
You, Spirit of the Earth, are nearer me,
I feel more potent energy,

---

5. In the difficult lines which follow, the written symbol of the macrocosm
(universe) is imagined as coming alive before Faust's eyes. Essentially it is
a vision of the starry sky with all the stars complexly moving by immutable
laws like a cosmic watchworks. The moving parts, however, are also angels,
for the metaphor is blended with Jacob's dream from Genesis 28:12: "And
he [Jacob] dreamed, and behold a ladder set up on earth, and the top of it
reached to heaven: and behold the angels of God ascending and descending
on it." Regularly ordered movement is suggested by the passing of the golden
pails from angel to angel; possibly they are fetching light from the well and
source of all light, which is God. The angels, by piercing through the earth,
include our planet in the cosmic vision.
6. The image is that of a mother-earth-goddess, perhaps like the ancient
Diana of Ephesus, who was represented with innumerable breasts which gave
suck to all creatures.
7. The much discussed Spirit is a personification of amoral Nature, Goethe's
own variation of the *Archaeus terrae* of the sixteenth-century natural philosophers and Giordano Bruno's *Anima terrae*. These philosophers, and later ones
as well, e.g., Swedenborg, conceived of a supernatural spirit dwelling at the
earth's core and controlling all earthly life of animals, vegetables, and even
minerals. Each planet had its own analogous spirit. In a jotting of 1800, reproduced by Witkowski (Vol. I, p. 526), Goethe defined the Earth Spirit as
Welt und Thaten Genius, the spirit of the world and of deeds.

I feel aglow as with new wine.
I feel the strength to brave the world, to go
And shoulder earthly weal and earthly woe,
To wrestle with the tempests there,
In shipwreck's grinding crash not to despair.
Clouds gather over me—
The moon conceals its light—
The lamp has vanished!   470
Mists rise!—Red lightnings dart and flash
About my head—Down from
The vaulted roof cold horror blows
And seizes me!
Spirit implored, I feel you hovering near.
Reveal yourself!
O how my heart is rent with fear!
With new emotion
My senses riot in wild commotion!
My heart surrenders to you utterly!   480
You must! You must! though it cost life to me!

(*He seizes the book and mystically pronounces the sign of
the Spirit. A reddish flame flashes. The* SPIRIT *appears in the
flame.*) [8]

SPIRIT. Who calls me?
FAUST (*cowering*).   Ghastly shape!
SPIRIT.   With might
    You have compelled me to appear,
    You have long sucked about my sphere,[9]
    Now—
FAUST.   No! I cannot bear the sight!
SPIRIT. You begged so breathlessly to bring me near
    To hear my voice and see my face as well;
    I bow before your strong compulsive spell,

---

8. See "Apparition of the Earth Spirit," illustrations.
9. According to Swedenborg, every spirit has its own "sphere"; spirits also
suck, leech-like, on human heads and leave a kind of wound. Paracelsus, one
of the chief alchemists whom Goethe had read, says the senses suck reason
from the sun the way a bee sucks honey from flowers.

And here I am!—What childish fear
Besets you, superman! [10] Where is the soul that cried?   490
Where is the heart that made and bore a world inside
Itself and sought amid its gleeful pride
To be with spirits equal and allied?
Where are you, Faust, whose voice called out to me,
Who forced yourself on me so urgently?
Are you the one who, having felt my breath,
Now tremble to your being's depth,
A terrified and cringing worm?
FAUST. Shall I give way before you, thing of flame?
I am your equal. Faust is my name!   500
SPIRIT. In tides of life, in action's storm
    I surge as a wave,
    Swaying ceaselessly;
    Birth and the grave,
    An endless sea,
    A changeful flowing,
    A life all glowing:
    I work in the hum of the loom of time
    Weaving the living raiment of godhead sublime.
FAUST. O you who roam the world from end to end,   510
    Restless Spirit, I feel so close to you!
SPIRIT. You are like the spirit you comprehend,
    Not me!

    (*Disappears.*)

FAUST (*overwhelmed*). Not you?
    Whom then?
    I, image of the godhead!
    Not even rank with you!

    (*A knock.*)

God's death! I know who's there—my famulus [11]—

---

10. "Superman" (*Übermensch*), probably the first occurrence of the word in
literature.
11. Famulus, a graduate assistant to a professor.
sense of "study" or "private library."

This puts an end to my great joy!
To think that dry-bones should destroy   520
The fullness of these visions thus!

(*Enter* WAGNER *in a dressing gown and nightcap, a lamp in his hand.* FAUST *turns around impatiently.*)

WAGNER. Excuse me! I heard you declaiming;
    It surely was a Grecian tragedy?
    There I would like some more proficiency,
    Today it gets so much acclaiming.
    I've sometimes heard it said a preacher
    Could profit with an actor for a teacher.
FAUST. Yes, if the preacher is an actor too,
    As may on some occasions be the case.
WAGNER. Oh, cooped up in one's museum [12] all year through   530
    And hardly seeing folks except on holidays,
    Hardly by telescope, how can one find
    Persuasive skills wherewith to guide mankind?
FAUST. Unless you feel it you will not succeed;
    Unless up from your soul it wells
    And all your listeners' hearts compels
    By utmost satisfaction of a need,
    You'll always fail. With paste and glue,
    By grinding others' feasts for hash,
    By blowing your small flame up too   540
    Above your paltry pile of ash,
    High praise you'll get in apes' and children's sight,
    If that's what suits your hankering—
    But heart with heart you never will unite
    If from your heart it does not spring.
WAGNER. Delivery makes the speaker's real success,
    And that's just where I feel my backwardness.
FAUST. Try for an honest win! Why rail
    Like any bell-loud fool there is?
    Good sense and reason will prevail   550

---

12. Museum, literally "a haunt of the Muses," used preciously here in the sense of "study" or "private library."

Without a lot of artifice.
If you have serious things to say,
Why hunt for words out of your way?
Your flashy speeches on which you have pinned
The frilly cutouts of men's artistry
Are unrefreshing as the misty wind
That sighs through withered leaves autumnally!

WAGNER. Oh Lord! How long is art,
How short our life! And ever
Amid my work and critical endeavor   560
Despair besets my head and heart.
How difficult the means are to come by
That get one back up to the source,[13]
And then before one finishes mid-course,
Poor devil, one must up and die.

FAUST. Is that the sacred font, a parchment roll,
From which a drink will sate your thirst forever?
Refreshment will delight you never
Unless it surges up from your own soul.

WAGNER. But what delight there is in pages   570
That lead us to the spirit of the ages!
In seeing how before us wise men thought
And how far glorious progress has been brought.

FAUST. O yes, up to the furthest star!
My friend, the eras and past ages are
For us a book with seven seals.[14]
What you the spirit of the ages call
Is only those men's spirits after all
Held as a mirror that reveals
The times. They're often just a source of gloom!   580
You take one look at them and run away.
A trash can and a littered storage room,
At best a plot for some heroic play [15]

13. I.e., it takes so long to master Greek and Latin in order to study the classics in the original.
14. Revelation 5:1.
15. "Heroic play" stands for the technical term *Haupt- und Staatsaktion,*

With excellent pragmatic saws
That come resoundingly from puppets' jaws.
WAGNER. But then the world! The mind and heart of man!
To learn about those things is our whole aim.
FAUST. Yes, call it learning if you can!
But who dares call a child by its right name?
The few who such things ever learned,   590
Who foolishly their brimming hearts unsealed
And to the mob their feelings and their thoughts revealed,
Were in all ages crucified or burned.
But it is late into the night, my friend,
We must break off now for the present.
WAGNER. I would have liked to stay awake and spend
The time in talk so learned and so pleasant.
But since tomorrow will be Easter Day,
I'll ask some further questions if I may.
I have industriously pursued my studying;   600
I know a lot, but would like to know everything.

(*Exit.*)

FAUST (*alone*). Why hope does not abandon all such brains
That cling forever to such shallow stuff!
They dig for treasure and are glad enough
To turn up angleworms for all their pains! [16]
May such a human voice presume to speak
Where spirits closed around me in full ranks?
And yet for this one time I give you thanks,
Of all earth's sons the poorest and most weak.
You pulled me back from the despair and panic   610
That threatened to destroy my very mind.

which describes drama of the French classical type involving the fates of
countries and their rulers, but more particularly the sorry 17th-century German works in that vein.
16. Here at l. 605 the scene ended in the *Urfaust,* though without the last
four lines of Wagner's parting speech, which were added only in the completed Part I of 1808. Thus both the *Urfaust* (before 1775) and the 1790
Fragment opened with the 248 lines of "Night." The *Urfaust* then skipped all
the way to l. 1868, whereas the 1790 *Fragment* next resumed with l. 1770.

That vision loomed so vast and so titanic
That I felt dwarfed and of the dwarfish kind.
  I, image of the godhead, who supposed
Myself so near eternal verity,
Who reveled in celestial clarity,
My earthly substance quite deposed,
I, more than cherub, whose free strength presumed
To flow through Nature's veins, myself creating,
Thereby in godlike life participating,   620
How I must pay for my expostulating!
There by a word of thunder I was consumed!
  Your equal I dare not pretend to be;
If I had power to make you come to me,
I did not have the power to make you stay.
In that brief moment's ecstasy
I felt so small and yet so great;
You thrust me backwards cruelly
To my uncertain human fate.
Who will instruct me? What must I not do?   630
Should I give every impulse play?
Alas, our very actions, like our sorrows too,
Build obstacles in our life's way.
  On the most glorious things mind can conceive
Things strange and ever stranger force intrusion;
Once we the good things of this world achieve,
We term the better things cheat and delusion.
The noble feelings that conferred our life
Are paralyzed amid our earthly strife.
  If Fantasy once soared through endless space   640
And hopefully aspired to the sublime,
She is content now with a little place
When joys have foundered in the gulf of time.
Deep down within the heart Care builds her nest
And causing hidden pain she broods,
And brooding restlessly she troubles joy and rest;
Assuming ever different masks and moods,
She may appear as house and home, as child, as wife,
As poison, dagger, flood, or fire;

You dread what never does transpire,   650
And what you never lose you grieve for all your life.
    I am not like the gods! Too sharp I feel that thrust!
I am more like the worm that burrows in the dust,
That living there and finding sustenance
Is crushed beneath a passing foot by chance.
    Is all of this not dust that these walls hold
Upon their hundred shelves oppressing me?
The rubbish which with nonsense thousandfold
Confines me in this world of moths distressfully?
Should I find *here* the things I need?   660
When in perhaps a thousand books I read
That men have been tormented everywhere,
Though one may have been happy here and there?—
What is your grinning message, hollow skull,
But that your brain, like mine, once sought the day
In all its lightness, but amid the twilight dull,
Lusting for truth, went miserably astray?
And all you instruments make fun of me
With wheel and cog and drum and block:
I stood before the door, you should have been the key;   670
Your wards are intricate but do not turn the lock.
Mysterious in broad daylight,
Nature's veil can not be filched by you,
And what she keeps back from your prying spirit's sight
You will not wrest from her by lever or by screw.
You old contrivances unused by me,
You served my father's needs, hence here you stay.
You, ancient scroll, have blackened steadily
As long as dull lamps on this desk have smoked away.
Better if I had squandered my small estate   680
Than sweat and by that little be oppressed!
Whatever you inherit from your late
Forebears, see that it is possessed.
Things unused are a burden of great weight;
The hour can use what it alone creates, at best.
    But why does my gaze fix on that spot over there?
Is that small bottle then a magnet to my eyes?

Why is all suddenly so bright and fair
As when in a dark wood clear moonlight round us lies?
   Rare phial, I salute you as I draw   690
You down with reverence and with awe.
In you I honor human skill and art.
You essence of all lovely slumber-flowers,
You extract of all subtle deadly powers,
Unto your master now your grace impart!
I see you, and my suffering is eased,
I clasp you, and my strugglings have ceased,
The flood tide of my spirit ebbs away.
To open seas I am shown forth by signs,
Before my feet the mirror-water shines,   700
And I am lured to new shores by new day.
   A fiery chariot comes on airy pinions [17]
Down toward me! I feel ready now and free
To rise by new paths unto aether's wide dominions,
To newer spheres of pure activity.
This higher life! This godlike ecstasy!
And you, but now a worm, have you acquired such worth?
Yes, only turn your back decisively
Upon the lovely sun of earth!
By your presumptuous will, fling wide the portals   710
Past which each man would rather slink away.
Now is the time to prove by deeds that mortals
Yield not to gods in dignity's array:
To shrink not back from that dark cavern where
Imagination sees itself to torment damned,
To press on toward that thoroughfare
Around whose narrow mouth all hell is spanned:
To take that step with cheer, to force egress—
Though at the risk of passing into nothingness.
   Come down, you glass of crystal purity,   720
Come forth out of your ancient case to me
Who have not thought of you these many years.

---

17. In II Kings 2:11, Elijah was taken up to heaven in a "chariot of fire."

You used to gleam amid my father's feasts
And used to gladden earnest guests
As you were passed from hand to hand with cheers.
Your gorgeous braid of pictures deftly twined,
The drinker's pledge to tell of them in rhyme
And drain your hollow rondure at one time,
These bring back many youthful nights to mind;
I shall not this time pass you to a neighbor,   730
To prove my wit upon your art I shall not labor;
Here is a juice that makes one drunk with no delay.
Its brownish liquid streams and fills your hollow.
This final drink which now shall follow,
Which I prepared and which I choose to swallow,
Be it a festive high salute to coming day!

(*He lifts the glass to his lips.*)

(*A peal of bells and choral song.*)

CHORUS OF ANGELS.[18] Christ is arisen!
  Joy to the mortal
  Whom the pernicious
  Lingering, inherited   740
  Dearths encompassed.
FAUST. What bright clear tone, what whirring drone profound
  Makes me put this glass from my lips away?
  Do you deep bells already sound
  The solemn first hour of the Easter Day?
  Do you choirs sing the song that once such comfort gave
  When angels sang it by the darkness of a grave
  Assuring a new covenant that day?
CHORUS OF WOMEN. With spices embalmed
  Here we had carried Him,   750

---

18. Angel voices are heard in all poetic appropriateness in this scene, which
is a dialogue between Faust and "spirits." On a more literal plane, a nearby
church is to be assumed, where a miracle play of the Resurrection is being
enacted. Angels at the empty tomb make replies to the three Marys. See Luke
24. Regarding the rhyme scheme for the Chorus of Angels, see l. 807*n*.

We, His devoted,
Here we had buried Him;
With winding cloths
Cleanly we wrapped Him;
But, alas, we find
Christ is not here.

CHORUS OF ANGELS. Christ is arisen!
Blessed the loving
Who stood the troubling,
Stood the healing,   760
Chastening test.

FAUST. Why seek here in the dust for me,
You heavenly tones so mighty and so mild?
Ring out around where gentle souls may be.
I hear your tidings but I lack for faith,
And Miracle is Faith's most favored child.
As high as to those spheres I dare not soar
Whence sound these tidings of great joy;
Yet by these sounds, familiar since I was a boy,
I now am summoned back to life once more.   770
Once there would downward rush to me the kiss
Of heavenly love in solemn Sabbath hour;
Then plenitude of bell tones rang with mystic power
And prayer had the intensity of bliss;
Past comprehension sweet, a yearning
Drove me to wander field and forest where
Amid a thousand hot tears burning
I felt a world arise which was most fair.
The merry games of youth are summoned by that song,
And free delight of springtime festival;   780
And by that memory with childlike feeling strong
I am kept from this final step of all.
Sing on, sweet songs, in that celestial strain!
A teardrop falls, the earth has me again!

CHORUS OF DISCIPLES. If from the dead
He has ascended,
Living, sublime,
Glorious on high,

If He in His growth [19]   790
Nears creative joy,
We, alas, are still here
On the bosom of earth.
He has left His own
Behind here to languish;
Master, we mourn
Thy happiness.
CHORUS OF ANGELS. Christ is arisen
From the womb of decay;
Bonds that imprison
You, rend gladsome away!   800
For you as you praise Him,
Proving your love,
Fraternally sharing,
Preaching and faring,
Rapture proclaiming,
For you the Master is near,
For you He is here.[20]

Outside the City Gate

All sorts of people coming out for a walk.

SEVERAL APPRENTICES. But why go up the hill?
OTHERS. We're going to the Hunting Lodge up there.
THE FIRST ONES. We'd rather walk out to the Mill.   810
ONE APPRENTICE. I'd suggest you go to the Reservoir.

---

19. The word "growth" stands for the original *Werdelust* which can only be
roughly paraphrased as "delight in the process of becoming." The difficult—
and entirely unorthodox—idea underlying ll. 790–91 becomes clear by con-
frontation with ll. 11,934 to the end of the poem, and with l. 11,980n.
20. In view of the intricacies of rhyme which these Easter choruses combine
with uncommon verbal compression and with grammatical tours de force, the
translator has chosen to render them fairly literally and line for line, with only
occasional rhymes to suggest the lyric quality of the original.

THE SECOND. It's not a pleasant walk, you know.

OTHERS. How about you?

A THIRD.   I'll go where the others go.

A FOURTH.

Come on to Burgdorf! There you're sure to find good cheer,
The prettiest girls and also first-rate beer,
And the best fights you'll ever face.

A FIFTH. You glutton, do you itch to go
For your third drubbing in a row?
I have a horror of that place.

SERVING GIRL. No, no! I'm going back now, if you please.   820

ANOTHER. We'll surely find him standing by those poplar trees.

THE FIRST GIRL. For me that's no great lucky chance;
He'll walk at your side and he'll dance
With none but you upon the lea.
What good will your fun be to me?

THE OTHER GIRL. He won't be there alone today; he said
He'd bring along the curlyhead.

SCHOLAR.[1] Damn! How those lusty wenches hit their stride!
Brother, come on! We'll walk it at their side.
Strong beer, tobacco with a bite,   830
A girl decked in her best, just suit my appetite.

GIRL OF THE MIDDLE CLASS.

Just see those handsome boys! It certainly
Is just a shame and a disgrace;
They could enjoy the very best society,
And after serving girls they chase.

SECOND SCHOLAR (to the FIRST).

Don't go so fast! Behind us are two more,
Both very nicely dressed;
One is my neighbor from next door
In whom I take an interest.
They walk demurely, but you'll see   840
How they will overtake us finally.

THE FIRST. No, Brother, I don't like things in my way.
Quick! Let's not lose these wildfowl on our chase.

---

1. "Scholar" in the old-fashioned sense of "student."

The hand that wields the broom on Saturday
On Sunday will provide the best embrace.[2]

CITIZEN. No, this new burgomaster, I don't care for him,
And now he's in, he daily gets more grim.
And for the city, what's he done?
Don't things get worse from day to day?
More rules than ever to obey,   850
And taxes worse than any yet, bar none.

BEGGAR (*sings*). Kind gentlemen and ladies fair,
So rosy-cheeked and gay of dress,
Be good enough to hear my prayer,
Relieve my want and my distress.
Let me not vainly tune my lay.
Glad is the giver and only he.
Now that all men keep holiday,
Be there a harvest day for me.

ANOTHER CITIZEN.
There's nothing better for Sunday or a holiday   860
Than talk about war and war's alarms,
When off in Turkey people up in arms
Are battling in a far-off fray.
You sip your glass, stand by the window side,
And down the river watch the painted vessels glide,
Then come home in the evening all at ease,
Blessing peace and the times of peace.

THIRD CITIZEN. Yes, neighbor, that's the way I like it too:
Let them beat out each other's brains,
Turn everything up wrong-end-to,   870
So long as here at home our good old way remains.

OLD WOMAN (*to the* MIDDLE-CLASS GIRLS).
Heyday! How smart! My young and pretty crew!
Now who could help but fall for you?—
But don't act quite so proud. You'll do!
And what you're after, I could help you to.

MIDDLE-CLASS GIRL. Come, Agatha! I don't want to be seen

---

2. At this point the Scholars set off in pursuit of the Serving Girls, while the Middle-Class Girls remain waiting on the sidelines; the Citizens come along.

In public with such witches. It's quite true
My future lover last Saint Andrew's E'en
In flesh and blood she let me view— [3]

THE OTHER GIRL. She showed me mine too in her crystal glass,   880
A soldier type, with dashing friends behind him;
I look for him in every one I pass
And yet I just don't seem to find him.

SOLDIERS. Castles and towers,
Ramparts so high,
Girls of disdainful
Scorn-casting eye,
I'd like to win!
Keen is the contest,
Grand is the pay!   890
      We'll let the trumpets
Sound out the call,
Whether to joy
Or to downfall.
There's an assault!
That is the life!
Maidens and castles
Surrender in strife.
Keen is the contest,
Grand is the pay!   900
And then the soldiers
Go marching away.

(*Enter* FAUST *and* WAGNER.)

FAUST. From ice are released the streams and brooks
At springtime's lovely, life-giving gaze;
Now hope smiles green down valley ways;
Old Winter feebly flees to nooks
Of rugged hills, and as he hies
Casts backward from him in his flight
Impotent showers of gritty ice

---

3. On Nov. 30th Saint Andrew, the patron saint of the unwed, will, if properly invoked, grant visions of future spouses.

In streaks over meadows newly green.   910
But the sun permits of nothing white,
Everything is growth and striving,
All things are in colors reviving,
And lack of flowers in the countryside
By gay-clad humans is supplied.
Turn and from these heights look down
And backwards yonder toward the town.
From the hollow, gloomy gate
Streams a throng in motley array.
All want to sun themselves today.   920
The Lord's resurrection they celebrate
For they are themselves new risen from tombs:
From squalid houses' dingy rooms,
From tradesman's and apprentice' chains,
From crushing streets and choking lanes,
From roof's and gable's oppressive mass,
From their churches' everlasting night,
They are all brought forth into the light.
See now, just see how swiftly they pass
And scatter to fields' and gardens' grass   930
And how so many merry boats
The river's length and breadth there floats,
How almost sinking with its load
That last barque pushes from the quay.
From even the hillside's distant road
Bright costumes glimmer colorfully.
Sounds of village mirth arise,
Here is the people's true paradise.
Both great and small send up a cheer:
"Here I am human, I can *be* human here!"   940
WAGNER. Doctor, to take a walk with you
Is an honor and a gain, of course,
But come here alone, that I'd never do,
Because I am a foe of all things coarse.
This fiddling, shouting, bowling, I detest
And all that with it goes along;
They rage as if by fiends possessed

And call it pleasure, call it song!

(*Peasants under the linden tree. Dance and song.*)

The shepherd for the dance got dressed
In wreath and bows and fancy vest,   950
And bravely did he show.
Beneath the linden lass and lad
Were dancing round and round like mad.
Juchhe! Juchhe!
Juchheisa! Heisa! He!
So went the fiddlebow.

    In through the crowd he pushed in haste
And jostled one girl in the waist
All with his sharp elbow.
The buxom lass, she turned her head,   960
"Well, that was stupid, now!" she said.
Juchhe! Juchhe!
Juchheisa! Heisa! He!
"Don't be so rude, fine fellow!"

    The ring spun round with all its might,
They danced to left, they danced to right,
And see the coattails go!
And they got red, and they got warm,
And breathless waited arm in arm,
Juchhe! Juchhe!   970
Juchheisa! Heisa! He!
A hip against an elbow.

    "Don't be so free! How many a maid
Has been betrothed and been betrayed
By carrying on just so!"
And yet he coaxed her to one side,
And from the linden far and wide
Juchhe! Juchhe!
Juchheisa! Heisa! He!
Rang shout and fiddlebow.   980

OLD PEASANT. Doctor, it's really nice of you
    Not to shun our mirth today,
    And such a larnèd master too,

To mingle with the folk this way.
Therefore accept our finest stein
Filled with cool drink and let me first
Present it with this wish of mine:
May it not only quench your thirst—
May all its count of drops be added to
The sum of days that are allotted you.   990
FAUST. I take the cooling drink you offer me
And wish you thanks and all prosperity.

(*The people gather around in a circle.*)

OLD PEASANT. Indeed it was most kind of you
On this glad day to come here thus,
For in the evil days gone by
You proved a friend to all of us.
Many a man is here alive
Because your father in the past
Saved him from raging fever's fury
When he had stemmed the plague at last.   1000
And as a young man you went too
Among the houses of the pest;
Many a corpse they carried out
But you came healthy from the test.
You bore up under trials severe;
The Helper yonder helped the helper here.
ALL. Good health attend the proven man,
Long may he help, as help he can!
FAUST. Bow to Him yonder who provides
His help and teaches help besides.   1010

(*He walks on with* WAGNER.)

WAGNER. What feelings must be yours, O noble man,
Before the veneration of this crowd!
O fortunate indeed is one who can
So profit from the gifts with which he is endowed!
The fathers show you to their sons,
Each asks and pushes in and runs,
The fiddle stops, the dancer waits,

They stand in rows where you pass by,
And all their caps go flying high:
A little more and they would bend the knee   1020
As if there passed the Venerabile.[4]
FAUST. Only a few steps more now up to yonder stone
And we shall rest from our long walk. Up there
I often used to sit and brood alone
And rack myself with fasting and with prayer.
Then rich in hope, in faith secure,
By wringing of hands, by tears and sighs,
I sought the plague's end to assure
By forcing the Lord of the skies.
Praise sounds like mockery on the people's part.   1030
If you could only read within my heart
How little father and son
Were worthy of the fame they won!
My father was a man of honor but obscure
Who over Nature and her holy spheres would brood
In his own way and with capricious mood,
Though wholly upright, to be sure.
With other adepts of the art he locked
Himself in his black kitchen and from lists
Of endless recipes sought to concoct   1040
A blend of the antagonists.[5]
There a Red Lion—a wooer to aspire—
Was in a warm bath with the Lily wed,
And both were then tormented over open fire
From one into the other bridal bed.
If the Young Queen was then espied

---

4. The Blessed Sacrament, i.e., the consecrated wafer contained in a round,
glass-covered compartment in the center of a golden sun-burst monstrance,
which is carried aloft in procession.
5. Using actual 16th-century terms, though a trifle freely, Goethe describes
the manufacture of "the Philosopher's Stone" in an alchemist's laboratory
("black kitchen"). The male "antagonist," derived from gold and called "the
Blood of the Golden Lion" or "the Red Lion" (mercuric oxide), was "wed"
with the female "antagonist," derived from silver and called "the White
Eagle" or "the Lily" (hydrochloric acid), in a retort ("bridal bed"); the
"offspring" was "the Young Queen" or "the Philosopher's Stone."

In rainbow hues within the flask,
There was our medicine; the patients died,
And "Who got well?" none thought to ask.
Thus we with hellish tonics wrought more ills   1050
Among these valleys and these hills,
And raged more fiercely, than the pest.
I gave the poison out to thousands with my hand;
They withered, and I have to stand
And hear the ruthless killers blessed.

WAGNER. How can such things make you downcast?
Has not a good man done sufficient
In being conscientious and proficient
At skills transmitted from the past?
If you respect your father in your youth,   1060
You will receive his fund of knowledge whole;
If as a man you swell the store of truth,
Your son can then achieve a higher goal.

FAUST. O happy he who still can hope
To rise out of the sea of errors here!
What one most needs to know exceeds his scope,
And what one knows is useless and unclear.
But let us not spoil hours that are so fair
With these dark melancholy thoughts of mine!
See how beneath the sunset air   1070
The green-girt cottages all shine.
The sun moves on, the day has spent its force,
Yonder it speeds, new day eliciting.
O that I am swept upward on no wing
To follow it forever in its course!
Then I would see by deathless evening rays
The silent world beneath my feet,
All valleys calmed, all mountaintops ablaze,
And silver brooks with golden rivers meet.
No mountains then would block my godlike flight   1080
For all the chasms gashed across their ways;
And soon the sea with its warmed bays
Would open to my wondering sight.
But now the goddess seems to sink down finally;

But a new impulse wakes in me,
I hasten forth to drink her everlasting light,
With day in front of me and at my back the night,
With waves down under me and over me the sky.
A glorious dream, dreamed while the day declined.
Alas, that to the pinions of the mind   1090
No wing corporeal is joined as their ally.
And yet inborn in all our race
Is impulse upward, forward, and along,
When overhead and lost in azure space
The lark pours forth its trilling song,
When over jagged pine tree heights
The full-spread eagle wheels its flights,
And when across the seas and plains
Onward press the homing cranes.
WAGNER. I have had moody hours of my own,   1100
But such an impulse I have never known.
The spectacle of woods and fields soon cloys,
I'll never envy birds their pinionage;
But how we *are* borne on by mental joys
From book to book, from page to page!
How sweet and fair the winter nights become,
A blessed life glows warm in every limb,
And oh! if one unrolls a noble parchment tome,
The whole of heaven then comes down to him.
FAUST. By one impulse alone are you possessed,   1110
O may you never know the other!
Two souls abide, alas, within my breast,[6]
And each one seeks for riddance from the other.
The one clings with a dogged love and lust
With clutching parts unto this present world,
The other surges fiercely from the dust
Unto sublime ancestral fields.
If there are spirits in the air
Between the earth and heaven holding sway,

---

6. The two impulses are to repose and exertion, rather than Christian flesh
and spirit.

Descend out of your golden fragrance there   1120
And to new life of many hues sweep me away!
Yes, if a magic mantle were but mine,
And if to far-off lands it bore me,
Not for all costly raiment placed before me
Would I exchange it; kings' cloaks I would decline!
WAGNER. Do not invoke that well-known troop
    That stream above us in the murky air,
    Who from all quarters down on mankind swoop
    And bring the thousand perils they prepare.
    With whetted spirit fangs down from the north   1130
    They pitch upon you with their arrowy tongues;
    Out of the morning's east they issue forth
    To prey with parching breath upon your lungs;
    And if the south up from the desert drives
    Those which heap fire on fire upon your brain,
    The west brings on the swarm that first revives
    Then drowns you as it drowns the field and plain.
    They listen eagerly, on mischief bent,
    And to deceive us, willingly comply,
    They often pose as being heaven sent   1140
    And lisp like angels when they lie.
    But let us go. The world has all turned grey,
    The air is chill, mist closes out the day.
    With nightfall one enjoys a room.—
    Why do you stand and stare with wondering gaze?
    What so arrests you out there in the gloom?
FAUST. Do you see that black dog that through the stubble strays?
WAGNER. He looks quite unremarkable to me.
FAUST. Look close! What do you take the beast to be?
WAGNER. A poodle, searching with his natural bent   1150
    And snuffing for his master's scent.
FAUST. Do you see how he spirals round us, snail-
    shell-wise, and ever closer on our trail?
    And if I'm not mistaken, he lays welts
    Of fire behind him in his wake.
WAGNER. I see a plain black poodle, nothing else;
    Your eyes must be the cause of some mistake.

FAUST. I seem to see deft snares of magic laid
    For future bondage round our feet somehow.
WAGNER. I see him run about uncertain and afraid   1160
    Because he sees two strangers, not his master now.
FAUST. The circle narrows, he is near!
WAGNER. You see! It's just a dog, no phantom here.
    He growls, he doubts, lies belly-flat and all,
    And wags his tail. All doggish protocol.
FAUST. Come here! Come join our company!
WAGNER. He's just a foolish pup. You see?
    You stop, and he will wait for you,
    You speak to him, and he'll jump up on you,
    Lose something, and he'll fetch it quick,   1170
    Or go in water for a stick.
FAUST. You must be right, I see there's not a trace
    Of spirits. It's his training he displays.
WAGNER. A sage himself will often find
    He likes a dog that's trained to mind.
    Yes, he deserves your favor totally,
    A model scholar of the students, he.

(They go in through the city gate.)

Study Room

FAUST *entering with the poodle.*

FAUST. From field and meadow I withdraw
    Which deepest darkness now bedecks,
    With holy and foreboding awe   1180
    The better soul within us wakes.
    Asleep now are my wild desires,
    My vehement activity;
    The love of mankind now aspires,
    The love of God aspires in me.
        Be quiet, poodle! Why should you romp and rove?

What are you snuffing there at the sill?
Go and lie down behind the stove,
I'll give you my best pillow if you're still.
Out there on the hill-road back to town   1190
You amused us by running and frisking your best;
Now accept your keep from me; lie down
And be a welcome and quiet guest.
    Ah, when in our close cell by night
The lamp burns with a friendly cheer,
Then deep within us all grows bright
And hearts that know themselves grow clear.
Reason begins once more to speak
And hope begins to bloom again,
The brooks of life we yearn to seek   1200
And to life's source, ah! to attain.
    Stop growling, poodle! With the sacred tones that rise
And now my total soul embrace,
Your animal noise is out of place.
We are accustomed to having men despise
What they do not understand;
The good and the beautiful they misprize,
Finding it cumbersome, they scowl and growl;
Must a dog, like men, set up a howl?
    But alas! with the best of will I feel no more   1210
Contentment welling up from my heart's core.
Why must the stream so soon run dry
And we again here thirsting lie?
These things experiences familiarize.
But this lack can find compensation,
The supernatural we learn to prize,
And then we long for revelation,
Which nowhere burns more nobly or more bright
Than here in the New Testament. Tonight
An impulse urges me to reach   1220
Out for this basic text and with sincere
Emotion make its holy meaning clear
Within my own beloved German speech.

(*He opens a volume and sets about it.*)

It says: "In the beginning was the *Word*." [1]
Already I am stuck! And who will help afford?
Mere word I cannot possibly so prize,
I must translate it otherwise.
Now if the Spirit lends me proper light,
"In the beginning was the *Mind*" would be more nearly right.
Consider that first line with care,   1230
The pen must not be overhasty there!
Can it be mind that makes and shapes all things?
It should read: "In the beginning was the *Power*."
But even as I write down this word too,
Something warns me that it will not do.
Now suddenly the Spirit prompts me in my need,
I confidently write: "In the beginning was the *Deed!*"
    If I'm to share this room with you,
Poodle, that howling must be curbed.
And stop that barking too!   1240
I cannot be disturbed
By one who raises such a din.
One of us must give in
And leave this cell we're in.
I hate to drive you out of here,
But the door is open, the way is clear.
But what is this I see?
Can such things happen naturally?
Is this reality or fraud?
My poodle grows both long and broad!   1250
He rises up with might;
No dog's shape this! This can't be right!
What phantom have I harbored thus?
He's like a hippopotamus
With fiery eyes and ghastly teeth.
O, I see what's beneath!
For such a mongrel of hell

---

1. John 1:1, *En arkhê ēn o logos,* in which the word *logos* ("Word") has
a complex theological meaning of pre-Christian origin.

The Key of Solomon works well.[2]

SPIRITS (*in the corridor*).

Captive inside there is one of us,
Stay out here, follow him none of us.   1260
Like a fox in an iron snare
A lynx of hell is cornered in there.
But take heed!
Hover to, hover fro,
Above, below,
And pretty soon he'll be freed.
If you can help him in aught
Don't leave him caught.
Many a turn he has done
Helping us every one.   1270

FAUST. To deal with the beast before
Me, I'll use the spell of the four: [3]
    Salamander shall kindle,
Undine shall coil,
Sylph shall dwindle,
Kobold shall toil.

    Lacking the lore
Of the elements four,
Not knowing aright
Their use and might,   1280
None shall be lord
Of the spirit horde.

---

2. The *Key of Solomon* was a quasi-religious book composed in Hebrew, and enormously popular in Latin translation as *Clavicula Salomonis* from the 16th to the 18th centuries. It dealt with the rules and means for controlling spirits.

3. The "spell of the four" is Goethe's whimsical invention, based on the *Key of Solomon*. By pronouncing it, Faust seeks to compel the spirit which has assumed a dog's shape to appear in its true form: as fire, if it is a fire spirit (salamander); as water, if it is a water spirit (undine, nixie, nymph); as air —represented by a shooting star or meteor—if it is an air spirit; as personified earth (kobold, incubus, gnome, dwarf, pygmy), if it is an earth spirit. The incubi were particularly malevolent since, as nightmares, they bestrode and oppressed sleeping persons.

Vanish in flame,
Salamander!
Together rush and stream,
Undine!
In meteor glory gleam,
Sylph!
Bring help to the house,
Incubus! Incubus!   1290
Step forth and make an ending! Thus!
    None of the four
Lurks in the beast.
He lies and grins at me as before,
I have not harmed him in the least.
You'll hear me tell
A stronger spell.
    Do you, fellow, live
As hell's fugitive?
See this sign now [4]   1300
To which they bow,
The black hordes of hell!
    With hair abristle he starts to swell.
    Forfeiter of bliss,
Can you read this?
The never-created
Of name unstated,
Diffused through all heavens' expanse,
Transpierced by the infamous lance? [5]
    Back of the stove he flees from my spells,   1310
There like an elephant he swells,
He fills the room entire,

---

4. The sign INRI or JNRJ, abbreviation for "Jesus the Nazarene, King of the
Jews" (*Jesus Nazarenus Rex Judaeorum*), which Pilate had inscribed on the
cross that held the body of Jesus at the crucifixion (John 19:19). Faust apparently holds a crucifix over the shape-shifting spirit-beast.
5. John 19:34 states that one of the attendant soldiers thrust his lance into
the side of the dead Jesus. The three previous lines refer to Christ as un-
created, i.e., existent from all time, as inconceivable in terms of any earthly
name, and as "the same also that ascended up far above all heavens, that He
might fill all things" (Ephesians 4:10).

He melts like a mist of sleet.
Rise ceilingwards no higher!
Fall down at your master's feet.
You see that mine is no idle threat.
With sacred flame I will scorch you yet.
Await not the might
Of the triply burning light! [6]
Await not the sight   1320
Of my arts in their fullest measure!

(*As the mist falls away,* MEPHISTOPHELES *steps forth from
behind the stove, dressed as a traveling scholar.*[7])

MEPHISTOPHELES.
    Why all the fuss? What is the gentleman's pleasure?
FAUST. So this was what was in the cur!
    A traveling scholar? That's the best joke I've heard yet.
MEPHISTOPHELES. I salute you, learned Sir.
    You had me in a mighty sweat.
FAUST. What is your name? [8]
MEPHISTOPHELES.   For one so disesteeming
    The word, the question seems so small to me,
    And for a man disdainful of all seeming,
    Who searches only for reality.   1330
FAUST. With gentlemen like you, their nature is deduced
    Quite often from the name that's used,
    As all too patently applies
    When you are named Corrupter, Liar, God of Flies.[9]
    All right, who are you then?
MEPHISTOPHELES.   Part of that Force which would
    Do evil ever yet forever works the good.
FAUST. What sense is there beneath that riddling guise?
MEPHISTOPHELES. I am the Spirit that constantly denies!

---

6. The "sign" of the Trinity.
7. Traveling scholars were frequently rogues and adventurers.
8. To know a spirit's name was to give one "a name to conjure with," and
hence put the spirit in the knower's power.
9. The "Baal-zebub the god of Ekron" of II Kings 1:2, usually etymologized
as "the god of flies" or "the fly-god."

And rightly so; for everything that's ever brought
To life deserves to come to naught.   1340
Better if nothing ever came to be.
Thus all that you call sin, you see,
And havoc—evil, in short—is meant
To be my proper element.

FAUST.

You call yourself a part, yet stand quite whole before me there?

MEPHISTOPHELES.

It is the modest truth that I declare.
Now folly's little microcosm, man,
Boasts *him*self whole as often as he can. . . .
I am part of the part which once was absolute,
Part of the Darkness which gave birth to Light,   1350
The haughty Light, which now seeks to dispute
The ancient rank and range of Mother Night,
But unsuccessfully, because, try as it will,
It is stuck fast to bodies still.
It streams from bodies, bodies it makes fair,
A body hinders its progression; thus I hope
It won't be long before its scope
Will in the bodies' ruination share.

FAUST. I see your fine objectives now!
Wholesale annihilation fails somehow,   1360
So you go at it one by one.

MEPHISTOPHELES. I don't get far, when all is said and done.
The thing opposed to Nothingness,
This stupid earth, this Somethingness,
For all that I have undertaken
Against it, still remains unshaken;
In spite of tempest, earthquake, flood, and flame
The earth and ocean calmly stay the same.
And as for that damned stuff, the brood of beasts and man,
With them there's nothing I can do.   1370
To think how many I have buried too!
Fresh blood runs in their veins just as it always ran.
And so it goes. Sometimes I could despair!
In earth, in water, and in air

A thousand growing things unfold,
In dryness, wetness, warmth, and cold!
Had I not specially reserved the flame,
I wouldn't have a thing in my own name.

FAUST. So you shake your cold devil's fist
   Clenched in futile rage malign, 1380
   So you the endless Power resist,
   The creative, living, and benign!
   Some other goal had best be sought,
   Chaos' own fantastic son!

MEPHISTOPHELES. We really shall give this some thought
   And talk about it more anon.
   Right now, however, might I go?

FAUST. Why you should ask, I don't quite see.
   Now that we've made acquaintance, though,
   Come any time to visit me. 1390
   Here is the window, there the doors,
   The chimney too is practical.

MEPHISTOPHELES. Must I confess? To leave this room of yours
   There is a trifling obstacle.
   The witch's foot there on the sill— [10]

FAUST. The pentagram distresses you?
   But tell me now, O son of hell,
   If that prevents you, how did you get through?
   Could such a spirit be so blind?

MEPHISTOPHELES. Observe it carefully. It's ill designed. 1400
   One point there, facing outward as it were,
   Is just a bit disjoined, you see.

FAUST. Now what a lucky chance for me!
   And so you are my prisoner?
   And all by merest accident!

MEPHISTOPHELES. The poodle did not notice when in he went.
   Things now take on a different shape:
   The Devil's caught and can't escape.

---

10. The witch's foot, identical with the pentagram of the following line, is a symbol made up of interlocking triangles to form a five-pointed star. Known also as "the sign of Christ," it was inscribed to ward off evil spirits.

FAUST. But why not use the window to withdraw?
MEPHISTOPHELES. With devils and with spirits it's a law: 1410
    Where they slipped in, they must go out.
    The first is up to us, the second leaves no doubt:
    There we are slaves.
FAUST.   So hell has its own law?
    I find that good, because a pact could then
    Perhaps be worked out with you gentlemen?
MEPHISTOPHELES. What once is promised, you will revel in,
    No skimping and no spreading thin.
    But such things can't be done so fast,
    We'll speak of that when next we meet.
    And now I beg you first and last   1420
    To let me make my fair retreat.
FAUST. Just for a single moment yet remain
    And tell me of some pleasant news.
MEPHISTOPHELES. No, let me go now! I'll come back again,
    Then you can ask me all you choose.
FAUST. I never had a plan so bold
    As capturing you. You walked into the snare.
    Whoever holds the Devil, let him hold!
    A second time he will not have him there.
MEPHISTOPHELES. I am quite ready, if you choose,   1430
    To keep you company and stay,
    But on condition that I use
    My worthy skills to while the time away.
FAUST. I'd like to see them, so feel free,
    Just so the skills work pleasantly.
MEPHISTOPHELES. Your senses will, my friend, gain more
    In this hour than you've known before
    In one whole year's monotony.
    And what my dainty spirits sing you,
    The lovely images they bring you   1440
    Will be no empty magic play.
    Your sense of smell shall be delighted,
    Your sense of taste shall be excited,
    And feelings will sweep you away.
    No preparation shall we need;

We are assembled, so proceed!
SPIRITS.[11] Vanish, you gloomy
    Vaultings above!
    Lovelier hue
    Of aether's blue   1450
    Be shed in here!
    O might the darkling
    Clouds melt for once!
    Stars begin sparkling;
    Mellower suns
    Shine now in here.
    Sons of the air,
    Of beauty rare,
    Hover thronging,
    Wafting in light.   1460
    Ardent longing
    Follows their flight.
    Raiment in strands
    Shed as streamer bands
    Cover the lands,
    Cover the groves
    Where lovers vow,
    Lost in reverie,
    Lifelong loves.
    Arbors on arbors!   1470
    Lush greenery!
    Masses of grapes
    Tumble from vines
    Into presses and vats,
    Gush now as brooks
    Of foaming wines,
    Trickle as rills
    Through gorges that wind,
    Leaving the hills
    Far behind,   1480
    Widening to lakes

---

11. From the corridor, where they were gathered at l. 1259.

Around the abundance
Of verdant heights.
And then the birds
Drink delight,
Fly to the sun,
Fly to the bright
Islands that gleam
Drifting and glittering
Upon the stream;   1490
There we hear choirs
Of jubilant throngs,
See them on meadows
At dances and songs,
Disporting free
In festivity;
Climbing, some,
Over the peaks,
Skimming, some,
Over the lakes,   1500
Still others fly;
All toward the high
Joy of existence,
All toward the distance
Of loving stars.[12]

MEPHISTOPHELES.

He is asleep. Well done, my dainty, airy youngsters!
You lulled him loyally, my songsters!
I am much in your debt for such a concert.

---

12. The spirits speak Faust's incantatory dream: ll. 1447–54, the vaulted
arches of the Gothic room dissolve into cloud, which in turn dissolves into
starry sky (of this Easter night); 1455–62, a new and different day is reached
by Faust's spirit on its flight accompanied by other spirits, and ardent longing
projects the flight still further; 1463–74, the spirits "shed down" the beauties
of an Arcadian landscape with many pairs of lovers in leafy shade and with
the grape harvest in progress; 1475–90, the grapejuice spurting from the
presses becomes rivers flowing through mountain gorges to emerge as a flood
that turns hills into islands; birds drink the wines and become intoxicated
with rapture; 1491–1505, the vintage festivals become a Bacchic revel on the
newly made Isles of the Blessed. The dream is a wild upsurge of voluptuous
desire. The Greek scene anticipates motifs to be developed in Part II.

You are not yet the man to hold the Devil fast!
Around him your sweet dream illusions cast   1510
And steep him in a sea of fancy;
But now I need a rat's tooth to divest
This threshold of its necromancy.
No lengthy incantation will be needed,
Here comes one rustling up, and my word will be heeded.
The Master of the rats and mice,
Of bedbugs, flies, and frogs and lice,
Commands you boldly to appear
And gnaw this carven threshold clear
Where he has daubed a jot of oil— [13]   1520
Ah, there you scamper up to toil!
Get right to work! I'm hemmed in by the wedge
That's right there on the outer edge.
Just one more bite and then it's done.—
Now, till we meet again, Faustus, dream on!
FAUST (*waking*). Have I been once again betrayed?
    The spirit throng has fled so utterly
    That I but dreamed the Devil came and stayed
    And that a poodle got away from me?

Study Room [*II*]

FAUST   MEPHISTOPHELES

FAUST. A knock? Come in! Who now comes bothering me?   1530
MEPHISTOPHELES. It's I.
FAUST.   Come in!
MEPHISTOPHELES.   A third call there must be.
FAUST. Come in, then!
MEPHISTOPHELES.   That's the way I like to hear you.

---

13. Mephistopheles probably dips his finger in the oil of the lamp and smears
the imperfectly drawn angle of the pentagram on the threshold. Oil is bait for
rodents.

We shall, I trust, get on quite well,
For I have come here to dispel
Your moods, and as a noble squire be near you,
Clad all in scarlet and gold braid,
With my short cape of stiff silk made,
A rooster feather on my hat,
A long sharp rapier at my side,[1]
And I advise you to provide   1540
Yourself a costume just like that,
So you, untrammeled and set free,
Can find out just what life can be.

FAUST. No matter what might be my own attire,
I would feel life cramped anyway.
I am too old merely to play,
Too young to be without desire.
What can the world give me? Renounce,
Renounce shalt thou, thou shalt renounce!
That is the everlasting song   1550
Dinned in our ears throughout the course
Of all our lives, which all life long
Each hour sings until it's hoarse.
Mornings I wake with horror and could weep
Hot tears at seeing the new sun
Which will not grant me in its sweep
Fulfillment of a single wish, not one,
Which mars anticipated joys
Themselves with willful captiousness
And with a thousand petty frets destroys   1560
My eager heart's creativeness.
At nightfall I must lie down ill at ease
Upon my couch of misery where
There will be neither rest nor peace,
Wild dreams will terrify me even there.
The god that in my heart abides

---

1. Approximation of Spanish court costume of *ca.* 1500–1550, when the historical Faust (d. 1539?) was alive and when German lands formed part of the immense empire ruled by Charles V from Madrid.

Can stir my soul's profoundest springs;
He over all my energies presides
But cannot alter outward things.
Existence is a weight by which I am oppressed,   1570
With death desired, life something to detest.
MEPHISTOPHELES. And yet Death never is a wholly welcome guest.
FAUST. O happy he around whose brow Death winds
    The blood-stained wreath in victory's radiance,
    Or he whom in a girl's embrace Death finds
    After the hectic whirling of the dance!
    O, had I in my exultation sunk
    Down dead before the lofty Spirit's power!
MEPHISTOPHELES. And yet a brownish potion was not drunk
    By someone on a certain midnight hour.   1580
FAUST. Spying, it seems, amuses you.
MEPHISTOPHELES.   I dare
    Not claim omniscience, but of much I am aware.
FAUST. If from that harrowing confusion
    A sweet familiar tone drew me away,
    Belied me with a child's profusion
    Of memories from a former day,
    I now curse everything that holds the soul
    Enchanted by the lures of sorcery
    And charms it in this dreary hole
    By sweet illusion and duplicity!   1590
    Cursed be the lofty self-opinion
    With which the mind itself deludes!
    Cursed be phenomena's dominion
    Which on our senses so intrudes!
    Cursed be the cheating dream obsessions
    With name and fame that have us so beguiled!
    Cursed be what we have deemed possessions:
    Servant and plow, and wife and child!
    Cursed be old Mammon [2] when with treasure
    He lures to deeds adventurous   1600

---

2. The Aramaic word *mamona*, "riches," used by Jesus to personify the false
god of riches (Matthew 6:24 and Luke 16:13).

Or when for idleness and pleasure
He spreads the pillows soft for us!
Cursed be the nectar of the grape!
Cursed be love at its happiest!
And cursed be hope! And cursed be faith!
And cursed be patience more than all the rest!

CHORUS OF SPIRITS (*invisible*). Woe! Woe!
You have destroyed
The beauteous world
With mighty fist;   1610
It crumbles, it collapses!
A demigod has shattered it!
We carry
The fragments to the void,
We grieve
For beauty so destroyed.
More mightily,
Son of earth,
More splendidly
Bring it to birth,   1620
Rebuild it in the heart of you!
Begin a new
Life course
With senses clear,
And may new songs
Hail it with cheer! [3]

MEPHISTOPHELES. These are the minions
From my dominions.
Precociously wise,
Deeds and desires they now advise.   1630
Out of solitude
Where senses and saps are glued,
To the wide world's view

---

3. Interpretations differ as to the significance of this chorus and Mephisto's identifications of the singers. Witkowski plausibly argues for this one: the spirits are benevolent; their thoughts are the author's own; Mephisto's claim to the spirits is opportunistic, as is his seizing on their words, to which he lends his own flat, utilitarian, and unbenevolent meaning.

They lure and summon you.
  Cease toying with your sorrow then,
Which tears your life as vulture-talons tear;
The worst of company makes you aware
You are a man with other men.
This does not indicate
That you're to run with the pack;   1640
I am not one of the great,
But if you want a track
Through life together with me,
I'll adapt myself quite willingly
To be yours right here and now.
I am your fellow,
If it suits you, to the grave,
I am your servant and your slave.

FAUST. And what am I supposed to do for you?

MEPHISTOPHELES. There's lots of time before that's due.   1650

FAUST. No, no! The Devil is an egoist
And does not willingly assist
Another just for God's sake.[4] I insist
You make all your conditions clear;
Such a slave is one to fear.

MEPHISTOPHELES. I'll bind myself to be your servant *here*
And at your beck and call wait tirelessly,
If when there in the *yonder* we appear
You will perform the same for me.

FAUST. The yonder is of small concern.   1660
Once you have smashed this world to pieces,
The other one may come to be in turn.[5]
It is out of this earth that my joy springs
And this sun shines upon my sufferings;
Once free of them, this trouble ceases;

---

4. "For God's sake" (*um Gottes willen*) is the beggar's formula for asking alms.
5. If by any chance Goethe used the word *entstehn* ("come to be") in its obsolete sense of "to be lacking," the whole sense of the lines would be changed: If you smash this world to pieces, the other world may not exist either.

Then come what may and as time brings.
About all that I do not wish to hear,
Whether in future there is hate and love
And whether in that yonder sphere
There is a new beneath and new above.   1670

MEPHISTOPHELES. In this mood you dare venture it. Just make
    The compact, and I then will undertake
    To turn my skills to joy. I'll give you more
    Than any man has ever seen before.

FAUST. Poor, sorry Devil, what could you deliver?
    Was human mind in lofty aspiration ever
    Comprehended by the likes of you?
    Do you have food that does not satisfy? Or do
    You have red gold that will run through
    The hand like quicksilver and away?   1680
    A game that none may win who play?
    A girl who in my very arms
    Will pledge love to my neighbor with her eyes?
    Or honor with its godlike charms
    Which like a shooting star flashes and dies?
    Show me the fruit that rots right on the tree,
    And trees that every day leaf out anew!

MEPHISTOPHELES. Such a demand does not daunt me,
    Such treasures I can furnish you.
    But still the time will come around, good friend,   1690
    When we shall want to relish things in peace.

FAUST. If ever I lie down upon a bed of ease,
    Then let that be my final end!
    If you can cozen me with lies
    Into a self-complacency,
    Or can beguile with pleasures you devise,
    Let that day be the last for me!
    This bet I offer!

MEPHISTOPHELES.   Done!

FAUST.   And I agree: [6]

---

6. The German (*Und Schlag auf Schlag*) seems to indicate some sort of double handshake in token of both parties' agreement to the compact.

If I to any moment say:
Linger on! You are so fair!   1700
Put me in fetters straightaway,
Then I can die for all I care!
Then toll bells for my funeral,
Then of your service you are free,
The clock may stop, the clock hand fall,
And time be past and done for me!
MEPHISTOPHELES. Consider well, we shall remember this.
FAUST. And that would be quite right of you.
I have committed no presumptuousness.
I am a slave no matter what I do,   1710
Yours or another's, we may dismiss.
MEPHISTOPHELES. I will begin right with your doctoral feast [7]
And be your slave this very day.
For life and death's sake, though, just one thing, if I may:
Just write a line or two at least.
FAUST. You ask for written forms, you pedant? Can
You never have known man, or known the word of man?
Is it not enough that by the word I gave
The die of all my days is finally cast?
Does not the world down all its rivers rave,   1720
And should a promise hold me fast?
But this illusion in our hearts is set
And who has ever wanted to uproot it yet?
Happy the man whose heart is true and pure,
No sacrifice he makes will he regret!
A parchment, though, with seal and signature,

---

7. Goethe planned, sketched, and abandoned a "Disputation Scene" following the present one, in which Faust would defend a "thesis" before a board
of examiners and receive his degree to become "Doctor Faustus." Mephistopheles dressed as a traveling scholar was to appear at the examination and
defend his own "thesis" of worldly experience versus book learning. The plan
called for choruses of students, a "thesis defense" by Wagner, Mephisto's
intrusion, Faust's challenge to him to formalize his questions and answers,
Mephisto's mocking proposals of problems in natural science, and, at some
point, a speech by Faust which would culminate in the remark: "You have
won no knowledge unless it springs from your own soul!" (Witkowski prints
Goethe's tentative sketch of the scene and the extant fragments of text.)

That is a ghost at which all people shy.
The word is dead before the ink is dry
And wax and leather hold the mastery.
What, evil spirit, do you want from me?   1730
Bronze, marble, parchment, paper? And then
Am I to write with stylus, chisel, or a pen?
The choice is yours and wholly free.
MEPHISTOPHELES. Why carry on so heatedly
And force your eloquence so high?
Just any little scrap will do;
You sign it with a drop of blood.
FAUST. If that is satisfactory to you,
We'll let it stand at that absurdity.
MEPHISTOPHELES. Blood is a juice of very special kind.   1740
FAUST. I'll honor this pact, you need not be afraid!
The aim of all my strength and mind
Will be to keep this promise I have made.
I puffed myself up far too grand;
In your class I deserve to be.
The mighty Spirit spurned me and
Nature locks herself from me.
The thread of thought is snapped off short,
Knowledge I loathe of every sort.
Let us now sate our ardent passion   1750
In depths of sensuality!
Let miracles of every fashion
Be brought in veils of mystery!
Let us plunge in the flood of time and chance,
Into the tide of circumstance!
Let grief and gratification,
Success and frustration
Spell one another as they can;
Restless doing is the only way for man.
MEPHISTOPHELES. There is no goal or limit set.   1760
Snatch tidbits as impulse prompts you to,
Take on the wing whatever you can get!
And may you digest what pleases you.

Just help yourself and don't be coy.
FAUST. But I tell you there is no talk of joy.
I vow myself to frenzy, agonies of gratification,
Enamored hatred, quickening frustration.
Cured of the will to knowledge now, my mind
And heart shall be closed to no sorrow any more
And all that is the lot of human kind [8]   1770
I want to feel down to my senses' core,
Grasp with my mind their worst things and their best,
Heap all their joys and troubles on my breast,
And thus my self to their selves' limits to extend,
And like them perish foundering at the end.
MEPHISTOPHELES. Believe me, many a thousand year
I've chewed this rugged food, and I well know
That from the cradle to the bier
No man digests this ancient sourdough.
This whole, believe the likes of us,   1780
For deity alone was made.
He dwells in timeless radiance glorious,
Us he has relegated to the shade,
You, day and night alone can aid.
FAUST. But I am set on it.
MEPHISTOPHELES.   Easy said!
There's just one thing that could go wrong:
Time is short and art is long;
You could, I think, be taught and led.
Choose a poet for your associate,
Let the gentleman's thoughts have their free bent   1790
To heap upon your reverend pate
All noble qualities he can invent: [9]
The lion's nobility,
The fleetness of the hind,

8. L. 1770—here—and beginning with the word "And," the 1790 *Fragment* took up again directly after what is now l. 605.
9. Mephisto's ironic advice is to let an 18th-century tragic poet talk Faust into believing he is one of those stage heroes who are compendia of all virtues, impossible miniature universes (microcosms) in themselves.

The fiery blood of Italy,
The Northman's steadfast mind.[10]
Have him for you the secret find
Of magnanimity and guile combined,
Then make you fall in love by plan
While youthful passions are in flame.   1800
I'd like myself to meet just such a man,
I'd give him "Sir Microcosm" for a name.

FAUST. What am I then, if seeking to attain
    That toward which all my senses strain,
    The crown of mankind, is in vain?

MEPHISTOPHELES. You're after all—just what you are.
    Wear wigs of a million ringlets as you will,[11]
    Put ell-thick soles beneath your feet, and still
    You will remain just what you are.

FAUST. I feel that I have fruitlessly amassed   1810
    All treasures of the human mind,
    And now when I sit down at last
    No fresh strength wells within my heart, I find;
    I'm not one hair's breadth taller nor one whit
    Closer to the infinite.

MEPHISTOPHELES. These matters, my good Sir, you see
    Much in the ordinary light;
    We must proceed more cleverly
    Before life's joys have taken flight.
    What the Devil! You've got hands and feet,   1820
    You've got a head, you've got a prat;
    Are all the things that I find sweet
    Less mine for all of that?
    If I can buy six stallions, can
    I not call their strength also mine?
    I race along and am a proper man

---

10. Scandinavian gravity had been discussed by Lavater in a book which Goethe had reviewed.

11. The allusion is to the enormous curled wigs falling to the waist, worn in the 17th century by tragic actors. The following line refers to the "elevator shoes" worn by the same actors, though the word used is "sock" (the *soccus* of the ancient Roman stage).

As if their four-and-twenty legs were mine.
Come on, then! Let this brooding be!
And off into the world with me!
I tell you, any speculative fellow   1830
Is like a beast led round and round
By demons on a heath all dry and yellow
When on all sides lies good green pasture ground.
FAUST. But how do we begin?
MEPHISTOPHELES.   First we will get away.
What kind of dungeon is this anyway?
What kind of life do you lead if
You bore yourself and bore the youngsters stiff?
Leave that to Neighbor Sleek-and-Slow.
Why go on threshing straw? There is no doubt
The best things that you know   1840
You dare not tell the boys about.
I hear one now out in the hall.
FAUST. I simply cannot see him now.
MEPHISTOPHELES. The poor lad has been waiting, after all,
And must not go uncomforted somehow.
Come, lend your cap and gown to me;
The mask will suit me admirably.

(*He changes clothes.*)

Just trust my wits and I'll succeed.
A quarter of an hour is all I need.
Meanwhile get ready for your travels with all speed.   1850

(*Exit* FAUST.)

MEPHISTOPHELES (*in Faust's long gown*).
Scorn reason and the lore of mind,
Supremest powers of mankind,
Just let the Prince of Lies endow
Your strength with his illusions now,
And I will have you unconditionally—
Fate has conferred on him a mind
That urges ever onward with incontinency,
Whose eager striving is of such a kind

That early joys are overleaped and left behind.
I'll drag him through wild life at last,   1860
Through shallow insipidity,
I'll make him wriggle, stultify, stick fast,
And in his insatiety
His greedy lips will find that food and drink float past.
He will vainly beg refreshment on the way.
Had his lot not been with the Devil cast,
He would go to the Devil anyway.

(*Enter a* STUDENT.) [12]

STUDENT. I've been here just a short time, Sir,
    And come to you with deference
    To meet a man, and see and hear,   1870
    Of whom all speak with reverence.
MEPHISTOPHELES. I must approve your courtesy.
    A man like other men you see.
    Have you inquired around elsewhere?
STUDENT. Take me, I entreat you, in your care.
    I come with fresh blood, spirits high,
    And money in tolerable supply.
    My mother was loath to have me go,
    But I would like to learn and know.
MEPHISTOPHELES. Then this is just the place to come.   1880
STUDENT. Frankly, I'd rather be back home.
    I feel confined within these walls,
    I'm ill at ease amid these halls,
    The space is cramped, you never see
    Green country or a single tree,

---

12. At this point the unpublished *Urfaust* took up directly following the present l. 605, just after Wagner's departure, so that the "Freshman's" appearance
seemingly came as a second interruption to Faust's spirit-conjuring. The stage
direction then read: "Mephistopheles in a dressing gown and large wig. Student." A bewigged Leipzig University professor from 1765–68 must have
been the model.

   For the 1790 *Fragment* the 196 lines of the *Urfaust* version of the present
scene were cut to 183, with a fair number of textual changes besides, and
the 22-line dialogue between Faust and Mephisto was added at the end. No
further changes were made for the final text of 1808.

And in these rooms with benches lined
I lose my hearing, sight, and mind.
MEPHISTOPHELES. It all depends on habit. Right at first
  The infant will not take its mother's breast,
  But then it finds relief from thirst   1890
  And soon it feeds away with zest.
  So you to Wisdom's breast will turn
  And every day more strongly yearn.
STUDENT. I'll hang upon her neck with all affection
  If you will set me in the right direction.
MEPHISTOPHELES. First tell me, before we go on,
  What course have you decided on?
STUDENT. I want to be quite erudite;
  I'd like to comprehend aright
  What all there is on earth, in heaven as well,   1900
  In science and in nature too.
MEPHISTOPHELES. You're on the right track, I can tell;
  Just see that nothing distracts you.
STUDENT. With body and soul it shall be done.
  But to be frank, I would like in some ways
  A little freedom and some fun
  On pleasant summer holidays.
MEPHISTOPHELES. Make good use of your time, so fast it flies.
  You'll gain time if you just will organize.
  And so, dear friend, I would advise   1910
  First off *collegium logicum*.[13]
  There you will get your mind well braced
  In Spanish boots so tightly laced[14]
  That it will henceforth toe the taut
  And cautiously marked line of thought
  And not go will-o'-the-wisping out
  And in, across, and round about.
  They will spend days on teaching you
  About how things you used to do—

---

13. A course in logic.
14. The Spanish boot was an instrument of torture, consisting of metal greaves fastened to the victim's leg and screwed tighter and tighter.

Like eating, drinking—just like that,   1920
Need One! Two! Three! for getting at.
For with thought-manufacturies
It's like a weaver's masterpiece:
A thousand threads one treadle plies,
The shuttles dart back to and fro,
Unseen the threads together flow,
A thousand knots one movement ties;
Then comes the philosopher to have his say
And proves things have to be this way:
The first being so, the second so,   1930
The third and fourth are so-and-so;
If first and second were absent, neither
Would third and fourth be present either.
All scholars find this very clever,
None have turned weavers yet, however.
Whoever wants to know and write about
A living thing, first drives the spirit out;
He has the parts then in his grasp,
But gone is the spirit's holding-clasp.
Encheiresin naturae chemists call it now,[15]   1940
Mocking themselves, they know not how.
STUDENT. I don't just get all you imply.
MEPHISTOPHELES. It will go better by and by,
    Once you have all these things principified
    And properly classified.
STUDENT. I feel as dazed by all you've said
    As if a mill wheel spun inside my head.
MEPHISTOPHELES. Above all else you next must turn
    To metaphysics. See that you learn
    Profoundly and with might and main   1950
    What does not fit the human brain.
    For what fits in—or misfits—grand
    Resounding phrases are on hand.

---

15. "Nature's hand-hold," a pretentious Greek-plus-Latin term of J. R. Spiel-
mann in his *Institutiones chemiae* (1763), signifying the elusive factor that
holds biological components together in a living organism.

But this semester most of all
Keep schedule, be punctual.
You'll have five classes every day;
Be in there on the stroke of the bell.
See that you are prepared as well,
With paragraphs worked up in such a way
That you can see with just a look   1960
There's nothing said but what is in the book;
And take your notes with dedication
As if the Holy Ghost gave the dictation!
STUDENT. No second time need I be told,
   I see its usefulness all right;
   What one gets down in black and white
   One can take home and feel consoled.
MEPHISTOPHELES. But name your field of concentration!
STUDENT. I don't feel law is just the thing for me.
MEPHISTOPHELES. I cannot blame you there especially,   1970
   Well do I know the law school situation.[16]
   Laws are perpetrated like disease
   Hereditary in some families;
   From generation to generation they are bred
   And furtively from place to place they spread.
   Sense turns to nonsense, wise works to a mire.
   Woe that you are a grandson and born late!
   About the legal right that is innate
   In man, they do not so much as inquire.
STUDENT. You make my own aversion still more great.   1980
   He whom you teach is fortunate.
   I'd almost take theology, in a way.
MEPHISTOPHELES. I wouldn't want to lead you astray.
   That branch of learning, once you do begin it,
   It's so hard to avoid the path of sin,
   There's so much hidden poison lurking in it
   And you can hardly tell this from the medicine.

---

16. Goethe took a law degree at the University of Strasbourg in 1771 and served briefly in the hopelessly antiquated law court of the Holy Roman Empire at Wetzlar in 1772.

Again it's best to follow only one man there
And by that master's statements swear.
Cling hard and fast to words, in sum;   1990
Then through sure portals you will come
To Certainty's own templed home.
STUDENT. But words must have ideas too behind them.
MEPHISTOPHELES. Quite so! But just don't fret too much to no avail,
    Because just when ideas fail
    Words will crop up, and timely you will find them.
    With words you can most excellently dispute,
    Words can a system constitute,
    In words you can put faith and not be shaken,
    And from a word not one iota can be taken.   2000
STUDENT. Forgive me for so importuning you,
    But I must trouble you again.
    Would you say just a telling word or two
    About the course in medicine?
    Three years is a short time, and O my God!
    The field itself is far too broad.
    With just a little hint alone
    One feels it would not seem so great.
MEPHISTOPHELES (*aside*). I've had enough of this dry tone,
    I've got to play the Devil straight.   2010

    (*aloud*)

    The gist of medicine is grasped with ease;
    You study through the great world and the small
    To let it go on after all
    As God may please.
    In vain you'll go a-roving scientifically,
    There each learns only what he can;
    But one who grasps the moment, he
    Is truly the right man.
    You've got a good build on the whole,
    And you won't lack for impudence;   2020
    If you just have self-confidence
    You'll have the trust of many a soul.
    And learn to manage women, of that make sure;

For all their endless Ah!'s and Oh!'s
And thousand woes
Depend on one point only for their cure,
And if you're halfway decent about that,
You'll have them all under your hat.
First, by a title win their confidence
That your skills many skills transcend,   2030
Then you can finger every little thing and be
Welcome where others wait for years on end.
Know how to take her little pulse, and grasp her
With slyly passionate glances while you clasp her
Around her trim and slender waist
To see how tightly she is laced.
STUDENT. Now that's more like it! The where and how I see!
MEPHISTOPHELES. Grey, my dear friend, is all of theory,
And verdant is life's golden tree.
STUDENT. I swear it's all just like a dream to me.   2040
Might I come back another time to sound
Your wisdom to its depths profound?
MEPHISTOPHELES. I'll gladly do anything I may.
STUDENT. It's just impossible to go away
Unless you take my album here and sign.
Would you do me the honor of a line?
MEPHISTOPHELES. With pleasure.

(*He writes and gives the album back.*)

STUDENT (*reads*). *Eritis sicut Deus, scientes bonum et malum.*[17]

(*He respectfully closes the book and takes his leave.*)

MEPHISTOPHELES.
Just follow that old saying and my cousin, the snake,
And you will surely tremble for your God's-likeness' sake!   2050

(*Reenter* FAUST.)

---

17. ". . . ye shall be as gods, knowing good and evil" (Genesis 3:5). This is
the serpent's temptation to Eve in the Garden of Eden, slightly misquoted
from the Vulgate Bible—*Deus* (God) instead of *dii* (gods)—doubtless from
recollection of Luther's *Gott*.

FAUST. And where do we go now?

MEPHISTOPHELES.   The choice is up to you.
We'll see the small world first, and then the great one too.
What joy, what profit will be yours
As you sail glibly through this course!

FAUST. But with this long beard on my face
I lack for easy social grace.
This bold attempt will never work with me,
I never could get on in company,
In front of others I feel small and harassed,
I'll be continually embarrassed.   2060

MEPHISTOPHELES. Good friend, all that is needed, time will give.
Once you have confidence, you will know how to live.

FAUST. How do we travel, though, and get about?
Do you have servants, coach and pair?

MEPHISTOPHELES. All we need do is spread this mantle out
And it will take us through the air.
But see that on this daring flight
Beginning now you travel light.
A little fire gas I will now prepare [18]
Will lift us to the upper air,   2070
And if we're light, we'll go up fast from here.
Congratulations on your new career!

Auerbach's Tavern in Leipzig [1]

A drinking bout of jolly cronies.

FROSCH.[2] Will no one drink? Will no one laugh?
I'll snap you out of your gloomy daze!

---

18. The brothers Montgolfier made the first balloon ascension in 1783.

1. Auerbach's Tavern was an actual tavern in Leipzig, allegedly frequented by the historical Faust (see illustrations, the Auerbach Tavern murals). Goethe probably visited the tavern while at the University of Leipzig. This stage direction is unique in the poem for its geographical specificity.
2. The common noun "frog," but in dialect, "schoolboy."

Today you're all like sodden chaff
And usually you're all ablaze.
BRANDER.[3] It's your fault, you've been keeping mum,
   No horseplay and no jokes with sour scum.
FROSCH (*pours a glass of wine over his head*).
   There's both!
BRANDER.   You double pork-hog, you!
FROSCH. It's what you wanted me to do!   2080
SIEBEL. Whoever brawls here, throw him out!
   Sing chorus with full chest now, drink and shout!
   Ho! Holla! Ho!
ALTMAYER.   Help! I've been wounded here!
   Bring me some cotton, this chap's split my ear!
SIEBEL. Not till the rafters of the room
   Reecho, do you get the bass's boom.
FROSCH. That's right! Throw out the ones complaining of the noise!
   A! tara lara da!
ALTMAYER. A! tara lara da!
FROSCH.   Our throats are tuned up, boys!

(*sings*)

The good old Holy Roman Empire,   2090
How does it hold together?
BRANDER. A filthy song! A song of politics!
   The song's offensive. Thank God every time you wake
   You need not worry for the Roman Empire's sake!
   At least I count it luck that mine is not
   The Emperor's or the Chancellor's lot.
   But then again we mustn't be without a head,
   So let's elect a Pope instead.
   You know the qualities that can
   Distinguish and elect a man.[4]   2100
FROSCH (*sings*).
   Rise, Lady Nightingale, and soar,

---

3. Suggestive of *Brandfuchs* (literally "brant fox"), the term for a second-semester student.
4. The leader of a drinking bout was called "the Pope"; his "qualities" were his capacity for liquor.

Greet my sweetheart ten thousand times and more.
SIEBEL. No sweetheart's greetings here! We'll have no more of that!
FROSCH. Greetings and meetings too! You won't stop me, that's flat!

(*sings*)

Bolt shoved back! in stilly night.
Bolt shoved back! the lover wakes.
Bolt shoved to: the morning breaks.
SIEBEL. Yes, sing away, sing on, and praise and boast of her!
My time will come for laughing too,
She jilted me and she will do the same for you.   2110
For lover may she get some filthy gnome
To dally with her where the crossroads meet,[5]
And may an old goat from the Blocksberg bleat
Good night to her as he goes galloping home.[6]
For that wench it's a lot too good
To have a stout lad with real flesh and blood.
To smash her windows in will be
The only greeting she'll get from me.
BRANDER (*pounding on the table*).
Attention everybody! Give me ear!
You will agree, Sirs, I know how to live.   2120
There are some lovesick people here,
And so it's proper I should give
Them something for their good night cheer.
This song's new cut and tailored for us,
So come in loudly on the chorus:

(*He sings.*)

In a cellar once there lived a rat
And all he ate was lard and butter;
He grew a gut so sleek and fat
He looked like Doctor Luther.

---

5. Crossroads, from time immemorial, have been considered places dear to
evil spirits.
6. The Blocksberg, highest peak of the Harz Mountains, was the traditional
scene of devils' orgies on St. Walpurga's Night, April 30. Goat form was a
popular guise to assume for the occasion.

The cook, she put some poison out,   2130
And then the world closed in about,
As if he had love inside him.
CHORUS (*shouting*). As if he had love inside him!
BRANDER. He traveled forth, he traveled to,
    He swilled from every puddle,
    He gnawed, he scratched the whole house through
    In fury all befuddled.
    He jumped for pain to beat the band,
    But soon had all that he could stand,
    As if he had love inside him.   2140
CHORUS. As if he had love inside him!
BRANDER. Into the kitchen by light of day
    He ran in agony,
    Dropped on the hearth and twitched and lay
    And snuffled piteously.
    The poisoneress, she laughed and said,
    "One more squeak and then he's dead,
    As if he had love inside him."
CHORUS. As if he had love inside him!
SIEBEL. These dullard lads just relish that!   2150
    It seems a scurvy trick to me
    To poison that poor helpless rat!
BRANDER. You tend to see them favorably?
ALTMAYER. Our lard-gut with the balding head
    Must take the mishap much to heart;
    The swollen rat he sees in his own stead
    As a wholly lifelike counterpart.

(*Enter* FAUST *and* MEPHISTOPHELES.)

MEPHISTOPHELES. Before all else it's up to me
    To get you into jolly company
    So you can see how lightly life can run.   2160
    These lads make every day a day of fun.
    Long on pleasure, short on brains,
    Around in narrow circles each one sails
    Like kittens chasing their own tails.
    When they're not nursing hangover pains,

As long as credit's on the cuff,
They're carefree and quite pleased enough.
BRANDER. Those two have been on travels, they
   Act odd and dress in a peculiar way.
   They haven't been an hour in this town.   2170
FROSCH. You're right! O Leipzig, such is your renown!
   It's "little Paris" and it gives its people *ton*.[7]
SIEBEL. These strangers would be what, you think?
FROSCH. Just let me have free hand. I'll worm the truth
   Out of their noses with a drink,
   And faster than you pull an infant's tooth.
   They have the air of being nobly born,
   They act dissatisfied and full of scorn.
BRANDER. I'll bet they're mountebanks just come to town.[8]
ALTMAYER. Could be.
FROSCH.   Watch me, I'll pin them down.   2180
MEPHISTOPHELES (*to* FAUST).
   The Devil's never recognized by such
   Even when their collar's in his clutch.
FAUST. Good evening, gentlemen.
SIEBEL.   Thanks, and to you the same.

(*softly, scanning* MEPHISTOPHELES *from the side*)

   The fellow drags one foot; could he be lame? [9]
MEPHISTOPHELES. Would you let us come join you where you sit?
   Since decent drink is an impossibility,
   The company will take the place of it.
ALTMAYER. It seems that you are very finicky.
FROSCH. You must have started out from Rippach late.
   Did you stay on for supper there with Jack? [10]   2190
MEPHISTOPHELES. We passed him on the road but didn't wait.

---

7. Leipzig's proud boast in the mid-18th century.
8. The Leipzig Fair attracted all sorts of comers to the city.
9. Folklore attributed a limp to the Devil.
10. Frosch hopes to catch the traveling stranger with an allusion to a local joke. Rippach, a village near Leipzig, was, since at least 1710, the alleged home of Jack Ass (Hans Arsch), alias Jack Dull (Hans Dumm). Frosch expects Mephisto to inquire innocently, "Jack who?"

We talked with him the last time, a while back.
He spoke about his cousins at that meeting
And asked that we bring all of you his greeting.

(*He bows to* FROSCH.)

ALTMAYER (*softly*). You got it! He caught on!
SIEBEL.   Cool customer, I'd say!
FROSCH. Just wait, I'll get him yet some way!
MEPHISTOPHELES. We did hear, if I am not wrong,
    Trained voices singing chorus here?
    This ceiling must reecho song
    Magnificently loud and clear.   2200
FROSCH. Might you then be a virtuoso?
MEPHISTOPHELES. No, I enjoy it, but my talent's only so-so.
ALTMAYER. Give us a song.
MEPHISTOPHELES.   If you like, a quantity.
SIEBEL. Be sure it's in the latest vein!
MEPHISTOPHELES. We've only just come back from Spain,
    The lovely land of wine and minstrelsy.

(*sings*)

    A king once was, they tell,
    Who had a big pet flea—
FROSCH. Hark! He said "flea!" Did you all catch the rest?
    I find a flea a very proper guest.   2210
MEPHISTOPHELES (*sings*). A king once was, they tell,
    Who had a big pet flea;
    He loved him passing well,
    Just like a son, they say.
    His tailor he then bade,
    And up the tailor goes;
    "Here measure me this lad
    To make a suit of clothes."
BRANDER. Just don't forget to let the tailor know
    He's got to measure to a T,   2220
    Because I'll have his head if he
    Makes them so any wrinkles show.
MEPHISTOPHELES. In silks and velvet dressed

He stood now in his pride,
With ribbons on his chest
And many a cross beside.
Prime Minister by station,
He wore a star of state,
And all his flea relation
Were numbered with the great.   2230
   The gentlemen and ladies
At court were much distressed,
Both queen and maid were harried
Along with all the rest,
Yet didn't dare to scratch
However they might itch.
When we are bit, we catch
And squash them as they twitch.

CHORUS (*shouting*). When we are bit, we catch
   And squash them as they twitch.   2240

FROSCH. Bravo! Bravo! That was fine!

SIEBEL. That's what should happen to all fleas!

BRANDER. Just purse your fingers, nip, and squeeze!

ALTMAYER. Long live freedom! Long live wine!

MEPHISTOPHELES. To honor freedom I'd be glad to drink a glass
   If only you had wines of somewhat better class.

SIEBEL. We'd rather not hear that again.

MEPHISTOPHELES. I fear the keeper of the inn
   Might be offended, or I'd fetch the best
   Our cellar offers for each worthy guest.   2250

SIEBEL. Go to it! And on my head be the sin!

FROSCH.
   Come up with a good glass and our praises will be ample,
   But just don't be too stingy with the sample;
   If I'm to judge and not be doubtful,
   I need to have a good big snoutful.

ALTMAYER (*softly*).
   They're from the Rhine, they've got that smack.

MEPHISTOPHELES.
   Bring me a gimlet.

BRANDER.   Why? What would you use it for?

You surely don't have casks outside the door?
ALTMAYER. The host has got a tool chest out in back.
MEPHISTOPHELES (*takes the gimlet. To* FROSCH).
   Now tell me, what would be most to your mind?   2260
FROSCH. How do you mean? Do you have every kind?
MEPHISTOPHELES. To every man the choice is free.
ALTMAYER (*to* FROSCH). Aha! You start to lick your lips, I see.
FROSCH. If I can have my choice, it's Rhine wine any time.
   My homeland turns out products in their prime.
MEPHISTOPHELES (*as he bores a hole in the table edge at Frosch's*
   place). Get me some wax to use for stoppers. Quick!
ALTMAYER. Aw, this is some magician's trick.
MEPHISTOPHELES (*to* BRANDER).
   And you?
BRANDER.   Champagne's the thing for me.
   And let it bubble busily!

(MEPHISTOPHELES *bores a hole. Someone has meanwhile
made wax plugs and stops up the holes.*)

This foreign stuff you sometimes can't avoid,   2270
Good things are often far away.
A Frenchman's something no real German can abide
But he will drink their wines with relish any day.
SIEBEL (*as* MEPHISTOPHELES *comes to his place*).
   I don't like sour wine in any case.
   A glass of sweet wine, if I may.
MEPHISTOPHELES (*boring*). For you at once shall flow Tokay.
ALTMAYER. No, gentlemen, now look me in the face!
   You're making fun of us, I know you are.
MEPHISTOPHELES. That would be going much too far
   With such distinguished company.   2280
   Quick now, speak up! What shall it be?
   What kind of wine can I serve you?
ALTMAYER. Don't fuss too much, just any kind.

(*after the holes have been bored and plugged*)

MEPHISTOPHELES (*with weird gestures*).
   Grapes the vine stem bears!

Horns the he-goat wears!
The wine is juicy, of wood the vine,
The wooden table too gives wine.
Into the depths of Nature peer!
Have faith, a miracle is here.
   Now draw the corks and drink your fill!   2290
ALL (*as they draw the corks and as the wine of their choice runs
   into the glass*). O lovely fountain, flowing all for us!
MEPHISTOPHELES. Just watch that none of it should spill!

(*They drink again and again.*)

ALL (*singing*). We've got more fun than cannibals
   Or than five hundred sows!
MEPHISTOPHELES.
   Just look, they're in their glory, they are free!
FAUST. I would prefer to go away.
MEPHISTOPHELES. You watch now, bestiality
   Will gloriously come into play.
SIEBEL (*drinks carelessly; the wine spills on the floor and turns
   to flame*). Help! Fire! Help! This flame is out of hell!
MEPHISTOPHELES (*addressing the flame*).
   Be quiet, friendly element! All's well.   2300

(*to the fellows*)

   This time it was a drop of purgatory merely.
SIEBEL. What's this supposed to mean? You'll pay for this, and dearly!
   You don't know us much, I can tell.
FROSCH. Don't you try that a second time, you hear!
ALTMAYER. I think we'd better gently ease him on his way.
SIEBEL. What, Sir! Do you presume to play
   Your hocus-pocus with us here?
MEPHISTOPHELES. Quiet, old wine vat!
SIEBEL.   Spindling broomstick!
   You dare to add your insults yet?
BRANDER. Just wait! A rain of fists you'll get.   2310
ALTMAYER (*pulls out a cork from the table; fire leaps at him*).
   Help! I'm on fire!
SIEBEL.   It's magic flame.

Stick him, boys! He's anybody's game!

(*They draw their knives and go after* MEPHISTOPHELES.)

MEPHISTOPHELES (*gesturing in earnest*).
False forms be seen,
Shift sense and scene!
Be here, be there!

(*They stand in amazement and look at each other.*)

ALTMAYER. Where am I? What a lovely land!
FROSCH. And vineyards? Am I seeing right?
SIEBEL.   And grapes at hand?
BRANDER. Here under this green arbor, O!
Just see what grapes and grapevines grow!

(*He grabs* SIEBEL *by the nose. The others do likewise to one another and lift their knives.*)

MEPHISTOPHELES (*as before*).
Error, slip the fetters from their view!   2320
And see what jokes the Devil knows.

(*He disappears with* FAUST. *The cronies move apart.*)

SIEBEL. What's happened?
ALTMAYER.   How . . . ?
FROSCH.   Was that your nose?
BRANDER (*to* SIEBEL). And yours is here in my hand too!
ALTMAYER. I felt a shock go through my every limb!
Give me a chair, I'm caving in.
FROSCH. Just what did happen anyway?
SIEBEL. Where is he? Let me at him just once more
And he won't live to get away!
ALTMAYER. I saw him go out through the tavern door . . .
And he was riding on a cask. . . . Why, say!   2330
My feet are weights of lead.

(*turning toward the table*)

                                    You don't suppose
By any chance the wine still flows?

SIEBEL. It was all cheating lies and fraud.
FROSCH. Yet I drank wine, or so I thought.
BRANDER. And what about the grapes?
ALTMAYER.   Yes, what about them?
But miracles occur, you cannot doubt them!

Witch's Kitchen

*A large cauldron stands over the fire on a low
hearth. Amid the steam rising from it various
forms are seen. A* MONKEY [1] *sits by the kettle
skimming it and watching that it does not boil
over. The* HE-MONKEY *sits near by with the
young ones, warming himself. Walls and ceiling are hung with the most bizarre parapher-
nalia of witchcraft.*[2]

FAUST   MEPHISTOPHELES

FAUST. I am revolted by this crazy witchery;
    I shall be cured, you guarantee,
    In this stark raving rookery?
    Must I seek counsel from an aged crone?   2340
    And will her filthy cookery
    Take thirty years off from my flesh and bone?
    Alas for me if you can nothing better find!
    Already hope has vanished, I despair.
    Has neither Nature nor a wholesome mind
    Devised a balm to cure me anywhere?
MEPHISTOPHELES.
    Ah, now, my friend, you're talking sense once more.
    There is a natural way to make you young again,
    But that is in another book, and on that score

---

1. The text terms the beast a *Meerkatze*, a "long-tailed monkey," literally a
"sea-cat."
2. See the title page from Lavater's *De spectris*, illustrations.

It forms a curious chapter even then.   2350
FAUST. I want to hear it.
MEPHISTOPHELES.   Good! A way without recourse
    To money, medicine, or sorcery:
    Straight to the fields direct your course
    And start to dig immediately;
    There keep yourself and keep your mind
    Within a circle close confined,
    Eat only unadulterated food,
    Live with the beasts as beast, and count it good
    To strew the harvest field with your own dung;
    There is no better way, believe me,   2360
    Up to age eighty to stay young.
FAUST. I am not used to that, nor could I ever stand
    To take a shovel in my hand.
    For me that narrow life would never do.
MEPHISTOPHELES. Well, then it's to the witch for you.
FAUST. But why just this old hag? What makes
    You say that *you* can't brew the cup?
MEPHISTOPHELES. A pretty pastime that! I could put up
    A thousand bridges in the time it takes.[3]
    This work needs skill and knowledge, it is true,   2370
    But it requires some patience too.
    A quiet mind may work for years on end
    But time alone achieves the potent blend.
    And as for what there may be to it,
    There's many an odd ingredient.
    The Devil taught her how to brew it,
    But by himself the Devil cannot do it.

    (*catching sight of the* ANIMALS)

    Ah, see the cute breed by the fire!
    That is the maid, that is the squire.

    (*to the* ANIMALS)

___

3. "Devil's bridges" are both bizarre rock formations, as in l. 10,121 and note, and "underhanded methods."

Where is the lady of the house?   2380
THE ANIMALS. Out of the house
   On a carouse
   Up chimney and away.
MEPHISTOPHELES. How long does she rampage today?
THE ANIMALS. Until we get our paws warm, anyway.
MEPHISTOPHELES (*to* FAUST).
   How do you like these cunning creatures?
FAUST. Repulsive to the nth degree.
MEPHISTOPHELES. No, discourse such as this one features
   Is just the kind that most entrances me.

   (*to the* ANIMALS)

   Now, you accursed puppets you,   2390
   Why are you paddling in that broth, pray tell?
THE ANIMALS. We're cooking up some beggars' stew.
MEPHISTOPHELES. You'll have a good big clientele.
THE HE-MONKEY (*coming over and fawning on* MEPHISTOPHELES).
   O roll the dice
   And make me nice
   And rich with gains!
   My lot is bad,
   But if I had
   Some money, I'd have brains.
MEPHISTOPHELES. How happy would this monkey be   2400
   If he could play the lottery!

   (*Meanwhile the young monkeys have been playing with a
   large globe and now roll it forward.*)

THE HE-MONKEY. That is the world;
   Spun and twirled,
   It never ceases;
   It rings like glass,
   But hollow, alas,
   It breaks to pieces.
   Here it gleams bright,
   And here more bright,
   Alive am I.   2410

Dear son, I say
Keep far away,
For you must die.
It's made of clay,
And splinters fly.

MEPHISTOPHELES. And why the sieve?

THE HE-MONKEY (*takes it down*).
I'd know you if
You were a thief.[4]

(*He runs to the* SHE-MONKEY *and has her look through it.*)

Look through the sieve:
You see the thief   2420
And name him not?

MEPHISTOPHELES (*going over to the fire*).
And why the pot?

THE HE-MONKEY AND THE SHE-MONKEY.
The silly sot!
Not know the pot,
Not know the kettle?

MEPHISTOPHELES. Uncivil beast!

THE HE-MONKEY. Here, take the whisk [5]
And sit on the settle.

(*He has* MEPHISTOPHELES *sit down.*)

FAUST (*has all this time been standing in front of a mirror, now
going up to it, now stepping back away from it*).
What do I see with form divine
Upon this magic mirror shine?   2430
O Love, lend me the swiftest of your pinions
And take me off to her dominions!
Unless I stand right here in this one place
And do not venture to go near,
I see her misted only and unclear.—

4. Folklore claimed a thief became recognizable as such when viewed
through a sieve.
5. A thick-handled dusting instrument.

A woman of the utmost grace!
Can any woman be so fair?
In this recumbent body do I face
The essence of all heavens here?
Is there on earth the like of it? [6]   2440
MEPHISTOPHELES.
It's natural, if a god will six whole days expend
And then himself shout bravo! in the end,
That something smart must come of it. [7]
Go right ahead and gaze your fill;
Just such a sweetheart I can well provide,
And lucky is the man who will
Then take her with him as his bride.

(FAUST *keeps right on looking into the mirror.* MEPHI-
STOPHELES *sprawls on the settle and toys with the whisk as
he goes on speaking.*)

I sit here like a king upon his throne,
I hold a scepter, and I lack a crown alone.

(*The* ANIMALS, *who have been going through all kinds of
odd motions helter-skelter, bring* MEPHISTOPHELES *a crown
amid loud cries.*)

THE ANIMALS. O just be so good
As with sweat and blood   2450
To glue this crown and lime it.

(*They handle the crown clumsily and break it in two pieces,
then hop around with the pieces.*)

Now it is done!
We talk, look, and run,
We listen and rhyme it—
FAUST (*toward the mirror*). I'm going crazy here, I feel!

---

6. The magic mirror reveals an ideal female nude, such as Giorgione's
"Venus" (see illustrations).
7. The refrain in Genesis, especially Genesis 1:31: "And God saw that it
was good."

MEPHISTOPHELES (*pointing to the* ANIMALS).
  My own head now almost begins to reel.
THE ANIMALS. If we have luck
    And don't get stuck
    We'll make sense yet! [8]   2460
FAUST (*as before*). My heart is catching fire within!
  Let's get away from here, and fast!
MEPHISTOPHELES (*in his previous posture*).
  This much you'll have to grant at least:
  As poets they are genuine.

  (*The kettle, which the* SHE-MONKEY *has left unwatched, begins to boil over. A great flame flashes up the chimney. Down
  through the flame comes the* WITCH *with hideous screams.*)

THE WITCH. Ow! Ow! Ow! Ow!
  Damnable brute! Accursed sow!
  Neglect the kettle, scorch your mate!
  Accursed beast!

  (*catching sight of* FAUST *and* MEPHISTOPHELES)

  What have we here?
  Who are you here?   2470
  What do you want?
  Who has sneaked in?
  Flames and groans
  Consume your bones!

  (*She dips the skimmer into the kettle and scoops flames at*
  FAUST, MEPHISTOPHELES, *and the* ANIMALS. *The* ANIMALS
  whimper.)

MEPHISTOPHELES (*reverses the whisk he is holding and goes
  smashing the glasses and pots*). Crash! And smash!
  There goes your trash!
  Your glassware's done!
  It's all in fun,

---

8. The monkeys speak both as French revolutionists and as German Romantic lyric poets who sacrificed sense for sound.

I'm only beating time,
Carrion, to your rhyme.

(*as the* WITCH *falls back in fury and horror*)   2480

You recognize me, Bone-bag? Skeleton?
You know your master and your lord?
What keeps me now from going on
To pulverize you and your monkey horde!
For my red coat you have such small respect?
My rooster feather you don't recognize?
Is my face hidden? Or do you expect
I'll state my name and enterprise?
THE WITCH. O Sir, forgive this rude salute from me!
And yet no horse hoof do I see;   2490
And then where is your raven pair? [9]
MEPHISTOPHELES. This time I'll let you get away with it.
It has been quite some while, I will admit,
Since last we met. And to be fair,
The culture that has licked the world up slick
Has even with the Devil turned the trick.
The northern phantom is no longer to be found;
Where will you see horns, tail, or claws around?
As for the foot, which I can't do without,
It would work me much social harm, I fear;   2500
And so, like many a young man, I've gone about
With padded calves this many a long year.[10]
THE WITCH (*dancing*). I'll lose my mind for jubilation
To see Squire Satan back in circulation!
MEPHISTOPHELES. Woman, I forbid that appellation!
THE WITCH. Why? What harm has it ever done?
MEPHISTOPHELES.
It's long since passed to fable books and vanished.

---

9. The "northern" or Germanic Devil, as opposed to the Mediterranean one,
inherited the ravens attendant upon Wotan as well as a horse hoof instead of
a human foot, horse sacrifices having been made to Wotan.
10. Knee breeches left the lower leg cased in skintight silk stockings to the
disadvantage of some persons; padding supplied "muscles" to the calf of the
leg.

Yet people are no better off. The Evil One
They're rid of, but their evils are not banished.
Just call me Baron, that will do.   2510
I am a cavalier like any cavalier.
You do not doubt my noble blood, and you
Can see the coat of arms that I wear here.

(*He makes an indecent gesture.*) [11]

THE WITCH (*laughing immoderately*).
    Ha! Ha! Just like you, that I'll swear!
    Oh you're a rogue, just as you always were!
MEPHISTOPHELES (*to* FAUST).
    Learn this, my friend! This is the way
    To handle witches any day.
THE WITCH. Now, gentlemen, how can I be of use?
MEPHISTOPHELES. A good glass of the well-known juice,
    But of your oldest, is what I'm after;   2520
    It's years that put the powers in those brews.
THE WITCH. Why, sure! Here is a bottle on my shelf
    From which I sometimes take a nip myself
    And which no longer has a trace of stink.
    I'll gladly pour you out a little glass.

(*softly*)

But if this man here unprepared should drink,
You know he'll die before two hours pass.
MEPHISTOPHELES.
    He's a good friend, and I mean things to thrive with him;
    Give him the best your kitchen offers, serve him well.
    So draw your circle, speak your spell,   2530
    And fill his cup right to the brim.

(*With bizarre gestures the* WITCH *describes a circle and
places strange things inside it. Meanwhile the glasses begin
to ring and the kettle to boom and make music. Finally she*

---

11. The gesture is usually identified as "the fig" (Italian *fico*), thumb between forefingers, though 16th-century male costume would easily enable
Mephisto to display the reality in lieu of the symbol.

fetches a great book and disposes the monkeys within the circle to serve her as a lectern and to hold torches. She beckons FAUST *to come to her.*)

FAUST (*to* MEPHISTOPHELES).
Now tell me, what is all this leading to?
These frantic motions and this wild ado
And all of this disgusting stuff
I've known and hated long enough.
MEPHISTOPHELES.
Oh, nonsense! It's just for the fun of it!
And don't be such a prig! As a physician,
She needs to hocus-pocus just a bit
So that the juice can work on your condition.

(*He gets* FAUST *into the circle.*)

THE WITCH (*begins to declaim with great bombast out of a book*).
This must ye ken!   2540
From one take ten;
Skip two; and then
Even up three,
And rich you'll be.
Leave out the four.
From five and six,
Thus says the witch,
Make seven and eight,
And all is straight.
And nine is one,   2550
And ten is none.
This is the witch's one-times-one!
FAUST. I think the hag's in fever and delirium.
MEPHISTOPHELES. Oh, there is lots more still to come.
As I well know, the whole book's in that vein.
I've wasted much time going through its pages,
For total paradox will still remain
A mystery alike to fools and sages.
My friend, the art is old and new.
For ages it has been the thing to do,   2560

By Three and One, and One and Three,
To broadcast error in guise of verity.[12]
And so they teach and jabber unperturbed;
With fools, though, who is going to bother?
Man has a way of thinking, when he hears a word,
That certainly behind it lies some thought or other.

THE WITCH (*continues*). The lofty force
  Of wisdom's source
  Is from the whole world hidden.
  Once give up thinking,   2570
  And in a twinkling
  It's granted you unbidden.[13]

FAUST. What nonsense is she spouting now before us?
  My head is going to split before too long.
  I feel as if I'm listening to a chorus
  Of fools a hundred thousand strong.

MEPHISTOPHELES. Enough, O worthy Sibyl! Pray, no more!
  Bring on your potion now, and pour
  A goblet quickly to the brim;
  My friend is safe, your drink won't injure him.   2580
  He is a man of many titles,[14]
  And many a dram has warmed his vitals.

(*With many ceremonies the* WITCH *pours out the drink in a goblet. As* FAUST *raises it to his mouth a little flame arises.*)

Just drink it down. Go on! You'll love
The way it makes your heart soar higher.
What! With the Devil hand-in-glove
And boggle at a little fire?

(*The* WITCH *dissolves the circle.* FAUST *steps forth.*)

Come right on out! You must not rest.

THE WITCH. And may the dram do you much good!

MEPHISTOPHELES (*to the* WITCH).
  If you have any favor to request,

---

12. A jibe at the Trinity.
13. A jibe at blind faith in revelation as opposed to 18th-century Reason.
14. Magister, Doctor, Professor; or in modern terms, B.A., M.A., Ph.D.

Just tell me on Walpurgis, if you would.[15]   2590
THE WITCH. Here is a spell; say it occasionally
   And you'll see strange results without a doubt.
MEPHISTOPHELES (*to* FAUST).
   Just come along, entrust yourself to me.
   You must perspire now necessarily
   To get the force to penetrate both in and out.
   I'll teach you later all the joys of indolence,
   And soon to your heart's pleasure you'll commence
   To feel how Cupid rises up and hops about.
FAUST. Just one more quick look in the mirror there!
   That womanly form was O! so fair!   2600
MEPHISTOPHELES. No, no! For soon, alive before you here
   The paragon of women shall appear.

   (*aside*)

   With that drink in you, you will find
   All women Helens to your mind.

A Street

FAUST. MARGARET *passing by.*

FAUST. Fair lady, may I be so free
   As offer my arm and company?
MARGARET. I'm neither a lady nor fair, and may
   Go unescorted on my way.

   (*She disengages herself and goes on.*)

FAUST. By heaven, but that child is sweet!
   Like none I ever chanced to meet.   2610
   So virtuous and modest, yes,
   But with a touch of spunkiness.
   Her lips so red, her cheek so bright,

---

15. See above, l. 2114*n*.

I never shall forget the sight.
The shy way she cast down her eye
Has pressed itself deep in my heart;
And then the quick and short reply,
That was the most delightful part!

(*Enter* MEPHISTOPHELES.)

You must get me that girl, you hear?
MEPHISTOPHELES. Which one?
FAUST.   She just went by me here.   2620
MEPHISTOPHELES. That one? She just came from the priest,
  He absolved her from her sins and all;
  I stole up near the confessional.
  She's just a simple little thing,
  Went to confession just for nothing.
  On such as she I have no hold.
FAUST. And yet she's past fourteen years old.
MEPHISTOPHELES. Why, you talk just like Jack the Rake
  Who wants all flowers to bloom for his sake
  And fancies that no honor is,   2630
  Or favor, but the picking's his.
  It doesn't always work that way.
FAUST. Dear Master Laudable, I say
  Don't bother me with your legality!
  And I am telling you outright,
  Unless that creature of delight
  Lies in my arms this very night,
  At midnight we part company.
MEPHISTOPHELES. Remember there are limits! I
  Need fourteen days at least to try   2640
  And find an opportunity.
FAUST. Had I but seven hours clear,
  I wouldn't need the Devil near
  To lead that girl astray for me.
MEPHISTOPHELES. You're talking like a Frenchman. Wait!
  And don't be put out or annoyed:
  What good's a thing too soon enjoyed?
  The pleasure is not half so great

As when you first parade the doll
Through every sort of folderol   2650
And knead and pat and shape her well,
The way that all French novels tell.

FAUST. I've appetite enough without it.

MEPHISTOPHELES. With no more joking now about it:
I'm telling you that pretty child
Will not be hurriedly beguiled.
There's nothing to be gained by force;
To cunning we must have recourse.

FAUST. Get me some of that angel's attire!
Lead me to her place of rest!   2660
Get me the kerchief from her breast,
A garter for my love's desire!

MEPHISTOPHELES. Just so you see that I do heed
Your pain and serve your every need,
We shall not waste a single minute.
I'll take you to her room and put you in it.

FAUST. And shall I see her? have her?

MEPHISTOPHELES.   No!
She'll be at a neighbor's when we go.
And all alone there you can dwell
Upon the fragrance of her cell   2670
And hope for future joys as well.

FAUST. Can we go now?

MEPHISTOPHELES.   It's too soon yet.

FAUST. Get me a gift for her, and don't forget.

(*Exit.*)

MEPHISTOPHELES.
What! Gifts so soon! That's fine! He'll be right in his glory!
I know a lot of pretty places
Where there are buried treasure cases;
I must go through my inventory!

(*Exit.*)

Evening

A small, neat room. MARGARET *braiding
her hair and doing it up.*

MARGARET. I'd give a good deal if I knew
  Who was that gentleman today!
  He had a very gallant way   2680
  And comes of noble lineage too.
  That much I could read from his face—
  Or he'd not be so bold in the first place.

(*Exit.*)

(*Enter* FAUST *and* MEPHISTOPHELES.)

MEPHISTOPHELES. Come on! But softly. In you go!
FAUST (*after a silence*). I beg you, leave me here alone.
MEPHISTOPHELES (*peering about*).
  Not every girl's this neat, you know?

(*Exit.*)

FAUST (*looking all around*).
  Welcome, lovely twilight gloom
  That hovers in this sacred room!
  Seize on my heart, sweet love pangs who
  Both live and languish on hope's own dew.   2690
  How everything here is imbued
  With stillness, order, and content!
  Here in this poverty, what plenitude!
  Here in this prison, what ravishment!

(*He throws himself into the leather armchair beside the bed.*)

O you who have both joy and sorrow known
From times gone by, clasp me too in your arms!
How often at this patriarchal throne
Children have gathered round about in swarms!
Perhaps my sweetheart, plump-cheeked, used to stand

Here grateful for a Christmas present and   2700
Devoutly kiss her grandsire's withered hand.
I feel your spirit, maiden, playing
About me, breathing order, plenitude,
And every day in mother-fashion saying
The cloth upon the table must be fresh renewed
And underfoot clean sand be strewed.
Dear hand! so godlike! In it lies
What turns a cottage to a paradise.
And here!

(*He lifts the bed curtains.*)

What chill of rapture seizes me!
Here I could linger on for hours.   2710
Here, Nature, you with your creative powers
From light dreams brought the angel forth to be;
Here lay the child, her bosom warm
With life; here tenderly there grew
With pure and sacred help from you
The godlike image of her form.
And you? What purpose brought you here?
How I am touched with shame sincere!
What do you want? Why is your heart so sore?
O sorry Faust! I know you now no more.   2720
Does magic haze surround me everywhere?
I pressed for pleasure with no least delay,
And in a love dream here I melt away!
Are we the toys of every breath of air?
If she this moment now were to come by,
What punishment your impudence would meet!
The loud-mouth lummox—O how small!—would lie
Dissolved in shame before her feet.

(*Enter* MEPHISTOPHELES.)

MEPHISTOPHELES. Quick now! I see her at the gate.
FAUST. Away! And never to come back!   2730
MEPHISTOPHELES. Here is a casket of some weight,
I took it elsewhere from a rack.

Just put it in her clothespress there,
It'll make her head swim, that I'll swear.
I put some little baubles in it
To bait another bauble and win it.
A girl's a girl and play is play.

FAUST. I wonder . . . should I?

MEPHISTOPHELES.   You delay?
You wouldn't maybe want to keep the baubles?
In that case I advise Your Lust   2740
To save my pretty daytime, just
Don't bother me with further troubles.
You are not miserly, I trust!
I scratch my head, I rub my hands—

(*He puts the casket in the clothespress and pushes the lock shut again.*)

Off and away now!
To get that lovely child to play now
Into your heart's desires and plans.
And you stand all
Poised to proceed to lecture hall,
And as if in the flesh, and grey,   2750
Physics and Metaphysics led the way.
Come on!

(*Exeunt.*)

(*Enter* MARGARET *with a lamp.*)

MARGARET. It's close in here, there is no air.

(*She opens the window.*)

And yet it's not so warm out there.
I feel so odd, I can't say how—
I do wish Mother would come home now.
I'm chilled all over, and shivering!
I'm such a foolish, timid thing!

(*She begins to sing as she undresses.*)

There was a king of Thule
True even to the grave,   2760
To whom a golden goblet
His dying mistress gave.
    Naught did he hold more dear,
He drained it every feast;
And from his eye a tear
Welled each time as he ceased.
    When life was nearly done,
His towns he totaled up,
Begrudged his heir not one,
But did not give the cup.   2770
    There with his vassals all
At royal board sat he
In high ancestral hall
Of his castle by the sea.
    The old toper then stood up,
Quaffed off his last life-glow,
And flung the sacred cup
Down to the flood below.
    He saw it fall, and drink,
And sink deep in the sea;   2780
Then did his eyelids sink,
And no drop more drank he.

*(She opens the clothespress to put her clothes away and
catches sight of the jewel casket.)*

How did this pretty casket get in here?
I locked the press, I'm sure. How queer!
What can it have inside it? Can it be
That someone left it as security
For money Mother has provided?
Here on a ribbon hangs a little key—
I think I'll have a look inside it!
What's this? O Lord in heaven! See!   2790
I've never seen the like in all my days!
A noble lady with such jewelry
Could walk with pride on holidays.

I wonder how this chain would look on me?
Such glorious things! Whose could they be?

(*She puts it on and steps up to the mirror.*)

If just these earrings could be mine!
One looks so different in them right away.
What good does beauty do, young thing? It may
Be very well to wonder at,
But people let it go at that;   2800
They praise you half in pity.
Gold serves all ends,
On gold depends
Everything. Ah, we poor!

Promenade

FAUST *pacing up and down in thought.*
MEPHISTOPHELES *comes to him.*

MEPHISTOPHELES. Now by the element of hell! By love refused!
    I wish I knew a stronger oath that could be used!
FAUST. What's this? What's griping you so badly?
    I've never seen a face the like of this!
MEPHISTOPHELES. Why, I'd surrender to the Devil gladly
    If I were not the Devil as it is!   2810
FAUST. Have you gone off your head? I grant
    It suits you, though, to rave and rant.
MEPHISTOPHELES.
    Just think, those jewels for Gretchen [1] that I got,
    Some priest has made off with the lot!—
    Her mother got to see the things,
    Off went her dire imaginings;
    That woman's got some sense of smell,

---

1. Diminutives of Margaret include (Mar)gretchen, Margretlein (in l. 2827),
Gretel, Gretelchen, etc.

She has prayerbook-sniffing on the brain,
A whiff of any item, and she can tell
Whether the thing is sacred or profane.   2820
That jewelry she spotted in a minute
As having no great blessing in it.
"My child," she cried, "ill-gotten good
Ensnares the soul, consumes the blood.
Before Our Lady we will lay it,
With heaven's manna she'll repay it." [2]
Margretlein pulled a pouty face,
Called it a gift horse, and in any case
She thought he wasn't godless, he
Who sneaked it in so cleverly.   2830
The mother had a priest drop by;
No sooner did he the trick espy
Than his eyes lit up with what he saw.
"This shows an upright mind," quoth he,
"Self-conquest gains us victory.
The church has a good healthy maw,
She's swallowed up whole countries, still
She never yet has eaten her fill.
The church, dear ladies, alone has health
For digestion of ill-gotten wealth."   2840
FAUST. That's nothing but the usual game,
A king and a Jew can do the same.
MEPHISTOPHELES. Then up he scooped brooch, chain, and rings
As if they were just trivial things
With no more thanks, if's, and's, or but's
Than if they were a bag of nuts,
Promised them celestial reward—
All edified, they thanked him for it.
FAUST. And Gretchen?
MEPHISTOPHELES.   Sits lost now in concern,
Not knowing yet which way to turn;   2850
Thinks day and night about the gems,

---

2. Revelation 2:17: "To him that overcometh will I give to eat of the hidden manna."

But more of him from whom the present stems.
FAUST. I hate to see the dear girl worry.
  Get her a new set in a hurry.
  The first one wasn't too much anyway.
MEPHISTOPHELES. My gentleman finds this mere child's play.
FAUST. And here's the way I want it. Go
  Make friends there with that neighbor. Show
  You're not a devil made of sugar water,
  Get those new gems and have them brought her.   2860
MEPHISTOPHELES. Sir, I obey with all my heart.

(*Exit* FAUST.)

This fool in love will huff and puff
The sun and moon and stars apart
To get his sweetheart pastime stuff.

(*Exit.*)

The Neighbor's House

MARTHA *alone.*

MARTHA. Now God forgive my husband, he
  Has not done the right thing by me.
  Way off into the world he's gone,
  And leaves me on the straw alone.
  Yet he surely had no cause on my part,
  God knows I loved him with all my heart.   2870

(*She weeps.*)

He could be dead!—If I just knew for sure!
Or had a statement with a signature!

(*Enter* MARGARET.)

MARGARET. Dame Martha!
MARTHA.   What is it, Gretelchen?

MARGARET. My knees are sinking under me.
   I've found one in my press again,
   Another casket, of ebony,
   And this time it's a gorgeous set
   Far richer than the first one yet.
MARTHA. This time you mustn't tell your mother,
   Off it would go to church just like the other.   2880
MARGARET. O look at them! Just see! Just see!
MARTHA (*putting them on her*).
   You *are* a lucky creature!
MARGARET.   Unfortunately
   In church or on the street I do not dare
   Be seen in them, or anywhere.
MARTHA. You just come over frequently,
   Put on the jewels in secret here,
   Walk by the mirror an hour or so in privacy,
   And we'll enjoy them, never fear.
   There'll come a chance, a holiday, before we're done,
   Where you can show them to the people one by one,   2890
   A necklace first, pearl ear-drops next; your mother
   Won't notice it, or we'll make up some thing or other.
MARGARET. But who could bring both caskets here?
   There's something not quite right . . .

   (*A knock.*)

                            Oh, dear!
   Could that be Mother coming here?
MARTHA (*looking through the blinds*).
   It's a strange gentleman—Come in!

   (MEPHISTOPHELES *steps in.*)

MEPHISTOPHELES. I'm so free as to step right in,
   The ladies must excuse my liberty.
   (*Steps back respectfully before* MARGARET.)
   I wish to see Dame Martha Schwerdtlein, if I may.
MARTHA. Right here! What might the gentleman have to say?   2900
MEPHISTOPHELES (*aside to her*).
   I know you now, that is enough for me.

You have distinguished company.
Forgive my freedom, I shall then
Return this afternoon again.

MARTHA *(aloud)*. Child, think of it! The gentleman takes
You for some lady! For mercy's sakes!

MARGARET. I'm just a poor young girl; I find
The gentleman is far too kind.
These gems do not belong to me.

MEPHISTOPHELES. Oh, it's not just the jewelry.   2910
She has a quick glance, and a way!
I am delighted I may stay.

MARTHA. What is your errand then? I'm very—

MEPHISTOPHELES. I wish my tidings were more merry.
I trust you will not make me rue this meeting:
Your husband is dead and sends you greeting.

MARTHA. He's dead! That faithful heart! Oh, my!
My husband's dead! Oh! I shall die!

MARGARET. Dear lady, Oh! Do not despair!

MEPHISTOPHELES. Now listen to the sad affair.   2920

MARGARET. I hope I never, never love.
Such loss as this I would die of.

MEPHISTOPHELES.
Glad must have sad, sad must have glad, as always.

MARTHA. O tell me all about his dying!

MEPHISTOPHELES. At Padua, by Saint Anthony's
They buried him, and he is lying
In ground well sanctified and blest
At cool and everlasting rest.

MARTHA. And there is nothing else you bring?

MEPHISTOPHELES. Yes, one request and solemn enterprise: 2930
Three hundred Masses for him you should have them sing.
My pockets are quite empty otherwise.

MARTHA. What, not a luck-piece, or a trinket such
As any journeyman deep in his pack would hoard
As a remembrance token stored
And sooner starve or beg than use it!

MEPHISTOPHELES. Madam, it grieves me very much;
Indeed he did not waste his money or lose it.

And much did he his failings then deplore,
Yes, and complained of his hard luck still more.   2940
MARGARET. To think that human fortunes so miscarry!
    Many's the Requiem I'll pray for him, I'm sure.
MEPHISTOPHELES. Ah, you deserve now very soon to marry,
    A child of such a kindly nature.
MARGARET. It's not yet time for that. Oh, no!
MEPHISTOPHELES. If not a husband, then meanwhile a beau.
    It's one of heaven's greatest graces
    To hold so dear a thing in one's embraces.
MARGARET. It's not the custom here for one.
MEPHISTOPHELES. Custom or not, it still is done.   2950
MARTHA. But tell me more!
MEPHISTOPHELES.   I stood at his bedside—
    Half-rotten straw it was and little more
    Than horse manure; but in good Christian style he died,
    Yet found he had still further items on his score.
    "How I detest myself!" he cried with dying breath,
    "For having left my business and my wife!
    Ah, that remembrance is my death.
    If she would just forgive me in this life!"—
MARTHA (*weeping*). The good man! I long since forgave.
MEPHISTOPHELES.
    "God knows, though, she was more to blame than I."   2960
MARTHA. It's a lie! And he with one foot in the grave!
MEPHISTOPHELES. Oh, he was talking through his hat
    There at the end, if I am half a judge.
    "I had no time to sit and yawn," he said,
    "First children and then earning children's bread,
    Bread in the widest sense, at that,
    And could not even eat my share in peace."
MARTHA. Did he forget my love, how I would drudge
    Both day and night and never cease?
MEPHISTOPHELES. No, he remembered that all right.   2970
    "As I put out from Malta," he went on,
    "I prayed for wife and children fervently;
    Then heaven too disposed things favorably
    So our ship took a Turkish galleon

With treasure for the great Sultan aboard.
Then bravery came in for reward
And I got, as was only fair,
My own well calculated share."

MARTHA. What! Where? Do you suppose he buried it?

MEPHISTOPHELES.

Who knows where the four winds have carried it?   2980
A pretty girl took him in tow when he
Was roaming Naples there without a friend;
She showed him so much love and loyalty
He bore the marks right to his blessed end.[1]

MARTHA. The rogue! He robbed his children like a thief!
And all that misery and grief
Could not prevent the shameful life he led.

MEPHISTOPHELES. But that, you see, is why he's dead.
Were I in your place now, you know,
I'd mourn him for a decent year and then   2990
Be casting round meanwhile to find another beau.

MARTHA. Oh Lord, the kind my first man was,
I'll never in this world find such again.
There never was a fonder fool than mine.
Only, he liked the roving life too much,
And foreign women, and foreign wine,
And then, of course, those devilish dice.

MEPHISTOPHELES. Well, well, it could have worked out fine
If he had only taken such
Good care on his part to be nice.   3000
I swear on those terms it is true
I would myself exchange rings with you.

MARTHA. Oh, the gentleman has such joking ways!

MEPHISTOPHELES (*aside*). It's time for me to be pushing onward!
She'd hold the very Devil to his word.

(*to* GRETCHEN)

How are things with your heart these days?

MARGARET. What do you mean, Sir?

---

1. Syphilis, *le mal de Naples.*

MEPHISTOPHELES (*aside*).   O you innocents!
  Ladies, farewell!
MARGARET.   Farewell.
MARTHA.   One word yet! What I crave is
  Some little piece of evidence
  Of when and how my sweetheart died and where
      his grave is.   3010
  I've always been a friend of orderliness,
  I'd like to read his death note in the weekly press.
MEPHISTOPHELES. Good woman, what two witnesses report
  Will stand as truth in any court.
  I have a friend, quite serious,
  I'll bring him to the judge with us.
  I'll go and get him.
MARTHA.   Do that! Do!
MEPHISTOPHELES. This lady will be with you too?
  A splendid lad, much traveled. He
  Shows ladies every courtesy.   3020
MARGARET. The gentleman would make me blush for shame.
MEPHISTOPHELES. Before no earthly king that one could name.
MARTHA. Out in the garden to the rear
  This afternoon we'll expect both of you here.

A Street[1]

FAUST   MEPHISTOPHELES

FAUST. How is it? Will it work? Will it succeed?
MEPHISTOPHELES. Ah, bravo! I find you aflame indeed.
  Gretchen is yours now pretty soon.
  You meet at neighbor Martha's house this afternoon.

---

1. The present rendezvous of Faust and Mephisto is in the city and nearer
Margaret's home, whereas their former one was in the "suburb" beyond the
walls of an 18th-century town, as the stage direction "Promenade" indicated.
Goethe originally wrote *Allee*, i.e., a tree-shaded walk, impossible in towns
until *ca.* 1800.

The woman is expressly made
To work the pimp and gypsy trade!   3030
FAUST. Good!
MEPHISTOPHELES. Ah, but something is required of us.
FAUST. One good turn deserves another.
MEPHISTOPHELES. We will depose some testimony or other
   To say her husband's bones are to be found
   In Padua in consecrated ground.
FAUST. Fine! First we'll need to do some journey-going.
MEPHISTOPHELES. *Sancta simplicitas!* For that we need not fuss.
   Just testify, and never mind the knowing.
FAUST. Think of a better plan, or nothing doing.
MEPHISTOPHELES. O saintly man! and sanctimonious!   3040
   False witness then you never bore
   In all your length of life before?
   Have you not with great power given definition
   Of God, the world, and all the world's condition,
   Of man, man's heart, man's mind, and what is more,
   With brazen brow and with no lack of breath?
   And when you come right down to it,
   You knew as much about them, you'll admit,
   As you know of this Mister Schwerdtlein's death!
FAUST. You are a liar and a sophist too.   3050
MEPHISTOPHELES. Or would be, if I didn't know a thing or two.
   Tomorrow will you not deceive
   Poor Gretchen and then make her believe
   The vows of soul-felt love you swear?
FAUST. And from my heart.
MEPHISTOPHELES.   All good and fair!
   Then comes eternal faith, and love still higher,
   Then comes the super-almighty desire—
   Will that be heartfelt too, I inquire?
FAUST. Stop there! It will!—If I have feeling,
   And for this feeling, for this reeling   3060
   Seek a name, and finding none,
   With all my senses through the wide world run,
   And clutch at words supreme, and claim
   That boundless, boundless is the flame

That burns me, infinite and never done,
Is that a devilish, lying game?
MEPHISTOPHELES. I still am right!
FAUST.   Mark this and heed it,
And spare me further waste of throat and lung:
To win an argument takes no more than a tongue,
That's all that's needed.   3070
But come, this chatter fills me with disgust,
For you are right, primarily because I must.

A Garden

MARGARET *on* FAUST'S *arm,* MARTHA *with*
MEPHISTOPHELES, *strolling up and down.*

MARGARET. I feel, Sir, you are only sparing me
And shaming me by condescending so.
A traveler, from charity,
Will often take things as they go.
I realize my conversation can
Not possibly amuse such an experienced man.
FAUST. One glance of yours, one word delights me more
Than all of this world's wisdom-store.   3080

(*He kisses her hand.*)

MARGARET. How can you kiss it? It must seem to you
So coarse, so rough a hand to kiss.
What kinds of tasks have I not had to do!
You do not know how strict my mother is.

(*They pass on.*)

MARTHA. And so, Sir, you are traveling constantly?
MEPHISTOPHELES. Business and duty keep us on our way.
Many a place one leaves regretfully,
But then one simply cannot stay.
MARTHA. It may well do while in one's prime

To rove about the world as a rolling stone,   3090
But then comes the unhappy time,
And dragging to the grave, a bachelor, alone,
Was never good for anyone.
MEPHISTOPHELES. Ah, such with horror I anticipate.
MARTHA. Then act, dear Sir, before it is too late.

(*They pass on.*)

MARGARET. But out of sight is out of mind!
Your courtesy comes naturally;
But you have friends in quantity
Who are more clever than my kind.
FAUST. Dear girl, believe me, clever in that sense   3100
Means usually a close self-interest.
MARGARET. Really?
FAUST.   To think simplicity and innocence
Are unaware their sacred way is best,
That lowliness and sweet humility
Are bounteous Nature's highest gifts—
MARGARET. Think only for a moment's time of me,
I shall have time enough to think of you.
FAUST. Then you are much alone?
MARGARET. Yes, our house is a little one,
And yet it must be tended to.   3110
We have no maid, hence I must cook and sweep and knit
And sew, and do the errands early and late;
And then my mother is a bit
Too strict and strait.
And yet she has no need to scrimp and save this way;
We could live better far than others, you might say;
My father left a sizeable estate,
A house and garden past the city gate.
But I have rather quiet days of late.
My brother is a soldier,   3120
My little sister died;
The child did sometimes leave me with my patience tried,
And yet I'd gladly have the trouble back again,
She was so dear to me.

FAUST.   An angel, if like you.

MARGARET. I brought her up; she dearly loved me too.
　She was born following my father's death.
　Mother we thought at her last breath,
　She was so miserable, but then
　She slowly, slowly got her strength again.
　It was impossible for her to nurse   3130
　The little mite herself, of course,
　And so I raised her all alone
　On milk and water; she became my own.
　In my arms, in my lap she smiled,
　Wriggled, and grew up to be a child.

FAUST. You must have known the purest happiness.

MARGARET. But many trying hours nonetheless.
　At night her little cradle used to stand
　Beside my bed, and she had but to stir
　And I was there at hand,   3140
　Sometimes to feed her, sometimes to comfort her,
　Sometimes when she would not be still, to rise
　And pace the floor with her to soothe her cries,
　And yet be at the washtub early, do
　The marketing and tend the hearth fire too,
　And every morrow like today.
　One's spirits are not always cheerful, Sir, that way;
　Yet food is relished better, as is rest.

(*They pass on.*)

MARTHA. Poor women! They are badly off indeed,
　A bachelor is hard to change, they say.   3150

MEPHISTOPHELES. Someone like you is all that I would need
　To set me on a better way.

MARTHA. But is there no one, Sir, that you have found?
　Speak frankly, is your heart in no wise bound?

MEPHISTOPHELES.
　The proverb says: A wife and one's own household
　Are worth their weight in pearls and gold.

MARTHA. But I mean, have you felt no inclination?

MEPHISTOPHELES.
   I have met everywhere with much consideration.
MARTHA. But has your heart in no case been impressed?
MEPHISTOPHELES. With ladies one must not presume to jest.   3160
MARTHA. Oh, you misunderstand me!
MEPHISTOPHELES.   What a shame! I find
   I understand—that you are very kind.

   (*They pass on.*)

FAUST. And so you did, my angel, recognize
   Me in the garden here at the first look?
MARGARET. Did you not see how I cast down my eyes?
FAUST. And you forgive the liberty I took
   And all my impudence before
   When you had just left the cathedral door?
MARGARET. I was confused, the experience was all new.
   No one could say bad things of me.   3170
   Ah, thought I, could he possibly
   Have noted something brazen or bold in you?
   He seemed to think here was a girl he could
   Treat in just any way he would.
   I must confess that then I hardly knew
   What soon began to argue in your favor;
   But I was angry with myself, however,
   For not becoming angrier with you.
FAUST. My darling!
MARGARET.   Wait!

   (*She picks a star flower and plucks the petals off it one by
one.*)

FAUST.   What is it? A bouquet?
MARGARET.
   No, just a game.
FAUST.   What?
MARGARET.   You'd laugh at me if I should say.   3180

   (*She murmurs something as she goes on plucking.*)

FAUST. What are you murmuring?
MARGARET (*half aloud*).   He loves me—loves me not.
FAUST. You lovely creature of the skies!
MARGARET (*continuing*). Loves me—not—loves me—not—

(*with delight as she reaches the last petal*)

He loves me!
FAUST.   Yes, my child! And let this language of
   The flowers be your oracle. He loves you!
   Do you know what that means? He loves you!

(*He takes both her hands.*)

MARGARET. I'm trembling!
FAUST. O do not tremble! Let this glance
   And let this pressure of my hands
   Say what is inexpressible: 3190
   To yield oneself entirely and to feel
   A rapture that must be everlasting!
   Eternal!—Its end would be despair.
   No! Without end! Without end!

(MARGARET *presses his hands, disengages herself, and runs
off. He stands in thought for a moment, then follows her.*)

MARTHA (*coming along*). It's getting dark.
MEPHISTOPHELES.   We must be on our way.
MARTHA. I'd ask you gentlemen to stay,
   But this is such a wicked neighborhood.
   It seems that no one has a thing to do
   Or put his mind to
   But watch his neighbor's every move and stir.   3200
   No matter what one does, there's always talk.
   What of our couple?
MEPHISTOPHELES.   They've flown up the arbor walk.
   The wanton butterflies!
MARTHA.   He seems to take to her.
MEPHISTOPHELES. And she to him. Such is the world's old way.

A Summer House[1]

MARGARET *comes running in, hides behind the door, puts her finger to her lips, and peeps through the crack.*

MARGARET. He's coming!

(FAUST *comes along.*)

FAUST.   Little rogue, to tease me so!
I'll catch you!

(*He kisses her.*)

MARGARET (*embracing him and returning his kiss*).
         From my heart I love you so!

(MEPHISTOPHELES *knocks.*)

FAUST (*stamping his foot*).
Who's there?
MEPHISTOPHELES.
         A friend!
FAUST.   A beast!
MEPHISTOPHELES.   It's time for us to go.

(MARTHA *comes along.*)

MARTHA. Yes, it is late, Sir.
FAUST.   May I not escort you, though?
MARGARET. My mother would—farewell!
FAUST.   Ah, must I leave you then?
Farewell!
MARTHA.   Adieu!
MARGARET.   But soon to meet again!   3210

(*Exeunt* FAUST *and* MEPHISTOPHELES.)

---

1. Usually construed as following without interruption upon the preceding, this scene was intended, at least in the *Urfaust,* to come some days later, as l. 3206 originally read, "For a long time I have loved you so."

Dear Lord! What things and things there can
Come to the mind of such a man!
I stand abashed, and for the life of me
Cannot do other than agree.
A simple child, I cannot see
Whatever it is he finds in me.

(*Exit.*)

Forest and Cavern[1]

FAUST *alone.*

FAUST. Spirit sublime, thou gavest me, gavest me all
    For which I asked. Thou didst not turn in vain
    Thy countenance upon me in the fire.
    Thou gavest me glorious Nature for my kingdom,   3220
    And power to feel it and enjoy it. No
    Cold, marveling observation didst thou grant me,
    Deep vision to her very heart thou hast
    Vouchsafed, as into the heart of a friend.
    Thou dost conduct the ranks of living creatures
    Before me and teachest me to know my brethren
    In quiet bush, in air, and in the water.
    And when the storm in forest roars and snarls,
    And the giant fir comes crashing down, and, falling,
    Crushes its neighbor boughs and neighbor stems,   3230
    And hills make hollow thunder of its fall,

---

1. For the completed Part I of 1808, Goethe placed this scene so as to demarcate the first third of the Margaret story, hence balancing the "Walpurgis Night" which marks the end of the second "act" of that story. In the 1790 *Fragment* it constituted a kind of flashback to Faust and came between "At the Well" and "Zwinger"; in the *Urfaust* only ll. 3342–69 existed at all, and they came after the cathedral scene. Faust's blank-verse monologue was composed separately, in Rome in 1788. The artistically problematical scene is highly interesting but need not detain the attention upon first reading of the total work.

Then dost thou guide me to safe caverns, showest
Me then unto myself, and my own bosom's
Profound and secret wonders are revealed.
And when before my sight the pure moon rises
And casts its mellow comfort, then from crags
And rain-sprent bushes there come drifting toward me
The silvery forms from ages now gone by,
Allaying meditation's austere pleasure.
   That no perfection is to man allotted,   324
I now perceive. Along with this delight
That brings me near and nearer to the gods,
Thou gavest me this companion whom I can
No longer do without, however he
Degrades me to myself or insolently
Turns thy gifts by a breath to nothingness.
Officiously he fans a frantic fire
Within my bosom for that lovely girl.
Thus from desire I stagger to enjoyment
And in enjoyment languish for desire.   325

(*Enter* MEPHISTOPHELES.)

MEPHISTOPHELES.
Won't you have had enough of this life presently? [2]
How can it in the long run do for you?
All well and good to try it out and see,
But then go on to something new!
FAUST. I do wish you had more to do
Than pester me on a good day.
MEPHISTOPHELES. All right, then, I won't bother you.
You dare not mean that anyway.
In you, friend, gruff, uncivil, and annoyed,
There's nothing much to lose, indeed.   326
The whole day long you keep my time employed!
But from my master's nose it's hard to read
What pleases him and what one should avoid.

---

2. Mephisto's words are a *reply* to the monologue on which he has eave
dropped. More strikingly than any other Faust-Mephisto interchange in t]
poem, this passage sounds like a dialogue of the divided self.

FAUST. Now there is just the proper tone!
  He wants my thanks for having been annoying.
MEPHISTOPHELES. What kind of life would you now be enjoying,
  Poor son of earth, without the help I've shown?
  But I have long since cured you anyhow
  From gibberish your imagination talked,
  And if it weren't for me you would have walked   3270
  Right off this earthly globe by now.
  Why should you mope around and stare
  Owl-like at cave and rocky lair?
  Why suck up food from soggy moss and trickling stone
  Just like a toad all, all alone?
  A fine sweet pastime! That stick-in-the-mud
  Professor still is in your blood.
FAUST. Can you conceive the fresh vitality
  This wilderness existence gives to me?
  But if you could conceive it, yes,   3280
  You would be devil enough to block my happiness.
MEPHISTOPHELES. A superterrestrial delight!
  To lie around on dewy hills at night,
  Clasp earth and heaven to you in a rapture,
  Inflate yourself to deity's great size,
  Delve to earth's core by impulse of surmise,
  All six days' creation in your own heart capture,
  In pride of power enjoy I know not what,
  In ecstasy blend with the All there on the spot,
  The son of earth dissolved in vision,   3290
  And then the lofty intuition—

(*with a gesture*)

  To end—just how, I must not mention.
FAUST. O vile!
MEPHISTOPHELES.
            That does not please you much; meanwhile
  You have the right to speak your moral "Vile!"
  Before chaste ears one must not talk about
  What chaste hearts cannot do without.

All right: occasional pleasure of a lie
To yourself, is something I will not deny;
But you won't last long in that vein.
Soon you will be elsewhere attracted,   3300
Or if it goes too long, distracted
To madness or to anguished pain.
Enough of this! Your sweetheart sits there in her room,
Around her everything is gloom.
You never leave her thoughts, and she
Loves you just overwhelmingly.
Passion came to flood first on your part,
As melting snow will send a brooklet running high;
You poured all that into her heart,
And now your brook is running dry.   3310
It seems to me, instead of playing king
In woodland wilds, so great a lord
Might help the childish little thing
And give her loving some reward.
Time hangs upon her like a pall,
She stands by the window, watches the clouds along
And past the ancient city wall.
"If I were a little bird!" so goes her song
Half the night and all day long.
Sometimes cheerful, mostly sad and of   3320
No further power of tears,
Then calm again, so it appears,
And always in love.

FAUST. Serpent! Serpent!

MEPHISTOPHELES (*aside*). Admit I've got you there!

FAUST. Infamous being! Begone! And do not dare
So much as speak that lovely creature's name!
Do not arouse desire in me to where
Half-maddened senses burst in open flame!

MEPHISTOPHELES. What, then? She thinks you fled from her,   3330
And more or less that's just what did occur.

FAUST. I am near her, and even if I were
Afar, I could not lose her or forget;

The very body of the Lord, when her
Lips touch it, rouses envy and regret.[3]
MEPHISTOPHELES. My friend, I've often envied you indeed
The twin roes that among the lilies feed.[4]
FAUST. Pander, begone!
MEPHISTOPHELES.   Fine! I laugh while you rail.
The God that created girls and boys
Saw that the noblest power He enjoys   3340
Was seeing that occasion should not fail.
Come on, then! What a shame this is!
You're going to your sweetheart's room
And not off to your doom.
FAUST. What if I do find heaven in her arms?
What if in her embrace my spirit warms?
Do I not still feel her distress?
Am I not still the fugitive, the homeless,
The monster without rest or purpose sweeping
Like a cataract from crag to crag and leaping   3350
In frenzy of desire to the abyss?
While at one side, she, with her childlike mind,
Dwells in a cottage on the Alpine slope
With all her quiet life confined
Within her small world's narrow scope.
And I, the God-detested,
Had not enough, but wrested
The crag away and scattered
Its ruins as they shattered
To undermine her and her peace as well!   3360
The victim you demanded, fiend of hell!
Help, Devil, make this time of anguish brief!
Let it be soon if it must be!
Let her fate crash in ruins over me,
Together let us come to grief.
MEPHISTOPHELES. Ah, now it seethes again and glows!

---

3. Witkowski suggests that the crucifix is meant, not the Eucharistic wafer.
4. Song of Solomon 4:5: "Thy two breasts are like two young roes that are
twins, which feed among the lilies."

Go in and comfort her, you lout!
A head like yours beholds the close
Of doom as soon as he sees no way out.
Hurrah for men that bravely dare!   3370
You're half bedeviled anyway;
There's nothing sillier in the world, I say,
Than being a devil in despair.

Gretchen's Room

GRETCHEN *at her spinning wheel, alone.*

GRETCHEN. My peace is gone,
  My heart is sore,
  I'll find it never
  And nevermore.
    When he does not come
  I live in a tomb,
  The world is all   3380
  Bitter as gall.
    O, my poor head
  Is quite distraught,
  And my poor mind
  Is overwrought.
    My peace is gone,
  My heart is sore,
  I'll find it never
  And nevermore.
    I look from my window   3390
  Only to greet him,
  I leave the house
  Only to meet him.
    His noble gait
  And form and guise,
  The smile of his mouth,
  The spell of his eyes,

The magic in
Those words of his,
The clasp of his hand,   3400
And oh!—his kiss.
　My peace is gone,
My heart is sore,
I'll find it never
And nevermore.
　My bosom aches
To feel him near,
Oh, could I clasp
And hold him here
　And kiss and kiss him   3410
Whom I so cherish,
Beneath his kisses
I would perish!

Martha's Garden

MARGARET   FAUST

MARGARET. Promise me, Henry!
FAUST.   If I can!
MARGARET. About religion, what do you feel now, say?
　You are a good, warmhearted man,
　And yet I fear you're not inclined that way.
FAUST. Leave that, my child! That I love you, you feel;
　For those I love, my flesh and blood I'd give,
　And no one's church or feelings would I steal.   3420
MARGARET. But that is not enough! One must believe!
FAUST. Must one?
MARGARET.   O, if I had some influence!
　You do not even revere the sacraments.
FAUST. I do revere them.
MARGARET.   But without desire.
　It's long since you have gone to Mass or to confession.
　Do you believe in God?

FAUST.   My darling, who can say:
  I believe in God?
  Ask priest or sage you may,
  And their replies seem odd
  Mockings of the asker.
MARGARET.   Then you do not believe?   3430
FAUST. My answer, dear one, do not misconceive!
  Who can name
  Him, or proclaim:
  I believe in Him?
  Who is so cold
  As to make bold
  To say: I do not believe in Him?
  The all-embracing,
  The all-sustaining,
  Does He not hold and sustain   3440
  You, me, Himself?
  Does heaven not arch high above us?
  Does earth not lie firm here below?
  And do not everlasting stars
  Rise with a kindly glance?
  Do I not gaze into your eyes,
  And do not all things crowd
  Into your head and heart,
  Working in eternal mystery
  Invisibly visible at your side?   3450
  Let these things fill your heart, vast as they are,
  And when you are entirely happy in that feeling,
  Then call it what you will:
  Heart, Fortune, Love, or God!
  I have no name for it.
  Feeling is everything,
  Names are sound and smoke
  Obscuring heaven's glow.
MARGARET. That is all very good and fair;
  The priest says much the same, although   3460
  He used a different wording as he spoke.
FAUST. It is said everywhere

By all hearts underneath the sky of day,
Each heart in its own way;
So why not I in mine?

MARGARET. It sounds all right when you express it so;
There's something not quite right about it, though;
You have no Christianity.

FAUST. Dear child!

MARGARET.   It has this long time troubled me
To find you keep the company you do.   3470

FAUST. How so?

MARGARET.   The person whom you have with you,
In my profoundest being I abhor,
And nothing in my life before
So cut me to the heart
As this man's face when he came near.

FAUST. My darling, have no fear.

MARGARET. His presence roils my blood, yet for my part,
People otherwise win my heart;
Much as I yearn to have you near,
This person inspires in me a secret fear,   3480
And if I take him for a scoundrel too,
God forgive me for the wrong I do!

FAUST. Such queer fish also have to be.

MARGARET. To live with him would never do for me!
Let him but so much as appear,
He looks about with such a sneer
And half enraged;
Nothing can keep his sympathy engaged;
Upon his brow it's written clear
That he can hold no person dear.   3490
In your embrace I feel so free,
So warm, so yielded utterly;
His presence chokes me, chills me through and through.

FAUST. O you intuitive angel, you!

MARGARET. This so overwhelms me, that when
He joins us, be it where it may,
It seems that I no longer love you then.
With him there, I could never pray.

This eats my very heart; and you,
Henry, must feel the same thing too.   3500
FAUST. This is a matter of antipathy.
MARGARET. I must be going.
FAUST.   O, when will it be
That I may for a little hour rest
In your embrace in quiet, breast to breast?
MARGARET. If I but slept alone, this very night
I'd leave the door unbolted, you realize,
But Mother's sleep is always light,
And if she took us by surprise,
I would die on the spot, I think.
FAUST. There is no need for that, my dear!   3510
Here is a little phial. A mere
Three drops into her drink
Will shroud up Nature in deep sleep.
MARGARET. What will I not do for your sake?
It will not harm her, though, to take?
FAUST. Would I propose it, Love, if that were so?
MARGARET. I look at you, dear man, and do not know
What so compels me to your will;
Already I have done so much for you
That there is little left for me to do.   3520

(*Exit.*)

(*Enter* MEPHISTOPHELES.)

MEPHISTOPHELES.
The little monkey's gone?
FAUST.   You spied again?
MEPHISTOPHELES.   I could
Not help but hear it word for word:
Professor had his catechism heard;
I hope it does you lots of good.
Girls have a way of wanting to find out
Whether a man's conventionally devout.
They think: he gave in there, he'll truckle to us, no doubt.
FAUST. You, monster, do not realize
How this good loyal soul can be

So full of faith and trust— 3530
Which things alone suffice
To make her bliss—and worry holily
For fear she must look on her best beloved as lost.
MEPHISTOPHELES. You supersensual sensual wooer,
A girl has got you on a puppet wire.
FAUST. You misbegotten thing of filth and fire!
MEPHISTOPHELES. She's mighty clever too at physiognomy:
When I am present, she feels—how, she's not just sure,
My mask bodes meaning at a hidden level;
She thinks beyond a doubt I'm a "Genie," [5] 3540
And possibly the very Devil.
Tonight, then—?
FAUST.   What is that to you?
MEPHISTOPHELES. I have my pleasure in it too!

At the Well

GRETCHEN *and* LIESCHEN *with pitchers.*[1]

LIESCHEN. About Barbie, I suppose you've heard?
GRETCHEN. I get out very little. Not a word.
LIESCHEN. Why, Sibyl was telling me today.
She's finally gone down Fools' Way.
That's what grand airs will do!
GRETCHEN.   How so?
LIESCHEN.   It stinks!
She's feeding two now when she eats and drinks.
GRETCHEN. Ah!

---

5. The French word *génie* ("genius")—pronounced with an initial "sh" sound and with the accent on the second syllable—was German jargon of the 1770's for a young fellow of mighty passions and insensitive conscience, something between Casanova and a Byronic hero.

1. "Lieschen" would be similar to our "Lizzy." "Barbie" (the text calls her Bärbelchen) is a familiar form for Barbara. The diminutives designate girls of the lower class who are fetching water from the public well.

LIESCHEN.   Serves her right! And long enough   3550
She hung around that fellow. All that stuff!
It was walk and jaunt
Out to the village and dancing haunt,
And everywhere she had to shine,
Always treating her to pastry and wine;
She got to think her good looks were so fine
She lost her self-respect and nothing would do
But she accepted presents from him too.
It was kiss and cuddle, and pretty soon   3560
The flower that she had was gone.
GRETCHEN. O the poor thing!
LIESCHEN.   Is it pity that you feel!
When our kind sat at the spinning wheel
And our mothers wouldn't let us out at night,
There she was with her lover at sweet delight
Down on the bench in the dark entryway
With never an hour too long for such play.
So let her go now with head bowed down
And do church penance in a sinner's gown! [2]
GRETCHEN. But surely he'll take her as his wife!   3570
LIESCHEN. He'd be a fool! A chipper lad
Finds fun is elsewhere to be had.
Besides, he's gone.
GRETCHEN.   O, that's not fair!
LIESCHEN. If she gets him, she'll find it bad.
The boys will rip her wreath, and what's more,
They'll strew chopped straw around her door! [3]

(*Exit.*)

---

2. Unwed mothers were required by law to do church penance publicly in
a prescribed costume of humiliation. As early as 1763 the Weimar government
considered repeal of the law in order to reduce the high incidence of infanti-
cide. Repeal was enacted on May 15, 1786, partly at Goethe's urging, and
over the objections of Herder! (Herder, five years older than Goethe and
Goethe's most famous teacher, was a distinguished philosopher and, upon
Goethe's recommendation, had been appointed official chaplain to the Weimar
court.)
3. Like other details in this connection, to be understood quite literally. In
the language of the flowers, broken straw means broken agreement.

GRETCHEN (*walking home*). How firmly I could once inveigh
  When any young girl went astray!
  For others' sins I could not find
  Words enough to speak my mind!   3580
  Black as it was, blacker it had to be,
  And still it wasn't black enough for me.
  I thanked my stars and was so game,
  And now I stand exposed to shame!
  Yet all that led me to this pass
  Was so good, and so dear, alas!

Zwinger [1]

In a niche of the wall a statue of the Mater
dolorosa *with jugs of flowers in front of it.*

GRETCHEN (*puts fresh flowers in the jugs*).
  O deign
  Amid your pain
  To look in mercy on my grief.
    With sword thrust through   3590
  The heart of you,

---

1. *Zwinger* is an untranslatable term for the open space between the last houses of a town and the inside of the city walls, sometimes the open space between two parallel city walls. Gretchen has sought the most out-of-the-way spot in the city for her private devotions. The *Mater dolorosa* is a statue of Mary, the mother of Jesus, in an attitude of grief as she beholds the crucifixion; in accordance with Luke 2:35 her visible heart is pierced with a sword. The text freely adapts the famous 13th-century hymn, *Stabat mater dolorosa,* probably by Jacopone da Todi though sometimes attributed to Pope Innocent III:

Stabat mater dolorosa	The sorrowful mother was standing
juxta crucem lacrimosa	beside the cross in tears
dum pendebat filius;	while her Son hung [there],
cuius animam gementem	[she] whose soul grieving
contristantem et dolentem	compassionating and sorrowing,
pertransivit gladius.	a sword pierced through.

The hymn has a total of sixty lines.

You gaze up to your Son in death.
  To Him on high
You breathe your sigh
For His and your distressful grief.
  Who knows
What throes
Wrack me, flesh and bone?
What makes my poor heart sick with fear
And what it is I plead for here,   3600
Only you know, you alone!
  No matter where I go,
I know such woe, such woe
Here within my breast!
I am not quite alone,
Alas! I weep, I moan,
My heart is so distressed.
  The flowerpots at my window
Had only tears for dew
When early in the morning   3610
I picked these flowers for you.
  When bright into my room
The early sun had come,
Upon my bed in gloom
I sat, with sorrow numb.
  Help! Rescue me from shame and death!
O deign
Amid your pain
To look in mercy on my grief!

Night

The street in front of GRETCHEN'S *door.*
VALENTINE, *a soldier, Gretchen's brother.*

VALENTINE. When I used to be in a merry crowd   3620
  Where many a fellow liked to boast,

And lads in praise of girls grew loud
And to their fairest raised a toast
And drowned praise in glasses' overflow,
Then, braced on my elbows, I
Would sit with calm assurance by
And listen to their braggadocio;
Then I would stroke my beard and smile
And take my brimming glass in hand
And say: "To each his own! Meanwhile   3630
Where is there one in all the land
To hold a candle or compare
With my sister Gretel anywhere?"
Clink! Clank! the round of glasses went;
"He's right!" some shouted in assent,
"The glory of her sex!" cried some,
And all the braggarts sat there dumb.
But now!—I could tear my hair and crawl
Right up the side of the smooth wall!—
Now every rascal that comes near   3640
Can twit me with a jibe or sneer!
With every chance word dropped I sweat
Like one who has not paid a debt.
I'd knock the whole lot down if I
Could only tell them that they lie.
    What have we here? Who's sneaking along?
There are two of them, if I'm not wrong.
If he's the one, I'll grab his hide,
He won't get out of here alive!

(*Enter* FAUST *and* MEPHISTOPHELES.)

FAUST. How from the window of that sacristy   3650
    The vigil lamp casts forth its flickering light
    Sidewise faint and fainter down the night,
    And darkness closes around totally.
    So in my heart the darkness reigns.
MEPHISTOPHELES. And I feel like a cat with loving-pains
    That sneaks up fire escapes and crawls
    And slinks along the sides of walls;

I feel so cozy at it, and so right,
With a bit of thievery, a bit of rutting to it.
Through all my limbs I feel an ache for   3660
The glorious Walpurgis Night.
Day after tomorrow brings us to it;
Then one knows what he stays awake for.
FAUST. Will it come to the top, that treasure
I see glimmering over there? [1]
MEPHISTOPHELES. You very soon will have the pleasure
Of lifting the pot to upper air.
Just recently I took a squint:
It's full of ducats shiny from the mint.
FAUST. Not a jewel, not a ring   3670
To add to others of my girl's?
MEPHISTOPHELES. I do believe I saw a string
Of something that looked much like pearls.[2]
FAUST. That's good. I really hate to go
Without a gift to take with me.
MEPHISTOPHELES. You needn't fuss and trouble so
About enjoying something free.
But now that all the stars are in the sky,
You'll hear a real art work from me:
I'll sing her a moral lullaby   3680
To befool her the more certainly.

(*He sings to the zither.*)

What dost thou here [3]
With dawn so near,

---

1. Abruptly and not altogether felicitously Goethe brings in the motif of buried treasure working its way up through the ground under the force of the Devil's magical presence. The motif is frequent in the background readings which Goethe did in preparation for the "Walpurgis Night" scene.
2. In the language of gems, pearls represent tears.
3. The song is imitated from Ophelia's song in *Hamlet,* IV.v:

> And I a Maid at your Window,
>   To be your Valentine.
> Then up he rose, & don'd his clothes,
>   & dupt the chamber dore,
> Let in the Maid, that out a Maid,
>   Never departed more.

O Katie dear,
Outside your sweetheart's door?
Maiden, beware
Of entering there
Lest forth you fare
A maiden nevermore.
  Maidens, take heed! 3690
Once do the deed,
And all you need
Is: Good night, you poor things!
If you're in love,
To no thief give
The thing you have
Except with wedding rings.

VALENTINE (*steps forward*).
Who is it you're luring? By the Element!
You accursed rat-catcher, you!
To the Devil first with the instrument! 3700
Then to the Devil with the singer too!

MEPHISTOPHELES. The zither's smashed, there's nothing left of it.

VALENTINE. And next there is a skull to split!

MEPHISTOPHELES (*to* FAUST).
Don't flinch, Professor, and don't fluster!
Come close in by me, and don't tarry.
Quick! Whip out your feather duster!
Just thrust away and I will parry.

VALENTINE. Then parry this!

MEPHISTOPHELES.   Why not?

VALENTINE.   This too!

MEPHISTOPHELES. Of course!

VALENTINE.   I think the Devil fights in you!
What's this? My hand is going lame. 3710

MEPHISTOPHELES (*to* FAUST).
Thrust home!

VALENTINE (*falls*). O!

MEPHISTOPHELES.   There, the lummox is quite tame.
Come on! It's time for us to disappear.
Soon they will raise a murderous hue and cry.

With the police I always can get by,
But of the court of blood I stand in fear.[4]
MARTHA (*at the window*). Come out! Come out!
GRETCHEN (*at the window*).   Bring out a light!
MARTHA (*as before*). They swear and scuffle, shout and fight.
PEOPLE. Here's one already dead!
MARTHA (*coming out*). Where are the murderers? Have they fled?
GRETCHEN (*coming out*).
    Who's lying here?
PEOPLE.   Your mother's son.   3720
GRETCHEN. Almighty God! I am undone!
VALENTINE. I'm dying! That's a tale
    Soon told and sooner done.
    Why do you women stand and wail?
    Come close and hear me, everyone!

(*They all gather around him.*)

My Gretchen, see! too young you are
And not yet wise enough by far,
You do not manage right.
In confidence I'll tell you more:
You have turned out to be a whore,   3730
And being one, be one outright.
GRETCHEN. My brother! God! What do you mean?
VALENTINE. Leave our Lord God out of this farce. What's done
    Is done, alas! and cannot be undone.
    And what comes next will soon be seen.
    You started secretly with one,
    It won't be long till others come,
    And when a dozen more have had you,
    The whole town will have had you too.
        When shame is born, she first appears   3740
    Stealthily amid the world
    And with the veil of darkness furled

---

4. With the lower courts Mephistopheles could "arrange" most matters; but in the "court of blood" (*Blutbann*), originally under the jurisdiction of no one less than the emperor or king, where capital crimes were tried and where the death sentence was passed "in the name of God," he is out of his depth.

About her head and ears.
First one would gladly slay her outright.
But as she grows and waxes bold,
She walks quite naked in the daylight,
But is no fairer to behold.
The uglier her visage grows,
The more by open day she goes.
  The time already I foresee 3750
When all the decent citizenry
Will from you, harlot, turn away
As from a plague corpse in their way.
Your heart will sink within you when
They look you in the eye! No more
Golden chains will you wear then! [5]
Or stand by the altar in church as before!
No more in collars of fine lace
Will you come proudly to the dancing place!
Off to a dismal corner you will slouch 3760
Where the beggars and the cripples crouch.
And even though God may forgive,
Accursed here on earth you still will live.
MARTHA. Commend your soul to God! Will you
  Take blasphemy upon you too?
VALENTINE. If I could reach your withered skin and bone,
  You shameless, pandering, old crone,
  I do believe that I could win
  Full pardon for my every sin!
GRETCHEN. My brother! What pain of hell for me! 3770
VALENTINE. I tell you, let your weeping be!
  When you gave up your honor, you gave
  The fiercest heart-stab I could know.
  Now through the sleep of death I go
  To God, a soldier true and brave.

(*Dies.*)

---

5. As Goethe had observingly read, a Frankfurt police ordinance of the 15th century forbade fallen women to wear jewelry, silk, satin, or damask, and denied them the use of a pew in church. This latter requirement would force them to remain at the rear with the "beggars and cripples."

Cathedral

Service, organ, and choir. GRETCHEN *among many people. An* EVIL SPIRIT *behind Gretchen.*[1]

EVIL SPIRIT. How different, Gretchen, it was
  When still full of innocence
  You approached this altar,
  From your little dog-eared prayer book
  Murmuring prayers,   3780
  Half childish play,
  Half God in heart!
  Gretchen!
  Where are your thoughts?
  Within your heart
  What deed of crime?
  Do you pray for your mother's soul that slept
  Away unto the long, long pain because of you?
  Whose blood is on your doorstep?
  —And underneath your heart   3790
  Does not a new life quicken,
  Tormenting itself and you
  With its premonitory presence?
GRETCHEN. Alas! Alas!
  If I could be rid of the thoughts
  That rush this way and that way
  Despite my will!
CHOIR. *Dies irae, dies illa*
  solvet saeclum in favilla.[2]

(*The organ sounds.*)

---

1. The *Urfaust* has the significantly different stage direction: "Obsequies of Gretchen's mother. Gretchen (and) all relatives. Service, organ, and choir."
2. The opening of the greatest of medieval hymns, the *Dies irae*, composed before 1250, probably by Thomas of Celano, and used in Masses of the dead:
    The day of wrath, that day
    Shall dissolve the world in fire. . . .
Through nineteen three-line stanzas the hymn describes the end of the world and the Last Judgment.

EVIL SPIRIT. Wrath seizes you! 3800
  The trumpet sounds!
  The graves shudder!
  And your heart
  From ashen rest,
  For flames of torment
  Once more reconstituted,
  Quakes forth.[3]
GRETCHEN. If I were out of here!
  I feel as if the organ were
  Stifling my breath, 3810
  As if the choir dissolved
  My inmost heart.
CHOIR. *Judex ergo cum sedebit,*
  quidquid latet adparebit,
  nil inultum remanebit.[4]
GRETCHEN. I cannot breathe!
  The pillars of the wall
  Imprison me!
  The vaulted roof
  Crushes me!—Air! 3820
EVIL SPIRIT. Concealment! Sin and shame
  Are not concealed.
  Air? Light?

---

3. The Evil Spirit paraphrases stanzas three and four of the same hymn:

Tuba mirum spargens sonum	The trumpet scattering wondrous sound
per sepulchra regionum	Through the sepulchers of the lands
coget omnes ante thronum.	Will drive everyone up before the throne.
Mors stupebit et natura	Death and nature will stand aghast
cum resurget creatura	When the creature shall resurrect
judicanti responsura.	In answer to the Judge's call.

The Evil Spirit's lines also refer to the doctrine that from death until the Last Judgment the soul will be either in heaven, in hell, or in purgatory, while the body will be in its grave; at the sound of the last trumpet, however, the body will resurrect, be rejoined with its soul, submit to judgment, and then, together with the soul, be assigned either to heaven or to hell for all eternity. (Purgatory will be abolished on the Last Day.)

4. Stanza six: Therefore when the Judge shall sit,
                   Whatever is hidden shall appear,
                   Nothing shall remain unavenged.

Woe to you!

CHOIR. *Quid sum miser tunc dicturus?*
Quem patronum rogaturus?
Cum vix justus sit securus.[5]

EVIL SPIRIT. The clarified avert
Their countenances from you.
The pure shudder to reach   3830
Out hands to you.
Woe!

CHOIR. *Quid sum miser tunc dicturus?*

GRETCHEN. Neighbor! Your smelling-bottle!

(*She falls in a faint.*)[6]

Walpurgis Night

The Harz Mountains. Vicinity of Schierke and Elend.[1]

FAUST   MEPHISTOPHELES

MEPHISTOPHELES. Now don't you long for broomstick-transportation?
I'd like the toughest he-goat there can be.
We're far yet, by this route, from destination.

FAUST. Since my legs still are holding out so sturdily,
This knotty stick will do for me.

---

5. Stanza seven: What shall I, wretched, say?
                         What patron shall I call upon?
                         When scarcely the just man is safe.

6. Here the text of the 1790 *Fragment* ended.

1. Saint Walpurgis (Walpurga, Walburga, Valburg, d. 780), was a niece of Saint Boniface and herself a missionary to Germany. By coincidence, her church calendar day, April 30th, fell together with the pagan festivals on the eve of May Day, the end of winter and the beginning of summer. Under the Christian dispensation those festivals, like the Hallowe'en festivals (Oct. 31st) at the end of summer and the beginning of winter, passed into folklore as devils' orgies. (See the Blocksberg scenes, illustrations.) Folklore further localized those orgies on the Brocken, highest peak of the Harz Mountains in central Germany. From the village of Elend a two- or three-hour walk leads past the village of Schierke to a desolate plateau and finally to the top of the Brocken.

Why take a short cut anyway?   3840
Slinking through this labyrinth of alleys,
Then climbing cliffs above these valleys
Where streams plunge down in everlasting spray,
Such is the spice of pleasure on this way!
Springtime over birches weaves its spell,
It's sensed already by the very pine;
Why should it not affect our limbs as well?
MEPHISTOPHELES. There's no such feeling in these limbs of mine!
Within me all is winter's chill;
On my path I'd prefer the frost and snow.   3850
How drearily the reddish moon's disc, still
Not full, is rising with belated glow
And giving such bad light that any step now
Will have us bumping into rock or tree!
I'll call a will-o'-the-wisp, if you'll allow.[2]
I see one burning merrily.
Hey, there, my friend! May I request your flare?
Why flash for nothing over there?
Just be so good and light our way up here.
WILL-O'-THE-WISP. I hope sheer awe will give me mastery   3860
Over my natural instability;
Most commonly we go a zigzag career.
MEPHISTOPHELES. Ho, ho! It's man you want to imitate!
Now in the Devil's name, go straight!
Or else I'll blow your flicker-life right out.
WILL-O'-THE-WISP. You are the master here beyond a doubt,
And so I'll do my best to serve you nicely.
Remember, though! The mountain is magic-mad tonight,
And if you want a will-o'-the-wisp to lend you light
You mustn't take these matters too precisely.   3870

(FAUST, MEPHISTOPHELES, WILL-O'-THE-WISP *in alternating song.*)

---

2. A will-o'-the-wisp (*ignis fatuus,* Jack-o'-Lantern) is a conglomeration of phosphorescent gas from decayed vegetation in swamps. By night it resembles an eerily swaying lantern.

Having entered, as it seems,
Realms of magic and of dreams,
Guide us well so that we may
Get along our upward way
Through the vast and empty waste.
    Tree after tree, with what mad haste
They rush past us as we go,
See the boulders bending low,
And the rocks of long-nosed sort,
How they snore and how they snort.[3]   3880
    Athwart the turf, the stones athwart,
Brook and brooklet speeds along.
Is it rustling? Is it song?
Do I hear love's sweet lament
Singing of days from heaven sent?
What we hope and what we love!
And the echo is retold
Like a tale from times of old.
    To-whit! To-whoo! it sounds away,
Screech owl, plover, and the jay;   3890
Have all these stayed wide awake?
Are those efts amid the brake?
Long of haunch and thick of paunch!
And the roots that wind and coil
Snakelike out of stone and soil
Knot the bonds of wondrous snares,
Scare us, take us unawares;
Out of tough and living gnarls
Polyp arms reach out in snarls
For the traveler's foot. Mice scurry   3900
Thousand-colored by drove and flurry
Through the moss and through the heather!
And the fireflies in ascent
Densely swarm and swirl together,
Escort to bewilderment.

---

3. The Snorer (*Schnarcher*) is a curious rock formation near the Brocken.

Have we stopped or are we trying
To continue onward flying?
Everything is whirling by,
Rocks and trees are making faces,
Wandering lights in many places   3910
Bloat and bulge and multiply.
MEPHISTOPHELES. Grab my cloak-end and hold tight.
Here's a sort of medium height
Which for our amazement shows
How Mammon in the mountain glows.[4]
FAUST. How oddly in the valley bottoms gleams
A dull glow like the break of day,
And even in the chasm's deepest seams
It probes and gropes its searching way.
There steam puffs forth, there vapor twines,   3920
Here through the mist the splendor shines,
Now dwindling to a slender thread,
Now gushing like a fountainhead.
It fans out in a hundred veins
A long stretch of the valley run,
Then where the narrow pass constrains
Its course, it merges into one.
There sparks are gusting high and higher
Like golden sand strewn on the night.
Look! There along its entire height   3930
The cliff-face kindles into fire.
MEPHISTOPHELES. Has not Sir Mammon done some fine contriving
To illuminate his palace hall?
You're lucky to have seen it all.
But now I scent the boisterous guests arriving.
FAUST. How the wind's bride rides the air!
How she beats my back with cuff and blow!
MEPHISTOPHELES. Grab on to this cliff's ancient ribs with care
Or she will hurl you to the chasm far below.
A mist has thickened the night.   3940

---

4. "Mammon" here is gold.

Hark! Through the forests, what a crashing!
The startled owls fly up in fright.
Hark! The splitting and the smashing
Of pillars in the greenwood hall!
Boughs strain and snap and fall.
The tree trunks' mighty moaning!
The tree roots' creaking and groaning!
In fearful entanglement they all
Go tumbling to their crushing fall,
And through the wreckage-littered hollows   3950
The hissing wind howls and wallows.
Do you hear voices there on high?
In the distance, or nearby?
Yes, the mountain all along
Is bathed in frenzied magic song.

WITCHES (*in chorus*). The witches to the Brocken ride,
The stubble is yellow, the corn is green.
There with great crowds up every side,
Seated on high, Lord Urian is seen.[5]   3960
And on they go over stock and stone,
The he-goat st——s from the f——ts of the crone.

A VOICE. Old Baubo by herself comes now,[6]
Riding on a farrow sow.

CHORUS. Pay honor where honor is due!
Dame Baubo, up and on with you!
A mother astride a husky sow,
The whole witch crew can follow now.

A VOICE. Which way did *you* come?

A VOICE.   By Ilsenstein crest.[7]
And I took a peep in an owlet's nest:
What eyes she made at me!

A VOICE.   O go to hell!   3970
Why must you drive so hard!

---

5. Urian is a name for the Devil.
6. In classical mythology Baubo was Demeter's nurse; she is the archetype
of the lascivious old woman.
7. The Ilsenstein is the topmost point on the Brocken.

A VOICE. She skinned me alive,
  I'll never survive!
WITCHES (*chorus*). The way is broad, the way is long,
  O what a mad and crazy throng!
  The broomstick scratches, the pitchfork pokes,
  The mother bursts open, the infant chokes.
WITCHMASTERS (*semi-chorus*).
  We creep along like a snail in his house,
  The women are always up ahead.
  For traveling to the Devil's house,   3980
  Women are a thousand steps ahead.
THE OTHER HALF. Why, that's no cause for sorry faces!
  Women need the thousand paces;
  But let them hurry all they can,
  One jump is all it takes a man.
A VOICE (*above*). Come on along from Felsensee there, you!
VOICES (*from below*). We'd like to make the top there too.
  We wash and are as clean as clean can be,
  And still the same sterility.
BOTH CHORUSES. The wind has died, the star has fled,   3990
  The dull moon hides, and in its stead
  The whizzings of our magic choir
  Strike forth a thousand sparks of fire.
A VOICE (*from below*). Wait! Wait! Or I'll get left!
A VOICE (*from above*). Who's calling from that rocky cleft?
A VOICE (*from below*). Take me with you! Take me with you!
  Three hundred years I have been climbing
  And still can't make the top, I find.
  I'd like to be with my own kind.
BOTH CHORUSES. A broom or stick will carry you,   4000
  A pitchfork or a he-goat too;
  Whoever cannot fly today
  Is lost forever, you might say.
HALF-WITCH (*below*). Here all these years I've minced along;
  How did the others get so far ahead?
  I have no peace at home, and yet
  Can't get in here where I belong.

CHORUS OF WITCHES. The salve puts courage in a hag,[8]
 A sail is made from any rag,
 For a ship any trough will do;   4010
 None flies unless today he flew.
BOTH CHORUSES. And when the topmost peak we round
 Just coast along and graze the ground,
 So far and wide the heath will be
 Hid by your swarm of witchery.

 (*They alight.*)

MEPHISTOPHELES. They push and shove, they bustle and gab,
 They hiss and swirl, they hustle and blab!
 They glow, shed sparks, and stink and burn!
 The very witches' element!
 Hold tight to me, or we'll be swept apart in turn.   4020
 Where are you?
FAUST.   Here!
MEPHISTOPHELES.   What? Swept so far so soon?
 I must invoke my house-right and call the tune.
 Squire Voland comes! Give ground, sweet rabble, ground![9]
 Grab on to me, Professor! In one bound
 We'll give this mob the slip quite easily;
 It's too mad even for the likes of me.
 There's something shining with a very special flare
 Down in those bushes. Curiosity
 Impels me. Come! We'll drop in there.
FAUST. You Spirit of Contradiction! Be my guiding light!   4030
 I think it was a move that made good sense:
 We travel to the Brocken on Walpurgis Night
 To isolate ourselves up here by preference.
MEPHISTOPHELES. Just see the jolly fires! Why here
 A club has gathered for good cheer.
 In little circles one is not alone.

---

8. Witches rub a special salve over their whole bodies in preparation for an expedition.
9. Voland is another name for the Devil.

FAUST. I'd rather be up there, I own.
  I see the glow and twisting smoke.
  The crowd streams toward the Evil One;
  There many a riddle must be undone.   4040
MEPHISTOPHELES. And many a riddle also spun.
  But let the great world revel away,
  Here where it's quiet we shall stay.
  It is a usage long since instituted
  That in the great world little worlds are constituted.
  I see young witches naked and bare,
  And old ones clothed more prudently;
  For my sake, show them courtesy,
  The effort is small, the jest is rare.
  I hear some tuning up of instruments.   4050
  Damned whine and drone! One must get used to it.
  Come on! Come on! Now there's no help for it,
  I'll go in first and prepare your entrance,
  And you will owe me for another work of mine.
  This is no little space, you must admit, my friend.
  Look, and your eye can hardly see the end.
  A hundred bonfires burn there in a line;
  There's dancing, chatting, cooking, drinking, making love;
  What better things than these can you think of?
FAUST. In which of your roles will you now appear,   4060
  Magician or Devil, to introduce me here?
MEPHISTOPHELES. Most commonly I go incognito,
  But on such gala days one lets one's Orders show.
  I have no Garter to distinguish me,
  But here the cloven hoof is held in dignity.
  You see that snail that's creeping toward us there
  Its feelers have already spied
  My presence somehow in the air;
  I couldn't hide here even if I tried.
  Come on! We'll stroll along from fire to fire,   4070
  I'll be the wooer and you can be the squire.

(*to some people who are sitting around some dying embers*)

Old gentlemen, what are you doing here?

I'd praise you if I found you in the midst of cheer
Surrounded by the noise and youthful riot;
Alone at home we get our fill of quiet.

GENERAL. Who can put any faith in nations,
Do for them all you may have done?
With women and with populations
Youth is always number one.

PRIME MINISTER.
They're too far off the right course now today,   4080
I still stick with the men of old;
For frankly, when we had our way,
That was the actual Age of Gold.

PARVENU. We weren't so stupid either, you'll allow,
And often did what we should not;
But everything is topsy-turvy now
Just when we'd like to keep the things we've got.

AUTHOR. Where can you read a publication
With even a modicum of sense?
As for the younger generation,   4090
They are the height of impudence.

MEPHISTOPHELES (*who suddenly looks very old*).
I feel men ripe for doomsday, now my legs
Are climbing Witches' Hill in their last climb;
And since my cask is running dregs,
The world is also running out of time.

HUCKSTER WITCH. O Sirs, don't pass me by this way!
Don't miss this opportunity!
Just give my wares some scrutiny,
All sorts of things are on display.
Across the earth you will not find   4100
A booth like this; no item here, not one
But what has good sound mischief done
At some time to the world and human kind.
No dagger here but what has dripped with gore,
No cup but what has served to pour
Consuming poison in some healthy frame,
No jewel but what has misled to her shame
Some lovely girl, no sword but of the kind

That stabbed an adversary from behind.

MEPHISTOPHELES. Cousin, you're out of date in times like these.   4110
   What's done is past, what's past is done.
   Get in a stock of novelties!
   With us it's novelties or none.

FAUST. If I don't lose my mind! But I declare
   This really is what I would call a fair!

MEPHISTOPHELES. The whole mad rout is pushing on above;
   You're being shoved, though you may think you shove.

FAUST. Now who is that?

MEPHISTOPHELES.   Observe her with some care,
   For that is Lilith.

FAUST.   Who?

MEPHISTOPHELES.   Adam's first wife.[10]
   Beware of her resplendent hair,   4120
   The one adornment that she glories in,
   Once she entraps a young man in that snare,
   She won't so quickly let him out again.

FAUST. That old witch with the young one sitting there,
   They've kicked their heels around, that pair!

MEPHISTOPHELES. No rest for them today. Ah! They're beginning
   Another dance. Come on! Let's get into the swing.

FAUST (*dancing with the* YOUNG WITCH).
   A lovely dream once came to me;
   In it I saw an apple tree,
   Two lovely apples shone upon it,   4130
   They charmed me so, I climbed up on it.

THE BEAUTY. Apples always were your craze
   From Paradise to present days.
   I feel joy fill me through and through
   To think my garden bears them too.

MEPHISTOPHELES (*with the* OLD WITCH).
   A dismal dream once came to me;

---

10. Lilith (Hebrew, "she of the night") figures in medieval Jewish folklore as
Adam's first wife from whom demons were begotten. Genesis 1:27 speaks of
God's creation of humans "male and female" *before* the creation of Eve de-
scribed in chap. 2. The name is taken from Isaiah 34:14, though the King
James version translates it as "screech owl."

In it I saw a cloven tree,
It had a —— —— ——;
Yet —— as it was, it charmed my soul.
THE OLD WITCH. I proffer now my best salute   4140
To the Knight with the Horse's Hoof!
So if your —— —— ——, go to it,
Unless —— —— won't let you do it.
PROKTOPHANTASMIST.[11] Accursed mob! This is presumptuous!
Was it not long since proved to you
Ghosts do not have the same feet humans do?
And here you dance just like the rest of us!
THE BEAUTY (*dancing*). And what does *he* want at our ball?
FAUST (*dancing*). Oh, he turns up just anywhere at all.
What others dance, he must evaluate.   4150
If there's a step about which he can't prate,
It's just as if the step had not occurred.
It bothers him the most when we go forward.
If you would run in circles round about
The way he does in his old mill,
He'd call it good and sing its praises still,
Especially if his opinion were sought out.
PROKTOPHANTASMIST. But you're still here! Oh! This is insolent!
Begone! Why, we brought in Enlightenment!
This Devil's pack, with them all rules are flouted.   4160

---

11. Proktophantasmist (Greek, "buttocks-mage") is an allusion to Friedrich
Nicolai, the tedious and superannuated writer-publisher-"philosopher" who
denounced every innovation in German thought and letters after 1770 (including Kant). In the midst of the popularity of Goethe's novel *The Sorrows
of Young Werther*, he published a silly parody called *The Joys of Young
Werther* and somehow conceived the notion that *Faust* was a parody of him
by way of retaliation. The specific allusions here, however, are recondite to
the point where only a few people understood them in 1808. Nicolai had
long denounced belief in ghosts, but in 1797 seriously announced that a certain castle in Tegel was haunted. Then he compounded his self-contradictions
by saying that he himself had been plagued by ghosts back in 1791, but had
found an effective antidote in the application of leeches to his buttocks.
   The untranslatable pun in l. 4175 on *Geist* as "ghost," and *Geist* as "mind,"
"intelligence," may echo Friedrich Schlegel's caustic comment in an issue of
the *Athenäum* to the effect that Nicolai was looking for a vision of his own
Geist. L. 4169 alludes sarcastically to Nicolai's twelve-volume *Description of
a Trip through Germany and Switzerland in 1781*, published 1783–96.

We are so clever, yet there is no doubt about it:
There's still a ghost at Tegel. How long have I swept
Illusions out, and still I find they're kept.
THE BEAUTY. Then go away and let us have the field.
PROKTOPHANTASMIST. I tell you spirits to your faces
    I will not stand for any traces
    Of spirit despotism I can't wield.

(*The dancing goes on.*)

I just can't win today, no matter what I do.
But I can always take a trip;
And I still hope, before I'm done, to slip   4170
One over on the devils and the writers too.
MEPHISTOPHELES. Down in the nearest puddle he will plump,
    That is the best assuagement he can find;
    If leeches feast upon his rump,
    He will be cured of ghosts and his own mind.

(*to* FAUST, *who has left the dance*)

Why do you leave that pretty girl
Who in the dance so sweetly sang?
FAUST. Because a little red mouse sprang
    Out of her mouth while she was singing.
MEPHISTOPHELES.
    What's wrong with that? The mouse was still not grey.   4180
    Why raise such questions and be bringing
    Them to a trysting hour anyway?
FAUST. Then I saw—
MEPHISTOPHELES.   What?
FAUST.   Mephisto, do you see
    A pale girl standing over there alone?
    She drags herself but slowly from the place
    And seems to move with shackled feet.
    I must confess she has the sweet
    Look of my kindly Gretchen's face.
MEPHISTOPHELES. Let that be! That bodes well for no one.
    It is a magic image, lifeless, an eidolon.   4190
    Encounters with such are not good;

The fixed stare freezes human blood
And one is turned almost to stone—
You've heard of the Medusa, I suppose.

FAUST. Indeed, a corpse's eyes are those,
Unshut by loving hand. That is the breast
That Gretchen offered for my rest,
That is the dear, sweet body I have known.

MEPHISTOPHELES. You easily misguided fool, that's magic art.
She looks to every man like his own sweetheart.   4200

FAUST. What suffering! And what delight!
My eyes can not shift from that sight.
How oddly round that lovely throat there lies
A single band of scarlet thread
No broader than a knife has bled.

MEPHISTOPHELES. Quite right! And I can see it likewise.
Beneath her arm she also carries that same head
Since Perseus cut it off for her.
And you crave for illusion still!
Come, let us climb that little hill,   4210
The Prater is no merrier,[12]
And if I haven't been misled,
I actually see a theater.
What's being given?

SERVIBILIS.[13]   A minute yet before it starts.
A new play, last of seven in a row;
That is the number given in these parts.
A dilettant made up the show,
And dilettanti take the parts.
Forgive me, Sirs, if I now disappear;
I just delight in running up the curtain.   4220

MEPHISTOPHELES. I'm glad to find you on the Blocksberg here,[14]
It's just where you belong, that's certain.

---

12. The Prater is a famous park in Vienna.
13. Latin, "officious."
14. Blocksberg is an alternate name for the Brocken.

Walpurgis Night's Dream

Or Oberon's and Titania's Golden Wedding

Intermezzo[1]

THEATER MANAGER. Loyal sons of Mieding,[2] we
    Shall repose today.
Ancient hills and valleys may
    Provide the scenery.
HERALD. For a marriage to be golden,
    Must fifty years be ended;
I would far prefer that "golden"
    Where quarrels were suspended.   4230
OBERON. If you are a spirit crew,
    Let such now appear;
King and Queen have pledged anew
    Troth and marriage here.
PUCK. Puck comes leaping left and right
    Tripping it and dancing;
Come to share in his delight,
    Hundreds are advancing.
ARIEL. Ariel uplifts his song
    In tones celestial ringing,   4240
Luring ugly forms along
    With fair ones he is bringing.
OBERON. Spouses, if you would agree,
    Choose us for imitation;
Two who would forever be
    In love, need separation.
TITANIA. Brooding husband, pouting wife,

---

1. The subtitle "Intermezzo" is inappropriately retained from an earlier plan of the "Walpurgis Night," where it came between the witch passages and the orgiastic finale. (Fragments preserved from the originally planned finale indicate that it would have been a monstrous travesty of the Last Judgment.)
2. Johann Martin Mieding was stage manager of the Weimar theater.

Apart with them henceforth,
Off with her to southland life,
With him to furthest north.   4250
ORCHESTRA TUTTI (*fortissimo*).[3] Nose of gnat and snout of fly
   With all their family,
Tree toad and the cricket's cry
   Make up our symphony.
SOLO. Yonder see: the bagpipe comes,
   A soap bubble he blows.
Schnecke-schnicke-schnack he hums
   Through his turned-up nose.
MIND IN EMBRYO. Spider-foot and hop-toad's belly
   And winglets on the mite   4260
Add up to no wee animal
   But *do* to a poem-ette.
A LITTLE COUPLE. [*a*] Little steps and lofty leaps
   Through honey-dew and light.
[*b*] True, you mince and mince along
   But never rise in flight.
INQUISITIVE TRAVELER. Is this a masquerade? How odd!
   Can I believe my eyes?
Oberon the handsome god
   Here *too* beneath these skies?   4270
ORTHODOX. Lacking claws and tail maybe,
   And yet no doubt it's true:
Like the gods of Greece, so he,
   He is a devil too.
NORTHERN ARTIST. What I have achieved already
   Is sketchy, that is sure;

---

3. Group I (ll. 4251–90), miscellaneous and social. Orchestra Tutti: a transition stanza; the insect orchestra plays throughout. Solo: a soap bubble playing like a bagpipe—any loud and empty person. Mind in Embryo: some trivial eclectic poet (unidentified) who puts together incongruous oddments. A Little Couple: (*a*) "*I* write poems that soar"; (*b*) "You don't get off the ground." Inquisitive Traveler: Nicolai (see above, l. 4144*n*). Orthodox: Count Friedrich Leopold von Stolberg, who had attacked Schiller's poem *The Gods of Greece* for its paganism. Northern Artist: the native German painter waiting until he gets to Italy to begin serious work. Purist: an academic critic insisting on the neoclassical rules. Young Witch, Matron: female representatives of the younger and older generations.

But I'm starting to get ready
    For my Italian tour.
PURIST. Ah! What bad luck brings me to!
    They're lewd jades here, I swear!   4280
Of all these witches only two
    Are wearing powdered hair.
YOUNG WITCH. Powder, like the petticoat,
    Suits grannies old and grey,
So I sit naked on my goat
    With my charms on display.
MATRON. We are too well-bred by far
    To haggle with you here;
Young and tender as you are,
    I hope you rot, my dear.   4290
ORCHESTRA CONDUCTOR.[4] Nose of gnat and snout of fly,
    Don't crowd the naked lady!
Tree toad and the cricket's cry,
    Beat time and keep it steady!
WEATHER VANE (*in one direction*).
Company of first-rate sort,
    And nothing but sheer brides!

---

4. Group II (ll. 4291–4330), miscellaneous and personal. Orchestra Conductor: a transition stanza; the insect musicians are distracted by the Young
Witch. Weather Vane: an insincere flatterer of both factions; possibly Orchestra Conductor Reichardt, possibly Weimar Rector Böttiger (who has also
been proposed for Servibilis, l. 4214). "Xenien": the title of a collection of
satirical quatrains by Goethe and Schiller. The present scene is the outgrowth
of Goethe's plan for a larger and artistically ordered collection of such quatrains. Hennings: the Danish critic August von Hennings, a determined foe of
Goethe and Schiller. "Musaget": *Der Musaget* (Latin, *Musagetes*, "Leader
of the Muses"), title of a two-volume poetry anthology published by Hennings in 1798–99. *Ci-devant* "Genius of the Age": *Genius of the Age* (*Genius
der Zeit*) was the title of Hennings' magazine—the vehicle of his attacks on
Goethe and Schiller—up to 1800; from 1800 to 1802 it was called *Genius of
the Nineteenth Century*, hence the use of *ci-devant*, "formerly." Inquisitive
Traveler: Nicolai again, as traveler and as baiter of Jesuits. Crane: Lavater,
the phrenologist and Goethe's onetime friend; his walk was awkward like
that of a crane. Child of the World: Goethe himself; see the poem "Dîné zu
Coblenz," which begins, "Between Lavater and Basedow" (another onetime
friend of Goethe), and ends:

      Prophets to the right, prophets to the left,
      The child of the world in between.

Bachelors to a man, besides,
   To lend them proper escort.
WEATHER VANE (*in the other direction*).
   Unless a yawning of the ground
     Opens to receive them,   4300
   I will with a sudden bound
     Jump into hell to leave them.
"XENIEN." As small insects we appear
   With sharpened scissors here,
   Showing how much we revere
     Satan, our papa dear.
HENNINGS. Just see them milling there and jesting,
   So innocently too!
   They will wind up yet protesting
     Their hearts are tried and true.   4310
"MUSAGET." How I'd like to be absorbed
   Into these witches' crews;
   I could lead them on much sooner
     Than I could the Muse.
CI-DEVANT "GENIUS OF THE AGE."
   With proper people, one arrives,
     Come, grab my coattails now!
   The Blocksberg like the German Parnassus
     Has a broad, lofty brow.
INQUISITIVE TRAVELER.
   Tell me, who's that stodgy man?
     He struts about and fidgets.   4320
   He snoops as much as snoop he can.
     —"He's after Jesuits."
CRANE. I like to fish in waters clear,
   In troubled ones as well;
   That's why you see the pious man
     Mix with devils from hell.
CHILD OF THE WORLD.
   Yes, for pious men, believe me,
     All things are vehicles;
   On the Blocksberg here they hold
     Their own conventicles.   4330

DANCER.[5] What! Another chorus coming?
  I hear a distant drumming—
"Have no fear! It's bitterns booming
  And withered sedge grass humming."
BALLET MASTER. How each one hists his legs and jounces
  And as he can, gains clearance!
The crooked jumps, the clumsy bounces,
  Not caring for appearance.
FIDDLER. This rabble hate and most would like
  To see each other expire;   4340
They are united by the bagpipe
  Like beasts by Orpheus' lyre.
DOGMATIST. Doubts and critics will not shout
  Me out of certainty.
The Devil's real beyond a doubt,
  Else how could devils be?
IDEALIST. The fantasy of my mind is
  My master, willy-nilly.
Indeed, if I am all of this,
  I must be pretty silly.   4350
REALIST. Existence is a torment and
  There's worse yet I must meet;
This is the first time that I stand
  Unsteady on my feet.
SUPERNATURALIST. It's a pleasure to be here
  Among this motley crew,
For from the devils I infer
  That there are angels too.
SKEPTIC. They chase their will-o'-the-wisps and fancy
  That buried treasure's near.   4360
"Doubt" and "devil" start with *d*,
  So I'm in my true sphere.

---

5. Group III (ll. 4331–66), schools of philosophy. Dancer, Ballet Master,
Fiddler: transition stanzas describing the arriving philosophers. The latter
state in turn their conflicting opinions on the existence of devils. The Idealist
represents the school of Fichte: only the ego actually exists and all things are
its moment-to-moment creations. The Supernaturalist represents the followers
of Friedrich Jacobi. The Skeptic represents the tradition of Hume.

ORCHESTRA CONDUCTOR.[6] Tree toad and the cricket's cry,
    O dilettants accursed!
  Nose of gnat and snout of fly,
    In music you're well versed!
THE CLEVER ONES. *Sans souci* this host is called
    That merrily here treads;
  Walking's no more done on feet,
    So we walk on our heads.   4370
THE AWKWARD ONES. We sponged a lot in our time, true,
    Goodbye to all that, though;
  Our shoes have all been danced right through,
    And barefoot now we go.
WILL-O'-THE-WISPS. We come out of marshes dank
    From which we first arose,
  Here we are, rank after rank,
    The most resplendent beaux.
SHOOTING STAR. I came shooting from on high
    In starry flame and heat;   4380
  Sprawled now on the grass I lie—
    Who'll help me to my feet?
BRUISERS. Gangway there! We're coming through!
    The grass is bending low;
  Spirits come, and spirits too
    Have brawny limbs, you know.
PUCK. Don't go plowing through that way
    With elephantine tramp!
  Let the clumsiest one today
    Be Puck himself, the scamp.   4390

---

6. Group IV (ll. 4367 to the end), political types from the era of the French Revolution; finale. Orchestra Conductor: a transition stanza. The Clever Ones: "shrewd operators," political opportunists who change sides blithely (*sans souci*) as the tides of politics shift. The Awkward Ones: "weak sisters," émigrés stranded without capacity for earning their living. Will-o'-the-wisps: upstarts "made" by the Revolution. Shooting Star: a leader who rose from obscurity, had his day, and fell. Bruisers: brutal demagogues. Finale: Puck spurns the Bruisers; Ariel bids all the spirits follow him to the Hill of Roses, which, as was well known to readers of Wieland's *Oberon,* was the site of Oberon's palace; the Orchestra, playing to an empty stage, concludes the "scherzo."

ARIEL. If mind or Nature gave you wings
    And any wing discloses,
Follow where my leading brings
    You to the Hill of Roses.
ORCHESTRA (*pianissimo*).
    Gauze of mist and cloud-bank's edge
        Are touched with streaks of dawn.
    Breeze in branch and wind in sedge,
        And everything is gone.

Gloomy Day

A field.

FAUST   MEPHISTOPHELES

FAUST. In misery! Desperate! Long wandering pitifully upon the earth and now in prison! Locked up as a wrongdoer for ghastly torments in a jail, that lovely, unfortunate creature! To come to this! To this!—Perfidious, worthless Spirit, and this you kept from me!—Stand there, yes, stand there! Roll those devilish eyes furiously in your head! Stand and defy me with your unbearable presence! In prison! In irrevocable misery! Delivered over to evil spirits and to judging, heartless humanity! And meanwhile you lull me with insipid dissipations, conceal her increasing misery from me, and let her go helpless to destruction!

MEPHISTOPHELES. She is not the first.

FAUST. Cur! Monster of abomination!—Turn him, Infinite Spirit, turn the worm back into his canine form, the way he used to like to trot along in front of me often in time of night, and roll at the feet of the harmless traveler, and cling to the shoulders of one who fell. Turn him back into his favorite shape, so he can crawl on his belly in the sand up to me and I can kick him, the reprobate!—Not the first!—Grief! Grief beyond the grasp of any human soul, that more than one creature has sunk to the depths of such misery, that the first did not atone for the guilt of all the others in her writhing and deathly agony before the eyes of Eternal Forgiveness! It grinds through my marrow and my life, the misery of this one alone; you grin complacently over the fate of thousands!

MEPHISTOPHELES. Now we are once again at the limit of our wits, where the minds of you mortals go overboard. Why do you make common cause with us if you can't go through with it? You want to fly and are not proof to dizziness? Did we force ourselves on you, or you on us?

FAUST. Do not bare your ravening fangs at me that way! I loathe it!—Great and glorious Spirit who didst deign to appear to me, who knowest my heart and my soul, why dost thou forge me together with this infamous associate who gloats on harm and revels in destruction?

MEPHISTOPHELES. Are you through?

FAUST. Save her! Or woe to you! The ghastliest of curses upon you unto millenia!

MEPHISTOPHELES. I cannot loose the avenger's bonds, nor open his locks.—Save her!—Who was it plunged her into ruin? I or you?

(FAUST gazes wildly about.)

So you reach for thunderbolts? Lucky they were not given to you miserable mortals! To pulverize an innocent person in his path is the way of the tyrant, in order to relieve his feelings.

FAUST. Take me there! She shall be free!

MEPHISTOPHELES. And the risk you run? Remember: blood-guilt from your hand still lies upon the city. Over the place where the slain man fell hover avenging spirits in wait for the returning murderer.

FAUST. This yet from you? A world of murder and death upon you, monster! Take me there, I say, and set her free!

MEPHISTOPHELES. I will take you, and what I *can* do: hear! Do I have all power in heaven and on earth? The jailer's senses I will becloud, *you* get possession of his keys and lead her

out yourself with your human hand. I will stand watch! The
magic horses are ready, I will carry you away. This much I
can do.

FAUST. Up and away!

Night, Open Country

FAUST, MEPHISTOPHELES, *rushing on black horses.*

FAUST. What are they doing yonder on Gallows Rock?
MEPHISTOPHELES. I don't know what they're brewing or doing.   4400
FAUST. They soar and swoop, bending and stooping.
MEPHISTOPHELES. A crew of witches.
FAUST. They strew and bless.
MEPHISTOPHELES. On past! On past!

Dungeon

FAUST *in front of a little iron door, with a
bunch of keys and a lamp.*

FAUST. A horror long unfamiliar over me crawls,
Grief seizes me, grief common to human kind.
She is imprisoned in these clammy walls,
Her crime a fond illusion of the mind.
You shrink back from her door
Afraid to see her once more!   4410
On! Delay brings Death up from behind.

(*He seizes the lock.*)

(*Singing is heard from inside.*) [1]

1. Margaret sings a distorted form of the song in the old fairy tale of the
juniper tree, which Goethe knew long before it was set down as No. 47 in

My mother, the whore,
She murdered me!
My father, the rogue,
He has eaten me!
Little sister has laid
My bones away
In a place of cool, cool shade.
And I am turned into a woodland bird;
Fly away! Fly away!   4420
FAUST (*unlocking the door*).
She does not dream her lover can thus hear
Her clanking chains, her rustling straw so near.

(*He enters.*)

MARGARET (*cowering on her pallet*).
They're coming. O how bitter it is to die!
FAUST (*softly*). Be still! Be still! I come to set you free.
MARGARET (*throwing herself at his feet*).
If you are human, feel my misery.
FAUST. You'll wake the jailer with your cry!

(*He takes hold of the chains to unlock them.*)

MARGARET (*on her knees*). Who was it, headsman, who could give
You so much power!
You take me at the midnight hour.
Have pity on me, let me live!   4430
Is tomorrow morning not time enough?

(*She stands up.*)

Grimm's Fairy Tales in 1812. In *Von dem Machandelboom* a bird, representing the ghost of the boy slain by his wicked stepmother, sings:

Mein' Mutter der mich schlacht',	My mother who slew me,
Mein' Vater der mich ass,	My father who ate me,
Mein' Schwester der Marlenichen	My sister, little Marlene,
Sucht' alle meine Benichen,	Gathered up all my bones,
Bind't sie in ein seiden Tuch,	Tied them up in a silken cloth,
Legt's unter den Machandelbaum.	And buried them beneath the juniper tree.
Kywitt, Kywitt, wat vör'n schöön Vagel bün ik!	To-whit, to-whit, what a fair bird am I!

Am I not still so young, so young!
To die so soon!
And I was beautiful, and that was my undoing.
My friend was near, now he is near no more.
My wreath lies torn, the flowers scattered that I wore.
O do not seize me so violently!
What have I done to you? O pity me!
Let me not in vain implore,
I never saw you in my life before!   4440
FAUST. Will I survive such misery!
MARGARET. I am now wholly in your might.
First let me nurse my child again.
I fondled it all through the night;
They took it from me just to cause me pain,
And now they say that I have slain
My child. Now I shall never more be glad.
And they sing songs about me! How can they be
So wicked! So runs an ancient story, but who bade
Them make that tale fit me!   4450
FAUST (*falling on his knees*). A lover at your feet implores
You to come forth out of these woeful doors.
MARGARET (*kneels with him*).
O let us kneel and call upon the saints in prayer!
Look! Underneath that stair,
Beneath that threshold there,
Hell seethes! Beneath the floor
The Evil One
Makes ghastly noise
Of tumult and uproar!
FAUST (*loudly*). Gretchen! Gretchen!   4460
MARGARET (*attentively*). That was my beloved's voice!

(*She jumps up. Her chains fall off.*)

Where is he? I heard him calling me.
No one can stop me. I am free!
To his arms I will fly,
And at his heart I'll lie!
Gretchen, he called! He stood there at that door.

And through the howling din of hell's uproar,
Through the wrath of devils' mocking noise
I recognized that sweet, that loving voice.

FAUST. I *am* here!

MARGARET.   You! O say that once again!   4470

(*embracing him*)

It *is* he! Where is anguish now, or pain?
Where is my prison's agony?
You come to set me free!
And I am saved!—
There is the street once more where I
That first time saw you passing by.
There is the cheerful garden too
With Martha and me waiting for you.

FAUST (*trying to lead her away*).
Come with me! Come with me!

MARGARET.   O tarry!
I gladly tarry where you tarry.   4480

(*caressing him*)

FAUST. Hurry!
Unless you hurry,
It will cost us a bitter price.

MARGARET. What! Can you no longer kiss?
So briefly gone, so soon returned,
My friend, and kissing all unlearned?
Why am I frightened with such strange alarms,
When from your words, your glances, overwhelmingly
I once felt all of heaven in your arms,
When you would kiss as though to stifle me?   4490
Kiss me now, or
I will kiss you!

(*She embraces him.*)

Alas! your lips are cold,
And dumb.
What has become

Of your loving?
Who has robbed me of it?

(*She turns away from him.*)

FAUST. Come! Follow me! My darling, be bold!
  I'll love you with a passion thousandfold,
  Only come with me! That's all I'd have you do!   4500
MARGARET (*turning toward him*).
  But is it you? But is it really you?
FAUST. It is! But come with me!
MARGARET.   You loose my chain,
  And take me back into your arms again.
  How is it that you do not shrink from me?—
  Do you know who it is, my friend, you're setting free?
FAUST. Come! Come! Deep night will soon be done.
MARGARET. I sent my mother to her death,
  I drowned my child—the one
  Born to both you and me—yes, to you too.
  It *is* you! I can not believe it yet.   4510
  Give me your hand! It is no dream!
  Your dear hand!—O! But it is wet!
  Wipe it off. But still I seem
  To see blood on it.
  My God! What have you done!
  Put up your sword,
  That much I ask!
FAUST. O let the past be past and done
  Or you will be my death.
MARGARET. No, you must stay alive!   4520
  The graves I will describe for you,
  And you must see to them
  This coming morning;
  The best spot give to my mother,
  And next to her my brother;
  Bury me off a little way,
  But not too far away;
  And the babe at my right breast.
  No one else will lie by me!—

To nestle at your side so lovingly,   4530
That was a rapture sweet and blest!
But for me that will never come again.
It seems as if I had to force my way to you,
As if you spurned me away from you;
Yet it is you, and your look is so winsome.

FAUST. If you feel it is I, then come!

MARGARET. Out there?

FAUST. To freedom.

MARGARET.   If the grave is there,
If Death is waiting, come!
From there to my eternal bed   4540
But not one step beyond—
You go? O Henry, if I could go too!

FAUST. You can! If you but will! There is the door.

MARGARET. I cannot go! For me hope is no more.
What good is flight? They only hunt me down.
It is so wretched to have to beg,
And with an evil conscience too!
It is so wretched to wander far from home,
And they would catch me anyway!   4550

FAUST. I will stay with you.

MARGARET. O quick! O quick!
Save your poor child.
Go up the path
That skirts the brook
And across the bridge
To the woods beyond,
Left, where the plank is
In the pond.
Catch it quick!
It tries to rise,   4560
It struggles still!
Save it! Save it!

FAUST. Control yourself!
One step, and you are free!

MARGARET. If only we were past the hill!
There sits my mother on a stone,

And I am cold with dread!
There sits my mother on a stone
And shakes her head.
She does not beckon, does not nod, her head sinks lower,   4570
She slept so long, she wakes no more.
She slept so we might love.
O those were happy times!

FAUST. If all things fail that I can say,
Then I must carry you away.

MARGARET. No, let me go! I will not suffer violence!
Let go the hand that murderously holds me so fast!
I did all things to please you in the past.

FAUST. The day shows grey. My love! My love!

MARGARET. Yes, daylight penetrates. The final day.   4580
It was to be my wedding day.
Tell no one you have been with Gretchen.
Alas! rough hands
Have ripped the wreath I wore.
And we shall meet once more,
But not at the dance.
The crowd wells forth, it swells and grows
And overflows
The streets, the square;
The staff is broken, the death knell fills the air.[2]   4590
How I am seized and bound!
I am already at the block.
The neck of every living soul around
Foresenses the ax blade and its shock.
The crowd is silent as a tomb.

FAUST. Would I were never born!

(MEPHISTOPHELES *appears outside.*)

MEPHISTOPHELES. Up! Or it is your doom.
Useless dallying! Shilly-shallying!

---

2. After reading the death sentence, the judge broke a staff to symbolize the forfeiture of the condemned person's life; the death knell was rung throughout the execution ceremony.

Goethe, "Apparition of the Earth Spirit" (2nd version)   (ll. 460–517)
Weimar, Goethe National Museum

"Faust Among the Students"

"Faust's Ride on the Cask"

Engravings after murals from Auerbach's Tavern in Leipzig
(ll. 2073–2336)
Leipzig City Historical Institute

Title page from Lavater's *De spectris, lemuribus* . . . (1687)
("Witch's Kitchen," ll. 2337–2604)

Giorgione, "Venus" (ll. 2429–40)
Dresden, Gemäldegalerie

Frontispiece from Prätorius' *Blockes-Berges Verrichtung* (1669)
("Walpurgis Night," ll. 3835–4398)

p.166.

Blocks Berg.

Illustration from Caspar Schneider's *Saxonia vetus et magna* (1727)
("Walpurgis Night," ll. 3835–4398)

Roman Carnival Masks,
after Valentini

Giardiniere (Garden Girls, ll. 5088–5157)

Marinaro (Gardeners, ll. 5158–77)

Uomo e Donna Pulcinella
(Pulcinelle, ll. 5215–36)

Gianunculo   (Zoilo-Thersites, ll. 5457–70)

From Mantegna, "Triumph of Caesar" (ll. 5065–5986)

From Mantegna, "Triumph of Caesar"   (ll. 5065–5986)

Le Sueur, "Diana and Endymion"   (l. 6509)

From Correggio, "Leda"   (ll. 6903–20, 7271–7312)
Berlin, National Galleries

Chiron as Teacher of the Young Achilles   (ll. 7199, 7324–7487)
From a wall painting in Herculaneum

Goethe, "Thessalian Witches Conjuring the Moon"   (ll. 7920–23)
Weimar, Goethe National Museum

Lemurs   (ll. 11511–11603)
From a wall painting in the graves at Cumae

Raphael, "Triumph of Galatea"   (ll. 8144–49, 8424)
Rome, Villa Farnesina

Ceiling of St. Ignatius' Church, Rome   (ll. 11845 to end)

My horses shudder outside the door,[3]
It is the break of day.   4600
MARGARET. What rises out of the floor?
  He! He! Send him away!
  What does he want in this sacred place? [4]
  He comes for me!
FAUST.   You shall live!
MARGARET. Judgment of God! Myself to Thee I give!
MEPHISTOPHELES (*to* FAUST).
  Come on! Come on! Or I'll leave you here with her.
MARGARET. Father, I am Thine! Deliver me!
  You angels! Sacred hosts, descend!
  Guard me about, protect me and defend!
  Henry! I shudder to behold you.   4610
MEPHISTOPHELES. She is condemned!
A VOICE (*from above*).   Is saved!
MEPHISTOPHELES (*to* FAUST).   Hither to me!

(*Disappears with* FAUST.)

A VOICE (*from within, dying away*). Henry! Henry!

---

3. They are magic horses of the night and cannot bear the light of day.
4. A condemned person's place of confinement was inaccessible to evil spirits;
that Mephisto dares intrude is a sign of his desperation lest he lose Faust.

The Second Part of the Tragedy

Act One

Pleasant Region[1]

FAUST *reclining on flowery greensward, rest-*
less, trying to sleep. Twilight. A ring of spirits
hovering and flitting, graceful tiny forms.

ARIEL (*song accompanied by Aeolian harps*).
　When the blossoms of the spring
Float as rain down to the earth,
When green fields are shimmering
For all who are of this world's birth,
Elfins of high spirit race
Haste to help where help they can;
Be he holy, be he base,
They grieve for the grieving man.　　　　　　　　4620
　You airy hoverers where this head now lies,
Reveal yourselves in noble elfin guise,
Assuage the frantic turmoil of his soul,
Withdraw the fiery bitter arrows of remorse,
From horror lived through, purge and make him whole.
　Four are the watches of night's course,
Be prompt to keep them gladly and in full.
First, on cool pillows let his head be laid,
Then bathe him in the Lethe of the dew;
Lithe shall his strained and stiffened limbs be made　　4630
And rest deliver him to day, all new.
Perform the fairest elfin rite,
Restore him to the holy light.
CHORUS (*singly, by twos, and in combination, alternately and*
　　　together).[2] When the air lies warm and calm

---

1. Swiss Alpine scenery is intended.
2. According to the composer Eberwein, Goethe's manuscript entitled these
four stanzas, respectively, *Serenade, Notturno, Matutino,* and *Reveille.*

Over green-hemmed field and dale,
Twilight wafts a fragrant balm,
Wafts sweet mists in veil on veil,
Whispers softly of sweet peace,
Rocks the heart to childlike rest,
Grants this weary man's eyes ease,   4640
Shuts the portals of the west.
   Night has come with total dark,
Holily star moves to star,
Sovereign fire and feeble spark
Glitters near and glows afar,
Glitters here lake-mirrored, glows
High up in the clear of night;
Sealing joy in deep repose,
Reigns the moon in fullest light.
   Now these hours are snuffed out,   4650
Pain and joy have died away;
Health is certain; banish doubt,
Put your trust in coming day.
Green dawn valleys, hills are pillows
Fluffed for shadowed rest and sweet,
Harvestwards in silver billows
Sway and surge the tides of wheat.
   Wish on wishes to obtain,
Look to skies all bright aloft.
Lightest fetters still restrain,   4660
Sleep is seed coat: sluff it off!
Though the many shrink and waver,
Do not tarry to make bold;
All things tend in that man's favor
Who perceives and takes swift hold.

(*Tremendous tumult proclaims the approach of the sun.*)

ARIEL. Hark! the horal tempest nears!
   Sounding but to spirit ears
   Where the newborn day appears.
   Cliff gates, rasping, open; under
   Phoebus' chariot wheels rolls thunder;   4670

What mighty din the daylight brings!
Drumrolls pounding, trumpets sounding,
Eyesight-dazzling, ear-astounding,
Unheard be such unheard things.[3]
Into headed flowers dart!
Lie there still in deepest part,
Under leaves, in clefts of rock:
Deafness comes of such a shock!

FAUST. Life's pulse, renewed in vigor, throbs to greet
Aethereal dawning of the gentle light.   4680
New-quickened, Earth, thou breathest at my feet,
Thou who wert also constant through the night;
Already thou conferrest joy once more
And rousest resolution of great might
To strive for highest being evermore.
 In shimmering dawn revealed the world now lies,
The thousand voices of the forest soar,
A radiance streams in glory from the skies
Though mists in valleys still are drifted deep,
And branches fresh with life emerge and rise   4690
From fragrant glens where they were drowned in sleep;
By dull depths yielded up, hue clears on hue
Where pearls from glistening bloom and petal weep,
And paradise emerges to my view.
 Lift up your eyes!—Each giant mountain height
Proclaims the solemnest of hours anew.
They soonest catch the everlasting light
Which will thereafter unto us descend.
Now down the Alpine lawns steep-sloping, bright
New radiance and clarity extend   4700
And step by step their last objectives gain.
The sun comes forth! But when I that way tend,
I am struck blind, I turn aside in pain.
 So is it with our yearning hopes that tried
And finally their utmost wish attain

---

3. I.e., because such sounds ("sounding but to spirit ears") would, if received by physical ears, drive the hearer to madness, if not annihilate him.

When portals of fulfillment open wide.
And now as those eternal depths upraise
Flame so tremendous, we stand terrified;
We sought to set the torch of life ablaze
And find ourselves engulfed in seas of fire!   4710
Is it great love, or hate, whose burning gaze
Strikes now a mighty grief, now vast desire,
Till we turn backwards to the earth and run
And veil ourselves in youth's soft cloud attire? [4]
   Behind me only be the shining sun!
The cataract that through the cleft rock roars
To ever mounting rapture has me won;
From plunge to plunge it overflows and pours
Itself in thousands and uncounted streams
While high in air mist-veil on mist-veil soars.   4720
But O how glorious through the storm there gleams
The changeless, ever changeful rainbow bent,
Sometimes distinct, sometimes with shattered beams,
Dispensing showers of cool and fragrant scent.
Man's effort is there mirrored in that strife.
Reflect and by reflection comprehend:
There in that rainbow's radiance *is* our life. [5]

---

4. A mixed metaphor seems to account for the puzzling line, *Zu bergen uns in jugendlichstem Schleier*, namely, in our attempt to confront the overwhelming sun, we are routed and we make haste to shield ourselves from its fierce light by wrapping mists of the "youthful morning" around us.
5. The complex thought may be paraphrased: man is no match for the sun; his vital force is more appropriately symbolized by the cataract which rushes onward because its nature is to rush onward; human achievement is a by-product like the rainbow, sometimes realized in full, more often realized only in segments of its shattered arch.

Imperial Palace[1]

*Throne Room. The State Council awaiting
the Emperor. Trumpets. Enter* COURTIERS *of
all ranks, magnificently attired. The* EMPEROR
ascends the throne, the ASTROLOGER *at his
right.*

EMPEROR. I greet my loyal friends and dear
  Assembled thus from far and wide;—
  I see the wise man at my side,   4730
  But why then is the Fool not here?
A SQUIRE. Just where your mantle hem was trailing
  He fell against the stairway railing;
  They carried Tub-of-guts away:
  Dead or drunken, who can say?[2]
SECOND SQUIRE. Then in a sudden moment's space
  Another one assumed his place.
  Garb so rich yet queer he wears
  That each man startles, each man stares.
  There at the threshold guardsmen brace   4740
  Their halberds crosswise—and yet cool
  With impudence here is the Fool!
MEPHISTOPHELES (*kneeling at the throne*).
  What is accursed yet welcome still?
  What is desired and yet refused?
  What is defended with a will?
  What is denounced and hard abused?
  Whom do you dare not summon here?
  Whose name is everyone's delight?

---

1. Two modern words for palace are avoided (*Schloss, Palast*) in favor of the
archaic *Pfalz*, which suggests a remote era. The Emperor is left unnamed for
the sake of artistic liberty, though the historical personage connected with the
Faust saga was Maximilian I (1493–1519).
2. Mephistopheles, of course, struck down the old Fool, as Goethe expressly
told his secretary Eckermann on Oct. 1, 1827 (recorded in *Conversations with
Eckermann*).

What to your throne-steps now draws near?
What banished itself from your sight? [3]   4750
EMPEROR. For now, spare me your riddling words!
   Riddles are out of place right here.
   That is the business of these lords.—
   Solve some! Then I would gladly hear.
   My old Fool's gone, I fear I am bereft;
   Come take his place and stand here at my left.

(MEPHISTOPHELES *ascends and stands at his left.*)

MURMURS OF THE CROWD. A new fool's here—New trouble too—
   Where'd he come from?—How'd he get through?
   The old one dropped—He's all played out—
   He was a tub—And this a rain spout.   4760
EMPEROR. And now, my loyal friends and dear,
   I welcome you from near and far,
   You've come with an auspicious star,
   Up there our happiness is written clear.
   But tell me why, on such a day,
   When we would drive all care away
   And masquerade in strange array
   Enjoying only cheerful occupations,
   Why bore ourselves with state deliberations?
   But since you feel there is no other way,   4770
   We do so; be it as you say.
CHANCELLOR. The highest virtue like a halo glows
   About our Emperor's head, he only knows
   How justice can be dealt effectively!—
   What is beloved by all humanity,
   What all men seek, wish, cannot do without,
   It is for him alone to mete it out.
   But what use is intelligence to mind,
   Goodness to heart, or willingness to hand
   When fever rages up and down the land   4780
   And wrongs are breeding wrongs of every kind?

3. The answer to the riddle is: the court Fool.

To one who looks down from this height supreme
Upon the realm it seems an ugly dream
Where evils are in evil shapes arrayed,
Where laws are legally by wrongs outweighed,
And where a world of error is displayed.
　　One steals a woman, one steals herds,
Cross, chalice, altar lamps, yet he,
With skin unscathed, gets off scot-free
And boasts the feat for long years afterwards.　　　　　　4790
Now to the court the plaintiffs crowd,
On cushioned throne the judge presides,
And meanwhile uproar waxes loud
And surging swell the angry tides.
He brags of shame and impudence,
Accomplices remove his fears;
But at the trial of innocence
"Guilty!" 's the verdict that one hears.
Thus on the seemly all make war,
Destroy it, maim it, make it less;　　　　　　　　　　　　4800
How can a sense be fostered for
What can alone guide us to righteousness?
The upright man himself, in time,
To briber and to flatterer yields;
A judge who cannot punish crime
Supports the criminal he shields.
I've painted black, and yet I would
More densely shroud the picture if I could.

(*pause*)

Postponed decisions we can't afford;
When all work harm, all suffer pain,　　　　　　　　　　　4810
Then majesty itself falls prey.
FIELD MARSHAL. What license rages wild today!
　　Now each man slays, now each is slain,
And orders given are ignored.
The burgher safe behind his wall,
The knight high on his craggy nest,

Have both conspired to do their best
To keep their power and work our fall.[4]
Our restive mercenaries vow
With vehemence to have their pay,   4820
And if we did not owe them now
They would desert and run away.
Denying what all want would be
Like stirring up a hornets' nest;
The empire that should give security
Lies plundered, wasted, and distressed.
We tolerate their ravagings,
Half of the world has been undone;
In lands abroad there still are kings,
But none thinks it is his concern, not one.[5]   4830
TREASURER. Who will rely on allies thus!
The subsidies they promised us,
Like water conduits, fail. And, Sire,
Who are the ones who now acquire
Possessions in your far-flung states?
Go where you will, some upstart plants his gates
And tries to live quite independently.
We have to look on while he has his way;
We have bestowed so many rights that we
Have no rights left to anything today.   4840
On so-called parties of the state
There's no relying nowadays;
No matter if they blame or praise,
Their love comes to the same thing as their hate.
The Ghibelline is like the Guelph:
Both are in hiding and at rest.
Who helps his neighbor now? At best,
Each one is busy for himself.

---

4. 16th-century conditions in the age of the robber barons are here accurately
described.
5. Presumably meant are the kings who were vassals of the Holy Roman
Emperor, but Goethe had also observed what sluggish efforts had been put
forth by the monarchs of Europe in support of the French monarchy during
the Revolution of 1789.

The gates of gold are locked up tight,
All scrape and hoard with all their might,   4850
And still our coffers empty stand.
MARSHAL. What troubles plague me too! We slave
Every day to scrimp and save
And every day our needs expand.
And daily I face new distress.
No shortages annoy the cooks;
Wild boar and hare and venison,
Turkeys, chickens, geese, and ducks,
Tribute in kind—sure payment—these
Still do come in yet, more or less.   4860
And yet our stocks of wine are gone.
Where casks once heaped the cellar to the top,
From the best slopes and vintages,
The noble lords' unceasing ravages
And swillings have not left a single drop.
The City Council also drains supplies,
They reach for bumper, reach for cup,
And under the table the drunken party lies.
Then I must pay reward and fee;
The Jew is merciless to me;   4870
The promissory notes he grants
Devour years of harvests in advance.
No pigs are now to fatness fed,
Pawned is the pillow on the bed,
And to our tables comes pre-eaten bread.
EMPEROR (*to* MEPHISTOPHELES, *after some reflection*).
Well, Fool, don't you have some complaint to tender?
MEPHISTOPHELES. I? By no means! While gazing at this splendor,
On you and yours!—Can confidence give way
When majesty resistlessly holds sway,
When ready power scatters every fray,   4880
When good will, through intelligence made bold,
Is coupled with high actions manifold?
What things could for disaster here combine,
Or darkness either, when such bright stars shine?
MURMURS. He is a rogue—who knows his man—

He lies his way in—while he can—
I see already—what's his object—
What else could it well be?—A project—
MEPHISTOPHELES. Where in the world is there not something lacking?
    But money is the thing that's lacking here.   4890
    It can't be picked up off the floor, that's clear;
    But wisdom can produce profoundest things.
    In mountain veins, in caverns underground
    There's gold, both coined and uncoined to be found,
    And if you ask me who brings it to light:
    The gifted man's nature and mind's insight.
CHANCELLOR. Nature and mind—those words are infamous
    To Christians; for them atheists burn,
    Because such talk is highly dangerous.
    Mind is devil, Nature is sin.   4900
    Between them they beget in turn
    Their mongrel offspring, Doubt. Not so with us!
    The Emperor's ancient lands have nourished
    Two races only that have flourished
    And worthily support his throne:
    The clergy and the knights alone.
    These stand against all storms, and they
    Receive the church and state for pay.
    Thus there are set up barriers
    To keep the muddled minds of riffraff down;   4910
    These are the heretics, the sorcerers!
    They ravage countryside and town.
    And these you try to smuggle in
    To these high circles by your jest . . .
    Depraved hearts are what you like best!
    To the Fool they're close akin.
MEPHISTOPHELES. Ah, there the learned man I recognize!
    What you touch not, in furthest distance lies,
    What you grasp not, must simply be untrue,
    What you count not, you fancy is unreal,   4920
    What you weigh not, lacks any weight for you,
    What you coin not, will never pass, you feel.
EMPEROR. Our needs will not be met by all of that.

What is your Lenten sermon driving at?
I'm sick of this eternal if and when;
We lack for money: go and get some, then!
MEPHISTOPHELES. I will, and even more than you now ask.
    It's simple, yet the simple is a task.
    It's lying there right now, but to get to it
    Is quite a trick, and who knows how to do it?   4930
    Just think about those times of terror when
    The human tides submerged both lands and men,
    How one man here, another there, would hide
    Dearest possessions, they were so terrified.
    In mighty Romans' time things went that way,
    So things have gone down to the present day.
    Deep buried in the soil all that still lies;
    The Emperor owns the soil, his is the prize.
TREASURER. Now for a fool that's not such bad advice,
    These are indeed our ancient Emperor's rights.   4940
CHANCELLOR. It's golden traps this Satan sets for you,
    Things do not work that way if they are true.
MARSHALL. Let him bring welcome gifts to court and I
    Won't mind a little evil by the bye.
FIELD MARSHAL. The fool is shrewd, gives each man his desire;
    From whence it comes no soldier will inquire.
MEPHISTOPHELES. And if you think you're being hoodwinked, here
    Stands the astrologer: just ask this man,
    He knows the hours and houses, sphere on sphere.
    Now tell us how the starry aspects scan.   4950
MURMURS. Two rascals—each to other known—
    Phantast and fool—so near the throne—
    An old, old song—so trite, it reeks—
    The fool is prompting—as the sage speaks—
ASTROLOGER (speaks, MEPHISTOPHELES prompts).
    The sun itself is pure gold in its fire,[6]
    And Mercury, the herald, serves for hire,
    Dame Venus has bewitched you from above,

---

6. Goethe, the man of the Enlightenment, parodies the court astrologers
common in the 16th and 17th centuries.

Both late and soon she looks on you with love,
Chaste Luna moodily sulks in her bower,
Mars, though unstriking, lets you feel his power,   4960
And Jupiter is still the fairest gleam,
And Saturn, far and dim, is great in might;
As metal, we hold him in slight esteem
Yet of much weight, for all his worth is slight.[7]
When Luna joins with Sol and both appear,
Silver with gold, the world then finds its cheer,
Then all lies in the reach of him who seeks—
Parks, castles, little breasts, and rosy cheeks;
These things are all won by the learnèd man
Who can achieve what none of us now can.   4970
EMPEROR. I hear him double when he talks,
     And yet conviction fails and balks.
MURMURS. Why tell us stuff—such rehashed bluff—
     Almanachery—chemi-quackery—
     I've heard too much—pinned hopes on such—
     If he does pass—he's still an ass—
MEPHISTOPHELES. They gape and stare and stand around,
     Mistrust the finding of such loot,
     One babbling of the mandrake root,
     Another of the Midnight Hound.[8]   4980
     What matter if one jibes and rails
     And one complains of sorcery,
     When once their soles are tickling wickedly,
     When once their steady footing fails?[9]
        It is mysterious workings of
     Eternal Nature that you feel,
     And from her deepest regions steal

---

7. Alchemy associated metals with the planets: Saturn with lead; the sun (Sol) with gold; Mercury, quicksilver; Venus, copper; the moon (Luna), silver; Mars, iron; Jupiter, tin.
8. The spectral Midnight Hound was the necessary agent for pulling up the mandrake root (an actual herb, *mandragora officinalis*), whose scream when pulled from the ground would send a human being mad on the spot. Possession of the root conferred health, fertility, control of the weather, etc.
9. Ancient belief has it that sudden pains, itches, and the like indicate that one is standing over buried treasure.

Up living forces to the world above.
When every limb feels twinge and tweak,
When some place seems uncanny, on the spot   4990
Dig with a will and delve and seek:
There's treasure, there's your lucky spot.
MURMURS. My foot's like lead, I can't step out—
My arm's asleep—It's just the gout—
I've got an itch in my big toe—
My whole back is one aching woe—
Right here should be, with signs like these,
A tract of sumless treasuries.
EMPEROR. Be quick then! You shan't get away,
Put to the test this froth of lies,   5000
Set those high realms before our eyes.
My sword and scepter I will lay
Aside and with my hands complete—
If you're not lying—this high feat,
But if you're lying I'll send you to hell!
MEPHISTOPHELES. I know the way there pretty well
Myself—but I have not begun to tell
You all the unclaimed things lying around.
The peasant plowing up his ground
Turns up a gold crock with the sod,   5010
And looking for saltpeter from a lime wall,
Finds rolls of golden coins that fall
Into his startled hand that sought to prod.
O now to blow up basement vaults!
In through what passageways and faults
The treasure hunters now will scramble
Toward outskirts of the world below!
In ample cellars once well warded
They'll find the golden goblets hoarded
And plates and platters row on row.   5020
There winecups rich with rubies stand,
And there conveniently at hand
The super-ancient liquids bask.
Yet—trust in my experience—
The cask staves rotted ages since,

But tartar formed a second cask.
Not merely gold and jewels rare,
But essences of noble wines are there
Wrapped in the horrors of black air.
The wise will search here hard and long;   5030
To know by daylight is no task,
To darkness mysteries belong.

EMPEROR. What good is gloom? Such things I leave to you.
A thing of value must be brought to view.
Who knows a rascal in the dark of night?
All cows are black then, as all cats are grey.
Those crocks down there, and all the gold they weigh—
Go sink your plowshare, plow them up to light.

MEPHISTOPHELES. Take spade and fork yourself and dig—
You will grow great through peasant toil—   5040
A herd of golden calves both big
And fat will be wrenched from the soil.
With rapture and without delay
Yourself and your beloved you'll array,
For lustrous jewels go becomingly
With beauty as with majesty.

EMPEROR. Quick! Quick, then! Why wait any longer!

ASTROLOGER (*as above*).   Sire,
Pray moderate such vehement desire,
First let us have our merry carnival show;
Distraught minds will not lead us to our goal.   5050
First we must gain our calm, our self-control,
Through things above, deserve the things below.
Who craves good things must first himself be good;
Who craves for joy, must moderate his blood;
If wine is wanted, ripe grapes must be pressed,
And miracles require a strong faith stressed.

EMPEROR. Then let the time be spent in revelry
Until we greet Ash Wednesday eagerly!
Meanwhile we'll keep, whatever may befall,
More lustily our frantic carnival.   5060

(*Trumpets. Exeunt.*)

MEPHISTOPHELES. How luck and merit are close bound
　　Fools never see and never will;
　　And if the Wise Man's Stone were found,[10]
　　The stone would lack the wise man still.

Spacious Hall

*Adjoining apartments decked and adorned
for a masquerade.*

HERALD. Think not that we hold German revels
　　With dances of death and fools and devils;
　　Gay festival is yours tonight.
　　Our master journeying to Rome,[1]
　　To his advantage and your delight
　　Has crossed the high Alps and come home;　　　　　5070
　　A cheerful empire is his gain.
　　Before the sacred slipper he bowed down,
　　Requesting rights to his domain,
　　And when he went to claim the crown
　　He brought us back a fool's cap too.
　　Now we have all been born anew
　　And every wise and worldly man
　　Now gladly pulls it over head and ears;
　　Each like a crazy fool appears,
　　Each plays the sage as best he can.　　　　　5080
　　I see them gathering into groups,

---

10. The Wise Man's Stone, which conferred wealth, power, and long life, was the object of much alchemical research.

1. The whole masquerade scene is presented as part of the coronation festivities of the Holy Roman Emperor, who has just returned from Rome and the age-old ceremony of kissing the Pope's slipper and requesting the crown of the Holy Roman Empire. As a matter of fact, Maximilian I was the first Emperor to break that ancient custom. (To illustrate the masquerade's triumphal march, see illustrations, "The Triumph of Caesar"; for particular carnival characters in following lines, the Roman carnival masks.)

Dividing, straggling, pair and pair;
Groups force themselves on other groups,
Hither, thither, and everywhere.
Yet with its antics thousand score
The world remains, now as before,
One vast, huge fool forevermore.

GARDEN GIRLS (*song, accompanied by mandolins*).
    Your approval to obtain,
We have dressed for your delight,
Girls of Florence in the train   5090
Of the German court tonight.
    In our hair of auburn gloss
We are wearing flowers gay;
Silken ribbons, silken floss
Also have their role to play.
    That your praises should be ours
We believe to be quite clear,
For our bright, hand-woven flowers [2]
Bloom throughout the livelong year.
    Symmetry of fold and crease   5100
Blent these wisps of every hue;
You may spurn them piece by piece
But the whole still pleases you.
    We are dainty to behold,
Garden girls of carefree heart;
Women's way is known of old
To be close akin to art.

HERALD. Let us see your baskets there
Blown with color in your arms,
Balancing upon your hair;   5110
Let each choose what holds most charms.
    Hurry, so a garden's found
In the walks and thoroughfares.
They are worth the crowding round,
Both these sellers and their wares.

GARDEN GIRLS. Let your purchases be heard,

---

2. Making artificial flowers was a fad of Goethe's time.

But no haggling at this fair!
In a brief and pungent word,
What each has, let her declare.

OLIVE BRANCH WITH FRUIT.

I of blossoms envy none,   5120
All contention do I shun;
Such against my nature is.
I am the marrow of the land
And as a trusted pledge I stand,
To every field a sign of peace.
Be it my good fortune now
To adorn a worthy brow.

WHEAT WREATH (*golden*).

Ceres' gifts adorning you
Will become you and content;
Things most sought and useful too   5130
Be your fairest ornament.

FANCIFUL GARLAND. Colored flowers rich and strange
Mallows-like from moss are blooming;
They are not in Nature's range
But are bred by Fashion's grooming.

FANCIFUL BOUQUET. Theophrastus would not dare
Name for you the name I bear,[3]
Yet I trust I will please some
Of the ladies who have come.
There are some I would become   5140
If they wove me in their hair—
If they chose, on their own parts,
To grant me room inside their hearts.

CHALLENGE.

Let your fantasies be gay
In the fashion of the day,
Odd shapes with still odder wed
Such as Nature never bred;

---

3. Theophrastus of Lesbos (b. 372/369 B.C.), a disciple of Aristotle, wrote a
work on plants, a German translation of which was published in 1822. Goethe
originally wrote: "Even Humboldt would not dare," i.e., his friend and fel-
low-scientist Alexander von Humboldt.

Stem on stem of green unfurls
Golden bells among rich curls;
But we
ROSEBUDS. hide back from all glances;   5150
Happy he who on us chances.
  When once Summer cries his name,
Rosebuds kindle into flame:
Who would such delight forgo?
Promise and fulfillment, lo!
These in Flora's realm control
Sight and sense and heart and soul.

(*Under arcades of greenery the* GARDEN GIRLS *daintily set
forth their wares.*)

GARDENERS (*song, accompanied by theorboes*).[4]
  See how softly growing flowers
Wreathe your heads with gracious favor;
Fruits will not mislead you: savor   5160
And enjoy these fruits of ours.
  If sun-ripe faces you espy
On cherries, peaches, royal plums,
Buy them: truer judgment comes
From the tongue than from the eye.
  Taste with relish and delight
Fruit so luscious and so prized!
Roses can be poetized,
Into apples you can bite.
  Let us join you now in pairs   5170
In your show of flowery youth
And display our ripened wares
Booth by friendly neighbor booth.
  Underneath these leafy bowers
Gay with garlands intertwined
Everything at once you find:
Buds and leaves and fruit and flowers.

---

4. Theorboes are "bass lutes" contrasting with the "soprano mandolins and guitars."

(*In alternate song accompanied by guitars and theorboes, both choruses proceed to arrange their wares and set them out on display, level on level upwards.*)

(*Enter a* MOTHER *and* DAUGHTER.)

MOTHER. When, my girl, you first saw light,
   You had a lovely face;
   I decked you for your marriage night,   5180
   And you were full of grace.
   I saw you right away a bride
   Wed to the richest far and wide,
   I saw you in your wifely place.
    Alas! these many years are sped
   And wasted now in vain,
   The motley line of beaux has fled
   Swiftly in their train;
   With one you tripped a sprightly dance
   And to another gave a glance   5190
   And elbow nudge quite plain.
    All the parties we could plan,
   All were held for naught,
   Games of forfeit and "Third Man"
   Would not yield what we sought;
   The fools are on the loose today,
   Spread your lap, my dear! You may
   Yet see a suitor caught.

(*Young and beautiful playmates gather around them and confidential chats grow loud. Enter Fishermen and Fowlers with nets, fishing poles, limed twigs, and other gear; they join the pretty girls. Reciprocal attempts to win, catch, escape, and hold fast provide the occasion for the most pleasant interchanges of dialogue.*)

(*Enter* WOODCUTTERS, *boisterous and uncouth.*)

WOODCUTTERS. Make way! Stand clear!
   We need room!   5200
   When we fell trees
   They crash and smash,

And when we load,
You hear them boom.
This to our credit
Understand:
If rough men didn't
Work in the land,
Where then would
The gentry stand,   5210
How clever soever?
Do not forget:
You would freeze
But for our sweat.

PULCINELLE (*clumsy, almost silly*).[5]

You're fools! You're hacks!
Born with bent backs!
It's we who are clever
Because we never
Lug things. Our caps,
Our jackets and traps   5220
Are light to wear.
And to our pleasure
We're always at leisure
To run around
In slippered feet
Through market and street,
And gape and stare,
And crow aloud
To one another,
And by such sound   5230
To slip like eels
Through throng and crowd
And kick up our heels.
Praise us fair
Or cry us blame,
To us it's all the same.

---

5. Clown types from the Italian folk farces (*Commedia dell'arte*). See illustrations.

PARASITES (*fawning, lascivious*).
  You porters [6] lusty,
  And your trusty
  Charcoal-burner kin,
  You're our men!   5240
    All this kowtowing,
  Yes-yesing and bowing,
  Ingratiating
  Two-faced prating,
  This blowing hot,
  Then cold—now what
  Use are such things?
    We'd need the high
  Fires from the sky,
  The giant lightnings,   5250
  If we did not
  Have logs or kindling
  To heat our dwindling
  Hearth fires hot.
  There's roasting and brewing
  And toasting and stewing
  To do!—Gourmets
  And platter-lickers
  Can scent a roast
  And sniff a fish;   5260
  That makes them able
  At a patron's table.
DRUNKARD (*befuddled*).
    No one now shall say me nay!
  I feel so let loose and free;
  Cheer and lively roundelay
  I have brought along with me.
  So I drink! Drink with me, drink!
  Clink your glasses: clinkety-clink!
  You in back there, join the fun!
  Clink now! *That's* the way it's done.   5270
    How my wife did rant and rail

---

6. I.e., the woodcutters of ll. 5199 ff.

And turn her nose up at my coat;
Strutting was of no avail,
She called me a masking goat.
But I drink! Drink with me, drink!
Sound your glasses: clinkety-clink!
Masking goats, clink every one!
Here is how the clinking's done.
   Don't tell me that I'm confused,
I'm right where I want to be.   5280
The credit that mine host refused
His wife or maid'll extend to me.
I drink on! Drink with me, drink!
Everybody: clinkety-clink!
Each to other, every one!
That's the way I think it's done.
   Let me be wherever I
Find my pleasure and my treat;
Leave me lying where I lie,
I just can't stand on my feet.   5290
CHORUS. Brothers all, come on and drink!
Raise a toast now: clinkety-clink!
Sit your benches, every one!
Under the table all who are done.

(*The* HERALD *announces various poets, Nature poets, court
bards, and knightly minstrels, sentimental ones as well as
rhapsodic.*[7] *In the crush of competitors of all sorts none will
allow another to declaim. One, a satirical poet, sneaks past
with a few words.*)

SATIRIST. You know what would delight
My poet's heart with cheer?
To sing and to recite
What no one cares to hear.

---

7. The Nature poets probably represent a group of crude but then popular
amateurs with such forgotten names as Grübel, Fürnstein, and Hiller. The
bards and minstrels stand for the facile practitioners, in Goethe's day, of
romantic medievalism.

(*The Night poets and the Graveyard poets excuse themselves because they have just become engaged in a most interesting conversation with a freshly risen vampire, from
which experience a new kind of poetry might perhaps develop. The* HERALD *has to accept the excuse, and meanwhile
he announces Greek mythology, which, even in its modern
mask, loses neither its character nor its charm.*)

(*Enter the* GRACES.) [8]

AGLAIA. We are graciousness in living;
   Put graciousness into your giving.   5300
HEGEMONE. Put graciousness in your receiving;
   Joy is in desire's achieving.
EUPHROSYNE. And in quiet days what ranks
   Supremely gracious is your thanks.

(*Enter the* PARCAE.) [9]

ATROPOS. Me, the eldest, they advised to
   Come and spin for this occasion;
   Fragile life-thread does give rise to
   Lots of thought and rumination.
     So it might be soft and tender,
   Flax of finest kind I chose;   5310
   So it may be sleek and slender,
   The finger smooths it as it goes.
     If in dance and jubilation
   You too wantonly disport,
   Think of this thread's limitation:
   Caution! It may snap off short!
CLOTHO. Know that in these latter days

---

8. The Graces represent the social virtues, which are here identified in
slightly modified terms as gracious giving, gracious receiving, and gracious
thanking. For the second, whose name is usually said to be Thalia, Goethe
substituted the name Hegemone to avoid confusion with Thalia the Muse of
comedy.
9. The Parcae are the Fates, who are usually identified as Clotho ("the
spinner"), Lachesis ("the measurer," i.e., of the length of the strand), and
Atropos ("she who cannot be turned away," i.e., she who inevitably severs
the life-strand by death.)

I am trusted with the shears,
For our ancient sister's ways
Proved quite shocking through the years.   5320
   Threads of utter uselessness
To the light and air she gave,
Wefts of glorious hopefulness
She clipped and dragged to the grave.
   But time and time again the taint
Of error marked *my* ruling years;
Now to exercise restraint,
In their sheath I keep the shears.
   And I welcome such control,
With good will this place I see;   5330
Your free hours have no goal
But this endless revelry.
LACHESIS. To me, because I was so clever,
   Tidying was the task assigned;
My reel, ever living, never
Has outrun the speed defined.
   Threads appear and threads are reeled,
Each in proper course is guided;
I let none stray far afield,
Each goes to the skein provided.   5340
   Let me err but once and I
For the world in fear would stand;
Hours are totaled, years go by,
And The Weaver takes the strand.
HERALD. These coming next you doubtless do not know,
   For all you may be steeped in ancient books;
You might receive them, judging by their looks,
As welcome guests, these bringers of much woe.
   These are the Furies, for all you may doubt:
Attractive, pretty, shapely little loves;   5350
If you take up with them you will find out
How very like a snake they sting, these doves.
   They may be crafty, but when every clown
Boasts of his failings they will not essay

To be called angels; they admit today
They are the plague of country and of town.

(*Enter the* Furies.) [10]

ALECTO. How can you help but trust us? We are pretty,
And young, and expert in cajolery.
If one among you has a sweetheart, we
Will get his ear and in it sing our ditty   5360
    Till we can look him in the eye and say:
She flirts with more than one at once, she skimps
On brains, she's crooked in the spine, she limps,
And will prove worthless in a bridal way.
    We also can involve the girl in wrangles:
Why! her friend spoke just a few weeks ago
Contemptuously of her to so-and-so!
They may make up, but something clings and rankles.
MEGARA. That's nothing! Let me see them married once:
I go to work then, always with success,   5370
With moods that poison any happiness:
Uneven are both mortals and the months.
    And no one clasps a love in his embrace
Without a mad desire for more than this
Supreme but all too much accustomed bliss;
He flees the sun to warm frost in its place.
    I know just how to handle such affairs:
I have good old Asmodi come and sow
His mischiefs at the time when they best grow,[11]
And thus undo the human race by pairs.   5380
TISIPHONE. Poison I brew, daggers I whet,
Not tongues of slander, for a traitor;
Love another, and sooner or later
Ruin will befall you yet.

---

10. The Furies, here invested with a wholly new interpretation, were usually
construed by the Greeks and Romans as personifications of vengeance or
remorse, by name, Alecto ("unnameable"), Megaera ("grudge"), and Tisiphone ("avenger of blood").
11. Asmodi (or Asmodeus) is the demon of discord.

    Into froth and gall they turn
Sweetest of sweet moments' feelings.
Then no hagglings, then no dealings:
As he sinned, so he shall burn.
    Let none sing the word "Forgive!"
To stone crags my cause I bring,   5390
Hark!—"Revenge!" the echoes ring,
"Who changed lovers shall not live."

HERALD. Would you oblige me, please, and step behind:
    These now approaching are not of your kind.
    It is a mountain moving up you see,
    Its proud sides hung with colored tapestry,
    A head with tusks and snakelike trunk in the middle—
    Mysterious, but I have the key to the riddle.
    Athwart its neck an elfin lady rides,
    With dainty wand its every step she guides;   5400
    A second stands atop, her stately height
    Beshone with radiance dazzling to my sight;
    At either side walk ladies bound with chains,
    One full of cheer, while one with dread complains,
    One yearning, while the other feels quite free.
    Let each one now declare who she may be.

FEAR. Murky torch and lamp and flare
    Dimly through this revel shine;
    With false faces everywhere,
    I stand in these chains of mine.   5410
        Foolish funsters, go your ways!
    I mistrust your grinning sight;
    All my adversaries raise
    Hue and cry for me tonight.
        Here! A friend turned enemy!
    But I know his masked array.
    That one tried to murder me;
    Now, found out, he sneaks away.
        Oh, how I would like to flee
    To the wide world anywhere!   5420
    But destruction waits for me,
    Gloom is here, and horror there.

HOPE.[12] Hail, sweet sisters! Though you may
    Today perhaps and yesterday
    Have taken pleasure in disguise,
    All the same I realize
    Tomorrow you will doff these masks.
    If by torchlight we have not
    Especially enjoyed this spot,
    Cheerful days there yet will be   5430
    When we will be released from tasks,
    Alone or in good company
    To roam fair meadows for our pleasure,
    Resting, moving, at our leisure,
    And in life, glad and carefree,
    Never want, but strive forever.
    Each shall be a welcome guest
    Anywhere we may be bound.
    There is no doubt but the best
    Is surely somewhere to be found.   5440
PRUDENCE. Two of mankind's greatest foes,
    Fear and Hope, I hold in chains,
    Guarding people from their woes.—
    You are quite safe! Open lanes!
      I guide this colossus here,
    Howdah-laden, as you see,
    It advances with no fear
    Up steep paths undauntedly.
      Yonder goddess, though, up there
    On the ramparts, with swift pinions   5450
    Wide outspanned, looks everywhere
    To the gaining of dominions.
      Glory shines about her, she
    Sheds light on all she devises,
    And her name is Victory,
    Goddess of all enterprises.
ZOILO-THERSITES.[13] Bah! Bah! I'm just in time to call

---

12. Hope is here fatuous optimism and over-trustfulness.
13. Zoilus was a Greek grammarian of the third century B.C. who belittled

Your stupid errors one and all!
Right now my real attack concerns
The Lady Victory up there   5460
With her white wings outspread in air.
She thinks she is an eagle and
Whichever way she looks or turns
She owns all people and all land.
Let any glorious thing succeed:
I come out fighting with all speed.
When high is low and low is high,
When crooked is straight and straight awry,
Then only am I wholly sound;
That's how I want it on this earthly round.   5470
HERALD. Hah! Now, you filthy cur, you've found
The masterstroke my staff can deal!
Cringe and writhe with welt and weal!—
How fast the double dwarfish stump
Rolls up into a loathsome clump!—
The clump becomes an egg!—A wonder!
It puffs and swells and bursts asunder;
Out plops a pair of twins. See! That
One is an adder, this a bat.
Off through the dust one slithers while   5480
The other swoops up black and vile.
They will rejoin in outer air;
I'd hate to be a third out there.
MURMURS. Quick! There's dancing at the rear—
No, I'd rather get out of here—
Don't you feel this spectral rout
Has us hemmed in all about?—
Something whizzed right past my hair—
Past my foot I felt it go—
None of us is injured, though—   5490

Homer. Thersites is the abusive scoundrel in the *Iliad*. Mephistopheles here appears as this double figure wearing, like some persons in the carnival at Rome, one mask over his face with a corresponding half-costume in front and a different mask on the back of his head with a corresponding half-costume on his back (see illustrations).

But we all have had a scare—
But the prank got out of hand—
Just the way the rascals planned.
HERALD. Since upon me falls the task
   Of being Herald to this masque,
   I watch by the door with care
   Lest some harm steal unaware
   On you in this merry spot,
   Faltering never, yielding not.
   Yet I fear ghosts of the air   5500
   May come through the windows there,
   And I could not set you free
   From their spells of sorcery.
   If that dwarf caused you some doubt,
   Now here comes a mighty rout.
   As a Herald I must cry
   What these figures signify,
   But how can I well explain
   What I do not understand?
   You must help me make it plain!   5510
   Do you see them through the throng?
   Splendid with its four-in-hand
   Comes a chariot along,
   Yet through crowds it cleaves no lane,
   Nowhere see I crush or strain.
   Colored star on colored star
   Trails and glitters out afar,
   Such as magic lanterns cast;
   Those steeds ride the storm wind's blast.
   I am chilled with awe. Make way!   5520
BOY CHARIOTEER. Stay your wings, my coursers, stay!
   Own the wonted check-rein's sway,
   Be checked when I check your fire,
   Rush aloft when I inspire—
   These rooms let us honor here!
   See the people crowding near,
   Throng on throng, in wonderment.
   Herald, rise, as is your bent,

And before we go, proclaim
Our appearance and our name: 5530
We are allegories, true,
But we should be known to you.
HERALD. I know of no name for you,
    I had best describe you merely.
BOY CHARIOTEER. Try!
HERALD.   First off, one must declare
    Both of you are young and fair.
    You are a half-grown boy, yet women own
    They would be glad to see you fully grown.
    I see you in a future wooer's part,
    A downright charmer from the start.   5540
BOY CHARIOTEER. All well and good! But set about
    Sorting the riddle's cheerful meaning out.
HERALD. Your jet eyes' fire, your night-dark hair
    By jeweled circlet made more glowing,
    And what a graceful garment flowing
    From shoulder down to ankle there,
    Its purple hem and spangles showing!
    Too girlish, some would say, to please;
    And yet you could, for weal and woe,
    Pass muster with girls even so—   5550
    They would teach you the A B C's.
BOY CHARIOTEER. And he whose figure nobly gleams
    In splendor on his chariot throne?
HERALD. A monarch rich and mild he seems;
    Happy he to whom his grace is shown.
    He has achieved all goals of living,
    Dearth wheresoever he relieves,
    For him the pure delight of giving
    Outweighs all gifts that he receives.
BOY CHARIOTEER. You cannot stop short thus and fail,   5560
    You must describe him in detail.
HERALD. With dignity descriptions fail.
    And yet: that face full-moon and hale,
    A full mouth and fair cheeks that show

Beneath his jeweled turban's glow; [14]
What ease his flowing robes display!
And of his poise, what can I say?
A monarch to the last detail.

BOY CHARIOTEER. His name is Plutus, god of wealth,
 In gorgeous state he comes as such;   5570
 Our Emperor craves his presence much.

HERALD. But now disclose your own identity.

BOY CHARIOTEER. My names are Lavishness and Poetry.
 I am the poet who achieves his ends
 When he his inner substance most expends.
 I too have riches infinite, and here
 I look upon myself as Plutus's peer.
 I deck his dances, I am his banquets' pride,
 And what he lacks for, I provide.

HERALD. It suits you well to boast and claim,   5580
 But let us see these arts you name.

BOY CHARIOTEER. I snap my fingers: so! And right away
 Around the chariot glittering splendors play.
 A strand of pearls leaps flashing here.

(repeatedly snapping his fingers)

 Take golden clasps for throat and ear,
 A comb, a flawless coronet,
 And rings with precious jewels set;
 Sometimes I scatter flamelets and
 Then watch them kindle as they land.

HERALD. How this dear crowd does grab and rush!   5590
 The giver is half stifled in the crush.
 He snaps forth gems as in a dream
 And all grab for their flash and gleam.
 But now these are new tricks I see:
 What each one grabs so eagerly
 Proves actually a sorry prize:

---

14. Faust's Plutus costume includes a turban, hence is to be conceived as the opulent dress of a maharajah.

No sooner caught than off it flies.
The pearls come loose and slip their strand
And beetles wriggle in his hand;
The poor oaf flicks them off for dead   5600
And there they buzz around his head.
Others, instead of solid things,
Catch butterflies with wanton wings.
For all his promises, the bold
Rogue gives what only *gleams* like gold.
BOY CHARIOTEER. Masks, I observe, you recognize quite well,
But fathoming the essence in the shell
Is no task for a herald of the court;
That calls for insight of a sharper sort.
But I shun feuds with all and each;   5610
To you, my Sovereign, I address my speech.

(*turning to* PLUTUS)

Now was it not by your command
I got the storm wind for a four-in-hand?
Do I not drive just as you say?
Arriving where you point the way?
On daring wings did I not win
The palm for you time and again?
I have fought for you often and
I've won all battles up to now,
And if the laurel decks your brow,   5620
Did I not weave it with my wits and hand?
PLUTUS. If testimony is the thing you need,
I state: You are soul of my soul indeed;
You always act according to my will;
If I am rich, then you are richer still.
And to reward your services, I bear
Your green branch more esteem than all the crowns I wear.
Let this true statement be to all released:
Dear son of mine, in you I am well pleased.
BOY CHARIOTEER (*to the crowd*).
Supremest gifts my hand gives out,   5630
Behold how I strew them about.

On this one's head and that one's head
There glows a flamelet I have shed,
Sometimes from one to one it skips,
To some it cleaves, from some it slips,
Occasionally—though this is rare—
It blazes up with transient flare;
With most, before they realize,
It sinks down drearily and dies.

CHATTER OF WOMEN. Up in the chariot there, that man   5640
  Is certainly a charlatan.
  And there a clown behind him cringes,
  From thirst and hunger grown so lean
  The like of him was never seen;
  If pinched, he would not feel the pinches.

THE STARVELING.[15] Disgusting female trash, let me alone!
  I'll never please you, that's well known.
  When hearths were tended by a dame,
  Then Avaritia was my name.
  Ah, then the household throve throughout: 5650
  All things came in, no things got out;
  I gave my zeal for chest and bin—
  A thing you now claim is a sin!
  But since no women nowadays
  Care anything for thrifty ways,
  And since, like any dead beat, they
  Have more desires than they can pay,
  Their husbands have a lot to bear,
  With debts here, there, and everywhere.
  What needlework brings in they spend   5660
  Upon themselves or for a boy friend.
  They dine far better—drink more too—
  Amid their shiftless suitor crew.
  This boosts the charms of gold for me indeed:
  I'm masculine of gender now: I'm Greed.[16]

---

15. Mephistopheles in his second mask of the evening.
16. A bilingual grammatical play on the Latin feminine noun *Avaritia* and
the German masculine noun *der Geiz* ("Greed").

LEADER OF THE WOMEN.
  With dragons let this dragon sup,
  It's all a cheating lie, no more!
  He's here to stir the menfolk up,
  Who were stirred up enough before.
WOMEN (*all together*).
  The bag-of-bones! Give him a slap!   5670
  The gallows-pole would threaten us?
  His antics are preposterous!
  Those dragons are of wood and pap,[17]
  Let's close in on him, all of us!
HERALD. Now, by my staff! Be quiet there!—
  My help is hardly needed though.
  Just look at those grim monsters where
  They flap their double wings and go
  About the cleared space on rampage.
  They snap their scaly jaws with rage   5680
  And spew fire on all they come near.
  The mob has fled, the place is clear.

  (PLUTUS *descends from the chariot.*)

  He now descends, how like a king!
  The dragons at his beckoning
  Have lifted down his chest with speed
  And bring it forth with gold and greed;
  It stands there at his feet. For one,
  I marvel how it all was done.
PLUTUS (*to the* BOY CHARIOTEER).
  You're rid now of this all too heavy weight,
  And being free: Off to your sphere now, straight!   5690
  Here it is not! Wild, checkered, and unclear
  Are these deformed shapes crowded round us here.
  Only where clear in clarity you gaze,
  On self rely, to self belong, by ways
  Where nothing pleases but the good and fair,

---

17. A crew of maskers in dragon costume attends the chariot. Dragons guard
treasure-hoards.

In solitude—go found your kingdom there.

BOY CHARIOTEER. Then I shall be your worthy deputy,
I so love you as closest kin to me.
Where you dwell, plenty is; and where I bide
All sense the glorious benefit with pride.　5700
Men often waver in uncertainty:
Should they devote themselves to you? or me?
Your votaries can rest at ease, it's true,
But those who follow me have much to do.
In secret place I do not ply my trade,
Let me but breathe, and there I am betrayed.
Farewell! It is my happiness that you bestow,
But I am with you, if you but whisper low.

(*Exit as he came.*)

PLUTUS. The time has come to set the treasure free!
I smite the locks now with the Herald's rod.　5710
The chest is opened, and in bronze pots see
The seething and the foam of golden blood
Of ring, of necklace, and of jeweled crown;
The heat almost consumes and melts them down.

ALTERNATE CRIES FROM THE CROWD.
See how the foam swells to the rim
And fills the chest up to the brim!—
Golden vessels seethe and boil,
Rolls of coins there writhe and roil.—
New ducats spurt as from the mint,
O how my heart leaps to their glint!—　5720
How I behold my heart's desire!
They hit the floor like sparks of fire.—
They're free, just grab them as they pitch,
Just stoop and gather to be rich!—
Let's pounce like lightning on this pelf
And make off with the chest itself!

HERALD. What's this, you fools! Fall back there! Quick!
It's just a masqueraders' trick!
You do not ask for things tonight!
You fancy they give gold outright?　5730

Why, giving playing chips in such
A game as this would be too much!
You dolts! To take the glittering
And shining for the solid thing!
What's truth to you? In your confusion
You grab for dear life at illusion.—
Masked Plutus, hero of this ball,
Drive me this mob out of the hall.

PLUTUS. Your staff will neatly turn this trick,
Just lend it to me briefly. Quick!— 5740
Into the seething mass I dip
It for an instant.—Maskers, beware!
Behold the sparks that whiz and flare!
The staff has caught fire at the tip.
Now those who come too close will be
Singed straight away and mercilessly.—
I start around the circle now.

CRIES AND TUMULT. Look out or we'll be killed! Ouch! Ow!—
Escape now anyone who can!—
Fall back! Fall back there, hindmost man!— 5750
Right in my face the hot sparks lit.—
I felt the burning staff's weight hit.
We all are lost, we all are lost!—
Fall back, you masqueraders' host!—
Fall back, you senseless crowd, I say!—
If I had wings I'd fly away.—

PLUTUS. The crowd's pushed back, the circle's free,
With no one scorched that I can see.
The mob gives way
For sheer dismay.— 5760
But so they stay where I have bound them,
I draw an unseen circle round them.

HERALD. A splendid feat, to make them yield.
I thank you for the power you wield.

PLUTUS. Have still more patience, noble friend:
All sorts of tumult still impend.

GREED. It's quite a pleasure, quite a treat
To look upon this circle now.

For women always are up front, I vow,
When there's a thing to gape at or to eat.   5770
I'm not all rusted yet! In any place
A pretty face is still a pretty face;
And since it does not cost us anything,
Let's have a little courtship and a fling.
But since in crowded rooms not every word
Is comprehensible as it is heard,
I'll try some pantomiming to express
My meaning, and I hope for some success.
Hand, foot, and gesture will not be enough,
I'll have to go in for some funny stuff.   5780
I'll knead this gold as if it were wet clay,
This metal can be shaped up any way.
HERALD. That lanky fool, what's he about?
    Can there be wit in such a lout?
    He kneads the gold into a dough,
    Beneath his hands it softens so;
    Yet squeeze and punch it as he will,
    The lumpy mass is shapeless still.
    He turns to the women there, but they
    All scream and try to get away,   5790
    Protesting with marks of disgust.
    The rogue is evil bent and must,
    I fear, feel some especial glee
    In actions that shock decency.[18]
    Such things I cannot countenance.
    Give me my staff to drive him hence.
PLUTUS. He does not dream what threatens us outside;
    Allow him his tomfoolery,
    Soon he will have no objects to deride;
    Law is less mighty than necessity.   5800
TUMULT AND SINGING. From sylvan vale and mountain height
    This savage host comes on with might,[19]

---

18. Mephistopheles has kneaded the gold into a phallus, which he now
brandishes before the ladies.
19. Rather curiously, this chorus and others that follow speak of themselves

Resist them there is none who can.
They celebrate their great god Pan.
They know what no one else can guess [20]
And to this open space they press.

PLUTUS. I know you and I know your great god Pan!
Together you have formed a daring plan.
I know what is not known in every case
And, as my duty, yield this narrow space.   5810
And may good fortune with you go!
Most wondrous things may now befall.
Which way they move they do not know,
They have not looked ahead at all.

WILD SONG. Bedizened folk, you glittering brood!
They come on rough, they come on rude,
With lofty leaps, in wild career,
Tough and lusty they appear.

FAUNS. We fauns advance
In jolly dance,   5820
Oak crowns we wear
In our curling hair,
On each side a fine pointed ear
Pricks up from curls both here and here,
A snub nose and a platter face
Will lose us nothing of ladies' grace:
The prettiest will not withdraw
When once a faun holds out his paw.

SATYR. Here comes a satyr hopping in
With foot of goat and shriveled shin,   5830
Both must be sinewy and thin,
And chamois-like on mountain height
He gazes round with sportive delight.
Refreshed in freedom's air, he then
Makes sport of children, women, men,
Who deep in smoky valleys dim

---

in third person. For clarity, the translator has rendered some of the passages
in first person.
20. I.e., the "secret" that the Emperor is concealed beneath the mask of
great Pan.

Imagine they too live a life,
While the pure, high world exempt from strife
Belongs exclusively to him.

GNOMES. Here tripping comes a tiny crew   5840
    That dislikes going two by two.
    In mossy dress, with lamps alight
    They race and chase to left and right,
    Each with his own task that he plies,
    All helter-skelter like fireflies,
    Back and forth they teem and tumble,
    Rush in zigzags, toss, and fumble.
        Close kindred of the Good Folk we,
    Well known for our rock surgery:
    The towering mountain's depths we tap,   5850
    From their full veins we draw the sap;
    We heap and pile the metals high,
    "Good luck! Good luck!" is what we cry,[21]
    And from our depths we sound that call,
    For we are friends to good men all.
    And yet the gold that we unseal
    We give to men who pimp and steal,
    Nor does iron fail the haughty man
    With wholesale slaughter for his plan.
    Who scorns these three commandments bothers   5860
    Himself but little with the others.
    But all that is no fault of ours.
    Like us, have patience through all hours.

GIANTS. "The Wild Men" we are called, the same
    Of the Harz Mountains district fame.[22]
    Nature-naked now we come,
    Giants all from giantdom,
    A pine tree held in each right hand
    And round our loins a padded band,
    Crudest of aprons, leaf and twig;   5870

---

21. Their untranslatable call is *Glück auf!* (literally, "luck up!," i.e., from the mine shaft), the distinctive miners' greeting.
22. Such figures also appear on the Prussian coat of arms.

The Pope has no guards half as big.

CHORUS OF NYMPHS (*who surround* GREAT PAN).

He too draws near!—
Now recognize
In Great Pan's guise
The "world's All" here.[23]
You merriest, surround him now,
In whirling dance enclose him now.
Though grave, he is benevolent
And wants all to be merriment.
Beneath the sky's blue arch he keeps   5880
Unending watch that never sleeps,
Yet for him every brooklet flows
And light winds lull his soft repose;
And when he slumbers at midday,[24]
Stirs not one leaf on any spray;
Then wholesome plants shed balsams rare
Throughout the still and soundless air;
No nymph may then make merry noise,
She falls asleep in standing poise.
But when quite unexpectedly   5890
His voice peals forth with potency
Like thunderclap on bursting sea,
Then no one knows which way to flee,
Brave armies in the field then scatter
And in the tumult heroes shatter.[25]
So: Honor to whom honor is due,
Hail to him who brought us to you!

DEPUTATION OF GNOMES (*to* GREAT PAN).

If the shining precious goods [26]

---

23. The word *pan* in Greek is the neuter form of the adjective "all"; Goethe here translates it as *Das All der Welt* (the world's All).

24. The Greeks described the ominous silence of midday heat with the phrase: "Great Pan sleeps." The lines immediately following here paraphrase that concept.

25. The cry of Pan produces "pan-ic" (an ancient etymology), the sudden, unreasoning terror that spreads swiftly from person to person.

26. The Gnomes use miners' jargon, e.g., "the goods" is "gold," but other such terms have not been rendered here.

Stretch through clefts in veined outlays,
None but shrewd divining rods   5900
Trace their labyrinthine ways.
   Houses of the troglodyte
We in caves construct and measure,
And beneath the day's pure light
You bestow largesse of treasure.
   Now a fountainhead we find
Welling riches wondrously [27]
Close at hand and of a kind
We had never hoped to see.
   This you only can perfect;   5910
Into your keeping, Sire, take it: [28]
Any treasure you protect
Gives the whole world benefit.

PLUTUS (*to the* HERALD).

Our self-possession must now be displayed
And, come what may, we must be undismayed;
You always have shown lofty strength of soul.
A ghastly incident will soon betide,
One which will be by world and afterworld denied:
See that it's written in your protocol.

HERALD (*seizing the staff which* PLUTUS *is holding in his hand*).

Great Pan the dwarves now gently guide   5920
Up to the seething fire-chest's side.
From pits profound it heaves and swells,
Then sinks back down into deep wells,
Its open mouth is dark with spells.
Once more the surge of fiery tide!
Great Pan looks on well satisfied,
Delighted with the wondrous swirls
While left and right flies spray of pearls.
Can he trust such an agency?
He stoops to peer more eagerly.—   5930

---

27. Namely, the chest unloaded by the dragons.
28. The Gnomes act apparently at Faust-Plutus' instructions in luring the
Emperor up to the magic chest.

Now as he stoops, his beard falls in!—
Who is that man with shaven chin?
A hand conceals it from our view.—
Monstrous horrors now ensue:
His beard caught fire and backward flew,
Breast, head, and wreath are now ablaze,
His joys are turned to wild dismays.—
Up rush the crowd to quench and quell,
But all are caught by flames as well,
And though they clap and thwack and pound,   5940
New flames are fanned up all around;
A whole troop of the masking crowd
Is swathed within a fiery shroud.[29]

What cries are these now bruited here
From mouth to mouth, from ear to ear!
O night with endless sorrow fraught,
What sheer disaster you have brought!
The coming day will bring such word
As will by none be gladly heard;
On every side I hear quite plain: 5950
"The *Emperor* is in grievous pain."
O if some different news were true!
The Emperor burns with all his crew!
A curse on them who by their tricks
Got him to mask in pitch-smeared sticks
And romp about with roars of glee
For general catastrophe.
O Youth, O Youth, will you then never
Keep joy in proper bounds and season?
O Princes, Princes, will you never   5960
Subdue your might to sense and reason?
The mimic forest has caught fire.
Sharp tongues of flame lick high and higher
Up to the latticed rooves, and we
Face general calamity!
Grief's cup is brimmed, it overflows,

---

29. See Introduction, p. LIX.

And who can save us, no one knows.
The dawn will see imperial might
A heap of ashes in one night.
PLUTUS. Enough of terror is diffused,   5970
Now let help be introduced!—
Sacred staff, now smite this floor
So that it quakes with sound and roar!
Be filled, you wide and spacious air,
With cooling fragrance everywhere!
Approach and cover us, dense crowds
Of moisture-teeming mists and clouds,
Engulf this flaming turmoil here!
Curl, you cloudlets, curl and swirl,
Slip in, wavelike, drip and drizzle,   5980
Quench and quell and make fire fizzle,
You who moisten and allay,
Change to summer lightnings' play
These *imaginary* flames' display!—
If spirits seek to do us harm,
Magic must effect its charm.

Pleasure Garden

Morning sunlight. The EMPEROR *and courtiers.* FAUST *and* MEPHISTOPHELES, *dressed
becomingly but not ostentatiously in the pre-
vailing fashion; both kneel.*

FAUST. Then you forgive the fire-and-flame trick, Sire?
EMPEROR (*signifying to him to rise*).
More jokes like that are just what I desire.—
Why, there I was inside a burning ball,
Almost, it seemed, like Pluto in his hall.   5990
A floor of coals and darkness was aglow
With tiny flames, and from the pits below
Wild flames in untold thousands roared assault

And arched together toward a single vault;
Up to that round of dome they tongued and rose,
The dome would form and then again disclose.
Through halls of fiery twisted pillars I
Saw endless files of people moving by,
All pushing forward in a mighty crowd,
And as their custom was, all bowed;   6000
Some were from my own court, some were outlanders.
I felt much like a prince of salamanders.
ᴇᴘʜɪsᴛᴏᴘᴇʟᴇs. And so you are, Sire! All the elements
Hold majesty in total reverence.
Obedient fire you have put to the test.
Now plunge in ocean where it raves its wildest,
And hardly will you tread the deeps rich-pearled
Than you will be cased in a globe wave-swirled
And you will see the wavelets sink and swell,
Pale green with purple edge, to round the shell   6010
With you at midpoint. And, walk where you may,
The palaces will also walk that way.
The very walls are full of life, with dartings
And teemings, sudden meetings, sudden partings;
Up to the new and mellow light sea monsters ride,
They ram the globe, but none can get inside.
There colored dragons sport with golden claws,
Sharks yawn and gape and you laugh in their jaws.
Great as your courtiers' joy in you now is,
You never yet have seen a crowd like this.   6020
Nor will you long be parted from the fairest:
The curious Nereids will swarm to that rarest
Of dwellings in the deep to peer and pry,
The youngest eager as the fish, but shy,
The older ones more shrewd. Thetis will come,
And to a second Peleus give her kingdom.—
Then with your seat upon Olympus there . . .
ɪᴘᴇʀᴏʀ. O, I will leave to you the realms of air:
It's all too soon that one mounts to that throne.
ᴇᴘʜɪsᴛᴏᴘʜᴇʟᴇs. And, Sire, the earth already is your own.   6030
ɪᴘᴇʀᴏʀ. What fate can be so kind that it invites

You here straight out of the Arabian Nights?
If you can match Scheherazade's art,
I guarantee my favor from the start.
Stand ready when the world of commonplace
Most bores me—as is frequently the case.

(*Enter the* MARSHAL *in haste.*)

MARSHAL. Your Highness, never have I hoped to give
    You fairer tidings as long as I live
    Than these that fill me with delight
    As I now stand here in your sight: 6040
    Bill after bill of ours is paid,
    The usurers' talons have been stayed,
    I am released from pains of hell,
    In heaven I could not feel so well.
FIELD MARSHAL (*entering hurriedly*).
    The troops are paid up their full due
    And the whole army sworn anew;
    The mercenaries feel fresh blood,
    And bars and wenches have it good.
EMPEROR. Why, how your shoulders have been lightened
    And how your haggard face is brightened!   6050
    How swift and brisk your entrance is!
TREASURER (*who has come in*).
    Ask these men here who have accomplished this.
FAUST. It suits the Chancellor to state the case.
CHANCELLOR (*approaching slowly*).
    Sufficient happiness in my old days.—
    Now see and hear this fateful document
    Which has transformed our woe into content.

(*He reads.*)

"To whom it may concern we do announce:
The present note is worth a thousand crowns.
The holder is assured by guarantee
Of untold buried wealth in Imperial land.   6060
That treasure, once it is dug up, shall be
Redeemable for this sum on demand."

EMPEROR. Here is some monstrous treason, I feel sure!
   Who falsified the Emperor's signature?
   Is crime not punished in such instances?
TREASURER. Recall, Sire! You set your own name to this,
   And just last night. You stood as Great Pan when
   We heard the Chancellor speak these words to you:
   "Accord yourself a festive boon and do
   Your people good by one stroke of the pen." [1]   6070
   You wrote it fair, then conjurers took hold
   And multiplied the copies thousandfold.
   Then, so that all might share the profit, we
   Set seals on the whole lot immediately.
   Tens, thirties, fifties, hundreds are turned out.
   You cannot dream what joy there is about!
   Just see your city, moldered half to death,
   Just see it live, teem, and draw joyous breath!
   Long as your name has made the world rejoice,
   Never has it been viewed with looks so choice.   6080
   The alphabet has more signs than it had:
   In this sign every man will be made glad. [2]
EMPEROR. My people take it for real gold, you say?
   In camp and court it passes as full pay?
   I must consent, much as it baffles me.
MARSHAL. Held down these flying things will never be.
   They scattered on their ways with lightning stride.
   The changers' booths have propped their doorways wide
   And every note is honored totally
   In gold and silver, and, in fact, tax free.   6090
   To butcher, baker, vintner then they go,
   With food the only thought most people know,
   Though others strut around in their new clothes.

---

1. The Emperor's signing of the master copy of the new bank notes is nowhere hinted in either the text or stage directions of the foregoing masquerade scene. The incident must be conceived as byplay amid the confusion of maskers, most logically at the point where the Deputation of Gnomes addressed Great Pan, ll. 5898–5913, perhaps at ll. 5904–5.

2. A sly parody of Constantine's vision of the Cross: "In this sign thou shalt conquer" (*In hoc signo vinces*).

The mercer cuts off cloth, the tailor sews.
In taverns it's "The Emperor!" they toast
While clattering with their plates at stew and roast.
MEPHISTOPHELES. Lone strollers on the terrace promenade
May spy a lady splendidly arrayed,
One eye hid by her peacock fan; she sees
And smirks at us on seeing notes like these;   6100
Never were wit or eloquence so swift
Negotiating love's most precious gift.
No one will bother with a purse when these
Light papers fit the bosom with all ease—
Where they go well with love notes. Priests can carry
Them piously inside a breviary,
And soldiers will unload their belts and free
Their limbs for swifter action. Your Majesty
Will doubtless pardon me if I now seem
To hold the lofty work in small esteem.[3]   6110
FAUST. The superfluity of riches found
Within your borders, frozen underground,
Lies still unused. Thought in its widest measure
Sets paltry bounds and limits on such treasure,
Imagination in its furthest flight
Struggles in vain to estimate it right.
Yet worthy minds that see beyond the veil
Have boundless faith in things where limits fail.
MEPHISTOPHELES. Such paper used instead of pearls and gold
Is so convenient: we know what we hold!   6120
Now no more deals and barterings, in fine:
One can get drunk at will on love or wine.
If coin is needed, changers handle it,
And failing them, one digs around a bit.
Goblet and chain are auctioned off for bids,
And then the liquidated paper rids
Us of the doubter and his mockery.
Naught else is wanted, thus we'd have things be!

---

3. Paper money, commonplace today, first came into common use in the 18th century. Goethe had witnessed its ruinous inflation during French Revolutionary and Napoleonic times and here makes it an invention of the Devil.

Thus there will be throughout the Imperial land
Enough of paper, gold, and gems on hand. 6130
EMPEROR. To you our state owes this munificence;
The service should find equal recompense.
The realm's subsoil be henceforth in your care
As best custodians of the treasure there.
You know the vast, well-hidden hoard,
All exhumation shall be at your word.
Conjoin now, you two masters of our treasure,
Fulfill the honors of your post with pleasure
Where upper world and nether world converge,
Blessed in the unity wherein they merge. 6140
TREASURER. No slightest rift between us shall there be.
A conjuror for colleague just suits me.

(*Exit with* FAUST.)

EMPEROR. I give largesse to every man of you;
Let each one state what use he'd put it to.
PAGE (*receiving*). I'll live for merry, bright, and cheerful things.
A SECOND (*likewise*). I'll buy my sweetheart necklaces and rings.
CHAMBERLAIN (*accepting*).
I'll drink a brand of wine that's twice as heady.
A SECOND (*likewise*). The dice inside my pocket itch already.
COLOR-BEARER (*advisedly*). I'll get my land and castle out of debt.
A SECOND (*likewise*).
It's wealth to be put with more treasures yet. 6150
EMPEROR. I hoped for fresh deeds full of joy and zest,
But knowing you, one could have quickly guessed.
I see that in the midst of wealth galore
You still remain exactly as before.
FOOL (*coming up*). You're handing out largesse: give me some too.
EMPEROR. Back now in life, you'd only drink it through.
FOOL. These magic leaves, I don't know how to use them.
EMPEROR. That I can see from watching you abuse them.
FOOL. There drop some more; I'm not sure what to do.
EMPEROR. Just pick them up, there is your share for you. 6160

(*Exit.*)

FOOL. Five thousand crowns! Can that sum be correct?
MEPHISTOPHELES. Two-legged gut, so you can resurrect?
FOOL. I've had it happen, but not quite like this.
MEPHISTOPHELES. You're all asweat from the excess of bliss.
FOOL. Look here, is this thing worth real money yet?
MEPHISTOPHELES. With that, your gut's and gullet's wants are met.
FOOL. And can I buy a house and fields and herds?
MEPHISTOPHELES. No doubt of it! You need but speak the words.
FOOL. A castle, with hunting grounds and fishpond?
MEPHISTOPHELES.   Right!
    You as "Your Worship" would be quite a sight!   6170
FOOL. I'll snuggle down on my estate before
    Night falls.

    (*Exit.*)

MEPHISTOPHELES (*solus*).
    Who doubts our Fool's wits any more?

Dark Gallery

FAUST   MEPHISTOPHELES

MEPHISTOPHELES. Why drag me down these gloomy corridors?
    Is there not fun enough inside
    With motley throngs of servitors
    Where tricks and farces can be tried?
FAUST. Don't tell me that! You walked these ways
    Until your feet were tired in former days;
    Now all your rush and scurrying
    Is just to dodge my questioning.   6180
    But I have matters that distress me,
    The Marshal and the Chamberlain both press me:
    The Emperor wishes—hence it must take place—
    To look on Helen and Paris face to face;
    Those paragons of man and womankind
    He wants to see before him, well defined.

So quick to work! I must not break my promises.

MEPHISTOPHELES. It was foolhardy, mad, to promise this.

FAUST. You did not stop to think, my friend,
Of what your arts would lead us to;   6190
We made him rich, now in the end
We must give him amusement too.

MEPHISTOPHELES. You fancy these things take no time,
But steeper stairs confront us here;
You move into an alien sphere
And wind up stained with further crime;
You think that Helen from the deathly hosts
Is conjured like these paper-money ghosts.—
With witches' brats, with spectral floosies, and
With goiter-throated dwarves I'm right on hand,   6200
But devils' darlings, though not bad at all,
Won't pass for heroines upon my call.

FAUST. Still harping on that same old chord!
With you all things end in uncertainties.
You are the Father of All Hindrances,
For each device you want a fresh reward.
Some grumbling first, I know, then all is fine;
You'll fetch her in less time than it takes to tell.

MEPHISTOPHELES. The heathen folk are no concern of mine,
They dwell apart in their own hell.   6210
There *is* a way, though.

FAUST.   Speak! And no delay!

MEPHISTOPHELES. I grudge high secrets to the light of day.—
Goddesses throne in solitude sublime;
Around them is no space, and still less, time—
With them it's awkward, anything I say.
Those are the *Mothers!*

FAUST.   Mothers?!

MEPHISTOPHELES.   Does that scare
You?

FAUST. Mothers! Mothers!—That sounds strange and rare.

MEPHISTOPHELES. It is, too! Goddesses unknown to men,
Reluctantly acknowledged in *our* ken.
To their home deep is the descent and fall,   6220

And you're to blame that we need them at all.
FAUST. Where goes the road?
MEPHISTOPHELES.   No road! To the untrodden
  And never-to-be-trod! To the unmoved
  And never-to-be-moved or wrought by prayer.
  Will you face that? No locks or bolts are there,
  Around you solitudes will be deployed.
  Can you conceive of total void?
FAUST. Best skip such speeches! I can tell
  From time long past there is a smell
  Of witch's kitchen in the air.   6230
  Did I not have the world forced onto me?
  Did I not learn—and teach—vacuity?
  When I talked reason as I knew it,
  The paradoxes lent a double echo to it;
  I even had to flee from sheer excess
  Of adverse fortune to the wilderness;
  And not to live abandoned and alone,
  I gave the Devil the only life I own.
MEPHISTOPHELES. Suppose you swam the ocean's widest reach
  And looked upon infinity: 6240
  You still would see waves drive waves to the beach,
  Though your own fate struck you appallingly.
  But still you would see something. There would be
  Dolphins to cleave the green and silent sea,
  There would be cloud and sun and moon and star;
  But in the everlasting void afar:
  Nothing! Your foot falls with no sound,
  And where you stop there is no solid ground.
FAUST. You talk like the chief mystagogue of all
  Hoodwinking neophytes in mystic hall—   6250
  Only reversed. You send me to the void
  For increase of my skill and might; you treat
  Me like the well-known cat that you employed
  To snatch your chestnuts from the embers' heat.
  All right! We'll try it out! In what you call
  Sheer nothingness I hope to find the All.
MEPHISTOPHELES. I'll praise you now before you start your trip:

You know the Devil to his fingertip.
Here, take this key.
FAUST.   That little thing!
MEPHISTOPHELES. Grasp hold! It's not the trifle that it seems.   6260
FAUST. It grows beneath my hand! It glows! It gleams!
MEPHISTOPHELES. You see what great advantage it can bring?
    The key will scent the right place and skip others;
    Follow it down, it takes you to the Mothers.
FAUST (*shuddering*). The Mothers! Like a blow it strikes my ear!
    What is this word I cannot bear to hear?
MEPHISTOPHELES. So narrowminded? Scared by a new word?
    You hear none but the ones already heard?
    Do not fear any that the future brings,
    Long wonted as you are to strangest things.   6270
FAUST. In cool indifference I see no Good Law,[1]
    The best of man lies in his sense of awe.
    No matter how life wears his feelings dull,
    Once struck, he sees vast things as wonderful.
MEPHISTOPHELES. Sink, then! I could as well say: Rise!
    It makes no difference. From forms developed flee
    Into the realms which are from forms set free!
    Rejoice in things long vanished from our eyes,
    Whose files, like cloud processions, wend their way;
    Brandish the key and hold them all at bay.   6280
FAUST (*seized by enthusiasm*).
    Now as I clasp it tight, new strength be mine!
    My heart expands; now for the great design.
MEPHISTOPHELES.
    A glowing tripod last of all will show [2]
    That you have reached the deepest depths below,
    And by its gleam the Mothers you will see,
    Some seated there, or as the case may be,
    They walk or stand. Formation, transformation,

---

1. The rendering of *im Erstarren* as "In cool indifference" follows Witkowski's interpretation to the effect that the phrase reflects Horace's *nil admirari*, "to be astonished at nothing," *Epistles* I. 6.
2. The burning tripod, a common feature in ancient sanctuaries (such as Delphi), suggests oracular and spirit-summoning powers.

Eternal Mind's eternal recreation,
While round them float the forms of all the creatures.
They see the shadows only, not your features,   6290
Take heart then, though the peril is most grave,
And make your way straight to that tripod's light
And touch it with the key.

(FAUST *strikes a decisively imperious attitude with the key.*
MEPHISTOPHELES *observes him.*)

                        Yes, that is right!
The thing will walk behind you like a slave.
Then Fortune will lift you to upper air
And you'll be back before they are aware.
And once you have it here, you have the might
To call up hero and heroine from night,
The first to venture on such enterprise;
The deed is done and you have won the odds;   6300
Then by the power that in magic lies
The incense cloud will be transformed to gods.
FAUST. But right now, what?
MEPHISTOPHELES.   Stamp your foot to descend,
And once more stamp your foot to reascend.

(FAUST *stamps his foot and sinks downward.*)

That key now, will it keep him on the track?
I'm curious too to see if he gets back.

Brightly Lighted Rooms

EMPEROR *and* PRINCES; *the court in animation.*

CHAMBERLAIN (*to* MEPHISTOPHELES).
    You still owe us that spirit scene, you know;
    Our master is impatient for his show.
MARSHAL. His Highness just inquired of that from me.
    Delay is an affront to majesty!   6310

MEPHISTOPHELES. My comrade's on that very errand gone;
   He knows exactly how it's done
   And he is working on it privately.
   It takes a very special exercise;
   For raising beauty's treasure needs, you see,
   Supremest skill and magic of the wise.
MARSHAL. What skills are needed is all one,
   The Emperor's wish is that the thing be done.
A BLOND LADY (to MEPHISTOPHELES).
   A word, Sir! You see how my face is clear,
   But that's not so when nasty summer's here.   6320
   To my annoyance my white skin turns spotted
   Then, and a hundred brownish freckles dot it.
   A cure!
MEPHISTOPHELES. Such loveliness as yours, I say,
   Must not spot up like panther cubs in May.
   Take frog spawn and the tongue of toad together,
   Brew carefully in fullest moonlit weather,
   And as the moon wanes rub the ointment on;
   When springtime comes the spots will all be gone.
A BRUNETTE. The mob crowds round you with their fawning talk.
   I beg a cure. A frozen foot of mine   6330
   Impedes me when I dance or when I walk,
   My curtsey bow itself is out of line.
MEPHISTOPHELES. Let me step on it with this foot of mine.
BRUNETTE. But, only lovers do that sort of thing.
MEPHISTOPHELES. My footfall, child, has vastly more of meaning.
   Like unto like, no matter where you're sick;
   Foot heals a foot, and so on through the pack.
   Come here! Watch out! You need not give it back.
BRUNETTE (screaming).
   Ow! Ow! That burns! You deal a mighty kick,
   Like a horse's hoof.
MEPHISTOPHELES.   That stamp has done the trick.   6340
   Now you can dance as much as you are able
   And footsie with your lover while at table.
A LADY (pressing forward).
   Let me get through! Too monstrous is the smart

And sting of suffering deep within my heart;
In my glance *he* sought bliss till yesterday,
He talks with *her* now and from me turns away.

MEPHISTOPHELES. The case is touchy, but hear what I speak.
  You must somehow steal close up to this man;
  Here, take this piece of coal and make a streak
  On shoulder, coat, or sleeve as best you can;   6350
  His heart will feel sweet pangs of conscience' grips,
  But let no wine or water touch your lips;
  He'll sigh before your door this very day.

LADY. It isn't poison?

MEPHISTOPHELES (*indignant*). Please! Respect in proper place!
  For such a coal you'd have to travel far;
  The pyre from which it got its char
  Was raked more eagerly in olden days.[3]

A PAGE. I am in love, they think I'm underage.

MEPHISTOPHELES (*aside*).
  I don't know where to turn, and now this page.   6360

(*to the* PAGE)

On happiness with young ones set less store.
Those getting on in years appreciate you more.

(*Others crowd up.*)

More new ones yet! This rabble is uncouth!
I'll wind up yet by recourse to the truth—
The worst expedient! Grave grows my plight.
O Mothers, Mothers! Just lend Faustus flight!

(*looking about*)

The lights are burning dimly in the hall,
The court's in sudden movement, one and all.
I see processions winding decorously
Down long arcade and distant gallery.   6370
To the old Hall of Knights they now advance,

---

3. Relics of burned witches, sorcerers, and heretics were believed to contain
an especially powerful magic.

Which barely holds them in its vast expanse.
Along broad sidewalls tapestries are slung,
With suits of armor in the niches hung.
No magic words, I think, need here be known:
Ghosts will discover this place on their own.[4]

Hall of Knights

Dim light. EMPEROR *and court have entered.*

HERALD. The hidden might of spirits renders vain
　　My ancient office to announce the play;
　　It would be effort wasted to explain
　　This baffling business in a rational way.　　　　　　6380
　　Benches and chairs are in their proper places;
　　The Emperor has been seated so he faces
　　The pictured curtains where he may behold
　　In comfort battles from great times of old.[5]
　　In semicircle sit court and monarch here,
　　With benches jammed together at the rear,
　　And sweethearts, at this gloomy spirit-tide,
　　Have found sweet places at their sweethearts' side.
　　And now that all are in their seats, in sum,
　　We are all ready: let the spirits come!　　　　　　6390

(*Trumpets.*)

ASTROLOGER. The drama, at our Emperor's command,
　　Shall now begin its course. Ye walls, expand!
　　No further hindrance, magic makes its claim,
　　The curtains part as though rolled back by flame,

---

4. A deliberately spooky atmosphere has been established for the seance-like
raising of the ghosts of Paris and Helen of Troy, the "ghosts of classicism."
5. As in amateur court theatricals, the stage is improvised. Tapestries, which
part to left and right, form the "curtain." The battle scenes depicted on them
may be of the Hohenstaufen period.

The masonry divides, swings round on end.[6]
A deep stage seems to take shape and appear,
Casting a mystic radiance on us here,
And I to the proscenium ascend.

MEPHISTOPHELES (*emerging from the prompter's box*).
  I hope to please you from these nether reaches.
  The Devil's rhetoric consists of prompted speeches.   6400

(*to the* ASTROLOGER)

You know the tempo of the starry rounds
And masterfully will grasp my whispered sounds.

ASTROLOGER. By dint of magic there now meets our sight
  A rather massive ancient temple's height.[7]
  Like Atlas in his sky-supporting pose,
  Here rather numerous columns stand in rows;
  They doubtless can support the weight of stone—
  An entire house could rest on two alone.

ARCHITECT. You call that Greek! It gets no praise of mine,
  I'd sooner call it dumpy, elephantine.   6410
  Crude they call noble, clumsy they term great.
  I like slim columns, soaring and ornate;
  The pointed zenith lifts the soul on high;
  Such edifices truly edify.

ASTROLOGER. Receive with reverence star-granted hours,
  By magic words enthralled be reason's powers;
  But, on the other hand, let fantasy
  Rove wanton and magnificently free.
  The sight that you desired with craving bold,
  Impossible hence credible, behold!   6420

(FAUST *ascends from below at the other side of the proscenium.*)

In priestly vesture, crowned, see now a man
Of wonders who completes what he began.

---

6. The difficult line seems to mean that the castle wall itself opens like a magic gate to reveal the recessed stage.
7. This "Greek play" of Paris and Helen has the façade of a Doric temple as its setting, in recollection of ancient Athenian usage.

A tripod rises with him from the hole,
Already I guess incense from its bowl.
He starts to bless his lofty task: now all
Things of good fortune must henceforth befall.

FAUST (*grandiosely*).

In your name, Mothers, who maintain your throne
In emptiness, eternally alone,
Yet social too! The moving forms of life
Swarm round your heads, yet are devoid of life;   6430
Whatever once achieved the light diurnal
Is there astir and seeks to be eternal;
These you despatch beneath your boundless sway
To vaults of night or to the tent of day.
Life's lovely course the latter will invest,
The former are the bold magician's quest.
In rich profusion he brings to the light
The wondrous things craved by the common sight.

ASTROLOGER. The glowing key has barely touched the bowl
When bands of mist across the stage unroll,   6440
First softly drifting in, then cloudlike gliding,
Then swelling, shrinking, twining, twofold dividing.
Now note a spirit masterpiece as they
Make music in their movement and their play.
Ethereal tones pour forth mysteriously
And every motion turns to melody.
Each column-shaft, each triglyph-picture rings,
I do believe the very temple sings.
The mist subsides, and in its shimmering place
A comely youth steps forth with rhythmic pace.   6450
My office ends, I need not speak his name:
Who would not know fair Paris of high fame!

(PARIS *steps forth.*)

A LADY. O what a radiance of youthful grace!
A SECOND. How like a fresh and luscious peach, his face!
A THIRD. That finely chiseled, sweetly swelling lip!
A FOURTH. A cup, no doubt, from which you'd like to sip?
A FIFTH. He *is* good-looking, if not too refined.

A SIXTH. He could be somewhat nimbler, don't you find?
A KNIGHT. A shepherd lad is all that I can see,
  No breeding and no princely quality.   6460
ANOTHER. Oh well, half naked this lad is a charmer,
  But let's see how he looks when cased in armor!
A LADY. He seats himself with a soft dignity.
KNIGHT. His lap is just where you'd rest comfortably?
ANOTHER LADY. He bends his arm so well behind his head.
CHAMBERLAIN. The oafish manners of him! That's ill-bred!
LADY. You gentlemen find fault with everything.
CHAMBERLAIN. In the Emperor's presence, lolling and lounging!
LADY. He's only acting! He thinks he's alone.
CHAMBERLAIN. The drama should be courtly near the throne.   6470
LADY. Sleep gently overtakes the handsome youth.
CHAMBERLAIN. Soon he'll be snoring—art mimes nature's truth!
A YOUNG LADY (*enraptured*).
  What odors mingled with the incense soar
  To make my heart thrill to its very core?
AN OLDER LADY.
  A breath does strike my soul with fearsome power;
  It comes from him!
AN OLDEST LADY.   It is the vernal flower
  Ambrosially distilled in this youth here
  And wafted all about the atmosphere.

  (HELEN *steps forth*.)

MEPHISTOPHELES. So this is Helen! *My* peace she won't steal.
  She's pretty, but to me without appeal.   6480
ASTROLOGER. This time there isn't much for me to do,
  As a man of honor, I'll admit that's true.
  She comes, and were I touched with tongues of fire!—
  For beauty did from ancient times inspire;
  Who sees her is enraptured, and much blessed
  Was any man by whom she was possessed.[8]
FAUST. Do I have eyesight still? Have beauty's springs

---

8. A paraphrase of Plato, *Phaedrus* 30, 249d4 ff., which is also the source
for Faust's succeeding lines.

Deep in my mind been copiously revealed?
What glorious gain my fearful journey brings!
The world was null to me before, and sealed!   6490
But since my priesthood what has it become?
First-founded, lasting, and most pleasuresome!
May all my life-strength, all my breathing fail
If I recant or fall away from you!—
The lovely form that once enthralled my sight
And in the magic mirror waked delight,
Compared with beauty such as this, turns pale!—
I owe the impulse of all strength to you,
And passion's very fountainhead,
All love, all adoration—madness too.   6500

MEPHISTOPHELES (*from the prompter's box*).
Control yourself and stay in character!

AN ELDERLY LADY.
Tall and well shaped; her head's too little, though.

A YOUNGER ONE. Just see her foot! Could it be clumsier!

DIPLOMAT. I have seen princesses like this, you know.
To me she's beautiful from head to toe.

COURTIER. She comes up to the sleeper slyly, softly.

LADY. How brazen next to purity so lofty!

POET. He takes the radiance of her clarity.

LADY. Endymion and Luna! To a T! [9]

POET. Quite right! The goddess, as it were, descends   6510
To drink his breath as over him she bends.
A kiss!—Your cup is full, O enviable lad!

DUENNA. In front of all these people! This is mad!

FAUST. A fearsome favor to the boy!—

MEPHISTOPHELES.   Be still,
Be still, and let the ghost do as it will.

COURTIER. She steals away, he wakens from her touch.

LADY. She looks around again! I thought as much!

COURTIER. He marvels at this miracle of chance.

LADY. She feels no marvel in what meets her glance.

COURTIER. She now turns back to him with dignity.   6520

---

9. See "Diana and Endymion," illustrations.

LADY. She starts on his apprenticeship, I see.
All men are stupid at such times; no doubt
He thinks he is the first she has picked out.
KNIGHT. Just grant me she's majestic and refined!—
LADY. A hussy! Of the cheap and vulgar kind!
PAGE. If I had his place now, I wouldn't mind.
COURTIER. Who *would* mind being caught in such a net?
LADY. The jewel passed through many hands, I'll bet,
And its gold setting has worn thin since then.
ANOTHER LADY. She has been worthless since the age of ten.   6530
KNIGHT. When possible we all seize on the best;
With these fair leftovers I would feel blest.
SCHOLAR. I see her plainly, but I'll make so bold
As doubt that this is Helen we behold.
A presence misleads to exaggerations,
I stick to written texts with annotations,
And there I read: She gave exceeding joy
To all the ancient greybeard men of Troy.[10]
And how that tallies here I well can see:
I am no longer young, and she charms me.   6540
ASTROLOGER. A boy no longer! A heroic man
Embraces her so that she scarcely can
Resist. With strengthened arms he lifts her high.
Will he make off with her?
FAUST.   You fool! Just try!
Stop! You won't listen to me? Stop, I say!
MEPHISTOPHELES. You're spoiling your own silly specter-play!
ASTROLOGER. One word yet! From what happened here, I'd say
"The Rape of Helen" was the title of this play.
FAUST. Rape! Do I count for nothing any more?
In my hand do I not still hold this key?   6550
It guided me through horrors of the sea
Of solitude back to this solid shore.
I take firm footing here! Here is the real,
Here spirit may to spirit make appeal
And win the double realm: real and ideal.

---

10. *Iliad* III. 156 ff.

Far as she is, how can she be more near!
Once rescued, she is twice mine. Have no fear!
O Mothers! Mothers! You must grant my quest!
Who knew her once, without her cannot rest.

ASTROLOGER. What are you doing, Faustus! Faustus!—See!   6560
He seizes her by force, her form grows dim;
He turns the key against the youth and touches him!—
Woe! All is lost now instantaneously!

(*Explosion.* FAUST *lies unconscious on the floor. The spirits
vanish in mist.*)

MEPHISTOPHELES (*loading* FAUST *over his shoulder*).
Well, there you are! To lend a fool an arm
Will wind the very Devil up in harm.

(*Darkness. Tumult.*)

Act Two

Gothic Room

---

*High-vaulted, narrow; formerly Faust's, and
unchanged.* MEPHISTOPHELES *steps out from
behind a curtain. As he raises it and looks behind him,* FAUST *can be seen stretched out
on an old-fashioned bed.*

MEPHISTOPHELES. Lie here, unlucky fellow, lured
To love's entangled chains and ties!
Whom Helen's wiles once paralyze
Won't find his wits so quickly cured.

(*looking about*)

Look up or down or to the side,   6570
Nothing is changed or in disorder here.

The colored panes, I think, are still less clear,
And cobwebs everywhere have multiplied.
The ink is dried, the paper has turned yellow,
But everything is still in place;
Here is the very pen with which this fellow
Faust signed himself into the Devil's grace;
Here on one nib there is a tiny stain
Of blood which I teased from his vein.
A document unique as this one is   6580
Would be a great collector's bliss.
The old hook with the old fur cloak upon it
Recalls the bees I put in that boy's bonnet
When I was counseling him; the things I taught
May be—who knows?—the young man's food for thought.
I feel a hankering to be allied,
Old shaggy pelt, with you tonight
And strut once more with a professor's pride,
The way they think they are completely right.
Scholars still can play that part,   6590
The Devil long since lost the art.

(*He shakes out the cloak which he has taken down; crickets,
moths, and* INSECT-IMPS *fly out of it.*) [1]

CHORUS OF INSECTS. Welcome, O welcome,
    Our patron of yore!
    We buzz and we hum
    To see you once more.
    In silence and singly
    You sowed us, it's true;
    Father, by thousands
    We dance now to you.
    The rogue in the bosom   6600
    Lies deeply concealed,
    The lice in a mantle

---

1. The odd Italianism *Farfarellen,* translated here as "insect-imps," is usually
said to be Goethe's error, confusing Farfarello, a devil's name in Dante's *In-
ferno* (XXI, 123), with some diminutive form of Italian *farfalla,* "butterfly";
the translator believes it to be a deliberate pun.

Are sooner revealed.

MEPHISTOPHELES. Surprising what joy my young progeny bestows!
A man will reap in time if he just sows.
I give the good old rag another fling
And here and there another one takes wing.—
Be off into a hundred thousand nooks,
My darlings, and be quick to hide:
In those old boxes on that side,   6610
Here in these yellowed parchment books,
In dusty shards of ancient bowls,
And in the eye-pits of these skulls.
Amid such moldering junk must be
Whims for a whole eternity.[2]

(*He slips into the fur cloak.*)

Come, deck my shoulders as of yore,
I'm master of this house once more.
But how can I assume that name
With no one here to recognize my claim?

(*He pulls the bell, which sounds with a shrill, piercing tone
that makes the corridors tremble and the doors fly open.*)

FAMULUS [3] (*staggering down the long dark hall*).
What a din and what a quaking!   6620
Stairways sway and walls are shaking,
Past the window's clattering sash
I see summer lightnings flash,
Floorboards split as in disaster,
Ceilings sift down lime and plaster,
And some magic force has jolted
Open the door that was fast bolted.—
There! In Faust's old fleece I see
A giant looming monstrously!
At his gaze and beck I quail   6630
And my knees begin to fail.

---

2. The line puns on *Grillen* in its two senses of "whims" and "crickets."
3. See above, l. 518n.

Shall I stand or shall I flee?
O what will become of me!
MEPHISTOPHELES (*beckoning*).
  Come here, my friend!—Your name is Nicodemus.
FAMULUS. Yes, honored Sir, that is my name.—*Oremus.*[4]
MEPHISTOPHELES. Enough of that!
FAMULUS.   How nice that you know *me!*
MEPHISTOPHELES. A student yet, for all your years, I see;
  A mossback! Learned men keep studying too,
  Because there's nothing else that they can do.
  A middling house of cards is thus built neatly,   6640
  But greatest minds can not build it completely.
  Your master is an expert, though;
  The noble Doctor Wagner, who would deny him
  First in the learned world? Who does not know
  The world is only held together by him,
  The daily adder to all wisdom's store?
  Around him hearers by the score
  Gather in their thirst to know.
  He shines uniquely from his rostrum-throne,
  He wields keys like Saint Peter's own,   6650
  Unlocking things above and things below.[5]
  As he surpasses all for fire and spark,
  No name or glory but grows dim;
  The name of Faust himself grows dark,
  For sheer invention none can stand with him.
FAMULUS. Forgive me, reverend Sir, if I now say,
  And contradict you as I say,
  That he is not at all that way,
  That modesty is his allotted share.
  The great man's disappearance in thin air   6660
  Still baffles and disturbs him, and he yearns
  To see the blessed day when he returns.
  The chamber, as in Doctor Faustus' day,

---

4. Latin, "Let us pray."
5. Matthew 16:18: "And I will give unto thee the keys of the kingdom of heaven: and whatsoever thou shalt bind on earth shall be bound in heaven: and whatsoever thou shalt loose on earth shall be loosed in heaven."

Untouched since he has been away,
Awaits its master as of old;
For me to enter would be overbold.
What must the hour be among the stars?—
The house walls seem to quake with fear;
The doorposts sprang their bolts and bars,
Else you yourself could not be here.   6670
MEPHISTOPHELES. But tell me where the man can be,
    Lead me to him, bring him to me.
FAMULUS. Oh, his command could not be sterner,
    I don't know if I dare to try it.
    He has spent months there in his den
    At his great work in utmost quiet.
    The gentlest of all learned men,
    He now looks like a charcoal burner,
    His eyes begrimed from ears to nose
    And red from blowing of the bellows;   6680
    On every minute he hangs and longs,
    And music is the sound of tongs.
MEPHISTOPHELES. Would he refuse me some address?
    I am the man to hasten his success!

(*The* FAMULUS *goes out.* MEPHISTOPHELES *seats himself
with grave solemnity.*)

No sooner seated than I see
A guest approach, well known to me.
But this one's modern in the latest sense
And will show boundless impudence.
BACCALAUREUS [6] (*storming down the hallway*).
    Gate and door are open thrust!
    Well, at least I now may trust   6690
    That the living man no more
    Lies amoldering as before,
    Anguish-ridden, torment-rife,
    Dying of his very life.

---

6. Baccalaureus is the lowest title in the academic hierarchy. Though the lapse of a few years may be inferred since ll. 1868–2048, the present holder of the title is still in his twenties.

This house with its every wall
Bows and totters to its fall,
And unless we soon retreat,
Rack and ruin we will meet.
I'm as bold as bold can be,
Farther, though, you won't get me.   6700
   But the things I see today!
Is this not the passageway
I once walked in fear and woe
As a freshman years ago?
Trusting in these greybeards, all
Awe-struck with their folderol.
   Out of bookish crusts of mold
Lies of what they knew they told;
Disbelieving what they knew,
They stole my life and theirs too.   6710
What?—There in the study room
Sits one now in twilight gloom!
   He's still just the way I found him
With that same brown fur around him;
In that shaggy fleece he sat
When I left, I'm sure of that!
Then he seemed so wise and grand—
When I didn't understand.
That won't help him much today;
Go right up to him, I say!   6720
   Unless, O ancient Sir, dull Lethe's course
Winds through that sidewise-bent, bald head of yours,
Acknowledge me a student you have known—
Your academic switches all outgrown.
Just as you always were, I find you,
But I'm a different person, mind you!
MEPHISTOPHELES. I'm glad my ring made you come by.
   I once set no small store by you:
The grub and pupa always signify
The gorgeous butterfly that's due.   6730
Time was when you would simply dote
On mops of curls and lace at throat.—

A pigtail wig you've never worn?
Today I see you're Swedish shorn.[7]
You look so staunch and resolute—
But don't come home quite "absolute." [8]

BACCALAUREUS. My ancient Sir, this is an ancient *place*,
But think of how the *times* have changed!
And spare the *doubles entendres!* Nowadays
Things have been differently arranged.   6740
You hoodwinked the good, simple youth—
Which did not take much skill, in truth—
But just let someone try that trick today!

MEPHISTOPHELES. If one speaks naked truth to greenhorns, they
Don't relish it one little bit;
But then when they experience it
Years later, as hard upon their hides it comes,
They think it springs from their own craniums,
And then they say: The teacher was a nitwit.

BACCALAUREUS. A rogue perhaps!—Do teachers ever try   6750
To speak the truth and look us in the eye?
For little children they exaggerate
Too gravely, or too gaily underrate.

MEPHISTOPHELES. There is a learning time, but you are reaching
The later stage, I see, and are now ripe for teaching.
These many moons and several suns long since
You've gained a fullness of experience.

BACCALAUREUS. Experience! Froth and dust alone!
Compared with mind, it makes no showing.[9]
Admit that all things ever known   6760
Were absolutely not worth knowing . . .

7. The pigtail wig (*Zopf*) went out of fashion in the 1780's and tended thereafter to be worn by pedants. In the same period belligerently close-cropped hair became the mark of the radical; it was popularly thought of as Swedish in style. The English reader may imagine an analogous play on the terms "Cavalier" and "Roundhead."

8. A gibe at the overused philosophical term "the absolute"; here the word is used in its Latin sense of "cut off (from everything)," or possibly in the sense of "with *all* your hair cut off."

9. With some idealist philosophers experience and the evidence of one's senses were worthless, and the "mind" *created* the only reality.

MEPHISTOPHELES (*after a pause*).
  I've long thought that. For me, "fool" was the word;
  I see now I am hollow and absurd.
BACCALAUREUS. I'm glad to hear it! That's intelligence!
  The first old man I've found with any sense!
MEPHISTOPHELES. I sought for hidden gold and treasure-store
  And dredged up ghastly ashes to the air.
BACCALAUREUS. You grant that your bald pate is worth no more
  Than those skulls standing hollow there?
MEPHISTOPHELES (*good-naturedly*).
  Your rudeness is extreme, you realize? [10]   6770
BACCALAUREUS. When you're polite in German you tell lies.
MEPHISTOPHELES (*to the audience in the pit, as he rolls his
  rostrum chair further toward the proscenium*).
  Up here I'm being robbed of light and air,
  Can I take refuge with you folks down there?
BACCALAUREUS. When men are nothing any more, and they
  Still claim they're something, that is arrogance, I say.
  Man's life lives in the blood, and where, in truth,
  Does blood more lively stir than in a youth?
  That blood is living blood in vivid force,
  Creating new life in its old life's course.
  All impulse there begins, there things get done,   6780
  The weak falls and the able presses on.
  While we were winning half the world, what can
  You say you've done? You've nodded, drowsed, and spun
  Your dreams, and weighed and pondered plan on plan.
  Old age indeed is a cold fever spent
  In a capricious frost of discontent.
  Once past the age of thirty, men
  Already are as good as dead;
  It would be best to shoot you then.[11]
MEPHISTOPHELES. The Devil finds there's no more to be said.   6790

---

10. Here Mephistopheles drops the polite form of address (*Ihr*) and adopts
the familiar *du;* the Baccalaureus seems not to notice and continues in *Ihr*
form to Mephisto.
11. The idealist philosopher Fichte had made a remark more or less to this
effect in an essay of 1806, *Episode über unser Zeitalter.*

BACCALAUREUS. Unless I will them, devils don't exist.[12]
MEPHISTOPHELES (aside).
   The Devil's going to trip you up if you persist.
BACCALAUREUS. Youth's noblest mission is as I have stated it.
   The world was not, till I created it;
   I brought the sun up from the sea;
   The moon began its changeful course with me;
   The day adorned itself along my way,
   There earth grew green and put on its array;
   At my behest, across the primal night
   The stars all first displayed their splendid light.   6800
   Who, if not I, delivered you and brought
   You out of cramped Philistine thought? [13]
   But I am free to follow on the track
   Shown by my inner light and my mind's voice,
   I swiftly go my ways and I rejoice,
   Brightness before me, darkness at my back.

   (Exit.)

MEPHISTOPHELES. Queer duck, continue in your pompous show!—
   What pain to you this thought would bring:
   Who can think up a wise or stupid thing
   That was not thought of long ago?   6810
   But we are in no danger from this fellow,
   In just a few years he will mellow;
   Let grape juice act as silly as it will,
   There's wine to be made from it still.

   (to the younger section of the pit which has not applauded)

   My metaphor has left you cold,
   But I don't blame nice lads like you;

---

12. Fichte's doctrine held that the mind or ego willed all things into existence or out of existence from moment to moment, even to tables and chairs. (Compare ll. 6758–59, and note.)
13. "Philistine" had recently acquired currency as a derogatory term in the slang of student circles, who applied it to all who did not share their ideas. Goethe deeply distrusted the doctrinaire and para-political *Burschenschaften* (student societies).

Just think: the Devil, he is old:
Grow old to understand him too.

Laboratory

*In the medieval sense; complex, cumbersome
apparatus for fantastic purposes.*

WAGNER (*at the hearth*). The bell sounds and the sooty walls
    Quake at its dread reverberation.   6820
No longer will uncertainty
Attend my solemn expectation.
The dark spots now begin to lighten;
In the retort a fire dot grows
And like a living coal it glows,[1]
Yes, like a splendid ruby's spark
It flashes lightnings through the dark.
A clear, white light begins to brighten!
I mustn't miss this one time more!—
Oh Lord! What's rattling at the door?   6830
MEPHISTOPHELES (*entering*). Welcome! This is a friendly meeting.
WAGNER (*anxiously*).
    The star that rules the hour give you greeting!

(*softly*)

Let lips be of both words and breath relieved,
A mighty work is soon to be achieved.
MEPHISTOPHELES (*more softly*).
    What are you making there?
WAGNER (*still more softly*).
                  A human being![2]

---

1. To the alchemists, "living coals" took fire from their own inner spark.
2. The supreme objective of the alchemists. The details of Goethe's concept
are drawn from numerous writers of three centuries whose works he read in
1768 and again in the late 1790's, and who derive in many instances from

MEPHISTOPHELES. A human being? And what loving pair
　Have you got hidden in the smoke-hole there?
WAGNER. Why, none! Old-fashioned procreative ways
　We term mere idle trifling nowadays.
　The tender point from which life rose,　　　　　　　　　6840
　The sweet force born of inner throes,
　Which took, which gave—ordained to form itself,
　To add first near, then far things to itself—
　Has been deposed now from its dignity;
　Though animals may still delight therein,
　Man with his lofty gifts must henceforth be
　Assigned a higher, higher origin.

(*turning to the hearth*)

　It flashes! Look!—Now if we make selection
　From several hundred substances, and mix them—
　For on the mixing everything depends—　　　　　　　　6850
　And into human substance deftly fix them,
　And coat them in a jar with lime,
　And redistill them at the proper time,
　The job will quietly achieve its ends.

(*turning to the hearth*)

　It works! The mass is coming ever purer!
　Of this I'm sure and ever surer:
　What people used to call great Nature's mystery,
　We now dare probe with ratiocination,
　And what she once produced organically,

"Philippus Aureolus Paracelsus" (Theophrastus Bombastus von Hohenheim),
who died in 1541.

　Book I of Paracelsus' *De generationibus rerum naturalium* ("On the Generation of Natural Things") recommends: Allow male sperm to putrefy for
40 days in a covered jar until it visibly stirs with new life and somewhat resembles a man's form, though transparent and *without a body;* keep warm for
40 weeks (9 months) and feed daily with *arcano sanguinis humani* (secret
essence of human blood), after which time it will become a miniature living
child or "homunculus." Homunculi grow up as dwarves, giants, and other
specialized creatures; they have superhuman intelligence. Some writers
claimed they were clairvoyant. (Goethe knew the description of homunculi
in chap. 2 of *Tristram Shandy* but made no use of it in the present case.)

We now produce by crystallization.[3]   6860

MEPHISTOPHELES. One who lives long learns many things,
    By nothing new in this world can he be surprised;
    I have occasionally in my wanderings
    Seen human beings who were crystallized.[4]

WAGNER (*still attentively watching the retort*).
    It swells, it grows, and there are lightnings in it!
    It will be done at any minute.
    A great plan seems insane at the beginning,
    But in the future we shall laugh at fate,
    And in the future thinkers will create
    Just such a brain, which will do first-rate thinking.[5]   6870

    (*contemplating the retort with rapture*)

    The glass rings sweetly with a mighty sound;
    It clouds, it clears; the thing *must* come to be!
    Inside, a dainty form I see,
    A tiny little man that moves around.[6]
    What more can we or mankind hope to reach?
    The mystery lies plain as day.
    Lend ear to what he now may say,
    For he attains a voice, attains a speech.

HOMUNCULUS (*inside the retort, to* WAGNER).
    Well, Daddy, how are things? It was no jest,
    Come, press me tenderly against your breast,   6880
    But so the glass won't break, don't be too rough.
    That's how it is: when natural things seek place
    The universe has hardly room enough,
    But artificial things need bounded space.

    (*to* MEPHISTOPHELES)

    What! Scallywag and Cousin! You here too?

---

3. "By crystallization" means "synthetically" in alchemists' terminology.
4. I.e., "fossilized."
5. The matter in the retort resembles a brain, such as might be seen in a
dissecting room. The creature being manufactured is a mind without a body,
"the *idea* of a man."
6. "Little man" translates the Latin *homunculus*.

And in the nick of time! My thanks to you!
It was a lucky chance made you arrive.
I must be active while I am alive,
To gird my loins for work would best suit me
Right now, and short cuts are your specialty.   6890
WAGNER. A word yet! I have often been embarrassed
Why old and young had problems and were harassed.
For instance: no one yet has comprehended
How soul and body come to be so blended,
So locked together they can't get away
And yet torment each other all the livelong day.
Then—
MEPHISTOPHELES.
           Stop! And rather let the question be
Why man and wife get on so wretchedly!
Your question, friend, will never be made clear.
This little chap wants work, and that's right here.   6900
HOMUNCULUS. What's to be done?
MEPHISTOPHELES (*pointing to the side door*).
                          Right here your gifts employ!
WAGNER (*still gazing into the retort*).
   Oh, you are such a darling little boy!

(*The side door opens and* FAUST *is seen stretched out on the
bed.*)

HOMUNCULUS (*astonished*).
   Momentous!

(*The retort slips from* WAGNER'S *hands, swoops over* FAUST
and casts its shine upon him.) [7]

           Lovely scene!—Waters clear
In the dense grove, and women—they undress—
The fairest of the fair!—More loveliness!
One shows a radiance without a peer,
Descent from gods or heroes she must claim.
She sets her foot in the transparent gleam,

7. The clairvoyant Homunculus sees and tells aloud what Faust is dreaming.

Her noble body's gracious living flame
Is cooled in crystal of the yielding stream.—   6910
    But what a tumult of swift beating wings,
What rush and splash roils up the mirrored springs?
The maidens flee in panic, but the Queen [8]
Remains behind and calmly marks the scene;
With proud and womanly delight she sees
The prince of swans press fondly to her knees,
Importunately tame. More close he leans.—
Now suddenly moves in a mass of clouds
And with its densely textured veil enshrouds
In mist this loveliest of scenes.   6920
MEPHISTOPHELES. The things you don't know how to tell, and all!
    As phantast you're as great as *you* are small.
    Now, I see nothing—
HOMUNCULUS.   I believe it! Bred up north
    And from the Misty Ages issuing forth,
    From wastes of priestcraft and knight-errantry,
    How could your eye be free?
    In gloom alone you are at home.

    (*looking around*)

    Repulsive, whittled, time-browned stone,
    Arch-tapered and mold-overgrown!—
    If this man wakes, there'll be fresh cause for care,   6930
    Because he'll die right then and there.
    Swans, naked beauties, sylvan stream
    Made his premonitory dream;
    How could he put up with the likes of this
    When *I* can hardly stand it, as it is!
    Get him away from here.
MEPHISTOPHELES.   I'd like the chance!
HOMUNCULUS. Bid warriors go out and fight,
    Or bid a girl go to a dance,
    And everything will turn out right.

---

8. The Queen is Leda, the swan is Jupiter in his swan form, the event is the
begetting of Helen. (See "Leda," illustrations.)

It just occurs to me: tonight   6940
Is Classical Walpurgis Night;
That's just the thing to suit his bent:
Put him right in his element.
MEPHISTOPHELES. I've never heard of anything like that.
HOMUNCULUS. How could you hear of anything like that?
    Romantic ghosts are all that you would know;
    Real ghosts are Classical, and must be so.
MEPHISTOPHELES. But what direction would the journey take?
    These Classics colleagues give me bellyache.
HOMUNCULUS.
    Northwestwards, Satan, lies your pleasure ground;   6950
    Southeasterly this time our sails are bound.
    Across a vast plain there Peneus plies,[9]
    Shrub-lined, tree-lined, with cool and quiet bends;
    Up to the mountain clefts the plain extends,
    Pharsalus, old and new, above it lies.
MEPHISTOPHELES. O leave me out of that! Spare me
    That clash of servitude with tyranny! [10]
    It bores me, for no sooner is it done
    Than the whole struggle is once more begun,
    And no one sees how he's pushed to his fall   6960
    By Asmodeus, who's behind it all.[11]
    The struggle is, they say, for freedom's rights,
    Look closer, and it's slave with slave that fights.
HOMUNCULUS. Leave humans their perversity of whim,
    Each must defend himself as best he can
    From boyhood up, till he becomes a man.
    The only problem here

    [*pointing to* FAUST]

                    is curing *him*.

---

9. The Peneus River crosses the great plain of Thessaly in Greece.
10. Presumably meant is the clash between republic and empire in the persons of Pompey and Julius Caesar at the battle of Pharsalus, 48 B.C., though the more recent Greek-Turkish war may also be in the author's mind. See ll. 7005–24.
11. Asmodeus (compare Tobit 3:8) is the demon of discord, as in l. 5378 above.

If you can furnish us a remedy,
We'll try it, but if not, leave it to me.
MEPHISTOPHELES. I could test many a Brocken recipe,[12]   6970
But I find heathen bolts preventing me.
Those Greeks were not much good, though, anyway.
They dazzle you with frankly sensuous play
And lure men's hearts to cheerful sins, with our
Kind left to seem a gloomy sort and sour.
And so, what now?
HOMUNCULUS.   Well, you were never shy,
And with Thessalian witches mentioned, I
Believe I've said a thing or two.
MEPHISTOPHELES (*lasciviously*).
Thessalian witches![13] Well, now, there's a crew
I've long been curious about.   6980
Night after night with them no doubt
Would hardly be a pleasure. But, all right!
As a traveler I can try!
HOMUNCULUS. That mantle, wrap it round the "knight."
The rag will carry both of you
And fly just as it always flew.
I'll light the way.
WAGNER (*apprehensively*).
                   And I?
HOMUNCULUS.   Well, you
Stay home, where you have vital things to do.
Spread out your ancient parchments, note the rules,
Assemble living elements like tools,   6990
Join each to each with caution till they fit,
And meditate the *what*, still more the *why*.
Meanwhile, in roaming round the world a bit
I'll maybe find the dot that dots the *i*.
Your mighty goal will then be met,

---

12. The Brocken is the Harz Mountains summit mentioned in the Walpurgis
Night scene in Part I (see l. 3835*n*). Mephisto means that his powers, which
were effective in the "north-European" or "romantic" Walpurgis Night, will
not work in the "Classical Greek" one.
13. Thessaly, to the ancients, was witch country par excellence.

For which exertion this reward is set:
Fame, health, and wealth, and long life by the way,
And maybe truth and virtue—who can say?
Farewell.

WAGNER (*downcast*). Farewell. My heart is sad and sore,
    I fear I'll never see you any more.   7000

MEPHISTOPHELES. Down to Peneus then we go,
    We must not spurn my Cousin's aid.

    (*ad spectatores*)

    We do wind up depending so
    Upon the creatures we have made.

Classical Walpurgis Night

Pharsalian fields. Darkness.

ERICHTHO.[1] On this night's eerie feast, as often hitherto,
    I enter here, Erichtho, I, the gloomy one,
    Not so repugnant as the tiresome poets claim
    With their excessive slanders—never will they cease
    With praise and blame. To me the valley far ahead
    Appears paled over with the greyish wave of tents,   7010
    A reflex of the careworn and most anxious night.
    How often it has been repeated! And will be
    For all of time repeated . . . Neither yields the empire
    To other; none will yield it who with might acquired it
    And with might rules. For every man who cannot govern
    His inner self would far too soon and gladly govern
    His neighbor's will, according to his own proud mind.—
    But here there was fought out a great example of
    How force will block a force more potent, how the fair
    And thousand-blossomed wreath of liberty is torn   7020

---

1. A witch allegedly consulted by Pompey's son concerning the outcome of
the battle of Pharsalus, August 9, 48 B.C. (See Lucan, *Pharsalia* IV. 507 ff.)

And stubborn laurel bent around the victor's head.
Here Magnus [2] dreamed his flowering time of former greatness,
There Caesar watched and harkened to the flickering tongue.
Strengths will be matched. The world well knows
    which one prevailed.
  Watch fires are aglow, diffusing crimson flames,
The ground exhales reflection of the blood once shed,
And lured by the uncommon splendor of the night,
The legions of Hellenic saga gather now.
Round every fire uncertain waver, or at ease
Are seated, fabled figures of the olden days.   7030
The moon, not at the full but shining very bright,
Is rising, shedding mellow luster everywhere.
The spectral tents are disappearing; fires burn blue.
  But over me! What unexpected meteor?
It gleams, illuminating a corporeal ball.
I catch the smell of life. Me it does not beseem
To come near living things, for I work harm to them.
That brings me into bad repute and profits nothing.
Already it descends. I prudently retire!

(*She withdraws.*)

(*The aerial travelers above.*)

HOMUNCULUS. Circle once again around   7040
    Over flame and gruesome glow;
    Ghostly things are to be found
    In those valleys there below.
MEPHISTOPHELES. If I see some nasty ghosts
    Such as in the northland's gloom
    Crowd old windows with their hosts,
    Here as there I'll be at home.
HOMUNCULUS. See! There goes a lanky shade
    Beating her retreat down there.
MEPHISTOPHELES. Looks as though she were afraid   7050
    Seeing us come through the air.
HOMUNCULUS. Let her go! Set down your knight,

---

2. Pompey, called "the Great" (*Magnus*).

And right away he will be able
To regain his life and sight;
He seeks them in the land of fable.
FAUST (*touching the ground*).
Where is she?
HOMUNCULUS.   That we wouldn't know.
She still can be inquired for, though.
In haste from flame to flame you can
Go seeking her until the dawn;
No further trials await a man   7060
Who to the Mothers once has gone.
MEPHISTOPHELES. But don't forget that I'm here too;
Though I know nothing better we can do
Than have each one, among the fires,
Seek the adventure he desires,
Then meet once more when, Little Man,
You let your sounding beacon flash again.
HOMUNCULUS. It shall so flash, it shall so ring.

(*The glass booms and emits a mighty light.*)

Now off to many a wondrous thing!

(*Exit.*)

FAUST. (*alone*). Where is she!—Ask no more, no more invoke!   7070
If this is not the soil that bore her,
Nor this the wave that surged and broke before her,
Still this air heard the language that she spoke.
Here! By a miracle! In Helen's land!
I sensed the ground at once on which I stand.
As I in sleep was by new spirit fired,
So now I, like Antaeus, stand inspired.
If here are gathered all the rarest names,
I must search through this labyrinth of flames.

(*Withdraws.*)

MEPHISTOPHELES (*peering about*).
In threading through these bonfires as I came,   7080
I found myself an alien everywhere.

A few wear shirts, but most of them go bare;
Sphinxes shameless, griffins with no shame;
What I don't see, with flowing hair and wings,
With fore and aft views, in my wanderings . . . !
Of course, I am indecent, that I know;
This ancient stuff is much too lively though.
They need adjustment to the modern taste
And fashionable fixing up with paint and paste.
Repulsive lot! But I must not shirk lightly,   7090
Guest that I am, from greeting them politely . . .
Hello, there, pretty ladies, wise grey men!

GRIFFIN (*growling*). Not grey men! Griffin! No one likes to be
Called grey. It sounds too old. In every word
Some echo of its origin is heard:
Grey, gruesome, grizzled, graveyard, grim, and gripe
Are etymologically all of one stripe:
They put us out of temper.

MEPHISTOPHELES.   In your title
You do, however, find the "gri-" part vital?

GRIFFIN (*as above and consistently henceforth*).
Of course! The cognateship is no disgrace.   7100
Some do disparage it, but more give praise.
Have grit to grab a girl, a crown, or gold:
Fortuna grants a gritty man firm hold.[3]

ANTS (*of the colossal kind*).[4]
You mention gold. We had amassed whole piles
Of it in secret caves and rock defiles.
The Arimaspians over there now scoff

---

3. The fourfold pun defies translation. The "s" in *Greisen* ("old men") and "f" in *Greifen* ("griffin") resemble each other in Gothic type, causing a ludicrous schoolboy error in spelling. *Greifen* in turn sounds like a dialectal pronunciation of *Gräfin* ("Countess"). The verb *zu . . . greifen* is imitated, after a fashion, by "grab," though it means "to help oneself to, to go after," and "gritty" stands for *dem Greifenden,* "to one who does help himself, who does go after."
4. Herodotus, III. 102 speaks of ants in India, larger than foxes but smaller than dogs, which dig up gold with the sand when they scoop out their burrows. Herodotus, IV. 27 tells of the one-eyed Arimaspians and the gold-guarding griffins.

At us about how far they lugged it off.

GRIFFIN. We're going to force them to admit the deed.

ARIMASPIANS. Not on this free and gala night.

It'll all be gone by morning's light,   7110

This time we surely will succeed.

MEPHISTOPHELES (*has taken a seat between the* SPHINXES).

How soon I feel at ease among this crew,

I understand them to a man.

SPHINX. We'll breathe our spirit tones, and you

Embody them as best you can.

Until we know you better, state your name.

MEPHISTOPHELES. They give me lots of titles in my fame—

Are any Britons here? They always like to

Visit battlefields and waterfalls,

Old musty classic sites and ruined walls;   7120

They'd find this just the spot for them to hike to.

And they'd bear witness too: they used to like to

Give me stage roles as Old Iniquity.

SPHINX. Whence that name?

MEPHISTOPHELES.   I don't know.

SPHINX.   Well, let that be.

Do you have any astrological power?

What can you say about the present hour?

MEPHISTOPHELES (*looking up*).

Star shoots past star, the pared-down moon is bright,

And in this cozy spot I feel just right,

Your lion skin is warm where I lie tight.

It's no good soaring upwards, pretty maids,   7130

Let's have some riddles, better still, charades.

SPHINX. Explain yourself, and there will be our riddle.

Try stating yourself quintessentially:

"By good and bad men needed equally,

Mask for the one's ascetic fencing bout,

The other's crony and mad roustabout,

And both for Zeus to make a joke about."

FIRST GRIFFIN (*growling*). I just don't like him.

SECOND GRIFFIN (*growling louder*).   Why's he here?

BOTH. The vile brute has no business here.

MEPHISTOPHELES (*brutally*).

    Maybe you think the nails on your guest's paws   7140
    Can't match the scratching of your own sharp claws?
    Just try it!

SPHINX (*gently*). There's no harm done if you stay.

    In time you'll drive yourself out anyway.
    On home ground you may do much as you please,
    But here, if I'm not wrong, you're ill at ease.

MEPHISTOPHELES. You're a tasty dish to look at in your upper part,

    But lower down, that beast-half breaks my heart.

SPHINX. False creature, bitter will be your reproof:

    Our claws are sound. For you there'll be,
    You with your shriveled horse's hoof,   7150
    No joy in our society.

    (SIRENS *prelude overhead.*[5])

MEPHISTOPHELES. What birds are those that sway up there

    On branches of the poplar brook?

SPHINX. That singsong good men once mistook

    To their destruction. Have a care!

SIRENS. O, why let your taste go wrong

    With all this ugly fantasy?
    Hark, we flock with minstrelsy
    Of well modulated song,
    As befits the Siren throng.   7160

SPHINXES (*mocking them in the same melody*).

    Force them down out of those trees!
    In the branches no one sees
    Their filthy hawk claws curving back
    For a murderous attack
    Once you lend ear to their cry.

SIRENS. Banish envy! Banish hate!

    Gather we both soon and late
    The brightest joys beneath the sky.
    On the sea and in all lands
    Let the cheerfulest of hands   7170

---

5. Half women, half birds, whose enchanting song lured men to their death.

Greet the welcome passerby.

MEPHISTOPHELES. These are the newest offerings,
Where out of throats and from the strings
Tones intertwine with devious art.
This caroling is lost on me;
It wiggles in my ears, maybe,
But never gets down to my heart.

SPHINXES. Don't mention heart; that's sheer pretense.
With your face it would make more sense
To have a shriveled leather pouch.   7180

FAUST (*coming along*).
How wonderful is all I see! Odd creatures
Ill-favored, yet with great and sturdy features.
I sense auspicious outcome for it all.
But what do I at this stern glance recall?

(*gesturing toward the* SPHINXES)

Once Oedipus from these heard riddling words.

(*gesturing toward the* SIRENS)

At such as these Ulysses writhed in hempen cords.[6]

(*gesturing toward the* ANTS)

By these the greatest treasure once was stored.

(*gesturing toward the* GRIFFINS)

And these watched faithfully above the hoard.
I feel myself refreshed with energies.
The forms are great, great are the memories.   7190

MEPHISTOPHELES.
Once you would have cursed them from your soul,
Now you find they serve your ends.
When a beloved is the goal
Monsters themselves are seen as friends.

FAUST (*to the* SPHINXES).
You ladies must vouchsafe me one reply:

---

6. in the *Odyssey* XII. 155–200, Ulysses fills his crew's ears with wax and has them tie him to the mast of the ship, so that he can sail near the Sirens without succumbing to them.

Has either of you seen Helen passing by?
SPHINXES. We don't go back to her time. Hercules
    Killed off the last of those far ancestries.
    But ask of Chiron, if you please.[7]
    He's galloping about this ghostly night,   7200
    And if he stops for you, you've done all right.
SIRENS. No good reason why you should fail! . . .
    When Ulysses with us tarried,
    Spurning not, by haste unharried,
    He would tell us many a tale.
    We would show all things to you
    If you came with us down to
    Our bailiwicks by the green sea.
SPHINX. Be not gulled by trickery.
    Allow our good advice to hold you   7210
    As Ulysses was fast bound.
    Once great Chiron has been found,
    You will learn what I foretold you.

(FAUST *withdraws*.)

MEPHISTOPHELES (*peevishly*).
    What's all that croaking going by
    With wings a-flap so fast the eye
    Can't see them? One by one they fly.
    They would tire a huntsman out.
SPHINX. Like gusts of winter wind they go,
    Outranging old Alcides' bow,[8]
    Birds of the swift Stymphalian rout.   7220
    They croak with kind intent and seek,
    With goose-foot and with vulture-beak,
    To come and join us in the name

---

7. Chiron, the centaur, was skilled in medicine, music, and astronomy; he was the teacher of Hercules, Aesculapius, Jason, Achilles, and many others. (See illustrations.) The source of this information was Hederich's *Basic Mythological Lexicon* (*Gründliches mythologisches Lexikon*, 1770), which supplied the bulk of the material for the "Classical Walpurgis Night."
8. Hercules, grandson of Alceus. With his bow he shot, as his sixth labor, the man-eating birds of the war-god, which flocked in the Stymphalian Marsh between Arcadia and Argolis.

Of old blood kinship that they claim.

MEPHISTOPHELES (*as though frightened*).

What's that other stuff that hissed?

SPHINX. No need for you to fear and quake,
Those are the heads of the Lernaean snake
Lopped from the trunk; they think they still exist.
But why your sudden great distress?
And why these signs of restlessness?   7230
You want to leave us? Feel quite free! . . .
It's yonder chorus, I can see,
That makes you rubberneck. There's a whole pack
Of charming faces. Go on! Don't hold back!
Those wenches are the Lamiae
Of smiling mouth and sluttish eye;
The Satyr fellows like those sorts,
With them a Goatfoot dares all sports.

MEPHISTOPHELES. But you'll stay here so I can find you later?

SPHINX. Yes! Mingle with the merry mob, old Satyr.   7240
We, being out of Egypt, often stay
Up on a throne a thousand years this way.
Just respect our situation
And we will regulate sun and lunation.
   By the pyramids sit we,
Judging nations in our session;
War and peace and flood we see
But never vary our expression.

Middle Course of the Peneus River

[*The river-god*] PENEUS, *surrounded by
waters and* NYMPHS.

PENEUS. Sedges, sigh your whispers slow,
   Sister reeds, breathe soft and low,   7250
   Rustle, willows, where you cluster,
   Quiver, poplars, all a-fluster,
   To my interrupted dreams.

Dire forebodings made me wake,
Mysterious commotions shake
My rest within my flowing streams.
FAUST (*stepping up to the river*).
There, unless my ear deceives,
Past the masses of those leaves
Interlaced on bush and bough
I heard human sounds just now.   7260
The wave seems like a prattling guest,
With zephyrs jolly from his jest.
NYMPHS (*to* FAUST). Best would it be to
Recline at your ease, and
Rest from the road in
Coolness of trees, and
Know peace that evades you
For all you pursue;
We'll ripple and rustle
And whisper to you.   7270
FAUST. I am awake! Grant them full sway there,
My eye would have them be at play there,
Those peerless forms that are my quest.[1]
What wondrous rapture through me streams!
Can these be memories? Or dreams?
Yet once before you were thus blessed.
   Through copses softly stirring spills
A host of rivulets and rills
That barely murmur as they flow.
A hundred crystal brooks unite   7280
From every side to form a bright
Pool in the hollow down below.
Girls' wholesome limbs in youthful pose
Twofold the liquid mirror shows:
My eye is ravished at the sight.

---

1. The scene is that of Faust's vision as described by Homunculus in ll.
6903 ff. above, but without the girls, the swans, or Leda the Queen. The girls
now arrive, and then the swans; Leda must be nearby, for Jupiter as "prince
of swans" is swimming toward her. His embrace was described in the previous vision, which is realized here. From that embrace Helen will be born.

Now happily together bathing,
Now boldly swimming, shyly wading,
Now cries at last, and water fight.
I should be satisfied with these,
My eye should dwell on what it sees,   7290
But on and onward strives my mind.
My glance peers sharply through the blind
Mass of those leaves in their dense green
Where still concealed is the high Queen.
    Wondrous! Swans too make their way
Floating out from cove and bay,
Regal-motioned, pure, and still.
Smoothly drifting, pair by pair,
Yet so proud and self-aware,
How they lift up head and bill . . .   7300
One more grandly than the rest
Rears himself and swells his breast
Swiftly cutting through the surges;
Plumage ruffled and distending,
Himself a wave through wavelets wending,
Toward the sacred spot he urges . . .
The others calmly swim together
Agleam in every plume and feather,
Until by lusty, splendid strife
They drive the timid girls away;   7310
Abandoning their service,[2] they
Then think of nothing but their life.
NYMPHS. Sisters, come and lay an ear
    To this grassy bank's green mound;
    Tell me if I rightly hear
    Horses' hooves that thud and pound.
    Who could be so fast in flight
    Bringing tidings of this night?
FAUST. I seem to feel the earth resounding
    Beneath a horse's rapid bounding.   7320
        Yonder flies my glance.

---

2. The girls are ladies in waiting who desert their Queen.

Can such a lucky chance
Befall as I stand here?
O marvel without peer!
　Here gallops up a horseman proud,
He seems with mind and might endowed,
Upon a steed of dazzling white . . .
I know him now, he is the one,
It is Philyra's famous son!
Halt, Chiron! I must speak with you tonight . . .　　　　7330
CHIRON. What's this? What's this?
FAUST.　　　　　　　　　　Abate your rapid pace.
CHIRON. I never rest.
FAUST.　　　　　　　Then take me with you on your race!
CHIRON. Get on! Then I can ask you at my leisure
　Where you are bound. You stand here on the shore,
　And I will ford you through the stream with pleasure.
FAUST (*mounting*). Ride where you will. I'll thank you evermore . . .
　Great man and pedagogue of noble name,
　You reared a race of heroes to your fame;
　The noble fellowship of Argo's crew
　And all the poets' great were schooled by you.　　　　7340
CHIRON. We'll let all that be as it may.
　Pallas herself as Mentor counts for naught.[3]
　And in the end each goes along in his own way
　As if they never had been taught.
FAUST. O healer who profoundly knows
　Every plant and herb that grows,
　Who cures the sick and eases pain, I find
　My arms around your health of body and of mind!
CHIRON. With wounded heroes in the past
　I could prescribe a remedy,　　　　7350
　But I gave up my art at last
　To herb-women and the monkery.
FAUST. You are the truly great man who
　Rejects the praise that is his due,

---

3. In the second book of the *Odyssey*, Pallas Athene, goddess of wisdom, assumes the form of the tutor Mentor, in order to guide the youth Telemachus.

Who modestly disclaims, pretending
That he has peers of equal standing.
CHIRON. You sound adept at ways to please
    Prince or people with equal ease.
FAUST. You will admit that in your prime
    You knew the greatest figures of your time,   7360
    Vied with the noblest in accomplishment,
    And that your days were demigod-like spent.
    Among those heroes which one did you call
    The finest and the ablest of them all?
CHIRON. In the high Argo company [4]
    Each man was brave as his own way might be,
    And in that strength where he prevailed
    He was sufficient where the others failed.
    The Dioscuri always won the day
    When youthful strength and beauty were in play. [5]   7370
    Resolve, swift acts for others' welfare, these
    Were the fair lot of the Boreades. [6]
    Reflective, wary, strong, in council wise,
    Thus Jason triumphed, fair in women's eyes.
    Then Orpheus, tender, contemplative, still,
    He played the lyre outranking others' skill. [7]
    The sacred ship was steered by day and night
    Past rock and shoal by Lynceus' wondrous sight.
    Only comrades cope with danger best:
    What one achieves is praised by all the rest.   7380
FAUST. Of Hercules you speak no word?
CHIRON. Alas! There mournful chords are stirred . . .
    Phoebus I never saw of old,
    Nor Ares, Hermes, and the rest,
    But with my eyes I did behold
    What men call godlike at its best.

---

4. In the saga of the Argonauts, Jason assembled the noblest of Greek heroes
to accompany him in the ship Argo to fetch the Golden Fleece.
5. The Dioscuri, Castor and Pollux, were brothers of Helen.
6. The Boreades, Zetes and Calais, sons of Boreas (the north wind), were
winged warriors who fought the ravaging Harpies.
7. By playing his lyre more beautifully than the Sirens sang, Orpheus saved
the Argonauts from destruction by the Sirens.

He was a born king like no other,
A youth most glorious to the view,
Submissive to his elder brother,
And to all lovely women too.   7390
Earth will not yield his like again,
Nor Hebe guide him to the sky; [8]
Songs try to tell of him in vain,
Stone baffles sculptors as they try.

FAUST. Hammer sculptors all they can,
They will not limn his mighty brow.
You have told of the fairest man,
Tell of the fairest woman now.

CHIRON. What! . . . Woman's beauty is a thing
Of naught, often a lifeless toy.   7400
Such creatures only can I sing
As brim with zest for life and joy.
True loveliness is self-contained,
Its grace can never be constrained,
Like Helen, whom I once transported.

FAUST. You carried her?

CHIRON.   Yes, on this back.

FAUST. My wits already are unsorted,
And now I cling to this same back!

CHIRON. She clutched my mane and held it close
As you are doing.

FAUST.   I shall lose   7410
My mind completely. Tell me now—
She is my one supreme desire!—
Whence did you bring her, where, and how?

CHIRON. Easily told, what you inquire.
The Dioscuri had delivered their
Young sister from a robbers' lair.
But they, unused to losing any fight,
Took courage and pursued, and in their flight
The brothers and the sister found their way

---

8. Hebe, the daughter of Zeus and Hera and cupbearer to the gods, became the wife of Hercules after the latter's death and assumption of immortal form.

Blocked by the swamps that near Eleusis lay.   7420
The brothers waded, I splashed in and swam across.
Then down she jumped, stroked and caressed
My dripping mane, and, self-possessed,
Stated her thanks astutely, gravely coy.
O, she was charming! Young, an old man's joy!

FAUST. Just ten years old! . . .[9]

CHIRON.   The scholars, I can see,
Have fooled themselves and you preposterously.
Mythological ladies are unique,
Poets use them for effects they seek.
They never grow up, never age;   7430
Appetizing at every stage,
They're kidnapped young and still wooed when they're old.
For poets, time restrictions do not hold.

FAUST. Then let her also by no time be bound!
Himself outside of time, Achilles found
Her there on Pherae.[10] By what fortune he
Won her love counter to his destiny!
Should I not by the force of yearning now
Evoke that peerless form to life somehow?
That deathless creature, goddess' peer by birth,   7440
Great, tender, lovable, of lofty worth!
You saw her once, but I saw her today,
Longed for and lovely, ruled by sweet charm's sway.
I can no longer live unless I find
Her, for I am enthralled in heart and mind.

CHIRON. As man you are enraptured, that is plain;
But with us spirits you seem quite insane.
It happens you are lucky here:
To Manto, Aesculapius' child, each year
For a few moments only I repair.   7450

9. "Seven to ten," Hederich's dictionary of mythology stated. Goethe wrote "seven" but changed it to "ten."
10. Hederich's dictionary relates how Helen, after her death, was married to Achilles, who was himself living a posthumous life on the island of Leuce. Pherae is Goethe's mistaken substitution of the name of a town in Thessaly for the island.

She lives in constant, silent prayer
And begs her father, to his honor's gain,
To grant physicians' minds illumination
And cure them of their murderous inclination . . .
She is my favorite of the Sibyl guild,
Unfrenzied, and with helpful mildness filled.
Stay with her for a time, and from her wealth
Of herbs she will restore you to full health.

FAUST. I have no wish for cures, my mind is whole;
    That would be cheap of me and base of soul.   7460

CHIRON. Fail not the healing of the noble fount.
    But we are at the place. Dismount!

FAUST. Where have you brought me through the pebbled streams
    To land amid this night of dreadful dreams?

CHIRON. Here Rome with Greece in desperate battle vied—
    Peneus right, Olympus on the left-hand side—
    For the greatest empire ever lost in sand.
    The King retreats, and now victorious stand
    The burghers.[11] Look up! See how near
    The ageless temple stands in moonlight clear.   7470

MANTO (*dreaming within*).
    With horse's hoof
    Resounds my sacred roof.
    Half-gods I surmise.

CHIRON. Quite right!
    Only lift your sleeping eyes!

MANTO (*waking*). Welcome! I see you have not failed to come.

CHIRON. And here still stands your temple home!

MANTO. You still rove tireless in endeavor?

CHIRON. Peace-surrounded you dwell ever,
    While circling round is joy for me.   7480

MANTO. I bide, time circles around *me*.
    And he?

CHIRON.   The ill-famed night upcast
    Him here out of its vortex vast.

---

11. In 168 B.C. the Roman republican army ("the burghers") defeated the last King of Macedonia near the town of Pydna, thus ending the empire of Alexander the Great.

Helen, with senses all distraught,
He seeks for Helen and has sought;
Of where and how to start, knows naught.
Aesculapian cure advisable.
MANTO. I love the cravers of the impossible.

(CHIRON *is already far away.*)

Enter, rash man, and follow me.
The dark way leads down to Persephone.   7490
Within Olympus' hollow core
She bides forbidden greetings evermore.
I smuggled Orpheus once through here.
Use it more wisely[12] Quick! Good cheer!

(*They descend.*)

At the Upper Peneus

As before.

SIRENS. Plunge into Peneus' flood!
Seemly is it there to swim
And to lift up hymn on hymn
For unhallowed people's good.[1]
Without water life is none.
Troop we swift in company   7500
Down to the Aegean Sea,
Every joy will there be won.

(*Earthquake.*)

Wave upfoaming backward rushes,

---

12. Manto's conducting of Orpheus is Goethe's invention. Orpheus, after
rescuing his beloved Eurydice from the underworld, unwisely looked at her,
as he had been forbidden to do before regaining the upper air, and thus
forced her return among the shades.

1. Unhallowed are those who do not acknowledge the life-conferring quality
of water.

Flows within its bed no more,
Quakes the earth, the water gushes,
Bursts in smoke the pebbled shore.
Flee we now, come every one!
Bodes this marvel good to none.
   Joyous guests, come one and all
To the sea's glad festival.   7510
Glittering waves there each by each
Lightly swelling wet the beach,
Luna gleams with double flare,[2]
Sacred dew anoints the air.
Life moves freely in the ocean,
Here is earthquake's dire commotion.
Haste to flee, all who are wise!
Round this place a horror lies.

SEISMOS (*blustering and thumping in the depths*).[3]
Once more heave with might and main,
With your shoulders thrust and strain,   7520
Thus the upper world we gain,
Where everything must yield to us.

SPHINXES. What a weird vibration, hateful
With foreboding dire and fateful!
What a lurching, what a sway,
This way rock, rock then that way!
What commotion hideous!
But we will not shift position
Though all hell explodes perdition.
   Now a dome forms curiously,   7530
Upward surging. It is he,
He who built, when old and hoary,
Delos Island famed in story,
Built it for a mother-to-be,[4]
Heaving it up through the sea.
He by thrust and stress of brawn,

---

2. I.e., the moon and its reflection in the water.
3. "Seismos" is the Greek word for "earthquake."
4. Leto in birthpangs came to Delos, said to be a floating island, and there
bore Artemis and Apollo.

Back hunched down and arms taut drawn,
Atlas-postured in his toil,
Now lifts this ground, grass, and soil,
Stones and gravel, sand and clay,   7540
Once the bed where our stream lay.
Now our valley's quilt he rips,
Tearing it to jagged strips,
He, by labors unaffected,
A colossal caryatid.
Dread stone scaffoldings still rest
Deep in earth up to his chest.
But no further shall it go,
Sphinxes stand and gaze below.

SEISMOS. That I accomplished this alone   7550
Mankind will now at last confess.[5]
And had I not so shattered and so strown,
Would this world not be beautiless?—
How would yonder mountains stand
Amid the aether's gorgeous blue,
Had I not heaved them with my hand
So picturesquely into view,
When under my great parents' eye—
Chaos and Night—I made a show of strength
With Titan playmates, to the length   7560
Of tossing Pelion and Ossa toward the sky.
We romped, as boys will, all around the map
Till we got tired and it got dark,
And then those twin peaks like a double cap
We struck up on Parnassus for a lark.
Apollo has a gay retreat
Up there now with the Muses' choir.[6]
I also lifted up a seat
For Jupiter with all his bolts of fire.
Just so now with a mighty strain   7570

5. The events described by Seismos in ll. 7550 ff. are Goethe's invention,
based on hints in Hesiod's *Theogony*.
6. On the slope of twin-peaked Mt. Parnassus stood Delphi, the site of
Apollo's famous shrine. The Muses also inhabited the mountain.

I burst up from the nether sphere,
And summoning with might and main
Cry new life for all dwellers here.
SPHINXES. Primeval we would call them now,
    These things that here have come to birth,
    Had we not seen ourselves just how
    They were wrenched up out of the earth.
    A bushy forest reaches out afar,
    While here come thronging cliff and rocky scar.
    Before such things no Sphinx retreats,   7580
    And we shall not give up our sacred seats.
GRIFFINS. Tinsel gold and golden foil
    Glitter through the rifts of soil.
    Up and pick it, Emmets! Rise! [7]
    None shall cheat you of this prize!
CHORUS OF ANTS. Just as the giants
    Shoved the stuff up,
    You wriggle-foot clients
    Will get it atop.
    In and out you come!   7590
    In rifts like these
    Every little crumb
    You quickly seize.
    Don't overlook
    The least little thing
    In any nook;
    Fetch it and bring.
    Busy, busy ever!
    Swarm with a will!
    Just get the gold, and never   7600
    Mind the hill.
GRIFFINS. Fetch in! Fetch in! Bring gold and heap it!
    We lay our claws on it and keep it.
    No better bolts were ever made
    In all the treasure-guarding trade.
PYGMIES. We have laid claim to this spot,

---

7. Emmets are ants. See above, l. 7104n.

How it happened is not clear.
Where we come from, question not:
We are here because we're here.
Space for living may be given   7610
Anywhere in any land,
But let a rock or cliff be riven,
And your dwarf is right on hand.
He-dwarf, she-dwarf work in pairs
Noted for their industry,
We don't know how this fact squares
With facts in Eden anciently,
But we take things for the best
And thank our stars with all good will;
In the east as in the west   7620
Mother Earth is teeming still.

DACTYLS.[8] If she in one short night
Brought little ones to light,
Littlest too she will create,
And each will find a mate.

PYGMY ELDERS. Swift to the race
For living space!
Swiftly and long
Work to be strong!
While peace holds steady   7630
Get foundries ready,
Weapons with speed
Is the army's need.
    You Emmets all,
Busy at call,
Fetch minerals.
You Dactyls many,
Though smallest of any,
It's understood
You fetch the wood.   7640
On hidden fire
Stack layers higher,

---

8. "Fingerlings," tiniest of dwarves. They were metalworkers on Mt. Ida.

Make the coals good.

GENERALISSIMO. With arrow and bow,[9]
    Swift to the foe!
    Herons galore
    On the fishpond shore
    Build countless nests
    And swell their breasts:
    Shoot them all down,   7650
    Not one of them spare;
    Then our helmets can wear
    A feathered crown.

EMMETS AND DACTYLS. Will no one save us!
    The iron we got,
    But chains they gave us.
    This is still not
    The time to escape,
    So bow and scrape.

THE CRANES OF IBYCUS.[10] Cries of murder, slaughter, wailing!   7660
    Throbbing wings in anguish flailing!
    What groans of pain, what dying cries
    Pierce the pathways of our skies!
    All are slain now; red the lake
    Roils with bloodshed in their wake.
    Loathsome greed its force has spent
    Getting heron ornament.
    Stuck as crests on caps it waves
    On those lard-paunch, crook-leg knaves.
    Fellows of our confederacy,   7670
    Long-lined sailers of the sea,
    Vengeance be with all our powers
    Done in case so close to ours!
    Spare not either strength or blood

---

9. The Pygmies (see *Iliad* III. 6) fought annually with the cranes as the latter came north in the spring.

10. *The Cranes of Ibycus*, a ballad by Schiller, told the story of how the murderers of Ibycus betrayed their guilt by publicly crying out his name upon seeing again the cranes which had flown overhead at the moment of their crime.

In deathless hatred toward this brood.

(*They scatter croaking in the air.*)

MEPHISTOPHELES (*in the plain*).
  With. northern witches I had quite a knack,
  But with these foreign ones it's what I lack.
  The Blocksberg is a cozy place to roam,
  Go where you may, it's always just like home.
  Dame Ilse on her stone waits up for us,   7680
  On his Height there Heinrich is a cheery cuss,
  The Snorers snuff and snort at Elend some,[11]
  But all is made for a millennium.
  While here, go where you will, you never know
  But what the ground will blow up from below . . .
  There I am walking down a level spot,
  And up behind me pops a mountain—not
  A mountain really, just a hill; but high
  Enough so I'll have trouble getting by
  To find my Sphinxes.—Lots of fires still rally,   7690
  Enough to light the sideshows down the valley . . .
  The gallant chorus dances on, cavorting
  Like rascals, and eluding me, and sporting.
  But just you wait! When one is used to sweets,
  He tries for them with anyone he meets.
LAMIAE (*luring* MEPHISTOPHELES *after them*).
  Faster and faster,
  On and on,
  Then stop to smile
  And chat awhile.
  It is such fun   7700
  Luring the master
  Sinner on
  So frustratingly.
  We start to run,

---

11. Dame Ilse's Stone (*Ilsenstein*), Heinrich's Height (*Heinrichshöh*), and
the Snorers (*die Schnarcher*) are physical features of the Blocksberg peak,
above the village of Elend, in the Harz Mountains. All except the *Heinrichshöh* were mentioned in the earlier, Romantic, Walpurgis Night.

And his clubfoot stumbles
Along and bumbles
Along to find us,
As he drags himself
Along behind us.

MEPHISTOPHELES (*stopping*).

Accursed fate! How men are cheated!   7710
From Adam down, gulled and defeated!
Older we get, but who gets wise?
Haven't you lost enough of these tries?
  It's known that they are good-for-nothing creatures
With midriffs laced too tight and painted features.
Touch where you will, there's not one spot about
Them that is healthy; they are rotted out.
We see this, touch this, yet the riddle
Is that we dance the tune these bitches fiddle.

LAMIAE (*stopping*). Halt! He's debating, thinks he'll stay.   7720
Get to him now or he will get away!

MEPHISTOPHELES (*going ahead*). Push on! Don't be a silly lout
Caught in a tangled web of doubt.
Without witches, who the Devil *would*
Be a devil if he could!

LAMIAE (*most charmingly*). Surround this hero amorous;
Inevitably within his heart
Love will declare for one of us.

MEPHISTOPHELES. Here in this uncertain light
You ladies seem to be all right,   7730
And so I won't find any fault.

EMPUSE [12] (*forcing her way in*). I'm all right, I'm all right too!
Admit me to your retinue!

LAMIAE. She's one too many, not our sort,
Always spoils our fun and sport.

EMPUSE (*to* MEPHISTOPHELES).

Empuse greets you with good cheer,

---

12. A bogey that scares travelers, assuming various forms for that purpose. Hederich's dictionary of mythology listed "plant, cow, snake, fly, beautiful woman, etc." The ass's head in l. 7746 is Goethe's whimsical addition to the list.

Your cousin with the ass's foot;
Yours is just a horse's foot,
Still, Cousin, greetings and good cheer!
MEPHISTOPHELES. I had mere strangers on my mind,   7740
And here it's relatives I find.
But so it goes, and by the dozens,
From Harz to Hellas, always cousins.
EMPUSE. I *can* act with resolve and take
On many forms, but for your sake
I thought this ass's head would be
The best thing in this company.
MEPHISTOPHELES. I notice that with people such
As these, blood kinship counts for much;
This may offend, but just the same,   7750
This ass's head I do disclaim.
LAMIAE. O leave the nasty thing! She'd scare
Off anything that's fine and fair;
And what was fine and fair before,
Once she comes near, is so no more.
MEPHISTOPHELES. These cousins too, dainty and small,
I find suspicious one and all.
And from those lovely cheeks of roses
I look for ugly metamorphoses.
LAMIAE. But try! There's lots of us to choose   7760
From, and with luck you cannot lose,
You'll get the best one of the lot.
Why this lascivious palaver?
You're a washout as a lover,
Strutting around with such an air.—
Now he joins our company;
Let your masks down gradually
And show your essence to him bare.
MEPHISTOPHELES. I've picked the fairest one in sight . . .

   (*embracing her*)

What a dried-up broom! A fright!   7770

   (*grabbing another*)

And this one? . . . Ignominious face!

LAMIAE. You think you merit better grace?
MEPHISTOPHELES. That little one I'd like to catch . . .
    The lizard slips me when I snatch!
    Her braid is slippery as a snake.
    I'll take that tall one there instead . . .
    She's like a thyrsus wand you shake
    And has a pine cone for a head.
    What will I end with? . . . There's a fat one,
    Maybe I'll have some fun with that one.   7780
    Now one last try! That's what I'll do.
    A squishy, squashy sort of fry,
    The kind that Orientals buy . . .
    Oh dear, the puffball split in two.
LAMIAE. Scatter now! Swoop down and hover
    Like lightning, and with black flight cover
    The witch's son who went too deeply!
    Fly uncertain, ghastly rings
    Like flittermice on soundless wings!
    He's getting out of it too cheaply.   7790
MEPHISTOPHELES (*shaking himself*).
    I haven't got much wiser, that is clear.
    Things are absurd up north, absurd down here.
    Both there and here ghosts are foul-faced,
    Nation and poets have bad taste.
    It's masquerade both here and there
    And dance of the senses everywhere.
    I seized on maskers I believed
    Were lovely; what I caught set me aghast . . .
    I would be glad to be deceived
    If the illusion would just last.   7800

    (*losing his way among the rocks*)

    Where am I? Which way should I travel?
    This was a path, now it's coarse gravel.
    I came by smooth roads with no trouble,
    And now it's boulders, wash, and rubble.
    I scramble up and down in vain.
    How will I find my Sphinx again?

I would not have believed one night
Could raise a hill of such a height!
Now I call that some witch's ride:
They carry Blocksbergs at their side.   7810
OREAD (*from a natural cliff*).
　Up here! My mountain rock is old
　With shape unchanged through times untold.
　Revere steep mountain paths, revere
　The furthest spurs of Pindus here.
　I stood here with unshaken head
　When over me great Pompey fled.
　Those forms illusive fade away
　At cockcrow and the break of day.
　I see such fables come to be,
　Then vanish just as suddenly.   7820
MEPHISTOPHELES. All honor to you, reverend head
　With lofty oak-strength garlanded!
　The clearest moonlight ever known
　Has never yet through darkness shone.—
　　But sidelong through the bushes gleams
　A light of very modest beams.
　How things do come about for us!
　It is, in fact, Homunculus!
　Whither away now, Little Man?
HOMUNCULUS. I float from place to place as best I can   7830
　And would like, in the best sense, to evolve;
　I am on fire to break my glass;
　And yet, from what I've seen, I can't resolve
　For any of the forms I pass.
　But, confidentially, I'm looking
　For two philosophers I overheard,
　And with them "Nature! Nature!" was the word.
　And so I wouldn't want to miss
　Them: they must know what earthly being is.
　At last it may be I shall learn   7840
　Which way it would be best for me to turn.
MEPHISTOPHELES. You'd better do that on your own.

Where ghosts have set up shop, it's true
That your philosopher is welcome too.
To have his art the more appreciated,
He has a dozen new ones soon created.
You'll either get it wrong, or make no sense of it.
If you want to evolve, then do it on your own.
HOMUNCULUS. Good advice should never be turned down.
MEPHISTOPHELES.
Then go your ways. We'll see what comes of it.   7850

(*They separate.*)

ANAXAGORAS (*to* THALES). Your rigid mind will not be bent;
    What more must I add to the argument?
THALES. The wave is bent by all the winds that play,
    But from the rugged rock stays far away.
ANAXAGORAS. By work of fire this rock here was created.
THALES. From moisture living things originated.
HOMUNCULUS (*between the two*). I long to be evolving; do
    Let me walk along with you.
ANAXAGORAS. Have you, O Thales, ever in one night
    Produced from slime a hill of such a height?   7860
THALES. Never was Nature in her living power
    Dependent on the day and night and hour.
    She shapes all forms and regulates their course,
    But never, even in things huge, by force.
ANAXAGORAS. Yet such was here! Plutonic, savage fire
    And Aeolian vapors in explosion dire
    Burst through the ancient crusts of level earth
    Till a new mountain came to sudden birth.
THALES. But what else is accomplished now thereby?
    It's there, all well and good, and by the bye.   7870
    Such arguments waste time, they are mere pose,
    And just lead patient people by the nose.
ANAXAGORAS. The mountain swarms with myrmidons
    To colonize the clefts of stones;
    Pygmies, emmets, fingerlings,
    And other busy little things.

(*to* HOMUNCULUS)

You've never sought things of large scale
In your restricted hermit's pale;
Acquire the knack of governing,
And I will have them crown you king.   7880
HOMUNCULUS. What says my Thales?
THALES.   That's not wise.
　　Small actions from small men arise.
　　Great men will make the small man great.
　　But look! There cranes in a black cloud
　　Threaten the excited crowd,
　　And would so threaten any king.
　　Upon those little ones they wreak
　　Great slaughter now with claw and beak.
　　Fate strikes them like the lightning.
　　One crime led to the herons' slaughter   7890
　　In peaceful nests by quiet water.
　　Those previous showers of arrowed rain
　　Bring cruel revenge now in their train
　　As kindred cranes in outrage burn
　　For wanton pygmy blood in turn.
　　What good are helmets, spears, and shields?
　　What good to dwarves are herons' plumes?
　　How dactyls, emmets, meet their dooms!
　　Their army wavers—flees—and yields.
ANAXAGORAS (*after a pause, solemnly*).
　　If nether gods till now have had my praise,   7900
　　I turn to those above in present case . . .
　　O thou above, eternal, never old,
　　Threefold in name, in form threefold,
　　Amid my people's woe I cry to thee,
　　Diana, Luna, Hecate! [13]
　　Thou, heart-aggrandizing, mind of immensity,

---

13. The three forms of the moon divinity: Luna, as goddess in the sky; Diana, as goddess on earth; Hecate, as goddess in the dark underworld. Goethe's hot-headed Anaxagoras demands supernatural demonstration of the rightness of his arguments.

Thou, tranquil-seemingly, soul of intensity,
The dread gulf of thy shadows make thou known,
Be thy old might without enchantment shown!
(*pause*)

   Am I too quickly heard?   7910
Has my prayer
Ascending there
Marred Nature's order with a word?
   Now larger, ever larger looms in air
The goddess' circular, refulgent chair,
Stupendous, dreadful to the gaze!
Its fire shows redder through the haze . . .
 No closer! Disc of might so ominous,
You will destroy the land, the sea, and us!
   Did the Thessalian women, as they tell,   7920
In sacrilegious magic spell
Enchant you down, and by the charm
Wrest powers from you for great harm? . . .[14]
The bright shield darkens; suddenly
It bursts and blazes dazzlingly.
What crashing, hissing, all around!
What rush of wind and thunder sound!
A suppliant to the throne I fall!
Forgive me, for I caused it all!
(*Falls on his face.*)

THALES. What all this man has heard and seen in fear!   7930
   I don't just know what happened here,
   But I felt nothing of the kind.
   We grant these hours are mad, but I still find
   Luna floating as before
   Calmly down her path of yore.
HOMUNCULUS. Look where the pygmies were: the mound
   Is jagged where it once was round.
   I heard terrific noise, and soon

---

14. Thessalian witches were reputed experts at charming the moon down from the sky. (See Goethe's drawing, illustrations.)

That rock came tumbling from the moon;
Right off, unheeding, at a blow   7940
It squashed and killed both friend and foe.
Yet arts like these I can't help praising:
Working with creative might
Above and underneath, and raising
This mountain in a single night.

THALES. Be still! You only thought you saw the sight.
Good riddance to that nasty brood!
That you weren't king is to the good.
Now off to glad sea festival,
Where wonder-guests are honored one and all.   7950

(*They withdraw.*)

MEPHISTOPHELES (*clambering up the opposite side*).
Up steep stone stairs here I am toiling, crawling
Through roots of ancient oaks all gnarled and sprawling.
Home in my Harz the pine trees savor
Somewhat of pitch, which is my favorite flavor—[15]
After brimstone.—Here among these Greeks
You hardly get a whiff of those good reeks.
I'm curious though, I really must inquire
What fuel they use to make a hell and fire.

DRYAD. Be wise with local wisdom when at home,
Be more sophisticated when you roam   7960
Abroad and don't be hankering for the folks.
Revere the dignity of ancient oaks.

MEPHISTOPHELES. One thinks of what behind him lies;
What one is used to, that is paradise.
But tell me, what's that in that cave
Hunched triple-formed there over feeble light?

DRYAD. The Phorkyads.[16] Go speak to them, be brave—

---

15. Mephisto puns on *Harz*, the name of the mountains, and *Harz, harzig*, meaning "(pine tree) resin, resinous."
16. The Phorkyads were three aged sisters named Pemphredo, Enyo, and Deino, and were the daughters of Phorkys. According to Hederich's diction-

Or do you shrink from them in fright?
MEPHISTOPHELES. Why not! . . . I am aghast at what I see.
 Proud as I am, I must confess   7970
 I never saw such ugliness;
 Worse than mandrake by gallows tree—
 Will ever any sins arch-vile
 Seem ugly in the slightest, while
 This triple horror is on view?
 We wouldn't have them by the doors
 Of our hells' most appalling floors.
 Yet praised as "classic" here they stand
 Rooted right in beauty's land—
 They seem to notice me, they stir,   7980
 Like vampire bats they peep and churr.
ONE OF THE PHORKYADS. Give me the eye, sisters, to see who dares
 Come so close to our temples as he fares.
MEPHISTOPHELES. Most honored! Grant me to approach you now
 And feel your triple blessing on my brow.
 Though I come as a stranger, it may be
 I am a distant cousin of you three.
 Old reverend gods I have beheld ere now;
 To Ops and Rhea made my deepest bow; [17]
 The very Fates, sisters to Chaos and to you, 7990
 Just yesterday—or day before—I saw them too.
 But on the likes of you I never gazed.
 I stand in silence, ravished and amazed.
THE PHORKYADS. This spirit seems to have intelligence.
MEPHISTOPHELES. I marvel poets have not had the sense
 To praise you. Tell me now, how could it be
 I've never seen a picture of you three?

---

ary, they lived in a place where neither sun nor moon ever shone, and they possessed one eye and one tooth among them; these they used alternately whenever they wished to see or eat something.
17. Ops and Rhea were really one goddess, though Goethe seems to make two by using her alternate Latin and Greek names. As mother of Jupiter and consort of Saturn, Ops/Rhea belonged to a primeval time. Mephisto alleges equal age.

The sculptor should devote his skill to you,
Not Juno, Pallas, Venus, and that crew.
THE PHORKYADS. Immersed in solitude and stillest night,   8000
We never thought of such a thing, we three.
MEPHISTOPHELES. How could you, out of mind and out of sight,
With none to see you, none for you to see?
You ought to seek out places to reside
Where art and splendor throne in equal pride,
Where on the double every day they rustle
Some hero out of marble, where life's bustle—
THE PHORKYADS. Be still! Don't give us any hankerings!
How would it help if we knew better things?
Born of the night, to things of night allied,   8010
Ourselves unknowing, known to none outside.
MEPHISTOPHELES. In a case like this, that doesn't mean too much,
There can be transfer of the self as such.
One eye, one tooth suffices for you three,
Hence it is proper, mythologically,
To make two of the threefold entity,
With the remaining third transferred to me
Just briefly.
ONE OF THE PHORKYADS.
                    Do you feel it's worth a try?
THE OTHERS. Let's try it—but without the tooth and eye.
MEPHISTOPHELES. But now you're taking the best part away,   8020
How would the likeness be complete that way?
ONE OF THE PHORKYADS.
You just hold one eye shut, there's nothing to it,
And let one tooth stick out if you can do it,
And right away in profile there will be
A sibling likeness managed to a T.
MEPHISTOPHELES. I'm honored! Done!
THE PHORKYADS.   And done!
MEPHISTOPHELES (as a Phorkyad in profile).   And here I stand:
Chaos' well-beloved son!
THE PHORKYADS. We're Chaos' daughters by unchallenged right.
MEPHISTOPHELES. They'll call me now—O shame!—hermaphrodite.
THE PHORKYADS. What beauty in our new-formed triad lies!   8030

We sisters now have two teeth and two eyes.
MEPHISTOPHELES. I'm going to leave you all now for a spell
To go and scare the devils down in hell.

(*Exit.*)

Rocky Bays of the Aegean Sea

The moon pausing at the zenith.

SIRENS (*reclining about on the cliffs, caroling and singing*).
Thou, whom once in monstrous rite
Thessalian women of the night
Downward forced, gaze tranquilly
From the arched immensity
Of sky upon this glittering sea
Flashing far horizonwards,
And illumine untold hordes   8040
Rising now out of its waves.
We thy service gladly bear;
Show us favor, Luna fair.
NEREIDS AND TRITONS (*as marvels of the sea*).[1]
Louder lift your singing, steep
Down through the sea. From far and near
Summon dwellers of the deep!
Stormy rending of the waves
Drove us down to silent caves,
But gracious singing draws us here.
See how we in our delight   8050
Are with golden chains bedight,
How we add to brooch and gem
Jeweled belt and diadem.

---

1. Offspring of the sea-god Nereus by different mothers. Hederich described
them as human in shape from the waist up, though covered with bluish
scales and having sea ivy for hair and gills under their ears, and as dolphin-
shaped from the waist down, except for feet like those of sea horses.

Fruits of your kind will are they;
To treasures shipwrecked here and drowned
You guided us with pleasant sound,
You guardian spirits of our bay.

SIRENS. Fishes frolic, we well know,
Cool in ocean depths below,
Friskly living as they wish;   8060
But, you festive, lively band,
We should like to understand
If you are something more than fish.

NEREIDS AND TRITONS. We gave some thought, before we came,
To just the matter that you name.
Sisters, brothers, near and far,
Off we go! One journey brief,
And we have proofs to force belief
That more than fish we surely are.

(*They withdraw.*)

SIRENS. Off at once they race,   8070
Making straight for Samothrace,
Gone with a favoring wind.
What can they be hoping to gain
In the lofty Cabiri's domain? [2]
They are gods! yet uniquely odd,
Self-creating and perpetuating,
Yet never knowing what they are.
   Tarry at zenith there,
Luna gracious and most fair,
So the night may delay   8080
And we be not hurried toward day.

THALES (*by the shore, to* HOMUNCULUS).
I'd like to take you to old Nereus now,

---

2. The Cabiri were Hellenized Oriental deities whose mystery cult was prac-
ticed on the island of Samothrace. Goethe is here poking fun at the Romantic
philosophers Creuzer and Schelling, who speculated elaborately on the obscure nature of the Cabiri (Creuzer's *Symbolik und Mythologie der alten
Völker*, 1810–12, and Schelling's *Über die Gottheiten von Samothrace*, 1815).

We're not far from his cave here anyhow.
But he's an old hardheaded cuss,
Crusty and cantankerous;
The entire race of human kind
Is never right to his sour mind;
And yet he knows the future; hence
People pay him reverence
And honor him for his great fame.   8090
Besides, he has helped many too.

HOMUNCULUS. Let's knock and see what he will do.
It will not cost my glass and flame.

NEREUS. Are those human voices in my ear?
They give me gripes and colic just to hear!
Creatures striving to become like gods,
And yet condemned to be themselves, poor clods!
For years I could have had a godlike rest
If I had not felt bound to help the best.
But when at last their deeds materialized,   8100
It was as if I never had advised.

THALES. Yet, Old Man of the Sea, in you we trust;
You are the man of wisdom, do not thrust
Us off! This semblance of a man, this flame,
Will follow your advice, for which he came.

NEREUS. Advice! When did advice prevail with man?
On stubborn ear a wise word falls in vain.
Let them denounce their actions all they can,
Self-willed as ever mortals still remain.
I once warned Paris, fatherly, before   8110
He lured a foreign wife to break the law;
He stood there boldly on the Grecian shore
And I predicted as my mind foresaw:—
The pouring smoke, red floods of fire, the glow
Of blazing rafters, carnage and death below,
Troy's day of doom—fast bound by poets' rhyme,[3]
A terror and a portent for all time.

---

3. See Vergil, *Aeneid* II.

The scoffer jeered at all that I could tell,
He followed his own lusts, and Ilium fell.
That giant corpse, its agony once ceased,   8120
Gave Pindus' eagles a right welcome feast.
Ulysses too! I told him without error
Beforehand: Circe's wiles, the Cyclops' terror,
His own delay, the folly of his crew,
And more besides, and what good did it do?
Till he, much buffeted by storms was cast
By favoring wave on friendly shore at last.

THALES. Such behavior causes wise men pain,
But good men will, however, try again.
A grain of gratitude will still outweigh   8130
The tons of thanklessness of common pay.
It's no slight question we ask you to solve;
This lad here wisely wishes to evolve.

NEREUS. Don't spoil my pleasantest of moods this way.
Quite different things are on my mind today.
I've bidden all my daughters come to me,
The Dorides, the Graces of the sea.[4]
Neither Olympus nor your country bears [5]
Forms half so fine and beautiful as theirs.
They leap with the most agile grace of motion   8140
From water dragon to the steeds of ocean,
And in the element are so at home
They seem uplifted by the very foam.
In Venus' sea-shell-car of rainbow hues
Will come my Galatea, whom they choose
The fairest, whom in Paphos they adore
As goddess since great Cypris left our shore.[6]
My lovely girl has this long time been known
As heiress to the templed town and chariot-throne.
     Away! Heart must not hate, nor lips employ   8150

---

4. The Dorides are the daughters of Nereus and the nymph Doris and hence
are reckoned among the Nereids.
5. Thales came from Miletus in Asia Minor.
6. Cypris is Venus, whose favorite shrine was in the town of Paphos on the
island of Cyprus.

Harsh words in this hour of a father's joy.
Away to Proteus! He has information
Of evolution and of transformation.

(*Withdraws toward the sea.*)

THALES. Our coming here has gained us little ground,
And Proteus only vanishes when found.
If he replies at all, he vexes you
With things astounding, and perplexes you.
You really do need counsel, though; so let us
Try him out and see where that will get us.

(*They withdraw.*)

SIRENS (*on the cliffs above*). What things now may these be,   8160
Cleaving waves of sea,
As though the white of sail
Advanced before the gale?
A sea-nymph constellation
In bright transfiguration.
Let us climb down; more near
The voices will be clear.
NEREIDS AND TRITONS. What we so cherish here
Shall bring you all great cheer.
Chelone's giant shield [7]   8170
Bears grave shapes in its field:
Gods here to you we bring,
Hence you must paeans sing.
SIRENS. Little in height,
Potent in might,
Hoar gods of the wave
Who foundering sailors save.
NEREIDS AND TRITONS. To joyous banqueting
We the Cabiri bring;
Where these wield sacred sway,   8180
There Neptune grants smooth way.
SIRENS. We yield to you;

---

7. Chelone was a nymph who was transformed into a giant turtle.

In shipwreck's hour
With irresistible power
You rescue the crew.

NEREIDS AND TRITONS. Three have we brought with us,
The fourth would not come with us;
He said that only he
Thought for the other three.[8]

SIRENS. One god may, if he will,   8190
Mock other gods; but you
To all give honor due,
Shun every harm and ill.

NEREIDS AND TRITONS. They are seven actually.

SIRENS. Where are the other three?

NEREIDS AND TRITONS. We have no notion. Seek
Them on Olympus peak.
They say an eighth there dwells
Of whom none knows or tells.
All are kindly disposed;   8200
Their number is undisclosed.
    These incomparables aspire
Ever higher, ever higher,
Starvelings riddled with desire
For the unattainable.

SIRENS. We give its own
To every throne
Within the zone
Of sun and moon.

NEREIDS AND TRITONS. Our glory shines in utmost splendor,   8210
Conducting this festival.

SIRENS. The heroes of story
Lack for glory

---

8. From here to l. 8224 Goethe whimsically plays with the conflicting statements of ancient speculators (Varro, Augustinus) and of contemporary speculators (Creuzer, Schelling) as to the number, nature, function, and appearance of the Cabiri. The Nereids and Tritons rehearse the bewildering
information in the mythological handbooks like dutiful students returning from
a thankless library research project, while the Sirens reply with a mixture of
irony and sober counsel to revere all gods.

Wherever it shines in splendor,
Though once they won the golden fleece,
O ye Cabiri.

(*repeated in full chorus*)

Though once they won the golden fleece,
O we⎱
O ye⎰ Cabiri.

(*The* NEREIDS *and* TRITONS *pass on.*)

HOMUNCULUS. These shapeless figures look to me
   Like old pots made of lead   8220
   On which the wise man foolishly
   Knocks his stubborn head.
THALES. That's just the thing that they want most.
   The coin is valued for its rust.
PROTEUS (*unnoticed*). Here's something for the tales I spin,
   The odder things are, the more respect they win.
THALES. Where are you, Proteus?
PROTEUS (*ventriloquizing, now nearby, now far away*).
                     Here!—And here!
THALES. I pardon your stale joke. Appear!
   Don't trick a friend with words. You throw
   Your voice from some false spot, I know.   8230
PROTEUS (*as though in the distance*).
   Farewell!
THALES (*softly to* HOMUNCULUS).
         He's right close by. Now flash your light.
   He's curious as a fish at night.
   In any shape, hide where he may,
   A flame will lure him right away.
HOMUNCULUS. I'll flash as much light as I dare;
   My glass will smash if I don't take good care.
PROTEUS (*in the form of a giant turtle*).
   What shines with such a lovely light?
THALES (*muffling* HOMUNCULUS).
   Good! If you like, come up for closer seeing.
   Do not begrudge an effort that's so slight,

And come on two feet as a human being.   8240
Let it be with our pleasure, with our will,
Whoever wants to see what we conceal.
PROTEUS (*in a noble form*).
You still can do the sophist dodge, I see.
THALES. And shifting shapes is still your specialty.

(*He has unveiled* HOMUNCULUS.)

PROTEUS (*astonished*).
Well, this beats anything! A dwarf that lights.
THALES. He would like to evolve, and seeks advice.
I understand from him his birth
Bizarrely put just half of him on earth.
He has no lack of mental qualities
But sadly wants the practicalities.   8250
Without his glass he has no weight at all,
And so he craves to be corporeal.
PROTEUS. Real virginal nativity:
You are, before you were supposed to be.
THALES (*softly*). Another aspect would seem critical—
He is, I think, hermaphroditical.
PROTEUS. All the sooner to succeed:
Any place will suit his need.
This takes no long thought on our part,
It's in the far-flung sea that you must start.   8260
The first beginnings must be small,
Minutest things make up the diet,
Ensuing growth is gradual,
Till fuller consummation is won by it.
HOMUNCULUS. There is a softness in this air,
Green fragrance that I love wafts everywhere.[9]
PROTEUS. That, dear lad, I well understand.
And further on, the sweet smells get

---

9. "Green fragrance . . . wafts" renders Goethe's *es grunelt,* an expression
which he coined and used here and elsewhere, but which never made its way
into the German language. He intended the phrase to mean, "there is a fragrance abroad as of fresh green things," particularly the smell that follows a
summer rain.

Still sweeter, on this tongue of land
The fragrances are sweeter yet.   8270
See where the great processioned host
Is moving in along our coast.
Come on along!
THALES.   I'm with you too!
HOMUNCULUS. Here's a striking spirit trio!

[Finale]

TELCHINES *from Rhodes*[10] *arrive on hippo-*
campi[11] *and sea serpents, brandishing Nep-*
tune's trident.

CHORUS [OF TELCHINES].
The trident we forged wherewith Neptune assuages
The ocean's wild waves in their fiercest of rages.
If clouds are outspread at the Thunderer's word,
Still Neptune will counter the storms they have stirred,
And though from above jagged lightnings strike low,
Still wave after wave is pitched up from below;   8280
And all who amid them with anguish have striven
Are buffeted long, then to death they are given.
Today then the scepter to us he has lent,
Serenely we drift in our festive content.
SIRENS. To you who Helios profess,
Whom cheerful days forever bless,
We offer greeting in this hour

---

10. From various ancient authors, as well as from Hederich, Goethe has assembled information to create his Telchines: primeval inhabitants of the island of Rhodes, metal workers, worshipers of Helios (the sun) but reverent
with respect to Helios' sister Luna (the moon), and a people convinced that
the human body is the most perfect of all forms, hence alone worthy to represent the gods. In this matter they are higher than the worshipers of the
Cabiri, whose images were, like primitive funerary urns, pot-shaped with
heads on the top of them.
11. Hippocampi are sea beasts, fore part horse, rear part dolphin.

That witnesses high Luna's power.

TELCHINES. O loveliest goddess at zenith upraised,
  Thou hear'st with delight when thy brother is praised.   8290
  To Rhodes of fair blessing thy ear thou wilt lend,
  For paeans eternal to him there ascend.
  At start of his day-course and when it is done
  He gazes on us with the gaze of the sun.
  With mountains and cities the god finds delight,
  The shore and the wave are both fair in his sight.
  No fog shrouds us in, and should one appear,
  One sunbeam, one breeze, and the island is clear.
  His form the high god beholds multiplied there
  As youth, as colossus, the great and the fair.[12]   8300
  We were of all peoples the first who began
  To dignify gods with the aspect of man.

PROTEUS. Begrudge them not their boastful singing;
  To the holy and life-bringing
  Sun, their dead works are mere jest.
  Tirelessly they smelt and cast,
  And when the bronze is poured at last
  They claim a feat and are impressed.
  What does it come to, this renown?
  Their statues tower fine and grand—   8310
  An earthquake topples them in sand,
  And there's scrap metal to melt down.
  Earth-toil, whatever it may be,
  Is nothing more than drudgery;
  Life in water better fares.
  To water, Proteus-dolphin bears
  You now, to waves of ceaseless motion.

(*He transforms himself.*)

There best fortune will bestead you,
I'll take you on my back and wed you

---

12. The allusion is to the Colossus of Rhodes, once one of the seven wonders
of the ancient world, but overthrown by an earthquake. It represented Helios
with his huge legs straddling the harbor, high enough for ships to pass underneath.

To the everlasting ocean.   8320
THALES. Yield to this laudable desire,
  And from creation's start, aspire.
  Prepare for work at rapid rate.
  You'll pass there by eternal norms
  Through a thousand thousand forms,
  With time you will gain human state.

(HOMUNCULUS *mounts upon the back of* PROTEUS-*dolphin.*)

PROTEUS. In spirit follow to the liquid world,
  Life's length and breadth for you lie there unfurled;
  There you can move which way you will.
  But don't let higher orders lure you,   8330
  For, once a man, I can assure you,
  You've passed all grades there are to fill.
THALES. May be; but there are poorer stunts
  Than being a real man for once.
PROTEUS (*to* THALES). One of your stamp, I suppose!
  They last a good while, men like those;
  Wherever the wan ghost parade appears
  I've seen you now for several hundred years.
SIRENS (*on the cliffs*). What a ring of cloudlets gyres
  Richly round the moon tonight!   8340
  Doves they are, lit with love-fires,
  Pinions pure and snowy white.
  Only Paphos could so send
  Ardent bird droves here to us.[13]
  Our festival comes to an end
  In joy supreme and rapturous.
NEREUS (*coming up to* THALES).
  Nocturnal travelers might maintain
  That moon-ring was mere play of light,
  But we spirits entertain
  Different notions, and we are right.   8350
  Doves they are, and they escort
  My daughter's journey up the sea

---

13. Doves were Venus' birds; Paphos held her favorite shrine.

In homing flights of wondrous sort
Learned in lost antiquity.
THALES. That I would also deem the best—
What pleases this good man as well—
When in a warm and quiet nest
Sacred things have life and dwell.[14]
PSYLLI AND MARSI [15] (*on sea bulls, sea calves, and sea rams*).
In Cyprus' rugged cavern lairs
Unsilted by the sea-god,   8360
Unshaken by the earthquake-god,
Fanned by eternal airs,
And, as in ancient days afar,
With quiet contentment we are
The guards of the Cyprian's car,
And through the rustlings of night,
Through braided waves and bright,
Concealed from latter-day sight,
We escort this loveliest daughter here.
Neither Eagle nor Wingèd Lion [16]   8370
Deters the work they spy on,
Neither Cross nor Crescent
In power recrudescent
With empires shifting, swaying,
Exiling men and slaying,
Harvest and town in ashes laying.
Evermore
We escort our lady to this shore.

---

14. This distressingly lame and unpoetic quatrain is interpreted: "I agree with
Nereus in preferring an explanation that shows the marvels of an animate
Nature, rather than a crassly mechanical explanation which would see the
strange clouds as merely accidental effects of moonlight."
15. Actually snake charmers, of classical Africa and classical Italy respectively. Goethe makes them primeval inhabitants of windy and rugged Cyprus,
as opposed to lovely Rhodes, and assigns them both guardianship and escort
of the chariot-throne (l. 8149), once Venus' own but now the inheritance of
Galatea (8144–49), which was normally stored in a sacred place in the town
of Paphos (8147, 8343) at the western end of the island of Cyprus.
16. Successive conquerors of the island of Cyprus: the Roman empire (the
Eagle), and Venice (the Wingèd Lion). Two lines below, the Cross and the
Crescent stand, of course, for Christianity and Islam.

SIRENS. Lightly moving, in tempered haste [17]
    Round the chariot, ring on ring,   8380
    Line on line now interlaced,
    Now untwining, altering,
    Come, you lusty Nereides,
    Hearty women, sportive, wild,
    Bring, you tender Dorides,
    Galatea, her mother's child.
    Grave and godlike is her mien,
    Worthy immortality,
    Yet, like earthly women, seen
    Possessed of sweet amenity.   8390
DORIDES (*mounted all on dolphins and passing in chorus before*
    NEREUS).
    Lend us, Luna, light and shadow,
    On these youths shed clarity;
    We submit beloved bridegrooms
    To our father's charity.

    (*to* NEREUS)

    These youths we saved from savage surf,
    From breakers on the shipwrecked shore;
    On beds of reeds and mossy turf
    We warmed them back to life once more.
    They now must pay with ardent kisses
    For our care and tendernesses.   8400
    Show them favor, we implore.
NEREUS. Such double profit is a treasure:
    Showing mercy and obtaining pleasure.
DORIDES. If you approve of our endeavor,
    Grant us a joy well earned: say we
    May hold them in our arms forever,
    O father, youths immortally.

---

17. The marine vision of Galatea in this Finale is based partly on the description by Philostratus (born *ca.* A.D. 190) of a lost painting from antiquity, in his *Imagines* II. 18. Goethe was highly enthusiastic about this odd book, which consists of 65 rhetorical *tours de force* whereby paintings are evoked in words, and in 1818 wrote an essay on it entitled *Philostrats Gemälde.*

NEREUS. To profit from your handsome catch,
  You need to form these youths as men;
  But what you ask me to dispatch   8410
  Lies solely in great Zeus's ken.
  The wave in which you sway and swim
  Makes love unsteadfast in its stand,
  And if affection flickers dim,
  Set them conveniently on land.
DORIDES. We love you dearly, handsome youths,
  But sadly we must go;
  We wanted everlasting troths;
  Gods would not have it so.
THE YOUTHS. If only you would keep us on,   8420
  Each gallant sailor lad;
  This is the best life we have had,
  We want no other one.

(GALATEA *approaches on her chariot-shell.*) [18]

NEREUS. It's you, O my darling!
GALATEA.   O father! Delight!
  Linger, my dolphins! I cling to his sight!
NEREUS. Past, past already is their throng
  In an arc of widening wake!
  What heed for my heart's feelings do they take?
  O, if they would take me along!
  Yet such delight is in one gaze   8430
  As makes up for a year of days.
THALES. Hail! Hail! Pierced through
  With the beautiful and true,
  What youth I feel again!
  Everything out of water began!
  Everything does the water sustain!
  Ocean, grant us your ceaseless reign!
  Were there no clouds by you outspread,
  Were no rich brooklets by you fed,
  Nor rivers down their courses sped,   8440

18. See "Triumph of Galatea," illustrations.

Nor streams brimmed full bed after bed,
Where would our world be, or mountain, or plain?
It is you who the freshness of life still maintain.
ECHO (*chorus of all groups*).
Out of you is drawn all the life we sustain.
NEREUS. Again, far out, they pass this shore,
But glance to glance is brought no more;
In widening circles dancing,
Festively advancing,
Their countless hosts toward ocean veer.
But Galatea's chariot-shell   8450
I see across the surge and swell.
It gleams like a star
Through the crowd.
Things loved shine bright amid a crowd!
However far,
Shimmering bright and clear,
Ever true and near.
HOMUNCULUS. Amid this watery sphere
Things I shine on appear
Gloriously fair.   8460
PROTEUS.   Only in this sphere
Will your light send out clear
Its glorious ringing flare.
NEREUS. Ah, look! What new mystery, fraught with surprise,
Out there in those hosts is revealed to our eyes?
What flames by her shell at the feet of my child?
Immense is its glowing, now mellow and mild,
As if with love's throbbing and pulses it played.
THALES. That is Homunculus, by Proteus conveyed . . .
And those are the symptoms of masterly yearning,   8470
I sense the fierce torment and throes of his burning,
He will shatter his glass on that star-shining car.
There! There spurts the flame as it gushes afar!
SIRENS. What marvel of fire lights the waves as they dash
Against one another with glittering clash?
Such shining and waving and blazing of light,
All forms are aglow on the path of the night

And all things are bathed in a vastness of flame.
Prevail then great Eros whence everything came!
   Hail to the sea! Hail to the waves   8480
Which sacred fire in brilliance laves!
Hail to water! To fire, all hail!
Hail, rare marvel of this tale!
   Hail to gently coursing airs!
Hail to earth's mysterious lairs!
Honor be forevermore
To you elements all four!

Act Three

Before the Palace of Menelaus in Sparta

Enter Helen *and a* Chorus *of captive
Trojan women.* Panthalis *is the chorus
leader.*

HELEN. Admired so much, so much inveighed against, I, Helen,
  Now come here from the shore where first we disembarked,
  Unsteady still from all the tumbling motion of   8490
  The rocking waves that from the Phrygian plains [1] have brought
  Us on their crested backs, by favor of Poseidon
  And by the strength of Euros,[2] to these homeland bays.
  Down there King Menelaus now rejoices at
  Return together with the bravest of his warriors.
  But you should bid me welcome home, O lofty house
  Which Tyndareos, my father, after his return
  From Pallas' hill erected close beside this slope
  And which, while I with Clytemnestra for a sister

---

1. The plains of Troy.
2. The east wind.

Grew up at happy play, with Castor too and Pollux,   8500
He beautified above all houses here in Sparta.
You I salute as well, you double doors of bronze.
Upon your hospitable swinging wide I once
Saw Menelaus, chosen one from many, shine
In radiance as a bridegroom coming toward me.
Now open them once more so that, as suits a spouse,
I may perform the urgent bidding of the King.
Admit me, and let everything remain behind
Which has till now around me stormed so fatefully.
For since the time I left this threshold, free of care,   8510
To visit Cytherea's temple, as duty bade,
And was abducted by the Phrygian pirate there,
So much has come to pass, which people far and wide
Like to relate but which offends the ears of him
Of whom the growing saga has become a legend.
CHORUS. Do not, majestic lady, disdain
  Supremest honor of all possessions.
  For the greatest fortune is granted to you,
  The fame of beauty outreaching all others.
  A hero's name resounds before him,   8520
  Hence he walks proudly,
  And yet the mind of stubbornest man
  At the all-compulsion of beauty will bend.
HELEN. Enough! I sailed here with my husband in a ship
  And am now sent ahead by him into his city,
  With what intention, I, however, have not guessed.
  Do I come as his spouse? Do I come as his Queen?
  Do I come as a victim for his bitter pain
  And for the long endured misfortunes of the Greeks?
  Conquered I am, but if a captive, I know not.   8530
  My fame and fate were by the immortals predicted
  Ambiguously, those dubious ones attendant on
  A form of beauty, who upon this very threshold
  Stand at my side with presence dark and menacing.
  For even in the hollow ship my husband looked
  At me but rarely, and he spoke no heartening word.
  He sat across from me as if he brooded mischief.

But when the lead-ships' prows had barely greeted land
On their way up the deeply recessed shoreline of
Eurotas' bay, he said as though the god inspired him: 8540
"My men of war will disembark in order here,
And on the seashore I shall marshal them in ranks.
But you shall travel on ahead, proceeding up
The fertile bank of the Eurotas straight along,
Steering your steeds across the dewy meadow flowers
Until you have arrived upon the level plain
Where Lacedaemon, once a broad and fruited field
Surrounded by stern mountains close at hand, is built.
Then go within the princely house that towers aloft
And marshal all the maids whom I there left behind   8550
Together with the shrewd and aged stewardess.
Have her unlock for you the ample stores of treasure
Just as your father left them and which I myself
In peace and war had added to unfailingly.
You will discover everything in order there;
That is a prince's privilege, to find everything
Aright within his house at his return and each
Thing in its proper place exactly as he left it;
For menials have authority to alter nothing."
CHORUS. Regale your eye and heart on this hoard   8560
    Of treasure steadily thus replenished,
    For embellishment of chains and the crown's
    Adornment rest there in haughty repose.
    Go in at once and challenge them all,
    They muster with speed;
    I love to behold beauty contesting
    Against gold and pearls and the splendor of gems.
HELEN. Then followed the master's further word of command:
    "Now when you have examined everything in order,
    Then take as many tripods as you think required   8570
    And all the sorts of vessels which the sacrificer
    Desires to have at hand when performing solemn rites,
    The cauldrons and the bowls, flat altar plates as well,
    And let the purest water from the sacred spring
    Be in the cruets; further, let dry kindling wood

That eagerly accepts the flames, be ready there;
And finally let a whetted knife be not omitted.
All other things I will entrust to your sole care."
Such were his words as he pressed my departure; but
No living thing was signified in his commands   8580
That he might slay to honor the Olympians.
This is suspicious, but I take no further thought
And leave all things to the decision of high gods,
Who will fulfill whatever their minds have conceived,
No matter whether human beings deem it good
Or deem it evil; we as mortals must endure it.
And often priests have raised aloft the heavy ax
In consecration of the earth-bent animal
And yet could not complete the act, prevented by
The intervention of a nearby foe or god.   8590
CHORUS. What will happen now you cannot guess.
     Go on your way then, O Queen,
     Strong of heart.
     Evil and good befall
     Mankind unexpectedly.
     Though foretold, we credit it not.
     Troy was destroyed, and we did behold
     Death with our eyes, a death with shame.
     And are we not here
     Your companions, serving you,   8600
     Seeing the heavens' dazzling sunlight
     And the fairest of earth,
     Yourself, with homage, to our good fortune?
HELEN. Whatever may impend, it now beseems me to
     Ascend without delay into the royal house
     Which, so long missed, much yearned for, almost lost
          through folly,
     Stands once again before my eyes, I know not how.
     My footsteps do not bear me quite so nimbly up
     These high steps as when I raced up them as a child.

     (*Exit.*)

CHORUS. Cast, O my sisters, you   8610

Captives disheartened,
All your sorrows afar.
Share in your mistress' joy,
Share you in Helen's joy,
Who to her father's house and hearth
With, I grant, a tardy returning,
Yet with all the more gladsome
Foot, approaches here now.
  Praise all the holy,
Gladly restoring,   8620
Homeward-conducting gods.
Delivered ones float
As if upon wings
Over the harshest fate, while in vain
Captives full of yearning
Grieve from their prison battlements
With arms outstretched in anguish.
  But she was seized by a god,
This distant one,
And from Ilium's ruins   8630
He bore her, bringing her back
To the old, yet newly refurbished
House of her fathers
After unspeakable
Delights and torments,
To recall afresh
The former times of her youth.

PANTHALIS (*as leader of the* CHORUS).
Abandon now the joy-surrounded path of song
And turn your gaze up toward the double portal wings.
What do I see there, sisters? Does the Queen not come   8640
Back out to us with agitation's rapid step?
What is it, lofty Queen? What dreadful thing can have
Confronted you inside your house's halls instead
Of greetings from your people? You can not dissemble,
For I can well discern abhorrence on your brow
And noble anger there contending with surprise.

HELEN (*who has left the double doors open, excited*).

No vulgar fear beseems the daughter of high Zeus,
No lightly grazing hand of horror can touch her;
And yet the terror which, arising from the womb
Of ancient Night and time primeval, surges up   8650
As glowing clouds of many shapes out of the mountain's
Abyss of fire, will even shake a hero's heart.
The Stygian gods today have so with horror marked
My entrance to this house, that like a guest dismissed,
I feel as though I want to leave and go away
From this long-yearned-for threshold once so often crossed.
No! I came here, retreating toward the light, nor shall
You drive me further, Powers, whoever you may be.
I shall devise a consecrating rite; once cleansed,
The hearth may welcome both the consort and the lord.   8660
CHORUS LEADER. Discover, noble lady, to your serving-women
      Who reverently support you, what thing has befallen.
HELEN. What I saw, you yourselves shall see with your own eyes,
      Unless it be that ancient Night has re-engulfed
      Her creatures in her wondrous womb immediately.
      But so that you may know, I tell you now in words:
      As I stepped solemnly within the interior of
      The royal house, intent upon immediate duties,
      I wondered at the stillness of deserted halls.
      No sound of busy servitors fell on my ear,   8670
      No rapid industry was there to meet my gaze,
      Before me there appeared no maid, no stewardess,
      Who used to greet all visitors in friendly fashion.
      But then when I approached the bosom of the hearth
      I saw by the yet warm remains of smoldering ash
      A tall, veiled woman sitting there upon the floor,
      Not so much like one sleeping as like one in thought.
      In accents of command I summoned her to work,
      Supposing her to be the stewardess appointed
      Perhaps by foresight of my spouse as he departed;   8680
      But motionless she sat still muffled in her veil;
      Then at my threats at last she lifted her right arm
      As though she were dismissing me from hearth and hall.
      I turned away from her in anger, hurrying

Up toward the steps on which the thalamos is raised [3]
Aloft in splendor, and near by the treasure room.
But suddenly the marvel leaped up from the floor
Barring my way imperiously and showed herself
In haggard height and with her hollow bloodshot eyes,
A creature strange and weird, confusing sight and mind.   8690
Yet I speak to the winds, for words but vainly strive
To body forth a form with true creative power.
But there behold her! She is venturing to the light!
We are the masters here until the King arrives.
The hideous brood of Night will be expelled by Phoebus,
Friend of Beauty, into caves or subjugated.

(PHORKYAS *appears on the threshold between the door-*
posts.)

CHORUS. Much have I known, although my locks
   Youthfully wave around my temples.
   Horrible things I often have seen,
   Anguish of warfare, Ilium's night   8700
   When it fell.
      Through the beclouded, dust-overdarkened
   Tumult of warriors, gods I have heard
   Fearfully crying; I have heard Discord's
   Brazen voice resound through the field
   Rampartwards.
      Ah! They still were standing, Ilium's
   Ramparts, but the blaze of the flames
   Already was darting from neighbor to neighbor
   Spreading afar from here and from there   8710
   With the blowing of very tempest
   Over the night and the city.
      Fleeing I saw through smoke and blaze
   And the glaring of tongues of flame
   Gods approaching in ghastly anger,
   Stalking figures of wonder,
   Giant-sized through dismal

---

3. The nuptial chamber.

Mist underlighted with fire.
  Saw I such, or did my mind
Anguish-gripped only imagine   8720
Such confusion of things? That I
Cannot tell; but that I behold
Ghastliness here with my own eyes,
This much I surely know;
I could even reach out and touch it,
Did not fear restrain me now
From the perilous thing.
  Which one of Phorkys'
Daughters then are you?
For I must liken you   8730
To that race.
Are you perchance one of the Graiae,[4]
Grey-haired at birth and using only
A single eye and a single tooth
Alternately among you?
  How dare you, Horror,
Stand beside Beauty
In the all-seeing
Eye of Phoebus?
Nevertheless step forward now,   8740
For he sees no ugliness
Just as his sacred eye has never
Yet beheld the shadow.
  But we mortals, alas, are constrained
By a dismal and sorry fate
To our eyes' unspeakable pain,
Pain that is roused in beauty-lovers
By the contemptible, by the unholy.
  Therefore hear, if you now approach
In your insolence, hear curses,   8750
Hear all sorts of threats and abuse
From the cursing mouths of the happy
Who were created by the gods.

---

4. The commoner name for the Phorkyads.

PHORKYAS. Trite is the saying, but its sense retains high truth,
    That Shame and Beauty hand in hand have never yet
    Pursued their way together across green paths of earth.
    Deep-rooted dwells in both of them an old aversion
    So that, encountering one another on any road,
    Each one will turn its back upon its old opponent.
    Then each one hurries on again more speedily,   8760
    With Shame downcast, with Beauty insolent of mood,
    Until at last the hollow night of Orcus takes
    Them in, unless old age has overwhelmed them first.
    I find you now, you insolent ones, come here from lands
    Afar, exuding haughtiness, like the procession
    Of raucous cranes that croak their way above our heads
    And from a long outstretching cloud send down their cry
    That lures the quiet traveler to lift his gaze
    Into the sky; yet they pursue their onward way,
    As he goes his. And so it will befall with us.   8770
    Who, then, are you that you should rage about the King's
    High palace wild as maenads and like drunken women?
    And who are you that you should bay the stewardess
    Of this house as a pack of dogs bays at the moon?
    Do you think it is hidden from me of what race
    You come, you war-begotten, battle-nurtured brood?
    Man-crazy and seducing as well as seduced,
    Unnerving both the warrior's and the citizen's strength!
    Seeing your throng, I feel as though a swarm of locusts
    Were settling down and covering green planted fields.   8780
    Consumers of another's labor! Ravenous
    Destroyers of prosperity that had grown up!
    —And you a conquered article of sale and barter!
HELEN. Whoever in the mistress' presence rails at servants
    Presumptuously offends against her household rights,
    For it beseems no one but her to praise their merits
    Or to chastise in any case where wrong is done.
    And I am wholly satisfied with all the service
    They rendered me when the high might of Ilium
    Stood under siege and fell and lay; and no less so   8790
    When we endured the woeful shifts of fortune on

Our voyage where each one thinks usually of himself.
Here I expect the like from all this cheerful crew.
A master asks, not what a servant is, but how
He serves. Therefore be silent and stop grinning at them.
If you have watched the King's house carefully till now
And filled the mistress' place, that will count toward
      your praise;
But she herself has now arrived, therefore step down
Lest there be punishment instead of earned reward.

PHORKYAS. The threatening of menials is a privilege still   8800
Which a god-favored master's lofty spouse may earn
By long years of wise management of household matters.[5]
And now that you, acknowledged Queen and mistress of
This house, have once again resumed your former place,
Take up the reins that have long since gone slack, and rule;
Take charge now of the treasure and of all of us.
But first of all, protect me as the elder from
This crew, which here beside your beauty's swan are only
A flock of wretched-plumed and idly chattering geese.

CHORUS LEADER. How ugly ugliness shows up at beauty's side.   8810
PHORKYAS. How foolish folly looks beside intelligence.

*(From here on the chorus members reply individually as
they step forth out of the* CHORUS.*)*

FIRST CHORUS MAIDEN.
Of Father Erebus [6] tell us, tell us of Mother Night.
PHORKYAS. Then you tell me of Scylla, who is your born sister.
SECOND CHORUS MAIDEN.
Your family tree sprouts with a quantity of monsters.

---

5. Here, at l. 265 of the scene, ended the fragment entitled *Helena,* which
Goethe composed in 1800.
6. A round of name-calling in which each term denotes either the oldest of
the old or the ugliest of the ugly. Erebus is Darkness, brother of Night and
son of Chaos, primitive deities from the beginning of time. The six-headed
monster Scylla fed on six sailors at a time. Tiresias, the blind Theban seer
who had in his time lived as both man and woman, was immemorially old.
Orion is one of the earliest identifications in mythology. The winged Harpies
would carry off people and food, and often defile with their excrement what
was left behind.

PHORKYAS. Go down to Orcus and look up your relatives.
THIRD CHORUS MAIDEN.

All those that dwell down there are far too young for you.
PHORKYAS. Tiresias the ancient, go make love to him.
FOURTH CHORUS MAIDEN.

Orion's nurse was your great-great-great-granddaughter.
PHORKYAS. The Harpies, I imagine, fed you on their filth.
FIFTH CHORUS MAIDEN.

What do you feed on to keep up your tended leanness?   8820
PHORKYAS.

Not with fresh blood, for which you show yourselves so greedy.
SIXTH CHORUS MAIDEN.

While you are greedy for the corpses, loathsome corpses!
PHORKYAS. Long vampire fangs shine in your insolent big mouths.
CHORUS LEADER.

Yours I could shut right up by telling who you are.
PHORKYAS.

Tell your name first and then the riddle will be solved.
HELEN. Not in anger but in grief I step between you,
     Forbidding such alternate rounds of blustering;
     For nothing more prejudicial can befall a master
     Than loyal servants' secretly contrived cabals.
     The echo of his commands does not come back to him   8830
     Harmoniously in swiftly executed action.
     No, storming with self-will it rages all around him
     As in his own bewilderment he scolds in vain.
     Nor is that all. You have in your ill-tempered wrath
     Evoked unblessed images of horrid shape
     That throng around me till I feel myself dragged down
     To Orcus in despite of my ancestral fields.
     Is this remembrance? Did illusion seize on me?
     Was I all that? Am I? Or am I to become so?
     The dream and horror image of that town-destroyer? [7]   8840
     My maidens quail, but you who are the eldest, you
     Stand calmly. Speak to me in words of prudent sense.
PHORKYAS. Remembering long years of fortune manifold,

---

7. So Euripides contemptuously terms Helen in *The Trojan Women*.

One finds a dream the highest favor of the gods.
But you, high favored past all measure and all limit,
Saw in your life's course only men inflamed with love,
Swift-kindled to bold enterprise of every sort.
Aroused to passion, Theseus seized you while still young,
Like Heracles strong, a splendid figure of a man—

HELEN. And carried me away, a slim and ten-yeared fawn,   8850
Up to Aphidnus' citadel in Attica.[8]

PHORKYAS. By Castor and by Pollux presently set free,
You were sought for on every side by crowds of heroes.

HELEN. Yet silent favor, as I readily confess,
Patroclus won, Pelides' second self,[9] from me.

PHORKYAS. Your father's will betrothed you, though, to Menelaus,
Bold rover of the sea and house-sustainer too.

HELEN. He gave his daughter to him and his kingdom's rule.
But from his wedlock then was born Hermione.

PHORKYAS. But while he fought to gain the heritage of Crete   8860
An all too handsome guest came where you were so lonely.

HELEN. Why must you now recall that semi-widowhood?
And what disaster direly came of it for me?

PHORKYAS. That journey also brought captivity and long
Enslavement for me, who was once a free-born Cretan.

HELEN. But he immediately made you his stewardess,
Entrusting much, both citadel and treasure, to you.

PHORKYAS. Which you deserted, turning to the towered town
Of Ilium and never-ending joys of love.

HELEN. Do not recall those joys! for an infinity   8870
Of all too bitter grief afflicted my heart and head.

PHORKYAS. Yet people say that you appeared in double form
And were seen both in Ilium and Egypt too.[10]

---

8. Aphidnus was a friend of Theseus. Compare ll. 7414–33 above. In order to have a daughter of Zeus for his wife, after his first wife Phaedra had hanged herself, Theseus kidnapped the girl Helen; Aphidnus guarded her until she was marriageable. Variant versions of the story are given in Diodorus Siculus, IV. 63; Hyginus, Fable 79; and Plutarch, *Theseus* 31.

9. Pelides is Achilles. Their great friendship is a major theme in the *Iliad*.

10. Euripides made a play out of the ancient legend that the true Helen spent the time of the Trojan War in Egypt while her phantom double (eidolon) went to Troy and caused all the disasters there.

HELEN. Do not disrange completely sense already wild.
  Not even now do I know fully who I am.
PHORKYAS. They also tell that from the hollow realm of shades
  Achilles also in his ardor rose to join
  You, whom he loved despite the will of destiny.
HELEN. I, as eidolon, joined with him, eidolon also.
  It was a dream, as the reports themselves maintain.   8880
  I fade away, and to myself am an eidolon.

(*She sinks into the arms of the semi-chorus.*[11])

CHORUS. Silence! Silence!
  You evil-eyed speaker of evil!
  Out of such hideous, one-toothed
  Mouth, what could be exhaled from
  Such a loathsome gulf of horror!
    For the malignant posing as kindly,
  Wolf's fury under sheep's woolly fleece,
  Seems to me far worse than the three-
  headed dog-monster's jaws.   8890
  Anxiously harkening we stand here:
  When? How? Where will it burst forth,
  This monster's deeply
  Hidden guile as it stalks its prey?
    Now, instead of words rich in comfort,
  Lethe-conferring and gentlestly kindly,
  You arouse from the whole of the past
  More of evil than good,
  Darkening simultaneously
  Both the splendor of the present   8900
  And the future's
  Gently shimmering light of hope.
    Silence! Silence!
  So the soul of the Queen
  Poised for vanishing flight
  May yet hold, may firmly hold

---

11. Helen, whom Faust has re-evoked from the Mothers, senses that she is
not living a real life but a kind of ghostly second existence.

This form supreme among forms
Ever shone upon by the sun.

(HELEN *has revived and stands again in their midst.*)

PHORKYAS. Come forth out of fleeting clouds, resplendent sun
      that shines this day,
Which delighted while still veiled but dazzles in
      its glory now.   8910
As the world unfolds before you, you look down with
      gracious gaze.
Ugly they may call me, but I still know what is beautiful.
HELEN.
As I falter from the void that closed around me when I fainted,
I should like to find some peace again, for all my limbs are weary.
Queens, however, it beseems, as it beseems all human kind,
To have self-control no matter what surprise or peril threatens.
PHORKYAS.
As you stand before us in your greatness and your beauty now,
If your gaze proclaims command, then what commands have
      you to give?
HELEN. Be prepared to make up for delay occasioned by disputes,
Hasten to arrange the sacrifice commanded by the King.   8920
PHORKYAS.
All is ready in the house, the bowls and tripods and sharp ax,
For lustration and for censing. Indicate the victim now.
HELEN.
That the King did not disclose.
PHORKYAS.   He did not say? O word of woe!
HELEN.
What woe so afflicts you?
PHORKYAS.   Queen, you are the designated victim.
HELEN. I?
PHORKYAS. And these.
CHORUS.   O woe and sorrow!
PHORKYAS.   You shall fall
      beneath the ax.
HELEN.
Monstrous! Yet foresensed. Alas for me!

PHORKYAS.   There can be no escape.
CHORUS.
But what will become of us then?
PHORKYAS.   She will die a noble death,
But, within, from rafters that support the gabled roof
You will dangle in a row like thrushes at the fowling season.

(HELEN *and the* CHORUS *astounded and terrified in significant and carefully anticipated groupings.*)

Specters!—You all stand here like figures
        turned to stone,   8930
Afraid to leave the light of day, which is not yours.
And human beings, all of whom are ghosts like you,
Renounce no less reluctantly the blessed sunlight,
Yet no one pleads them free or saves them from that close.
All know of it, but there are few who find it pleasing.
Enough, you are all lost. Hence to the task with speed!

(*She claps her hands, whereupon there appear at the door
masked dwarves who immediately perform her spoken commands with alacrity.*)

Come on, you dismal, swollen-bellied goblin brood!
Come rolling out like balls, there's mischief to be done!
Clear space here for the altar with the golden horns,
And hang the gleaming ax over its silver edge;   8940
Fill up the water jars, there will be washing needed
When hideous soilure has been made by the black gore.
Spread out the carpet richly here upon the dust
So that the victim may kneel down in royal fashion,
And later, wrapped in it, although with severed head,
She may be buried with appropriate dignity.
CHORUS LEADER.
The Queen stands off to one side here, absorbed in thought,
The maidens wither like the meadow grass that's mown;
To me as eldest falls the sacred obligation
To speak to you, who are the ancient of the ancient.   8950
You are experienced, wise, and well disposed toward us,
For all this brainless crew misjudged and spoke you ill.

Speak, then, of any rescue for us you may know.

PHORKYAS. Easily said. But it depends upon the Queen
Alone to save herself and you along with her.
Resolve is necessary, and the quickest possible.

CHORUS.
Reverendmost of all the Parcae, wisest of the Sibyls, you,
Hold the golden shears tight shut and cry us daylight and
deliverance,
For we feel our little legs already swinging, swaying, dangling
Most unpleasantly, which we would rather swing in dances
first,   8960
Then at lovers' breasts rest on them.

HELEN. Leave fear to these; I feel no fear, but only grief.
But if you know of rescue, I shall hear it gratefully.
To wise minds and farsighted, things impossible
Still often seem quite possible. Speak, then, and tell us.

CHORUS. Speak and tell us, tell us quickly, how we can escape
the ghastly
Odious nooses, vilest of all necklaces, that threaten to
Gird around our necks. Already we poor things are going through
Suffocation, choking, if you, Rhea, mother of all gods,
Do not now take pity on us.   8970

PHORKYAS. Do you have patience to listen to the long-drawn-out
Recital of my plan? It is a complex story.

CHORUS. Patience enough! And while we listen we still live.

PHORKYAS. A man who bides at home and guards a noble treasure,
Who knows how to lay up the high walls of a house
And how to make the roof secure from gusting rain,
That man will prosper all the long days of his life.
But one who with a rash and hasty foot steps out
Lightly beyond his threshold's sacred boundary
Will find on his return the former place completely   8980
Transformed, if not destroyed in its entirety.

HELEN. Why all these old familiar adages just now?
You wanted to narrate; do not, therefore, be irksome.

PHORKYAS. It is part of the story, not a slur at all.
Pirate-wise rowed Menelaus from bay to bay,
Attacking shores and islands as an enemy,

Returning with the booty now hard-heaped inside here.
And ten long years he spent before the walls of Troy,
I do not know how many he spent getting home.
But how do things stand now with Tyndareos' house? [12]   8990
And how do things stand with the kingdom all around it?
HELEN. Is finding fault so totally ingrained in you
　That you can never move your lips except in blame?
PHORKYAS. So many years neglected lay the mountain valley
　That back of Sparta stretches upward to the north,
　Taygetus at the rear, from whence Eurotas rolls
　Down as a merry stream, then broadens out its flow
　Among the reeds here in our valley, feeding your swans.
　But back up in that mountain valley a bold race
　Has settled in, herding out of Cimmerian night   9000
　To raise a fortress mighty and impregnable,
　From where they harry land and people at their will.
HELEN. Could they achieve all that? It seems impossible.
PHORKYAS. They have had ample time, perhaps some twenty years.[13]
HELEN. Is one man master, or are they a horde of brigands?
PHORKYAS. They are no brigands, and there is one man as master.
　I speak no ill of him, though he has pestered me.
　He could take everything, but he is satisfied
　With a few voluntary gifts, he says, not tribute.[14]
HELEN.
　What does he look like?
PHORKYAS.　　　　　　　Not bad. He rather pleases me.   9010
　He is a cheerful, sprightly fellow, educated
　As few are here among the Greeks, a man of sense.
　They call his countrymen barbarians, but none,
　I think, is cruel as they were at Ilium,

---

12. Tyndareos was Leda's husband, and hence Helen's "earthly" father.
13. Ten years of the Trojan War plus ten more years of difficult homeward
wanderings in the manner of Ulysses. Actually, more than two thousand years
have passed, for Goethe has here in mind the Frankish kingdom of Achaia
established around Sparta in the Peloponnesus in 1205 by Guillaume de
Champlitte, just after the Fourth Crusade (1204) against Constantinople.
The kingdom lasted until the coming of the Turks, 1446–61.
14. The Germanic custom attested as far back as Tacitus, whereby subjects
gave their princes gifts of livestock and produce rather than rental money.

Where many a hero acted like a cannibal.
His greatness I respect; I trusted myself to him.
And then his fortress! You should see it for yourself!
It's something different from the clumsy masonry
Your ancestors piled up just any way it happened,
Cyclopean-wise like Cyclops, heaving unwrought stone   9020
On unwrought stone. Up there, by contrast, everything
Is vertical and horizontal and by rule.
Just see it from outside! It rises toward the sky
So straight and even, and as mirror-smooth as steel.
And scaling it—the very thought itself slips off.
Plenty of room for spacious courts inside, all built
Around with structures of all kinds and purposes.
There you'll see pillars, pillarettes, arches and archlets,
Projecting porches, galleries for looking out and in,[15]
And coats of arms.

CHORUS.   What is a coat of arms?

PHORKYAS.   You know   9030
How Ajax wore a winding serpent on his shield.
The Seven there at Thebes had figured emblems too,
Each one upon his shield, of rich significance.
There moon and stars were seen in the nocturnal sky,
And goddesses and heroes, ladders, swords, and firebrands,
Whatever grimly bodes good cities any harm.
Our band of heroes also wears just such an emblem
In colored splendor, handed down from ancestors.
There you see lions, eagles, and claws and beaks besides,
Buffalo horns, and roses, wings, and peacocks' fans,   9040
And bands of gold and black and silver, blue and red.
And these they hang up row on row along their halls,
Those halls so limitless, the world is not so wide.
There you could dance!

CHORUS.   Tell us, do they have dances too?

PHORKYAS. The best! Fresh bands of merry boys with golden hair.
They have youth's fragrance! Only Paris smelled so sweet

---

15. The description is that of any medieval castle. It is possible but not certain that Goethe had in mind Castle Mistra, a Crusaders' castle in the
Peloponnesus.

When he came too close to the Queen.

HELEN.   You're stepping out
Of character. But tell me now the final word.

PHORKYAS. That is for you to tell. Say "Yes" so I can hear it,
And I will set you in that citadel.

CHORUS.   O speak   9050
That little word, and save yourself and us as well!

HELEN. What! Would you have me be afraid King Menelaus
Would so demean himself as to work harm to me?

PHORKYAS. Have you forgotten how he maimed your Deiphobus,
Slain Paris' brother, with unheard-of cruelty
For having won against your stubborn widowhood
And making you his concubine? He cut off nose
And ears and more besides; it was a ghastly sight.[16]

HELEN. Yes, he did that to him, did it because of me.

PHORKYAS. And he will do the like to you because of him.   9060
Beauty can not be shared; the full possessor will
Sooner destroy her, cursing any partnership.

(*Trumpets in the distance; the* CHORUS *shudders.*)

How sharp the snarling trumpets clutch and claw the ear
And vitals, just the way that jealousy will claw
The bosom of a man who never can forget
What once he had, and lost, and now no longer has.

CHORUS. Do you not hear how the trumpets sound? and how
        the weapons flash?

PHORKYAS.
Welcome to my Lord and King. I gladly give my reckoning.

CHORUS. But what of us?

PHORKYAS.   You know quite well, you will see her
        death with your eyes
And then meet your own inside there. No, for you
        there is no help.   9070

(*Pause*)

HELEN. I have thought out what I shall first make bold to do.

---

16. Vergil relates these cruelties in the *Aeneid* VI. 494 ff.

You are an adverse daemon, that I clearly sense,
And fear that you may well turn good things into evil.
But first of all I will go with you to that fortress;
The rest I know in my own mind, but what the Queen
May secretly conceal within her own heart's depths
Shall be accessible to none. Lead on, old woman.
CHORUS. O how gladly we go
  With hastening feet,
  Death at the rear,   9080
  And to the fore
  A towering fortress'
  Inaccessible walls.
  May they afford protection
  Equal to Ilium's ramparts,
  Which succumbed at last
  Only to contemptible guile.

(*Mist is diffused, veiling the background and also the fore-
ground, at random.*)

  What! What is this?
Sisters, look around!
Was it not cheerfulest day?   9090
Bands of mist come eddying upwards
From the flood of sacred Eurotas;
Already hidden is the lovely
Sedge-engarlanded shore from our sight,
And the free, graceful-proud
Swans that were softly gliding,
Flocking and floating there,
I see, alas, no longer.
  And yet, and yet
I hear their singing still,   9100
Their hoarse and far-off song,
Death-announcing, so they say.
O may it not bode for us
Death's destruction too instead of
Help and rescue that were promised.
Unto us, the swanlike, the

Long-fair-white-throated,
And our swan-begotten
Queen, alas, is woe!
  Everything has been veiled   9110
Round about with mist.
We no longer see each other.
What has happened? Are we
Walking or only
Hovering in motion over the ground?
Do you see nothing? Does Hermes not [17]
Lead our flight? Gleams not his golden wand
Bidding us backward, commanding return
To the joyless, grey-lighted, eternally
Empty region of Hades full and   9120
Overfull of insubstantial forms?
  Darkness suddenly descends, and lusterless dissolves the mist,
Murky-greyish, stone-wall-brownish. Walls loom up before
      our sight,
Starkly fronting our free sight. Is it a courtyard or a tomb?
Frightening in either case! O sisters! We are prisoners,
Prisoners just as before! [18]

Inner Courtyard of a Castle

*Surrounded by rich and fantastic structures
of the Middle Ages.*

CHORUS LEADER. Typical, overhasty, foolish womenfolk!
  Dependent on the moment, toys of every wind
  Of bane and blessing, facing neither of the two
  With constancy. One contradicts with vehemence   9130
  The other, only to be gainsaid in her turn.
  In joy and grief you howl and laugh with equal tones.

---

17. Hermes Psychopompos ("soul-sender"), who herds the dead to Hades.
18. I.e., ever since their capture at the fall of Troy.

Be still, and wait to hear what our high-minded mistress
May now decide to do for her sake and for ours.

HELEN. Where are you, Pythonissa? [1] Be your name what it may,
Step from the vaulted archways of this gloomy fortress.
If you have gone in to announce my coming to
This hero-lord and to prepare for my reception,
I thank you, but now quickly take me in to him.
I wish an end of wandering, I wish for peace.   9140

CHORUS LEADER.
In vain, O Queen, you look to all sides round about.
Her loathsome form has vanished. Perhaps she stayed inside
The mist there, from whose bosom we, I know not how,
Descended here with speed and yet without a step.
Or she perhaps is lost amid the labyrinth
Of fortress, oddly one despite its many parts,
And looking for the lord to arrange a princely welcome.
But see, up there already many servitors
Are moving to and fro in throngs, and swiftly too,
In galleries, at windows, and beneath the portals.   9150
It must portend distinguished welcome to a guest.

CHORUS. Expands now my heart! O behold over there
How so decorously downward with tarrying tread
Comes, youthfully lovely, a dignified group
In ordered procession. What? Whose was the order
To have them appear in their ranks and arrayed
So early, this throng of magnificent youths?
What most shall I praise? Their admirable gait,
Or their locks with the curls at their dazzling brows,
Or their twin-blooming cheeks with the blush of the peach   9160
And touched like the peach with a softness of down?
For in similar case once my mouth was all filled,
I shudder to say, with ashes.
    Now in their beauty
Forward they come.
What are they carrying?
Steps for a throne,

---

1. A late Greek word signifying "wise woman, witch, prophetess."

Carpet and seat,
Hangings and tentlike   9170
Canopy.
This overspreads
The head of our Queen
Like clustering clouds,
For she has ascended
To that proffered chair.
Upward advance,
Level to level,
In solemn ranks.
Worthy, O worthy, threefold worthy   9180
Be praised such a welcome as this!

(*Everything described by the Chorus gradually takes place.
Enter* FAUST. *After a long procession of pages and squires
has come down, he appears at the top of the stairs in the
chivalric court costume of the Middle Ages, and slowly descends with dignity.*)

CHORUS LEADER (*observing him attentively*).
If to this man the gods have not, as is their wont,
For brief time only lent this marvel of a form,
This lofty dignity, this presence full of grace,
As merely transient gifts, he will in every instance
Win all he undertakes, be it in strife with men
Or in the petty warfare waged with beautiful women.
He is indeed to be preferred above a host
Of others whom I have seen held in high esteem.
With slowly solemn tread by reverence sustained   9190
I see the princely ruler. Turn to him, O Queen!
FAUST (*advancing, a man in fetters at his side*).
Instead of solemn greeting, as was fitting,
Instead of reverent welcome, I bring you
This knave fast manacled in chains, who by
Neglect of duty, kept me from my duty.
Kneel here at this supremest lady's feet
At once and make confession of your guilt.
This is, exalted potentate, the man

Appointed for his rarity of vision
To look from the high tower and to scan   9200
The range of heaven and the breadth of earth
For what may there or here present itself,
For anything that may move from the circle
Of hills into the valley toward this fortress,
Be it a wave of sheep or an army marching.
We shield the one and fight the other. But
What negligence today! You come, and he
Does not report it; due respect and welcome
Is not paid to so high a guest. His life
Is forfeit, and he would be lying now   9210
In death, except that it is yours alone
To punish or to pardon, as you please.
HELEN. It is so high an honor that you offer
Me now as judge and regent, even if,
As I surmise, it is to test me merely,
That I shall do a judge's solemn duty
By hearing the accused. Let him now speak.
TOWER WARDEN LYNCEUS. Let me kneel and let me gaze,
Let me live or let me die,
To this godlike lady I   9220
Pledge myself through all my days.
    Waiting for the morning light,
Eastward peering toward its source,
Suddenly I saw the bright
Sun from southward start its course.
    That way sought my wondering eye,
Not the chasm, not the peak,
Not the range of earth and sky,
But that sun, that sun unique.
    Eyesight such to me is given   9230
As to lynx in highest tree,
But I now was roused and riven
As from dream obscurity.
    Could I know where I had strayed?
Ramparts? Tower? Close-barred portal?
Vapors falter, vapors fade,

Forth then steps such an immortal!
  Eye and heart in full surrender,
I inbreathed that mellow light;
Blinding all, that beauty's splendor   9240
Blinded my poor senses quite.
  I forgot my watchman's duty,
And the horn I swore to use;
Threaten to destroy me: Beauty
Conquers anger and subdues.

HELEN. The evil I occasioned I may not
  Chastise. Alas for me! What a harsh fate
  Pursues me, so infatuating men's
  Hearts everywhere that they will neither spare
  Themselves nor any thing of worth. Abducting now,   9250
  Seducing, fighting, plundering back and forth,
  Gods, heroes, demigods, the very daemons
  Perplexed have led me wandering forth and back.
  Singly the world I troubled, doubly more so,
  Now triply, fourfold I add woe to woe.
  Release this good man now, let him go free,
  Let no shame fall upon the god-deluded.

FAUST. Amazed, O Queen, I here behold together
  The never-failing striker and the stricken.
  I see the bow that sped the arrow forth,   9260
  And this man wounded. Arrows follow arrows,
  Wounding me. I sense their slanted flight
  Feathered and whirring through these courts and walls.
  What am I now? You suddenly make rebels
  Of my most loyal men, you make my walls
  Unsafe. Already I fear that my army
  Obeys the conquering, unconquered lady.
  What can I do now but surrender to you
  Myself and everything I thought was mine?
  Here at your feet I loyally and freely   9270
  Acknowledge you my Queen, who had but to
  Appear to win possession and a throne.

LYNCEUS (*with a chest, followed by men bearing other chests*).
  You see me, Queen, return once more.

One sight of you the rich implore,
And gazing, feel immediately
Both princely wealth and beggary.
    What have I been? What now am I?
What can I wish? What can I try?
What use is vision lightning-keen?
Your throne deflects its ray, O Queen.   9280
    Out of the East we once descended,[2]
And then the West's dominion ended;
A line of peoples long and vast,
The first one knew not of the last.
    One fell, a second made a stand,
A third one's lance was close at hand,
Strength hundredfold was each one's gain,
Unnoticed went the thousand slain.
    We stormed our way with unstemmed pace,
We were masters from place to place,   9290
And where today my rule prevailed,
Tomorrow others sacked and assailed.
    We looked—the look was swift—and there
One seized the fairest of the fair,
One seized the stolid-gaited ox,
All horses had to join our stocks.
    But I liked to seek out and glean
The rarest objects ever seen;
What someone else owned *too*, I spurned
Like grass that sun has parched and burned.   9300
    On trail of treasure-trove went I,
And followed only my keen eye;
I saw what every pocket hid,
Transparent was each coffer lid.
    I hoarded heaps of gold combined
With gems of most resplendent kind;
None but the emerald's lustrous green
May lie against your heart, O Queen.

---

2. The four stanzas that follow impressionistically suggest, not so much the Crusades, as the migrations of the Germanic peoples toward south European lands in the centuries surrounding the breakup of the Roman Empire.

Let pearl-drops from the ocean sway
Between your ear and lip today;   9310
Rubies are routed and turn pale
Where cheeks of redness so prevail.
   Before your presence I display
Supremest treasures these men convey,
And at your feet in homage yield
Harvest of many a bloody field.
   For all these chests dragged from my store,
Of iron chests I have still more;
Admit me to your path, and I
Will heap your treasure chambers high.   9320
   You need but take this throne seat now,
And there will bend, and there will bow
Wealth, power, and intelligence
Before your peerless excellence.
   All I once held so guardedly
Becomes herewith your property;
I deemed it worthy and a gain,
I now see that its worth was vain.
   All things I once possessed now pass
And are as mown and withered grass.   9330
O with one gladsome glance restore
Them to their cherished worth once more!
FAUST. Remove with haste this burden boldly won
   That bears no blame but yet brings no reward.
   Already all is hers that in this fortress'
   Womb is hidden; offering special gifts
   Is futile. Go and heap up hoard on hoard
   In ordered ranks. Exhibit in sublime
   Display the unseen splendor. Let the vaults
   Gleam like morning skies, let paradises   9340
   Of lifeless life be ordered and arrayed.[3]
   In haste before her steps let carpet after
   Flowered carpet be unrolled, and let her step
   Encounter dainty footing, and her gaze,

---

3. The dead jewels are full of living fires.

Blinding to all but gods, meet highest splendor.
LYNCEUS. A slight thing is our lord's behest,
Compliance with it is mere jest.
This beauty's overruling sway
Guides lives and fortunes anyway.
The army is already tame,   9350
All our swords are blunt and lame,
Confronting her resplendent mold
The very sun shines dead and cold,
Before her wealth of countenance
All is empty impotence.

(*Exit.*)

HELEN (*to* FAUST). I wish to speak with you, but first ascend
And sit here at my side. The empty place
Requires its master and assures me mine.
FAUST. First, kneeling, let my true allegiance be
Accepted, noble Lady. Let me kiss   9360
The hand that elevates me to your side.
Confirm me as coregent of your realm
That knows no boundaries, and gain yourself
Adorer, server, warder, all in one.
HELEN. Marvels manifold I see and hear,
Amazement seizes me. Much would I ask.
I should first like to know why that man's speech
Sounded so strange to me, so strange and friendly.
One tone seems with another to accord,
And once a word has sounded in the ear,   9370
Another comes and fondly meets the first.
FAUST. If you find pleasure in our peoples' language,
O then be sure our song will ravish you,
Profoundly satisfying ear and mind.
It would be best to practice it at once;
Alternate speech invites, elicits it.
HELEN. But tell me, how may I speak with such art?
FAUST. Quite easily; you must speak from the heart.
And if the heart with yearning brims its measure,
One looks about and asks—

HELEN.   who shares our pleasure.   9380
FAUST. Past and future, mind may not possess;
    The present only—
HELEN.   is our happiness.
FAUST. It is possession, wealth, holdings and land.
    And who confirms its ownership?
HELEN.   My hand.
CHORUS. Who will blame our Princess if
    To the master of this fortress
    She shows friendly kindness?
    For we all, it must be granted,
    Are captives, as we have been often
    Since the shameful overthrow   9390
    Of Ilium and the fearful
    Labyrinthine voyage of sorrow.
        Women to men's love accustomed,
    Choosers they are not, but knowers
    From experience.
    Sometimes to gold-ringleted shepherds,
    Or perchance to black-bristled fauns,
    Quite as occasion befalls,
    Over their sumptuous limbs
    They confer an equal control.   9400
        Near and nearer they sit already,
    Leaning close together,
    Shoulder to shoulder, knee to knee,
    Hand in hand they sway together
    Over the throne's
    Cushioned magnificence and richness.
    Majesty does not deny itself
    Secretest raptures
    Before the eyes of the people
    In their indecent display.   9410
HELEN. I feel myself so distant, yet so near,
    And all too gladly say: Here am I! Here!
FAUST. I scarcely breathe, I tremble, my words fail.
    This is a dream, the day and place grow pale.

HELEN. I feel lived out, and yet life seems so new
  In your embrace, to unknown futures true.
FAUST. Yours is a fate unique: probe not within it.
  Existence is duty, though it last one minute.
PHORKYAS (*entering obstreperously*).
  Do Love's primer's A B C's,
  Dilly-dally, peck and tease,   9420
  Brood and fondle all you please,
  But this is no time for delight!
  Don't you feel low thunder pounding?
  Listen to those trumpets sounding!
  Your destruction is in sight.
  Menelaus by swift posts
  Comes against you with his hosts.
  Arm yourselves for a harsh fight!
  Stormed by troops victorious,
  Mangled like Deiphobus,[4]   9430
  You will pay for your women's flight.
  This trash once in noose and halter,
  He will take you to the altar
  Where the ax is whetted bright.
FAUST. Brash interruption! She offensively intrudes.
  Not even in danger do I care for senseless bluster.
  Bad news will make the handsomest message-bearer ugly,
  And you, the ugliest, only like to bring bad news.
  But this time you will profit nothing, you will blast
  The air with empty breath. There is no danger here,   9440
  And even danger would come as an idle threat.

(*Signals, explosions from the towers, trumpets and cornets,
martial music. A powerful army marches across the stage.*)

  No, you shall see the gathered might
  Of our united hero bands:
  Women's favor goes by right
  To those who show defending hands.

---

4. See above, ll. 9054 ff.

(to the COMMANDERS, *who detach themselves from their columns and step forward)*

With bridled rage and quiet power
Sure victory will crown your course,
You, of the north the youthful flower,
You, of the east the blooming force.
  Steel-mailed, lit by the lightning flash,   9450
Before this band the empires break;
They come—earth trembles at their clash,
They go—with thunder in their wake.
  At Pylos we set foot on land,
The ancient Nestor is no more,
And every petty chieftain's band
Was routed by our freemen corps.
  Back from these walls without delay
Drive Menelaus to the sea;
There let him prowl and rob his way,   9460
As was his will and destiny.
  As dukes my lady bids me greet
Each one of you. Lay hill and plain
Before the Queen of Sparta's feet,
And yours will be the empire's gain.
  At Corinth's bays erect defense,[5]
Germanic chief, with wall and tower,
Achaia of the hundred glens,

---

5. In the next two stanzas Faust lists the provinces of the Peloponnesus peninsula, beginning at the Isthmus of Corinth and proceeding in counterclockwise order: Corinth, Achaia, Elis, Messenia, and then skipping to Argolis in the northeast corner. The circuit is completed in the third stanza with the mention of Sparta, Helen's city and the capital of the province of Laconia. All these areas together encircle the region of Arcadia in the center of the Peloponnesus, and of Arcadia Faust will speak in ll. 9526–74. (See map, pp. LXXII–LXXIII.)

With the medieval Crusaders' kingdom of Achaia in mind, Goethe fancifully distributes the Germanic peoples, as of the period of their migrations (5th and 6th centuries) among these lands in order to dedicate them spiritually to the ideals of Hellas. The first mentioned of the Germanic peoples are the *Germanen,* here considered as the individual tribe they originally were along the lower Rhine. (The word *Deutsch,* "German," does not occur in the text.)

O Goth, I trust into your power.
   Let Frankish men in Elis be,   9470
Messenia be the Saxons' share,
And let the Norman sweep the sea,
Rebuilding Argolis the fair.
   Each one shall then have home domain,
Each outward face his force and fire,
But Sparta over all shall reign,
Our Queen's ancestral seat and shire.
   She sees each one enjoy these lands,
None knowing want before her sight;
Come confidently where she stands   9480
To find assurance, law, and right.

(FAUST *descends, the* PRINCES *form a circle around him in
order to hear more closely his commands and instructions.*)

CHORUS. He who wishes to have the fairest,
   Sturdily first of all
Let him wisely find him weapons.
Fondly he may well have won
What on earth is deemed the highest,
But he cannot hold it in peace.
Fawners slyly entice her from him,
Predators daringly steal her from him.
How to prevent this, let him take thought.   9490
   I commend our Prince and prize him
Higher than all of the others
For such a shrewd and daring alliance
That the mighty obey his order
Heeding his every gesture.
Loyally they perform his command,
Each to his own private advantage
And for grateful reward from their master
And for increase of fame to them both.
   For who shall wrest her away   9500
Now from her mighty possessor?
His she is, to him let her be granted,
Doubly granted by us, whom he

Has enclosed with her inside the securest of walls
And outside by mightiest armies surrounded.
FAUST. Our gifts to these are glorious—
   To each a rich and fertile land;
Let them march on victorious,
   Here in their midst we take our stand.
     O thou peninsula, they vie   9510
   For honor of protecting thee,
Ringed with the skipping waves, thy low hills lie
   The farthest branch of Europe's mountain-tree.
     This land, of other lands the sun,
   Be it the joy of all the races,
This land now for my Queen new won,
   Where first to her men raised their faces.
     When with Eurotas' reeds a-whisper
   She broke forth from her shell all gleaming,[6]
Her lofty mother, brothers, sister   9520
   Paled in the radiance from her streaming.
     This land yields you its finest flower,
   It favors you above the rest;
Though all of earth be in your power,
   Oh, love your native region best!
     Though frigid arrows of the sun now light[7]
On jagged backs of mountain crests all bare,
Still valley-upwards greenness climbs each height
And wild goats browse there, cropping scanty fare.
     The fountain leaps, down plunge the meeting rills,   9530
Already meadows, slopes, and glens are green.
Upon the smooth lawns of a hundred hills
The woolly flocks fan out across the scene.
     In groups, with cautious step lest they should fall,
Horned cattle venture to the fearful edges,

---

6. Helen was born from a hyacinth-colored egg produced by her mother Leda.
7. The next nine stanzas describe Arcadia, north of Sparta and the heartland of the Peloponnesus, by long tradition the land of pastoral simplicity and happiness, the scene of the Golden Age. The mountains are the Taygetus range.

But shelter is provided for them all,
A hundred caves arch in from rocky ledges.
    Pan guards them there, and living nymphs [8] abide
In gullies moist and cool with shrubbery,
And full of yearning up the mountainside   9540
Arises tree on densely branching tree.
    Primeval woods! The oak tree stark and regnant
Spreads jagged bough on bough in overlays;
The maple gently and with sweet sap pregnant
Soars clear aloft and with its burden plays.
    Maternally in quiet shadow-bower
Warm milk for child and lamb wells readily,
Fruit is not far, ripe food of plains in flower,
And honey trickles from the hollowed tree.
    Here comfort is a birthright, here   9550
Bright cheeks beside bright lips are found,
All are immortal in their proper sphere,
All are content and whole and sound.
    Thus in pure day the lovely child attains
To fatherhood's estate. And then
We are amazed, our question still remains:
Are they gods or are they men?
    Apollo thus took on a shepherd's form,
The fairest bore his form divine;
Let Nature in its purest state perform   9560
And all worlds then will intertwine.[9]

(*sitting beside her*)

    Let all past time for us be done and ended
Now that we both have come into our own.
O feel yourself from highest god descended,
For you belong to that first world alone.
    Nor shall a fortress hold you bound!
For us and for our bliss henceforth
In youthful strength still closes round

---

8. I.e., nymphs of life-giving water, personified mountain freshets.
9. I.e., distinction will cease to exist between gods and mortals.

Arcadia, Sparta's neighbor to the north.
 Lured to dwell in that blessed land,   9570
You flee to brightest destiny.
Change we these thrones for bowers and
For happiness Arcadian-free!

Arcadia

*Closed arbors lean against a series of caverns
in the cliff. A shady grove extends as far as
the surrounding cliffsides.* FAUST *and* HELEN
are not seen. The CHORUS *is lying dispersed
at various points, asleep.*

PHORKYAS. I do not know how long the maidens have been sleeping;
  And whether they have dreamed what I so clearly saw
  Before my eyes, is likewise quite unknown to me.
  So I shall wake them. Young folks now will be amazed;
  You oldsters will be too, who sit down there and wait [1]
  To see the outcome of these credible miracles.
  Wake up! Wake up! And quickly shake your tousled curls,   9580
  Rub sleep out of your eyes! Don't blink so! Listen to me!
CHORUS.
  Speak now, tell us, tell us what astounding thing has happened.
  We love best to hear of things we cannot possibly believe,
  For we are completely bored with looking at these rocky cliffs.
PHORKYAS.
  Bored already, children, with sleep barely rubbed out of your eyes?
  Listen then: amid these caves, these grottoes, and
       these arbors here
  Shield and shelter were accorded to that idyllic pair of lovers,
  To our lord and to our lady.

---

1. Direct address to the audience, as in Greek comedy, but also in the illu-
sion-breaking manner of Hans Wurst, the clown of native German drama.

CHORUS.   What? Inside there?

PHORKYAS.   Yes, secluded
From the world, they called on me, on me alone, for silent
    service.
Highly honored, I stood by, but as befits a confidante,   9590
Looked at something else, put my mind to one thing
    and another,
Looked for mosses, roots, and barks, acquainted
    with their properties,
And thus they were left alone.

CHORUS. Why, you talk as if whole continents existed down in there,
Fields and forests, brooks and lakes. What fairy tales
    you're making up!

PHORKYAS. To be sure, you simple greenhorns! Those are still
    unfathomed depths,
Hall on hall and court on court, and I explored them thoughtfully.
Suddenly a peal of laughter echoed through the cavern rooms.
I looked over, and a boy ran from the woman to the man,
From his father to his mother, and the fondlings and
    endearments,   9600
Banterings of foolish love, mirthful cries and shouts of joy
Alternating, deafened me.
    Naked ran a wingless spirit, faunlike, yet in no wise bestial,
Leaping on the solid ground. But then the ground
    with counteraction
Sent him flying up aloft, and at the second or third leap
He had touched the vaulted roof.
    Anxiously his mother cried, "Leap all the leaps you
    choose to leap,
But beware of flying; flight untrammeled is forbidden you."
And his father warned him, "In the earth lies the elastic force
That impels you upward; touch the ground with no more
    than a toe,   9610
And you will be, like Antaeus, son of Earth, renewed in strength."
Hopping then he goes about the rocky masses of this mountain
Bouncing like a ball from one ledge to the next ledge all around.
    Suddenly he vanished in a rugged chasm's sightless cleft

And we all thought he was lost. His mother wept, his father
    consoled,
Anxiously I shrugged my shoulders. And then what a
    reappearance!
Are there treasures hidden there? In garments all adorned
    with flowers
He with dignity emerged.
    Tassels swung along his arms, ribbons fluttered at his breast,
In his hands the golden lyre; exactly like a little Phoebus   9620
He comes gaily walking to the precipice. We were amazed.
And his parents rapturously then clasped each other in their arms.
For what radiance shone about his head! What shone, was
    hard to tell.
Was it gold? Was it the flame of preternatural force of spirit?
And he moved with gestures such as now proclaimed him,
    still a boy,
As a future master of things beautiful, through whose limbs will
Course eternal melodies. And as such you will hear him too,
And behold him to your own particular astonishment.
CHORUS. Do you call that a marvel,
    Crete-begotten?   9630
Have you never listened
To poets' instructive words?
Have you never heard Ionia's,
Or not even Hellas'
Treasure of ancestral
Lore about the gods and heroes?
    All of the things that happen
Nowadays
Are the pitiful echoes
Of glorious ancestral times.   9640
Your report cannot compare
With the beloved fiction
More credible than truth
Sung of Maia and her son.[2]

---

2. Hermes, the son of Zeus and Maia. The ensuing two-stanza ode on the
birth of Hermes paraphrases Hederich's dictionary, under "Mercurius," but

That so dainty yet powerful
Newborn infant was wrapped
Spotless in down of swaddling clothes,
Cramped in costly bedizened swathings
By a chattering bevy of nurses
Full of nonsensical notions.   9650
Powerful and dainty, he, the rascal,
Drew his supple but still
Wholly elastic limbs
Cleverly out, leaving his purple
Clamp of constraining shell
Unconcernedly behind,
As the full-grown butterfly
From its rigid pupa case
Agilely slips and spreads its wings
Out on the sun-flooded aether boldly   9660
Sailing with a will.
    So he too, the most agile,
Showing himself the patron
Daemon of thieves and rascals
And of all advantage-seekers,
Managed to accomplish these feats
By the most skillful of arts:
Quickly from the lord of the sea
He stole the trident; from Ares himself
Slyly the sword from its sheath;   9670
Arrows and bow from Phoebus too,
And from Hephaistos the tongs;
Zeus the Father's very lightning
He would have taken but for the fear for fire;
Eros too he downed in a
Leg-tripping boxing bout;
Even from Cypris as she caressed him
He stole her bosom's girdle.

---

also derives partly from Philostratus' description of a lost painting from antiquity in his *Imagines* I. 26 (See above, l. 8379n.) More ample details may
be found in Philostratus' own source, the *Hymn to Hermes,* attributed by the
ancients to Homer.

(A charming, purely melodic music of a lyre is heard from the cavern. All become attentive and presently appear to be inwardly moved. From here on, as far as the pause indicated below, there is full musical accompaniment.) [3]

PHORKYAS. Hear these tones that sweetly play,
   Set yourselves from fables free,   9680
   Your old gods have had their day,
   They are finished, let them be.
      No one knows them any more,
   We require a higher art:
   From the heart a song must pour
   If it is to touch the heart.

(She retires toward the cliffside.)

CHORUS. If, dread being, you incline
   Toward this music that endears,
   Even more do we incline,
   We are softened unto tears.   9690
      Let the sun's bright blaze go blind,
   If dawns in the soul arise,
   In our own hearts we will find
   What the entire world denies. [4]

(Enter HELEN, FAUST, and EUPHORION, the latter in the costume previously described.) [5]

EUPHORION. Hear me sing a childhood song
   And your own mirth sings in me;
   Watch me as I dance along

---

3. Antiquity looked upon music as a supporting art for poetry and for dancing. Music listened to by itself alone is a modern notion.

4. Romantic subjectivity, Goethe believed, created its own inner world in defiance of circumstances, whereas classical antiquity was sun-clear and "objective."

5. With the entrance of Faust and Helen at l. 9695—if not already in the throne scene with Lynceus—Goethe intended to use opera *singers* who would double for the regular speaking actors who had been playing the roles up to this point. His remarks on this point in his conversation with Eckermann of Jan. 25, 1827 are explicit except for the specific point at which the substitution of roles is to take place.

And your own hearts skip with glee.

HELEN. Love, for mortal gladness, mates
  Two together happily,   9700
  But for godlike joy creates
  From these two a precious three.

FAUST. All things sought for thus are found,
  You are mine and I am yours
  And we stand together bound.
  Never be a different course.

CHORUS. Many, many years of joy
  Will there for this couple be
  In the mild light of this boy.
  How this union touches me!   9710

EUPHORION. Now let me skip,
  Now let me leap!
  To scale the sky
  In upward sweep
  Is the desire
  That fills me now.

FAUST. But caution! caution!
  Not too rash,
  Lest you should meet
  With fall and crash,   9720
  Destroying our
  Beloved son.

EUPHORION. I will no longer
  Earth-bonds bear.
  Release my hands,
  Release my hair,
  Release my garments,
  For they are mine.

HELEN. O think of them
  To whom you belong.   9730
  You would condemn
  Us to great wrong,
  Withdrawing "his"
  From "mine" and "thine."

CHORUS. Their union, I fear,

Will soon disjoin.

HELEN AND FAUST. Curb, O curb
  For parents' sake
  Your will superb
  And immoderate!   9740
  Rustic peace
  Be yours on this plain.

EUPHORION. Only to please
  You, I refrain.

  (*winding in and out among the* CHORUS *and drawing them
  out to dance with him*)

  I circle this company
  Merrily light.
  Now is the melody,
  Now is the movement right?

HELEN. Oh yes, it is well done.
  Lead the fair ones on   9750
  In figured dance.

FAUST. If they would only stop!
  On this whirling like a top
  I look askance.

  (EUPHORION *and the* CHORUS, *dancing and singing, move
  in interlocking figures.*)

CHORUS. When you thus fling
  Your graceful arms so fair
  And toss and swing
  The glory of your hair,
  When you with foot so fleet
  Over the meadow skim,   9760
  Advance and then retreat
  With grace in every limb,
  Then you have gained your goal,
  Beautiful child,
  And we are heart and soul
  By you beguiled.

  (*A pause.*)

EUPHORION. You are so many
  Light-footed deer;
  Quick to new games
  Gather near: 9770
  I am the huntsman,
  You are the quarry.
CHORUS. To catch us, do not
  Too swiftly chase,
  For all we want
  Is an embrace.
  Handsome huntsman,
  Wait and tarry.
EUPHORION. But let us rove
  By cliff and grove!   9780
  The easily coursed
  I abhor,
  But triumph-forced
  I adore.

[*Exit the* CHORUS *with* EUPHORION *in pursuit.*]

HELEN AND FAUST. What wild raving! What self-will!
  No restraint is to be hoped for.
  Now like horncalls voices shrill,
  Over woods and valley ringing.
  What an uproar! What a din!
CHORUS ([*re-*]*entering swiftly one by one*).
  He outran us! Spurned our call!   9790
  Of our whole troop he is bringing
  Back the wildest one of all.
  Here he comes lugging her in!

([*Reenter*] EUPHORION *carrying a* YOUNG GIRL *in his arms.*)

EUPHORION. Here I lug this hardy lass
  For delights I'll take by force.
  To my pleasure, to my bliss,
  Her reluctant breast I'll press
  And her rebel lips I'll kiss,
  Proving my relentlessness.

THE MAIDEN. Let me go! In this frame   9800
  Is a spirit's strength and might!
  Equal will with yours we claim,
  Capturing us is nothing slight.
  You think I will cry and cringe?
  You trust too much to your arm.
  Hold me fast, and I will singe
  You, you fool, and to your harm!

  (*She bursts into flame and flashes aloft.*)

  Follow me in tenuous air,
  Follow me to rocky lair,
  Catch your prey that vanished there.   9810
EUPHORION (*shaking off the last flames*).
  Prison of cliffs I see
  Thicket and forest hung.
  What are these walls to me?
  I am still fresh and young.
  Past them are winds that roar,
  Waves pound a distant shore,
  Both from afar I hear.
  Would I were near!

  (*He goes leaping higher up the height.*)

HELEN, FAUST, AND CHORUS.
  Would you scale the chamois' ways?
  Fear a fall before your time.   9820
EUPHORION. Ever higher I must climb,
  Ever further I must gaze.
    Now I see where I stand,
  Midmost in island free,
  Midmost in Pelops' land,[6]
  Kin to both earth and sea.
CHORUS. Why not in wood and hill
  Find peace and a haven?
  Let us go seek our fill

---

6. Peloponnesus is "Pelop's island" in Greek.

Where vine rows brightly laden   9830
High on the hill-slopes stand
With figs and apple-gold.
Ah, in this winsome land
Live to grow old.
EUPHORION. You dream of times of peace?
Dreams such as those should cease.
Let "War!" the watchword be,
With cries of "Victory!" [7]
CHORUS. Whoever cries
In times of peace for war,   9840
Hopeless lies
With nothing to live for.
EUPHORION. All whom this country bore
From peril into peril,
Who free and staunch have stood,
Lavish of their blood—
Sacred mind
Nothing can constrain—
All battle-signed,
Theirs be the gain! [8]   9850
CHORUS. See how high he climbs! Yet he
Seems no smaller now. He seems
Armored as for victory,
All in bronze and steel he gleams.
EUPHORION. Leave the walls of your contriving,
On himself alone each man depends,
Strongest fortress for surviving

---

7. Euphorion, the Spirit of Romantic Poetry, now begins to take on the qualities of Lord Byron (1788–1824), the Romantic poet whose enthusiasm for
liberty took him to Greece to fight in the Greek war of independence. The
name, which signifies something like "graceful bearing," is borrowed from
Hederich's account of a late Greek legend in which Euphorion was the offspring of Helen and Achilles, during their ghostly posthumous life on the
island of Leuce in the Black Sea. See ll. 7435–36 and note.
8. This stanza has been rendered as faithfully as possible from the German,
which is printed in exact conformity with Goethe's manuscript. Editors have
repunctuated, emended, paraphrased, and commented, in disagreement with
each other as to the precise meaning of the passage.

Is the breast of bronze that he defends.
Who seeks to live unconquered, dons
Light arms and swiftly takes the field;   9860
Women become Amazons
And children force the foe to yield.
CHORUS. Sacred Poetry,
     Skyward may it climb,
     Gleam as furthest star
     Far and onward far,
     Yet come to us it will
     Forever; we hear it still,
     Hear it joyfully.
EUPHORION. I came not as a child in bearing,   9870
     It was a youth in arms who came,
     Leagued with the strong, the free, the daring,
     Whose mind already won a name.
     Away!
     Today
     There opens out the path toward fame.
HELEN AND FAUST. Scarcely summoned into life,
     Scarcely knowing daylight's gleam,
     Here you yearn for pain and strife,
     Climbing up to heights supreme.   9880
     Is nothing due
     To us from you?
     Is our union all a dream?
EUPHORION. You hear that thunder on the sea?
     And valley-thunder answeringly:
     Shock of armies, waves and dust,[9]
     And pain and torment, thrust on thrust.
     And to die
     Is the high
     Command delivered to their trust.   9890
HELEN, FAUST, AND CHORUS.
     O what horror! What dismay!
     Is death likewise for you decreed?

---

9. Naval battle with cannon, and battle on land.

EUPHORION. Shall I look on from far away?
  No! I will share their pain and need.
HELEN, FAUST, AND CHORUS.
  Peril and wanton pride,
  The lot of the dead!
EUPHORION. Yet—wings now open wide
  From my shoulders outspread!
  To them! I must! I must!
  Grant me flight!   9900

(*He casts himself aloft, his garments bear him up for an instant, his head gives forth a radiance, a trail of light streams after him.*)

CHORUS. Icarus! Icarus!
  Sorrowful sight!

(*A handsome youth falls at his parents' feet. In the corpse we seem to recognize a well-known figure.*[10] *But the corporeal part vanishes; the aureole rises as a comet into the sky; garment, mantle, and lyre are left lying on the ground.*)

HELEN AND FAUST. After joy, another
  Grief makes us moan.
EUPHORION'S VOICE FROM THE DEPTHS.
  In this dark realm, Mother,
  Leave me not alone!

(*A pause.*)

CHORUS (*a dirge*).[11] Not alone!—be where you may,
  For we feel we recognize you;
  Though departed from our day,
  There is no heart that denies you.   9910

---

10. I.e., Byron.
11. Details of this lament, especially those of its middle stanzas, more exactly fit Byron, for whom the lament was composed, than Euphorion. We are to understand that Euphorion signified the generalized Spirit of Romanticism, whereas Byron was the particularized incarnation of the spirit. The death of the former is at this point somewhat abruptly identified with the death of the latter in 1824 in Greece, where he had gone to fight in support of the Greek war of liberation from the Turkish empire.

How could we express our sadness?
Envying, we sing your fate,
For with you, in grief or gladness,
Song and spirit were fine and great.
　Born with Fortune's favor vested,
Lofty lineage, ample power,
From yourself all too soon wrested,
Cut down in your youthful flower;
Worldly vision keen discerning,
Sympathy with every wrong,   9920
Noble women's ardent yearning,
And unique, exalted song.
　Yet you rushed of free volition
Into nets you clearly saw,
Reckless in your opposition
Both to custom and to law.
Nonetheless the ends you sought for
Lent your noble courage force,
Glorious were the goals you fought for,
But attainment was not yours.   9930
　Who attains them?—At that dismal
Question Fate averts its eyes,
While a nation in abysmal
Doom, left voiceless, bleeds and dies.
Still, let fresh songs be raised too,
Bowed with grief no longer mourn:
Such the earth will bear anew
As it has forever borne.[12]

(*Full pause. The music ceases.*) [13]

HELEN (*to* FAUST). An ancient proverb proves itself, alas, in me:
That joy and beauty may not lastingly be joined.   9940

---

12. The Greek nation and the cause of freedom have lost their peerless poet-spokesman, but the soil of earth will inevitably engender new poets in the future.
13. The miniature opera which began at l. 9679 is now concluded. With the passing of Helen directly thereafter, "classic" and "Romantic" are disjoined, and the act concludes with verses in the "ancient" manner—without rhyme, and patterned after ancient Greek choral song.

The bond of life, like that of love, is wrenched asunder;
Lamenting both, I bid a sorrowful farewell
And throw myself one final time into your arms.
Persephoneia! Take me, as you took this youth!

(*She embraces* FAUST. *Her corporeal part vanishes, her garment and her veil are left in his arms.*)

PHORKYAS (*to* FAUST).
Hold firm to what is left to you from all of that.
This garment must not slip out of your hands.
Already demons tug upon its hems
To pull it to the underworld. Hold fast!
If it is not the goddess whom you lost,
It still is none the less divine. Use therefore   9950
This priceless gift to raise yourself aloft.
It will transport you over all things base
With speed through air, as long as you endure.
We'll meet again, far, far away from here.

(*Helen's garment is dissolved into a cloud. It surrounds* FAUST, *lifts him aloft, and carries him away.*)

(PHORKYAS *picks up Euphorion's garment, mantle, and lyre from the ground, advances to the proscenium, holds the exuvia aloft, and says:*)

A lucky find, though, all the same,
For all there may be no more flame.
But I don't feel the least bit bad.
Enough is here to start some poets going
And make their guild and members mad,
And if his talents aren't mine for bestowing,   9960
I *can* rent out the costume that he had.

(*She sits down in the proscenium against a pillar.*)

PANTHALIS. Make haste, you maidens! We are rid of all that magic
And crazy spirit-spells of that Thessalian hag,
As well as of that jinglejangle noise and nonsense
That bruised our ears and, what was worse, our inner minds.
Down now to Hades! There the Queen with solemn tread

Has hurried on before us. Where her foot has gone
Let her handmaidens' footsteps follow her at once.
CHORUS. Queens, to be sure, are happy anywhere.   9970
    Even in Hades they may take first rank,
    Proudly with their equals companioned,
    With Persephone intimately friendly.
    We, however, in the background,
    Deep in meadows of asphodel,
    With the gangling poplars
    And the sterile willows for companions,
    What amusement do we have there,
    High-thin-whistling like bats,
    Whispering, undelighted, and ghostly?   9980
PANTHALIS.
    All those who have achieved no name, nor willed great ends,
    Belong among the elements, therefore be gone!
    Desire is ardent in me to be with my Queen.
    Not merit only, devotion too preserves the self.

    (*Exit.*)

ALL. We are restored unto the light of day,
    Not as persons, of course—
    That we feel and recognize—
    But never shall we return to Hades.
    Eternally living Nature
    Makes on us spirits,   9990
    As we on her, a valid claim.
A PART OF THE CHORUS.[14] We, amid these thousand branches'
        whispering dance and rustling sway,
    Lightly lure and playfully entice the living fountains up from
    Roots to boughs; and now with leaves, and now with
        blossoms in profusion,
    We adorn our tresses flung out free to ripeness and the air.
    When the fruit is falling we assemble lusty herds and herdsmen

---

14. The four parts of the Chorus are transformed respectively into (1) trees
(Dryads), (2) mountains (Oreads and Echo), (3) brooks (Naiads), and
(4) the juice of the vine (Bacchantes).

For the plucking and the tasting as they hurry and crowd up,
And before us, as before the early gods, they all bow down.

A SECOND PART. We, beside the smooth and distant-gleaming
　　　　mirror of these cliffs,
　Nestle, cradled in the gentle waves, as we caress the stone,　10000
　Harkening to every sound, to song of birds,
　　　　to reed-flute tones,
　Or the dreaded voice of Pan, and we are ready with an answer:
　Rustlings we return as rustlings, we roll thunder back
　　　　as thunder,
　Though with crash redoubled, tripled, multiplied
　　　　in tenfold echo.

A THIRD PART.
　Sisters, we of mobile mind now hurry onward with the brooks,
　For those richly mantled hills far in the distance charm
　　　　us downward,
　Ever deeper downward, where we water with meandering waves
　First the meadow, then the pasture, then the garden by the house.
　All across that landscape slender shafts of cypress thrusting
　　　　skyward
　Trace the windings of our margin-banks and mark our
　　　　mirror-pools.　　　　　　　　　　　10010

A FOURTH PART.
　Flow, you others, as you please: we encircle and we rustle
　Round the closely planted hillside where the trellised vines
　　　　are green.
　There in every day and hour the vintager's concern and loving
　Industry give evidence of his uncertain enterprise.
　Now with mattock, now with spade, and by his hilling,
　　　　pruning, tying,
　He invokes all gods, but more than all the rest invokes
　　　　the sun-god.
　Bacchus, weakling that he is, cares little for his
　　　　faithful servant,
　Rests in arbors, lolls in grottoes, babbling with
　　　　the youngest faun.
　All he ever might require for his half-drunken reveries

Is stored up for him in wineskins and in jugs and
  earthen vessels   10020
Right and left along the cool recesses for eternal time.
Once, however, all the gods, and Helios more than all
  the others,
Airing, moistening, warming, glowing, heap the berries'
  horn of plenty,
Where the quiet vintager had worked, there life teems suddenly
With a stir down every vine row and a bustle by every stalk.
Baskets creak and buckets clatter and the laden vine hods
  groan,
All bound for the mighty wine vat and the pressers'
  lusty dance.
Thus the sacred plenitude of purebred, luscious,
  clustered grapes,
Brashly trampled, foams and spurts and squashes
  to a sodden pulp.
Now our ears are split by cymbals and the brazen crash
  of sistra: 10030
Dionysus has revealed himself out of his mysteries.
Now he comes with goat-foot satyrs and with reeling nymphs
  goat-footed,
With Silenus' long-eared beast unruly braying in between.
None are spared! The cloven claws tread down the last
  of moral scruples,
All the senses whirl and spin, and ears are deafened hideously.
To the wine cups drunkards stagger, overfull are heads
  and paunches,
One or two may still be cautious, but they only louden tumult,
For, to make room for the new, old wineskins must be
  emptied out.

(*The curtain falls.*)

(PHORKYAS *in the proscenium rises up gigantic, but steps
down from the cothurni, lays aside mask and veil, and reveals
herself as* MEPHISTOPHELES, *in order to comment—insofar
as may be necessary—by way of epilogue upon the play.*)

Act Four

High Mountains

Stark, jagged peaks. A cloud moves up, leans against the rock, and lowers itself to a projecting ledge. It divides. FAUST steps forth.

FAUST. Profoundest solitudes beholding here beneath my feet,
  I step in pensive thought upon this summit's ridge,   10040
  Releasing my transporting cloud which wafted me
  So gently over land and sea through sunny days.
  Unshattered, it detaches itself slowly from me.
  Eastward the mass strives on, up-piling as it moves;
  The eye, amazed with wonderment, strives after it.
  In motion it divides like billows, changefully.
  It seeks to take on shape.—My eye does not deceive me!—
  On sun-illumined pillows gloriously reclining,
  Of giant size and goddess-like, a feminine form
  I see! With Juno's semblance, yet like Leda, Helen,   10050
  How lovely and majestic it floats before my sight.
  Alas! Already it dissolves! Formless and vast
  It rests there in the east like distant icecaps piled,
  Reflecting in its brilliance fleeting days' high meaning.
    And yet a faint and fragile wisp of mist still hovers
  Around my brow and heart, enlivening, cool, and tender.
  It lightly rises now, and floating high and higher
  Assumes a shape. Does it delude me by its grace
  As my youth's first and highest and long-lost possession?
  The earliest treasures of my deepest heart well up;   10060
  Aurora's love with deftest touch it signifies,[1]
  That swiftly sensed, first, scarcely comprehended glance,
  Which, once possessed and held, outshone all other treasures.
  Like beauty of the soul this lovely shape floats up,

---

1. Gretchen is meant, a love from the "dawn" (Aurora) of youth.

Does not dissolve, ascends aloft into the aether,
And draws the best part of my inner self to follow.

(*A seven-league boot plants itself down. A second one follows directly.* MEPHISTOPHELES *alights. The boots swiftly
stride on of themselves.*)

MEPHISTOPHELES. I call this pre-arrived in haste!
  But tell me now, what do you mean
  By landing in this grisly waste   10070
  Where only gaping rocks are seen?
    I know it, though not just this spot, quite well,
  For actually this was the floor of hell.
FAUST. You never lack for legends with no sense,
  And right away with such stuff you commence.
MEPHISTOPHELES (*seriously*).
  When God the Lord—and I know why—sent us
  As exiles from the air down to the deep
  Where central fire acquired a heat tremendous
  And everlasting flames raged in their sweep,
  We found ourselves in an excess of light
  And in a sadly overcrowded plight.   10080
  The devils all began to cough and wheeze
  And then collectively to snort and sneeze,
  All hell was bloated with that sulphur stink.
  What gas was there! It flooded to the brink
  So that the flat crust of the lands on top,
  Thick as it was, burst with a mighty pop.
  Thus things are wrong-end-to here nowadays,
  With high peaks formed from what was once the base.
  Whence comes the doctrine rightfully asserted
  That nethermost to topmost is converted.[2]   10090
  For we escaped from slavish burning lair
  To an excess of mastery of free air.
  An open secret long and well concealed

---

2. Mephistopheles propounds essentially the same "Vulcanist" notions as
Anaxagoras advocated in the "Classical Walpurgis Night," creation of the
earth by sudden and violent combustion.

And to the nations only late revealed. (Ephesians 6:12) [3]
FAUST. To me, mountains are nobly mute, and therefore
I do not ask about their whence and wherefore.
When Nature in her workings once had founded
Herself, she took this globe of earth and rounded
It off, in peak and chasm found delight,
Piled rock on rock and mountain height on height;   10100
Then next she fashioned hills with gentle force
And downward to the valleys shaped their course;
There things grow green and thrive; she needs no mad
Convulsive cataclysms to make her glad.
MEPHISTOPHELES. So *you* say! All as clear as the sun's glory;
One who was there can tell a different story.
And I was there when, seething down below,
The abyss came flooding up in fiery tide,
When Moloch's hammer forged cliffs at a blow [4]
And scattered mountain fragments far and wide.   10110
Still strewn with alien boulders lies the land;
Who will explain such vast projectile powers?
This no philosopher can understand,
There stands the rock and there you let it stand,
All wasted is this puzzling thought of ours.—
Your loyal common folks alone, they know
And their conviction is not to be shaken,
Their wisdom came to ripeness long ago:
It is a marvel, a monument to Satan.
My pilgrim hobbles on the crutch of faith   10120

---

3. Ephesians 6:12: "For we wrestle not against flesh and blood, but against
principalities, against powers, against the rulers of darkness of this world,
against spiritual wickedness in high places." But Mephistopheles' remark is
based on Luther's translation, the final phrase of which reads: *mit den bösen
Geistern unter dem Himmel* ("with the evil spirits beneath the sky"). The
identification of Biblical source passages in Act IV was actually the work of
Friedrich Wilhelm Riemer (1774–1845), with Goethe's permission. Riemer
had been a close associate of Goethe since 1803 when he became the tutor
of the poet's son. For many years he served Goethe as secretary.
4. Moloch was an ancient Philistine god portrayed by Klopstock in *The
Messiah* (Canto II, ll. 354–71) as hammering mountains into defenses against
Jehovah. See also Leviticus 18:21, and Milton's *Paradise Lost*, Book II, ll.
43–108.

By devil's bridge, by devil's path.[5]

FAUST. It is worth while to see your point of view
And look at Nature the way the devils do.

MEPHISTOPHELES. Be Nature as she may, what do I care!
But it's a point of honor—I was there.
We're great achievers, all this ilk of mine.
Force, tumult, senselessness! Behold the sign!—
But just so I may make my meaning clear,
Don't you like any of our topside here?
You have beheld the kingdoms of the world   10130
In untold breadth of glory all unfurled; (Matthew 4) [6]
Insatiable as you are, the view
Arouses no desires in you?

FAUST. Yes! One great plan occurred to me.
Guess what.

MEPHISTOPHELES. I guess it easily.
I'd hunt me up a capital with a store [7]
Of burgher-feeding garbage at its core,
With crooked alleys, gabled peaks,
Markets selling kale and leeks,
Butchers' stalls where every prize   10140
Roast beef is full of bottle flies.
At any hour there you'd find
Activity and stink combined.
And then broad streets and spacious squares
Where you could put on genteel airs;
And lastly, where no gate confines,
Suburbs stretched in endless lines.
I'd love the coaches in their hurrying
And noisy hither-thither scurrying,

---

5. Bizarre rock formations may, in German, be termed "Devil's" construc-
tions. In Switzerland there is both a Devil's Cathedral overlooking Lake Uri
and a Devil's Bridge on the Gotthard pass.
6. Matthew 4 presents Jesus thrice tempted in the wilderness by Satan.
Verses 8–9 contain the third temptation: "Then the devil taketh him up into
an exceeding high mountain, and sheweth him all the kingdoms of the world,
and the glory of them; and saith unto him: 'All these things will I give thee,
if thou wilt fall down and worship me.'"
7. The "capital" in question is pre-1789 Paris.

And all the constant to and fro   10150
Like ant hills after overthrow.
And when I drove or rode I'd be
The hub of curiosity
Adored by hundred thousands there.
FAUST. But that would never do for me.
One likes to see a folk increase,
Comfortably gain their food and fare,
Develop, get learning, if you please—
But rebels all they prove to be.[8]
MEPHISTOPHELES. Then, with self-satisfaction filled,   10160
A lordly palace in some jolly spot I'd build,[9]
With hills, dales, woods, and fields all changed
And as a garden rearranged,
With green walls hedging velvet lawn,
Shade neat-contrived, paths ruler-drawn,
Cascades and rocks set by the pair,
And jets of fountains everywhere—
Some nobly soar in their regalities,
Most hiss and piss a thousand trivialities.
And then for prettiest ladies I'd devise   10170
Cute cozy houses small in size
For endless hours in jolly mood
Of sweet-companioned solitude.[10]
Ladies, I say; for, urbanized or rural,
I always think of them as plural.
FAUST. Modern [11] and vile! A Sardanapalus! [12]
MEPHISTOPHELES. Might one surmise your own craved boon?

---

8. These lines, written early in 1831, allude not only to the 1789 Revolution
but also to the July Revolution of 1830, when the French expelled their
Bourbon monarchs for a second and final time.
9. Versailles is meant.
10. Le Petit Trianon, which Louis XV built in the Versailles gardens for
Mme de Pompadour.
11. In Goethe's formula, "modern" was synonymous with Romantic and un-
healthy, as opposed to "classic" which was synonymous with healthy.
12. The luxurious tyrant of ancient Assyria as portrayed by Byron in a five-
act, blank-verse tragedy entitled *Sardanapalus,* dedicated "to the illustrious
Goethe."

It was no doubt sublimely daring.
Since you fly so much closer to the moon,
Could your desire be that way faring?   10180
FAUST. By no means! This earthly sphere of ours
Still offers room for feats undone.
Amazing goals shall yet be won,
For daring work I feel fresh powers.
MEPHISTOPHELES. So fame's the thing you want to win?
It's obvious you've just left a heroine.
FAUST. Rule and possession shall be sought!
Doing is all, and fame is naught.
MEPHISTOPHELES. Yet poets will arise to name
You for the ages in your fame   10190
And kindle folly at folly's flame.
MEPHISTOPHELES. No sense at all your mind inspires.
What do you know of man's desires?
Your adverse nature sharp with greed,
What does it know of man's true need?
MEPHISTOPHELES. Your will be done! However strange,
Confide your whims to me in their full range.
FAUST. My eye was drawn down to the sea below
Which surged in towers from the ocean floor,
Then it drew back and shook its waves as though   10200
To storm the broadness of the level shore.
And I was angered that the haughty flood
Should vex free mind which treasures every right
And by fierce agitation of the blood
Rouse discontent and trouble my clear sight.
I took it for mere chance, then looked once more;
The waves stood still, then rolled back from the shore
And from their proudly conquered goal withdrew;
The hour returned, the game began anew.
MEPHISTOPHELES (*ad spectatores*).
All this is nothing novel to my ears,   10210
I've known all this a hundred thousand years.
FAUST (*continuing passionately*).
Up to uncounted shores it finds access,
Barren itself and bringing barrenness;

It swells and surges, rolls and overwhelms
The desolation of those wasted realms.
There wave on blind-willed wave, one after one,
Rules and withdraws—and nothing has been done.
This could drive me to sheer despair, to sense
Unpurposed strength of untamed elements!
My spirit ventures to outfly its sphere: 10220
Here I would fight, achieve my triumph here.
    And it is possible!—Its liquid flow
Bends round all hills and must around them go.
No matter how its pride is overblown,
Against it puny heights can hold their own
And puny shallows draw it down by force.
My mind then quickly shaped its plan and course:
Win rare joy for yourself by evermore
Driving imperious sea back from the shore,
Narrow the limits of the watery deep   10230
And far within itself constrain its sweep.
I have with care detailed the steps to you.
This is my wish. Now dare to see it through!

(*Drums and martial music at the spectators' rear, from the
distance, and from the right-hand side.*)

MEPHISTOPHELES. How simple! Do you hear those drums afar?
FAUST. What! War again! No wise man wants a war.
MEPHISTOPHELES. War or peace, a wise man is at pains
    To extract from situations his best gains.
    One is alert to every favoring fact.
    Here is your opportunity. Now, Faustus, act!
FAUST. Spare me your riddles and tomfooleries.   10240
    Say what is to be done—and briefly, please!
MEPHISTOPHELES. My recent journey over several states
    Showed me our Emperor is in sorry straits.
    Well, you know how he is. With us at court
    Providing him false wealth of every sort,
    The entire world was his possession.
    He was still young at his accession
    And loved his error like a treasure—

That he could easily combine
Two things desirable and fine,   10250
His rulership and his own pleasure.
FAUST. A major error. One who would command
    Must in commanding find his true delight.
    His bosom must with lofty will expand,
    But what he wills, be hidden from men's sight.
    His slightest whisper in a faithful ear
    Becomes a deed, amazing all who hear.
    He must at all times be the worthiest.
    Enjoyment is in common with the rest.[13]
MEPHISTOPHELES. But not with him! He had his fun, did he!   10260
    His empire meanwhile came to anarchy,
    With great and small all feuding with each other,
    Expropriations, brother killing brother,
    Castle against castle, town against town,
    Guild against nobles of the crown,
    Bishops squabbling with their diocese—
    All men that met were enemies.
    Inside the churches death and murder reign,
    And outside merchants and travelers are slain.
    Thus boldness grew, and to no small extent;   10270
    To stay alive meant self-defense.—And so things went.
FAUST. They went, and limped, fell down, got up, and stumbled
    Till all together in a heap they tumbled.
MEPHISTOPHELES. No one dared to denounce such a condition,

---

13. Semantic difficulty besets the famous line, *Geniessen macht gemein*, the
question being whether Goethe used the word *gemein* in its archaic sense
of "in common" or in its rather strong modern sense of common, i.e., "vulgar,
vile, base." Witkowski quotes from Goethe's *Maxims and Reflections:* "Rulership and enjoyment [*Herrschen und geniessen*] do not go together. Enjoyment means joining others in merriment; rulership means acting for the good
of oneself and of others in the most serious sense."
    Faust, therefore, makes here only a shrewd observation about political life,
to the effect that a person in command cannot be "one of the boys" and still
maintain authority. His remark is *not* a general one to the effect that "Enjoyment vulgarizes." Much less is it a philosophic turning point in the poem, at
which Faust turns from projects dear to himself alone to projects of a socially
beneficial nature. Some critics have distorted the entire poem on the basis of
this misunderstood line.

All coveted, all got some high position,
Success and triumph graced the pettiest.
Then it got too bad even for the best.
The able ones then rose up in their might
And said, "Whoever gives us peace is lord by right.
This Emperor can't, or won't . . . Let's choose instead   10280
One who can resurrect this empire dead,
And guarantee our lives' protection,
And in a world of fresh direction
Show us sweet peace with justice wed."
FAUST. That smacks of priestcraft.
MEPHISTOPHELES.   Well, the priests *were* there—
With well-fed paunches as their chiefest care.
They took more active part than all the rest.
Revolt swelled louder still, revolt was blessed;
The Emperor whom we pleased while in his land
Now comes here for, perhaps, his final stand.   10290
FAUST. I pity him, so frank and generous.
MEPHISTOPHELES.
With life, there's hope. Come, let's look on. Let us
Deliver him out of this strait defile.
A miss this once is as good as a mile.
Who knows what dice he yet may throw? As long
As he has luck, he'll have his vassal throng.

(*They climb over the middle ridge of mountains and observe
the order of the army down in the valley. Drums and martial
music resound from below.*)

I see they've taken up a good position.
With us here, victory will crown their mission.
FAUST. But what can one expect? Deceit!
And sorcery! And hollow cheat!   10300
MEPHISTOPHELES. The wiles of war, to win thereby!
Just keep your great ideals high
But keep your purpose well in sight.
Once we have saved the Emperor's throne and land,
You will kneel down in feudal rite
And get yourself a fief of boundless strand.

FAUST. There's much you have already done,
   So now let's see a battle won.
MEPHISTOPHELES. No, you will win it! To be brief,
   You're now the General-in-Chief.   10310
FAUST. Well, that's the limit! To command
   Where there's not one thing that I understand!
MEPHISTOPHELES. Just let the General Staff provide;
   The Field Marshal is true and tried.
   Poor leaders I have long detected,
   And hence my men are precollected
   From primal mountains' primal forces;
   Lucky the one with such resources.
FAUST. What do I see there bearing arms?
   Have you called men from mountain farms?   10320
MEPHISTOPHELES. No, but like Master Peter Squenz [14]
   I've drawn the riffraff's quintessence.

   (*Enter the* THREE MIGHTY MEN.) (II Samuel 23:8) [15]

   Ah, here come my good lads for you!
   Of different ages, as you see,
   And different as to dress and armor too.
   With them you'll make out splendidly.

   (*ad spectatores*)

   Now every child adores historical
   Knights in armor and in capes;
   And since these tramps are allegorical,

---

14. In the 17th-century comedy by Andreas Gryphius, Master Peter Squenz
assembles from the dregs of the loutish peasantry men to play the roles in the
tragedy of Pyramus and Thisbe. Gryphius' long play is an elaboration of the
fifth act of Shakespeare's *A Midsummer Night's Dream*, and Peter Squenz is,
of course, Peter Quince.
15. II Samuel 23:8 (and 9): "These be the names of the mighty men whom
David had: The Tachmonite that sat in the seat, chief among the captains; the
same was Adino the Eznite: he lift up his spear against eight hundred, whom
he slew at one time. And after him was Eleazar the son of Dodo the Ahohite,
one of the three mighty men with David, when they defied the Philistines.
. . . ." The names here are Goethe's coinings in the manner of 17th-century
comedy.

They'll charm you all the better by their shapes.   10330
BULLYBOY (*young, lightly armed, colorfully attired*).
 If someone looks me in the eye
 I'll ram my fist right down his kisser, fair and square,
 And any coward running by,
 I'll grab him by the flying hair.
HAVEQUICK (*mature, well armed, richly dressed*).
 Such silly jobs are kids' tricks, breaking
 Up the comfort of your day.
 Just don't be bashful in the taking,
 The rest will come along the way.
HOLDFAST (*elderly, heavily armed, without attire*).
 There's little gained by either play.
 A large estate soon melts away,   10340
 Gone down life's river out of view.
 Taking is good, but holding on is better still;
 Give grey heads charge, and no one will
 Get anything away from you.

(*They go down the mountain together.*)

On the Promontory

*Drums and martial music from below. The
Emperor's tent is being set up.*

EMPEROR   GENERAL-IN-CHIEF
          GENTLEMEN-AT-ARMS

GENERAL-IN-CHIEF. It still seems that our plan was wisely drawn:
 To pack the entire army tight
 Within this valley where we have withdrawn;
 I trust our choice will turn out right.
EMPEROR. We soon must see what things befall.
 But I dislike the half-rout termed "withdrawal."   10350
GENERAL-IN-CHIEF. Observe, my Prince, our right flank where it seems
 We have terrain as in tacticians' dreams:
 Not steep the hills, and yet no facile slope,

Our own advantage, the enemy's false hope.
We on this rolling plain are half concealed.
No mounted force will venture such a field.

EMPEROR. I must admit it does seem best.
Here arms and hearts will meet their test.

GENERAL-IN-CHIEF. Here at mid-plain with level stretches either way
You see our phalanx eager for the fray.   10360
The pikes are glittering where they catch the rays
Of sunlight through the early morning haze.
How darkly moves the great four-square formation,
With great deeds kindling thousands' animation.
There you can judge what force this mass combines.
I trust it to break through the enemy's lines.

EMPEROR. So fair a sight has never met my eyes.
A force like this can face one twice its size.

GENERAL-IN-CHIEF. About our left flank nothing need be said.
Stout heroes man the precipice ahead.   10370
The cliffside now with weapons all ablaze
Controls the narrow pass's entrance ways;
Our enemy's disaster I foresee
In battle here joined unexpectedly.

EMPEROR. And there they come, false kinsmen who once named
Me uncle, cousin, brother, unashamed,
Who with presumption full and fuller blown
Stole strength from scepter, reverence from throne,
And then among themselves divided, raised
Their heads against me, laying empire waste.   10380
The crowd uncertain wavers to and fro,
Then plunges onward where the torrents go.

GENERAL-IN-CHIEF. A trusty scout is hurrying down the slope.
O may his mission bring us what we hope!

FIRST SCOUT. We met with complete success,
Penetrating here and there
Cunningly and with address;
Our report is not so fair:
Many now regret their treason
But they give excuses for   10390
Their inaction with the reason:

Inner ferment, civil war.

EMPEROR. Self-preservation is the egoist's creed,
    Not duty, honor, gratitude, or need.
    But will you not consider what you do?
    Your neighbor's house-fire may consume you too.

GENERAL-IN-CHIEF. The second comes, but slow is his descent,
    He trembles, and the weary man is spent.

SECOND SCOUT. First with satisfaction we
    Saw how their wrong courses veered;   10400
    Promptly, unexpectedly
    A new Emperor appeared.
    Off the mob through meadows hies
    To their several bidden goals,
    Following that flag of lies
    There unfurled.—Sheeplike souls!

EMPEROR. I hail a rival Emperor as a gain,
    I never felt till now my *right* to reign.
    As a mere soldier I have armor worn:
    For nobler purpose it shall now be borne.   10410
    At all my festivals with friend or stranger
    I lacked no splendor, but I lacked for danger.
    You had me charge at hoops in sports events
    When with a high heart I breathed tournaments,
    And had you not dissuaded me from wars, my name
    Would now shine bright with deeds and hero's fame.
    I felt my heart's true self-reliance proved
    When mirrored in that realm of fire I moved; [1]
    The element stormed at me hideously—
    A mere illusion, but how grand to me!   10420
    My fames and triumphs were mere dream forays;
    I shall make up for impious delays.

(*Heralds are dispatched to challenge the rival Emperor.
Enter* FAUST *in armor, with half-closed visor, and the* THREE
MIGHTY MEN *armed and attired as above.*)

FAUST. We come here—unrebuked, we hope—to you;

---

1. At the end of the masquerade scene of Act I, ll. 5953 ff.

Caution before distress is useful too.
You know the brooding ways of mountain races
And how they read the stone-script Nature traces.[2]
Spirits long since left the flatlands, far
Preferring mountain cliff and craggy scar.
They work through labyrinthine passes
Amid metallic fumes of noble gases,   10430
Distilling, mixing, putting to the test,
With new invention as their constant quest.
With fingers deft and quick with spirit-might
They build up forms transparent to the sight,
And then through crystal and its stillness gaze
To watch the upper world's events and ways.
EMPEROR. So I have heard. I trust you readily.
But, worthy man, why speak all this to me?[3]
FAUST. The necromant of Sabine Norcia[4] is
Most loyally devoted to your service.   10440
What ghastly fate threatened him on the pyre!
The kindling crackled, and there flickered tongues of fire,
Dry faggots all around him had been placed
With sticks of pitch and sulphur interlaced,
To man or god or devil help was vain:
Your Majesty then sprung the fiery chain.
That was in Rome. He is much in your debt;
Above your path his watch is ever set;
Oblivious of himself from that time on,
He scans the stars and depths for you alone.   10450
He bade us come to you by swiftest courses
To offer help. Great are the mountain's forces;
There Nature's work is so superbly free

---

2. The old divinities—e.g., elves, gnomes, who have retreated to remote mountains since the coming of the new religion—are expert in reading the mystic "script" in stones: cleavage lines, fossil marks, etc. The passage is deliberately mysterious in order to awe the Emperor.
3. The Emperor's manner of address seems to indicate that he does not recognize the man in the half-closed visor as Faust.
4. Norcia is a mountain town in Sabine country northeast of Rome. The necromant is non-historical. His story, doubtless known through Mephistopheles, gives Faust a pretext for coming to the Emperor.

That priests' obtuseness calls it wizardry.
EMPEROR. On festive days when guests come joyously
    And with joy share in our festivity,
    We are delighted when they throng the hall
    And by their crowding make the wide space small.
    But highest welcome to that man is paid
    Who comes with offer of support and aid   10460
    Amid a dawn where doubtful issues wait
    As over it are poised the scales of fate.
    But at this lofty moment you had best
    Withdraw your hand and leave your sword at rest.
    Respect this time, when thousands in their pride
    Contend against me or here at my side.
    Men are unique, and one who craves a crown
    Must personally deserve such high renown.
    Now may this ghost that here against us stands,
    This self-styled Emperor, this ruler of our lands,   10470
    Our nobles' lord, this general in our stead,
    Be thrust by his own fist down to the dead!
FAUST. Be that as it may be, it is unwise
    To risk your head in this great enterprise.
    Do crest and mane not on your helmet wave?
    It guards the head that cheered and made us brave.
    Without the head what would the members do?
    For if it drowses, all the rest sink too.
    If it is wounded, all the rest feel pain,
    Yet soon revive when it is well again.   10480
    The arm is swift in its display of might
    And guards the skull with lifted shield upright;
    The sword at once perceives its sacred trust,
    Wards off the blow, repeating its own thrust;
    The foot has its part in the general weal,
    On fallen foeman's neck it plants its heel.
EMPEROR. Such is my anger, I would have him dead
    And make a footstool of his haughty head! [5]

---

5. Psalms 110 begins: "The Lord said unto my Lord, 'Sit thou at my right
hand, Until I make thine enemies thy footstool.' "

HERALDS (*returning*). Little honor, small result
  Did we meet with over there,   10490
  Noble challenge they insult,
  Spurn as jesting, and declare:
  "Echo and your Emperor, they
  Died at yonder canyon wall;
  'Once upon a time,' we say
  When we think of him at all."
FAUST. It was done as your best men counseled you,
  Who at your side now stand faithful and true.
  There comes the foe. Your army is ambitious;
  Order the charge, the moment is propitious.   10500
EMPEROR. I here proclaim that I renounce command.

(*to the* GENERAL-IN-CHIEF)

  Your duty, Prince, be now in your own hand.
GENERAL-IN-CHIEF. Then let our right wing move out to the field.
  The enemy's left now starting up the climb,
  Before they take their final step, shall yield
  To tested loyalty of youthful prime.
FAUST. Then grant that this blithe-hearted hero may
  Have place among your ranks without delay,
  And so enrolled in full assimilation
  May act at his strong nature's inclination.   10510

(*He points to the right.*)

BULLYBOY (*steps forward*). No face that looks at me will turn away
  Except with broken jaws—lower and upper;
  No back will turn toward me but I will lay
  Head, scalp, and neck adangle down his crupper.
  I'll go my raging way, and then
  If your men strike with sword and club,
  The enemy and all his men
  Will drop and drown in their own blood.

(*Exit.*)

GENERAL-IN-CHIEF. Next, let our center phalanx follow slow
  And steal in all its might up on the foe;   10520

A little to the right, where they're already battered,
And soon our men will have their plan quite shattered.
FAUST (*pointing to the middle one*).
Then let this man do also as you say.
He's swift, and carries everything away.
HAVEQUICK (*steps forward*). Let thirst for booty be assigned
As partner to heroic mind,
And as the goal on which they're bent
The rival Emperor's sumptuous tent.
He will not boast for long upon his throne.
I'll take charge of this phalanx on my own.   10530

(*Enter* GRABSWAG, *a sutlerwoman, who nestles up to him.*)

GRABSWAG. Although I may not be his wife,
He's still the darling of my life.
What a harvest ripens now untold!
A woman grips when she takes hold,
Is ruthless when she robs, and hard.
To victory now! With no holds barred.

(*Exeunt.*)

GENERAL-IN-CHIEF. Against our left, as was to be expected,
The force of their right wing is now directed.
Now every man must use all strength he has
To stem their rage and win the mountain pass.   10540
FAUST (*beckons to the left*).
Then, Sire, be so kind as to note this one.
If strong men strengthen strength, no harm is done.
HOLDFAST (*steps forward*).
About the left wing have no fear,
Possession's guaranteed when I am near;
That is the sure test of the old,
No lightning bolt cleaves what I hold.

(*Exit.*)

(*Enter* MEPHISTOPHELES *coming down from above.*)

MEPHISTOPHELES. Now watch the men in armor flock
From jagged crevices of rock

And swarm and throng there at the back,
Close in on narrow path and track,   10550
And form a wall there at our rear
With shield and helmet, sword and spear,
Awaiting the sign to start their task.

(*aside, to the knowing*)

Where these come from, you must not ask.
I did not waste my time but found
And ransacked every armory around,
And these were there, on horse or standing,
Like lords of earth and still commanding;
These were the kings and knights of yore,
Now they are empty snail shells, nothing more.   10560
In them a lot of ghosts decked out for strife
Have perked the Middle Ages up to life.
If each one has an imp inside of it,
Still the effect is nice, you must admit.

(*aloud*)

Just hear them rage in angry din
And clout each other's suits of tin!
And on their standards flutter tattered rags
Too long in need of airing to be flags.
This is an ancient people, don't forget it,
Who'd love a modern scrap if they could get it.   10570

(*A tremendous blast of trumpets from above. Perceptible
wavering in the enemy army.*)

FAUST. The whole horizon has turned dark,
    With only here and there a spark
    Of ominous and ruddy light.
    Already weapons flash with blood,
    The cliff, the atmosphere, the wood,
    The very sky joins in the fight.
MEPHISTOPHELES. Our right flank strongly stands defiant,
    But towering in their midst I see
    Jack Havequick, that most agile giant,

Plying his trade, and vigorously.   10580
EMPEROR. Where I saw one arm raised before
    I now can see a dozen more.
    By natural laws it is not right.
FAUST. You've not heard of those misty ghosts
    That drift above Sicilian coasts? [6]
    Hovering clear in broad daylight
    And floating in the middle air,
    Mirrored in strange fragrance there,
    They offer an unusual sight:
    There cities waver to and fro   10590
    And gardens rise and sink below,
    Form toppling form in aether bright.
EMPEROR. But how improper! Now the head
    Of every tall spear blazes red,
    And on our phalanx' every lance
    I seem to see lithe flamelets dance. [7]
    All far too eerie, to my mind.
FAUST. Forgive me, Sire, those are the traces
    Of long-departed spirit races,
    A reflex of the Dioscuri pair   10600
    By whom all sailors used to swear; [8]
    This is their power's culmination.
EMPEROR. Tell me, to whom are we indebted
    That Nature should thus have abetted
    Our work by rarest combination?
MEPHISTOPHELES. To whom else but that noble master [9]
    Whose heart holds your fate in his breast?
    Fear lest your foes should wreak disaster
    Perturbed and made him most distressed.

---

6. The mirages called fata morgana, sometimes seen around the Strait of Messina.
7. St. Elmo's fire, a flame-shaped electrical discharge seen on masts of ships at sea.
8. The Dioscuri pair are the twin brothers, Castor and Pollux, patron divinities of sailors as well as the two stars known as Gemini, "the Twins."
9. The Necromant of Sabine Norcia of l. 10439, whom the Emperor had pardoned at the very moment of being burned at the stake for witchcraft and who in his gratitude for that pardon has sent Faust to be the Emperor's ally.

His gratitude would see you by,   10610
Even though he himself should die.

EMPEROR. They took me there in state with cry and shout;
I had new power and wished to try it out;
With no great thought the fancy took me there
To give his white beard back to the cool air.
By doing so I spoiled the clergy's sport
And, frankly, did not gain their favor for it.
Now after all these many years
I'm to collect that deed's arrears?

FAUST. Rich interest gathers on such a deed.   10620
Lift up your eyes toward the Divine,
I fancy He will send a sign.
Just watch! It will be shown with speed.[10]

EMPEROR. An eagle soars high in the skies,
A griffin hunts it as it flies.

FAUST. Watch now! The sign appears auspicious.
You know that griffins are fictitious,
So how can one work up the zeal
To tackle eagles, which are real?

EMPEROR. They fly wide circles for the best   10630
Point of attack;—now in a flash
They wheel to onset, swoop, and clash,
And rip each other, throat and breast.

FAUST. Mark there the sorry griffin's trail
As clawed and battered he now veers
And with his drooping lion's tail
Drops treetop-wards and disappears.

EMPEROR. Here be it done as there it went.
I accept the sign with wonderment.

MEPHISTOPHELES (*to the right*). Urgently repeated blows   10640
Force surrender on our foes.
As uncertain goes the fight
They crowd over to their right,
Thus disrupting by impingement

---

10. The bird omens of the following lines may be conjured, but, more likely, we may assume something like hypnotic suggestion from Faust.

The left side of their main contingent,
While our phalanx, lightning swift,
Makes a sudden rightward shift
Striking for their weakest place.—
Now like waves that tempests raise,
Equal forces foaming crash   10650
Wildly in this double clash.
Grander deed was never done,
Now the battle has been won!

EMPEROR (*on the left side, to* FAUST).
Look! Over here they harry us,
Our position stands precarious.
Not a stone do I see flung.
They have scaled the cliff's first rung
And the top ones are deserted.
Now! The foe in a concerted
Thrust has forged ahead, and has   10660
Possibly got to the pass.
Godless effort's fine conclusion!
All your skills are an illusion.

(*A pause.*)

MEPHISTOPHELES. Ah, here they come, my raven pair.
What news for us? How do we fare?
I greatly fear it's not aright.

EMPEROR. What can these wretched birds avail?
They hoist black pinions for a sail
To fly here from the cliff's hot fight.

MEPHISTOPHELES (*to the ravens*).
Beside my ears come on and perch.   10670
You never leave one in the lurch,
For your advice is always right.

FAUST (*to the* EMPEROR).
You've heard of pigeons, haven't you,
That come from furthest lands back to
Their nest and fledglings, food and roost?
The same is here with variations:
Pigeon post serves peacetime nations,

While war requires the raven post.

MEPHISTOPHELES. Their news reports a nasty fate.
Our left is caught in narrow strait   10680
There on the cliff's edge where it stands.
The nearest heights have now been climbed,
And if they take the pass behind,
We'd have a hard fight on our hands.

EMPEROR. And so I am betrayed at last!
You have me in your net, caught fast.
Right from the start I've loathed that net.

MEPHISTOPHELES. Courage! Disaster is not yet.
Patience slips the final knot.
The going's hardest at final stand.   10690
My trusty messengers I've got,
Command me now to take command.

GENERAL-IN-CHIEF (*who meanwhile has come up*).
These are the ones you let take part.
This has annoyed me from the start:
From magic comes no solid gain.
The battle can't be marred or mended,
If they began it, let them end it.
I give you back your staff again.

EMPEROR. Keep it for better times to come
Which Fortune yet to us may lease.   10700
I fear and loathe this filthy scum
And his raven intimacies.

(*to* MEPHISTOPHELES)

I cannot give this staff to you,
You do not seem the proper man;
Command, and do what you can do;
Happen then what happen can.

(*He goes into the tent with the* GENERAL-IN-CHIEF.)

MEPHISTOPHELES. Protect him then, dead stick of wood!
It would do us but little good,
It had some cross or other on it.

FAUST. And now what do we do?

MEPHISTOPHELES.   We've done it!—   10710
   Now, dusky cousins, to the mountain lake
   And greet the water nixies for my sake!
   Ask them to lend the semblance of their flood.
   By wiles of women, never understood,
   They can detach a semblance from its fact,
   Yet all will swear it is the fact.

(*A pause.*)

FAUST. Our ravens' flattery must have gratified
   The water nixies to their deepest tide.
   Already it begins to drizzle.
   By many a bald and barren rock there seems   10720
   To be the gush of full and rapid streams.
   Their victory is going to fizzle.
MEPHISTOPHELES. A greeting to which they're unused;
   The boldest climbers are confused.
FAUST. Already brooks with brooks in might converge,
   Redoubled out of gorges they emerge,
   One stream leaps as an arching bow,
   And now it lies within a stone bed flat and wide
   And rages with its foam from side to side,
   And stepwise seeks the valley down below.   10730
   What use to seek to stem this tide today?
   The mighty flood now sweeps them all away.
   I quail myself at its tumultuous flow.
MEPHISTOPHELES. Now I see nothing of these watery lies,
   Deception works for none but human eyes,
   But I'm delighted with the odd affair.
   Whole mobs of them go down with all their clowning,
   The fools imagine they are drowning,
   And while they snuff and snort on solid land
   They go through swimming motions where they stand.   10740
   Confusion now is everywhere.

(*The ravens have returned.*)

I'll tell High Master what fine work you do;
But now if you would be as masters too,

Hurry to those glowing forges
Where tireless dwarf-folk in the gorges
Beat stone and metal into sparks.
Talk much, and ask them for a fire,
A glittering, bursting, shining fire,
The kind that wildest fancy marks.
Now sheeted lightning flashes seen afar   10750
Or wink-swift plunge of furthest shooting star
Can happen any summer night;
But lightning flashes close in tangled brush,
Stars hissing on the damp ground as they rush,
Are not such a familiar sight.
These, with no great fuss, you understand,
You first request, and then demand.

(*The ravens leave. All happens as prescribed.*)

Thick dark engulfs the enemy.
Their step is in uncertainty.
Sparks glint to mislead everywhere,   10760
Blindness follows sudden glare.
It would be perfect all around
Except we lack for spooky sound.
FAUST. The hollow weapons from the armories
    Take on new strength out in the open breeze;
    They have a rattling clatter all their own,
    A wonderfully false-sounding tone.
MEPHISTOPHELES. Quite right! They're no more to be bound.
    As in the good old days, the sound
    Of knightly pommeling is rife;   10770
    Arm-guards and leg-guards equally
    As Guelph and Ghibelline you see
    Renew their everlasting strife.
    With their ancestral hates imbued
    Theirs is a never-ending feud,
    Their uproar fills the landscape far and wide.
    In every devil's festival
    Party hate works best of all
    Right to the final ghastly throes.

Now arch-repulsive din and panic   10780
Shrill-pierced and sharp with cries satanic
In horror round the valley close.

(*Tumult of war in the orchestra, passing over finally into
cheerful military music.*)

The Rival Emperor's Tent

Throne, sumptuous furnishings.

HAVEQUICK   GRABSWAG

GRABSWAG. We are the first ones here, I see.
HAVEQUICK. No raven flies as fast as we.
GRABSWAG. The treasure here! Oh, what a crop!
  Where do I start? Where do I stop?
HAVEQUICK. The place is crammed and fit to burst!
  I don't know what to seize on first.
GRABSWAG. The carpet is the thing for me.
  My quarters are so beggarly.   10790
HAVEQUICK. Here hangs a club of steel, all spiked.[1]
  And just the kind I always liked.
GRABSWAG. This scarlet mantle with golden hem,
  I've dreamed of owning one of them.
HAVEQUICK (*taking the weapon*).
  Quick work with this: you strike him dead
  And then go moving on ahead.
  You've grabbed a lot, and yet you lack
  A really good thing in your sack.
  So leave the plunder where it is
  And take one of these chests of his;   10800
  The army's pay is what they hold
  And in their bellies is pure gold.

---

1. A spike-studded sphere at the end of a club or swung on a chain, known
from its bizarre shape as a "morning star."

GRABSWAG. It weighs a murderous weight and more.
   Why, I can't lift it off the floor.
HAVEQUICK. Bend down a minute and I'll jack
   The thing up on your sturdy back.
GRABSWAG. Oh! Now I've done it! Now it's done!
   The weight has cracked my crupper bone.

   (*The chest falls and springs open.*)

HAVEQUICK. There lies the red gold in a pile.
   Quick, pick it up in rapid style.   10810
GRABSWAG (*squats down*). Quick in my lap here scoop the stuff,
   There still will surely be enough.
HAVEQUICK. There, hurry now! You've gained your goal.

   (*She stands up.*)

   O Lord! Your skirt must have a hole.
   With every move you make, you sow
   A trail of treasure as you go.
MEN-AT-ARMS (*of our Emperor*).
   Why are you in this sacred place?
   And meddling with the treasure case?
HAVEQUICK. We risked our lives! It's only fair
   For us to get our booty share.   10820
   It's what is done with enemy tents,
   And we are soldiers in every sense.
MEN-AT-ARMS. But in our circle this won't do.
   Soldiers—and thieving rabble too!
   To serve our Emperor you must be
   An honest kind of soldiery.
HAVEQUICK. Yes, honesty! We know that game,
   And "Contribution" is its name.[2]
   You're all alike and very skilled:
   "Give" is the password in your guild.   10830

   (*to* GRABSWAG)

   Be off with what you've got, my dear.

---

2. "Voluntary contributions" from civilians to occupation forces.

There's no warm welcome for us here.

(*Exeunt.*)

FIRST MAN-AT-ARMS. Say, while you had that loud-mouthed chap
  Why didn't you give him a slap?
SECOND MAN-AT-ARMS. I just can't say; my strength forsook
  Me, they had such a ghostly look.
THE THIRD. There was a dazzling of my sight,
  Things blurred, I could not see aright.
THE FOURTH. I do not quite know what to say;
  It was so hot the livelong day,   10840
  Oppressive and close with dread as well;
  Where one man stood, another fell,
  We groped, and groping struck the foe
  And they went down at every blow;
  Before our eyes hung veils of mist
  And in our ears things buzzed and hissed.
  And so it went; now here we fare,
  Not knowing quite what happened there.

(*Enter the* EMPEROR *with four sovereign* PRINCES. *The*
MEN-AT-ARMS *withdraw.*)

EMPEROR. Be with him as may be. The day is ours. Much battered,
  The enemy in flight across the plain are scattered.   10850
  Here stands the empty throne; with tapestries hung round,
  The traitor's treasure clutters and bestrews the ground.
  We, honorably protected by guards of our own,
  Imperially await the envoys to our throne.
  From every side the happy tidings come; they say
  The realm is pacified, with joy accepts our sway.
  If there was magic intermingled in our fight,
  It was ourselves alone who held our cause upright.
  Accidents do occur sometimes for warriors' good—
  From heaven falls a stone, upon the foe rains blood,   10860
  Mighty and wondrous tones from mountain caves we hear
  That lift our hearts and clutch the enemy's hearts with fear.
  The vanquished fell, the butt of never-ending taunts,
  The victor lauds his favoring God amid his vaunts.

All join with him—for this he need proclaim no word—
"Lord God, we praise Thee!" from a million throats is heard.
But I, as I have rarely done, shall turn my gaze
Upon my inner heart by way of highest praise.
A young and cheerful prince can squander youthful prime,   10870
The years teach him the value of a moment's time.
Hence I shall join at once in an association
With you four worthy men for hearth and home and nation.[3]

(*to the first*)

Yours was, O Prince, the wise arranging of my force
And at the crucial moment its heroic course;
Therefore work now as may with times of peace accord.
Chief Marshal I appoint you and confer the sword.
CHIEF MARSHAL. Your loyal army, active *in* your realm alone,
Shall at your borders soon assure you and your throne;
Then be it ours upon that day of festival
To dress the banquet in your great ancestral hall.   10880
I'll bear it at your side, I'll bear it you before,
Of highest majesty the escort evermore.
EMPEROR (*to the second*).
You who high valor and sweet courtesy unite,
Be my Chief Chamberlain; the duty is not slight.
You are the head of all my household retinue,
Where I find servants bad from bickering and ado;
Let your example be henceforth revered with pride
Of how lord, court, and all may be well satisfied.
CHIEF CHAMBERLAIN.
To further my lord's noble thought will bring me grace:

---

3. The next hundred lines recapitulate in detail the proceedings of investiture ordained by Charles IV in 1356 for the Holy Roman Emperor. In actuality, the Elector of Saxony became Chief Marshal; the Margrave of Brandenburg, Chief Chamberlain; the Count Palatine, Chief Steward; and the King of Bohemia, Chief Cupbearer. These were the four temporal princes who elected the Emperor. To their number were added the three spiritual princes, the Archbishops of Mainz, Trier, and Cologne. The present scene introduces only one Archbishop and his see is unspecified. At age sixteen Goethe had witnessed precisely this ceremony in Frankfurt on the Main, in 1765.

To aid the best and even not to harm the base, 10890
Without guile to be clear, calm without treachery.
If you, Lord, know my thoughts, it is enough for me.
If Fancy may anticipate that feast, be sure
That when you go to board, I'll proffer the golden ewer,
Your rings I'll hold, that in the time of your delight
Your hand may be refreshed, as I enjoy your sight.
EMPEROR. I feel too grave to think about festivities,
     And yet—we do have need of glad activities.

(*to the third*)

You I appoint Chief Steward. Henceforth to your charge
I give the chase, the poultry yard, and farms at large. 10900
Provide me with my favorite dishes all year through
As seasons bring them in, and dressed with care by you.
CHIEF STEWARD. Strict fasting shall be both my duty and my wish
     Until I set before you a fine savory dish.
     The kitchen staff shall work to bring far products near
     And to anticipate the seasons of the year.
     You seek no table heaped with products forced and rare,
     Of simple, wholesome ones you'd sooner have your fare.
EMPEROR (*to the fourth*).
     Since festivals perforce are being here debated,
     Young hero, as my Cupbearer be now elevated. 10910
     Chief Cupbearer, let it be your duty now to see
     Our cellar stocked with splendid wine most generously.
     Yourself be temperate, and amid the animation
     Be not misled by the allurements of the occasion.
CHIEF CUPBEARER.
     Youth's self, my Prince, if confidence in it be shown,
     Will stand, before one notices, to manhood grown.
     I too transport myself to that grand festive day;
     I'll sumptuously set out an imperial buffet
     With vessels of great price, gold ones and silver too,
     And yet reserve the fairest cup of all for you— 10920
     A clear Venetian glass where solace lingers long,
     Which precludes drunkenness, yet makes the wine more strong.

One may be overconfident with such a treasure;
But more protective, Sire, are your restraint and measure.
EMPEROR. What in this solemn hour I have conferred on you
You have heard trustingly from faithful lips and true.
The Emperor's word is great and all his gifts secure,
Yet confirmation still requires his signature.
To draft such documents in proper form with speed
I see the proper man come just at time of need.   10930

(*Enter the* ARCHBISHOP—HIGH CHANCELLOR.)

When trusted to the keystone is the vaulted dome,
It is assured for all the ages yet to come.
You see four princes here, and we have just ordained
The rules whereby this court and household are maintained.
But now as for the realm in its entirety,
Upon all five be that responsibility.
In their estates they shall all others far excel;
The heritage of those who from our standard fell
I give them that their borders may thereby expand.
You faithful ones, I grant you many a fair land   10940
And the high privilege of further growth as well
As chance may cause you to inherit, buy, or sell.
As landlords be it granted and ordained for you
Without impediment to have your rightful due.
As judges you will set the verdict's final seal
And from your seats supreme there shall be no appeal.
Then tax and toll and tithe, custom and lien and fee,
Levies on salt and coinage shall be your property.
To prove my gratitude and make it fully known,
I elevate you next to my imperial throne.   10950
ARCHBISHOP. Now in the name of all of us, profoundest thanks.
You make us strong and firm and strengthen your own ranks.
EMPEROR. To you five, dignities still higher I shall give.
I still live in my realm and hope there long to live;
But my ancestral line attracts my thoughtful gaze
Away from eager efforts toward more sombre ways.
In time I too must go forth from this world of men:
Be it your duty to choose my successor then.

Lift him upon the sacred altar with crowned head; [4]
Close then in peace what was so shocked with storm and
    dread.   10960

HIGH CHANCELLOR.[5]

With pride deep in their hearts, yet humble-postured now
The foremost princes of the earth before you bow.
As long as loyal blood still courses through our veins,
We are the body over which your high will reigns.

EMPEROR. Now in conclusion let these my decisions be
By writing ratified in perpetuity.
As lords, maintain your holdings as to you seems best,
Save only that no parcel be sundered from the rest,
And howsoever you increase what we provided,
The eldest son must have the holding undivided.   10970

HIGH CHANCELLOR.

For our weal and the realm's I shall at once commit
This all-important statute to a parchment writ.
Seal and fair copy then the Chancery shall procure,
To be confirmed, Sire, by your sacred signature.

EMPEROR. Then I dismiss you, so that everyone now may
Assemble and reflect on this momentous day.

(*The temporal* PRINCES *withdraw.*)

THE SPIRITUAL ONE (*remains and speaks loftily*).

The Chancellor has gone, the Bishop has remained,
By sense of solemn warning to your ear constrained.
His father's heart is troubled for you with distress.

EMPEROR. What fear besets you in this hour of happiness?   10980

ARCHBISHOP. With what a bitter pang at this so joyous hour
I see your sacred head thus leagued with Satan's power.
Assured upon your throne, so it appears, quite true,
But flouting God the Lord, and Holy Pontiff too.
The latter when he learns of it will overwhelm
With sacred fire both you and your sin-ridden realm.

---

4. Such was literally the custom immediately upon coronation.
5. I.e., the Archbishop, whose speeches are labeled according to which part
of his dual role he is filling.

For he has not forgotten how last-minutely
On coronation day you set that sorcerer free,
How from your diadem, to Christendom's disgrace,
That head accursed received the first ray of your grace.   10990
But beat your breast and in your impious success
Give back a middling mite to things of holiness.
That spacious knoll where once your tent stood in defiance,
Where evil spirits to protect you made alliance,
And where you lent your ear unto the Prince of Lies,
With humble mind grant it for sacred enterprise—
Together with the mountain and the forest dense
And heights that furnish pastures green with succulence,
Clear lakes well stocked with fish, and countless brooks that flow
In swift and winding courses to the vale below;   11000
Then the broad vale itself, with meadow slope, and plain.
Thus you show your remorse, and absolution gain.

EMPEROR. I am so terrified by this grave fault of mine
That I accept whatever boundaries you assign.

ARCHBISHOP. First, let the place defiled, by sin so desecrated,
Be to the service of the Highest consecrated.
Swift in the mind's eye massive walls rise and aspire,
Already morning sun illuminates the choir,
The structure grows, assumes Cross-form, the nave gains height,
And as it lengthens fills the faithful with delight;   11010
With fervor they throng through the noble entrance doors,
The first peal of the bells down hill and valley pours,
Sounding from lofty towers as heavenwards they strive,
And penitents for new-created life arrive.
And at the consecration—may that day come soon!—
Your presence will there constitute the highest boon.

EMPEROR. So great a work must make my good intentions known.
I wish to praise the Lord and for my sins atone.
Enough! My mind already feels edification.

ARCHBISHOP. As Chancellor I now require formalization.   11020

EMPEROR. Prepare a document which will such grants define
In favor of the Church, and I with joy will sign.

ARCHBISHOP (*takes his leave, then turns around again at the door*).
And you will further dedicate all revenue

To the advancing project, tithes and taxes due
Forever. Proper upkeep needs consideration
And heavy costs are run up by administration.
Construction being in so wild a spot, your duty
Will also be to share the gold you took as booty.
Moreover we shall need, as I cannot disguise,
Timber and lime and slate and such far-off supplies.   11030
Poor folk will do the carting, their pulpits guiding them;
The Church will bless such works and those providing them.

(*Exit.*)

EMPEROR. The sin I took upon me is a grievous weight;
    Those sorry sorcerers have me in a parlous strait.
ARCHBISHOP (*returning once again, with a profound bow*).
    Forgive me, Sire, but to that ill-reputed man
    The empire's coast was given; he is under ban
    Unless you guarantee the Church in this case too
    All tithes and taxes and all levied revenue.
EMPEROR (*with annoyance*).
    The land does not exist yet, it lies in the sea.
ARCHBISHOP.
    The time will come with patience and with regency.   11040
    Your promise may, for all we care, be left in force.

(*Exit.*)

EMPEROR (*alone*).
    I could dismember my whole empire by this course.

Act Five

Open Country

A TRAVELER. Those dark lindens, well I know them,
    Standing in their strength of age;

Once again I pass below them
After such long pilgrimage.
Here, then, is the place at last;
That same cottage sheltered me,
On those dunes I once was cast
By the tempest-ridden sea.   11050
I should like to bless my hosts,
Such a kindly, sturdy pair,
Who were old then on these coasts,
All too old still to be there.
What good folk they used to be!
Shall I knock? Call out?—Good greeting!
If your hospitality
Still brings good to strangers meeting.

BAUCIS (*a little old woman, very ancient*).
Welcome, comer, softly speak,
Do not break my husband's rest;   11060
From his sleep the old man, weak,
Draws brief waking's rapid zest.

TRAVELER. Tell me, Mother, is it you
Who once saved the young man's life?
To whom now fresh thanks are due,
Both to husband and to wife?
Are you Baucis, who to my
Half-dead lips new life once gave?

(*The husband appears.*)

You Philemon, who saved my
Drowning treasure from the wave?   11070
By the flames of your quick fire,
By your bell's sweet silver sound,
That adventure grim and dire
Safe conclusion from you found.
    Let me step down here a way,
Gazing on the boundless sea;
Let me kneel and let me pray,
For my heart oppresses me.

(*He walks forward on the dune.*)

PHILEMON (*to* BAUCIS). Hurry now to set the table
    Underneath the garden trees.   11080
    Let him go, he is not able
    To believe what his eye sees.

(*standing next to the* TRAVELER)

That by which you were mistreated,
Wave on wild wave foaming, lies—
See you!—as a garden treated,
As a scene from Paradise.
Aging, I was not on hand
To be helpful as before;
While my strength waned, waves were banned
Far out from the former shore.   11090
Clever lords set daring wights
Dredging ditches, damming, diking,
Curbing ocean's sovereign rights,
Ruling it to their own liking.
Field on field, see! green and sweet,
Meadow, garden, forest, town.—
Come, however, come and eat,
For the sun will soon be down.—
Sails loom there against the west
Seeking port and safe repair;   11100
Like the birds, they know their nest,
For the harbor now is there.
Thus at furthest range of sight
Lies the blue fringe of the main,
All the rest to left and right
Is a thickly peopled plain.

(*In the garden. The three at table.*)

BAUCIS. You are silent? do not eat
    Though your lips are starved for food?
PHILEMON. He is marveling at the feat;
    Tell him how those matters stood,   11110
BAUCIS. As for marvels, this was one!
    Even now it troubles me;

For the whole affair was done
Not as rightful things should be.
PHILEMON. Should the Emperor be to blame
　If he let him have this shore?
　Did a herald not proclaim
　That with trumpets at our door?
　Near our dunes they first were seen;
　Swiftly tents and shacks appeared.   11120
　But amid the verdant green
　Soon a palace was upreared.
BAUCIS. Daytimes, noisy varlets might
　Vainly hack and delve away;
　Where the flamelets swarmed by night
　Stood a dike the following day.
　Human sacrifices bled,
　Nighttime heard them shriek and wail,
　Seawards rolled the tides of red,
　Morning saw a new canal.   11130
　Godless is he, and he still
　Wants our cottage, wants our trees,
　As a swaggering neighbor, will
　Have us as dependencies.
PHILEMON. Yet he offered us a fine
　Homestead on the new-made land.
BAUCIS. Trust no bottom dredged from brine,
　On your headland make your stand!
PHILEMON. To our chapel come away
　Final sunlight to behold,   11140
　Let us sound the bells and pray
　Kneeling to the God of old.

Palace

Spacious ornamental garden; a large, straight canal. FAUST *in extreme old age,*[1] *walking and meditating.*

LYNCEUS THE TOWER WARDEN (*through a speaking-trumpet*).
The sun sinks down, the final ships
Are moving briskly into port.
One mighty barque makes for the slips
On the canal close by your court.
The colored ensigns flutter faster,
The sturdy masts stand tall and straight,
The boatman hails you as his master,
And Fortune hails you as most great.   11150

(*The little bell rings out on the dune.*)

FAUST (*starting up*). Accursed bell![2] In profanation,
Like spiteful shot it wounds my ear;
Before me lies my vast creation,
Vexation dogs me at the rear;
The envious sound reminds me still
Complete possession is not mine,
The brown hut on the linden hill,
The moldering church is still not mine.
If I desired its coolness, I
Would seek its alien shade with fear,   11160
A thorn to my foot, a thorn to my eye.
Would I were far away from here!
TOWER WARDEN (*as above*). How gaily comes the boat with sails
Before the gentle evening gales.
How swift its course looms up with hoard
Of boxes, bales, and chests aboard.

---

1. "It is my intention that Faust, as he appears in the fifth act, shall be exactly a hundred years old . . . ," Goethe to Eckermann, June 6, 1831.
2. Goethe detested the sound of bells.

(*A splendid ship richly and colorfully laden with produce
of foreign climes.* MEPHISTOPHELES. *The* THREE MIGHTY
MEN.)

CHORUS. And so we land,
    And so we meet.
    Our master and
    Our lord we greet.   11170

(*They disembark; the wares are brought ashore.*)

MEPHISTOPHELES. So we have proved ourselves, content
    If we our master's praises earn.
    We had but two ships when we went
    But now have twenty on return.
    The mighty things that we have wrought
    Show by the cargo we have brought.
    Free ocean is mind's liberation:
    Who there cares for deliberation!
    What counts is sudden grasp and grip
    To catch a fish or catch a ship,   11180
    And once you have control of three,
    A fourth is hooked quite easily;
    The fifth is in a sorry plight
    For you have might and therefore right.
    "What" is the question, never "How."
    If I don't mix up stern and bow,
    Then business, war, and piracy
    Are an unsevered trinity.
THE THREE MIGHTY MEN. No thanks we get!
    We get no thanks!   11190
    Our master thinks
    Our cargo stinks.
    He makes a face,
    He takes no pleasure
    For all we bring
    Him royal treasure.
MEPHISTOPHELES. Expect no more.
    What do you care?

After all,
You got your share.   11200
THE MEN. That was only
In sport. Now we
Demand to share
Equally.
MEPHISTOPHELES. First arrange
In hall on hall
These costly items
One and all.
Once he sees
The precious sight,   11210
Once he reckons
Costs aright,
He won't skimp
You in the least,
He'll give the fleet
Feast on feast.
The gay birds come with morning's tide [3]
And for them I can best provide.

(*The cargo is removed.*)

MEPHISTOPHELES (*to* FAUST). With solemn brow, with somber glance
You take these noble gifts of Chance;   11220
Your wisdom has been glorified,
The shore and ocean are allied,
In swift career from shore the sea
Accepts your vessels willingly;
Admit that now your arm extends
From here to earth's extremest ends.
Here it began, on this spot stood
The very first poor shack of wood;
A little ditch was scraped in loam
Where now the oar leaps swift with foam.   11230
Your own high thought, your servers' toil

---

3. The "gay birds" (*bunte Vögel*) are presumably the other nineteen colored
ships.

Have won the prize from sea and soil.
From here . . .
FAUST.   O be that "here" accursed!
It's just the thing I mind the worst.
I must tell you as my ally
I cannot bear it, I am maimed
In heart, blow after blow, thereby,
And telling you, I am ashamed.
Those old folks up there ought to move,
I'd like those lindens for my seat;   11240
Those few trees not my own disprove
My worldwide claims and spell defeat.
There for the prospect I would now
Build scaffolding from bough to bough
And open vistas looking on
All the things that I have done,
And have in one view all combined
This masterpiece of human mind,
With shrewd sense spurring active feats
Throughout far nations' dwelling seats.   11250
    This is the torment of the rack,
In wealth perceiving what we lack.
The sound of bells, the lindens' bloom
Give me the sense of church and tomb;
The will that nothing could withstand
Is broken here upon this sand.
What can I do about it? Tell
Me! I am frantic from that bell.
MEPHISTOPHELES. Such nuisance cannot help but gall
You, that is only natural.   11260
Who would deny it? Far and near
That jangling grates on every ear.
And that damned ding-dong-diddle, why!
It shrouds the cheerful evening sky,
It butts in on your every turn
From baby-bath to funeral urn,
As if between the ding and dong
Life were a mere dream all along.

FAUST. Resistance, stubborn selfishness
  Can spoil the lordliest success,   11270
  Until in angry pain one must
  Grow tired at last of being just.
MEPHISTOPHELES. Why should you fuss about things here
  When colonizing's your career?
FAUST. Then go and get them off my path!—
  You know the pretty homestead where
  I mean to move the aged pair.
MEPHISTOPHELES. We'll move them out to their new ground
  Before there's time to look around.
  For any violence that's done   11280
  A pretty place will soon atone.

(*He gives a shrill whistle.*)

(*Enter the* THREE MIGHTY MEN.)

Come! Do as your lord bids you do.
Tomorrow he will feast the crew.
THE THREE. The old man met us with a slight.
  A nice feast is no more than right.

(*Exeunt.*)

MEPHISTOPHELES (*ad spectatores*).
  What happed of old now haps anew:
  For there was Naboth's vineyard too. (I Kings 21.) [4]

Deep Night

LYNCEUS THE TOWER WARDEN (*on the watchtower, singing*).
  For sight I was born,
  For viewing was set;

---

4. I Kings 21 relates how Ahab, King of Samaria, sought to buy a vineyard from Naboth the Jezreelite, and when the latter refused to sell, became so vexed that he would not eat. Thereupon Queen Jezebel had Naboth falsely accused of a crime, arrested, and killed, and Ahab took possession of the vineyard.

To watchtower sworn,   11290
I love the world yet.
I gaze out afar,
I see what is near,
The moon and the star,
The forest and deer.
Thus splendors of ages
On all sides I view;
As I found them all good,
So I find myself too.
You fortunate eyes,   11300
For all you have seen,
Whatever it was,
It still was so fine!

(*A pause.*)

Not alone for my delight
Am I stationed here so high;
In the darkness of the night
Monstrous horror strikes my eye!
I see sparks that dart and blow
Through the linden trees' twin night,
Strong and stronger twists the glow   11310
As the wind's draft fans it bright.
Hah! the cottage is on fire!
Walls that moist and mossy stand;
Speedy rescue they require
And no rescue is at hand.
Oh! those kindly aged folk,
Always careful with their fire,
Now are victims of the smoke
In disaster dread and dire!
Flames flame up, red stands the shape   11320
Of that black and mossy shell;
If those good folk could escape
From that wildly burning hell!
Tongues of lightning lightly leap,
Through the leaves and branches sweep;

Withered boughs, they flare and burn,
Falling with a sudden blaze.
Must my eyes so much discern?
Alas for my far-sighted gaze!
Now the chapel goes down crashing,   11330
Crushed by weight of limb and bough,
Pointed flames go writhing, flashing
To the highest treetops now.
Scarlet burns each hollow tree
To the very roots at last.

(*A long pause. Song.*)

What was once a joy to see
After centuries has passed.
FAUST (*on the balcony, toward the dunes*).
Above me what a whimpering dirge.
The word is here, the sound is late;
My warder wails; my deep thoughts urge   11340
That this deed was precipitate.
But if the lindens have been wrecked
And left as charred stumps hideously,
A lookout I shall soon erect
To face out toward infinity.
I also see the new house where
In peace the aged couple stays,
Who, sensing my kind wish and care,
Will now enjoy their latter days.
MEPHISTOPHELES AND THE THREE (*below*).
We come at a good rapid trot,   11350
But go off well, the thing did not.
We rapped, we knocked, we rapped again,
And still they would not let us in.
We battered and we knocked away,
The rotten door fell in and lay;
We shouted out in threat and call
But found they heard us not at all.
As happens in such cases, they
Just would not hear, would not obey;

We had no time to waste or spare   11360
And soon we cleared them out of there.
The couple's sufferings were slight,
And all they did was die of fright.
A stranger there put up a show
Of force and had to be laid low.
Amid the brief course of the match
Some scattered coals got in the thatch,
And now the fire is blazing free
To the cremation of all three.

FAUST. To all my words then you were deaf!   11370
I wanted an exchange, not theft.
Upon this ruthless action be
My curse! Share in it equally!

CHORUS. The ancient saying still makes sense:
Bow willingly to violence;
But if you bravely make resistence,
Risk house and home—and your existence.

(*Exeunt.*)

FAUST (*on the balcony*).
The stars conceal their gaze and shining,
The fire sinks smoldering and declining;
A faint gust fans it fitfully   11380
And wafts its smoke and scent to me.
Too rashly bidden, too rashly done!—
What glides so spectrally toward me?

Midnight

Enter FOUR GREY WOMEN.

THE FIRST. My name is Want.
THE SECOND.   My name is Guilt.
THE THIRD. My name is Care.
THE FOURTH.   My name is Distress.

THREE (*together*). The door is fast-bolted, we cannot get in,
   The owner is wealthy, we'll never get in.
WANT. Here I turn to shadow.
GUILT.   Here I have no place.
DISTRESS. From me is averted the much-pampered face.
CARE. You sisters, you can not and may not get in,   11390
   But Care through the keyhole will make her way in.

   (CARE *disappears*.)

WANT. O sisters, grey sisters, away let us glide.
GUILT. I'll be your ally and walk close at your side.
DISTRESS. And close on your footsteps will follow Distress.
THE THREE. Hard rides now the cloud, disappears now the star,
   From behind, from behind, from afar, from afar
   There comes now our brother, and his name is—Death.

   (*Exeunt*.)

FAUST (*in the palace*). Four I saw come, but only three go hence,
   And of their speech I could not catch the sense.
   "Distress" I heard, and like caught breath   11400
   A gloomy rhyme-word followed—"Death." [5]
   It sounded hollow, hushed with ghostly fear.
   I've still not fought my way into the clear.
   If I could sweep my path from magic free
   And quite unlearn the spells of sorcery,
   If I could face you, Nature, as a man,
   It then would be worth while to be a man.
      Such was I once, before I cursed to doom
   Both myself and the world in that dark room.
   The air so teems with monsters ghostly shaped   11410
   That no one knows how they can be escaped.
   If *one* day laughs amid sweet reason's light,
   Dreams weave us round with cobwebs that same night.
   If vernal fields make our glad hearts beat faster,
   A bird croaks; and what does he croak? Disaster.
   Ensnared by superstition soon and late,

---

5. In German, *Not* and *Tod*.

It works and shows itself and hints our fate,
And daunted we stand helpless in the gloom.
　　The door creaks, yet no one comes in the room.

(*shaken*)

　　Is someone here?
CARE.　　　　　　　　Well may you ask. I am.　　　　　　11420
FAUST. And you, who are you then?
CARE.　　　　　　　　　　But here I am.
FAUST. Go back, then!
CARE.　　　　　　　I am in my proper station.
FAUST (*angered at first, then appeased; to himself*).
　　Then watch yourself and speak no incantation.
CARE. If no ear for me were found,
　　In the heart I still would sound.
　　In my ever changeful guise
　　Fearful force I exercise,
　　On the highroad, on the sea
　　Bearing you dread company,
　　Ever found though sought for never,　　　　　　　　11430
　　Cursed and yet cajoled forever.
　　　　But have you never yet known Care?
FAUST. I have but raced on through the world;
　　I seized on every pleasure by the hair;
　　What did not satisfy, I let go by,
　　And what eluded me, I let it be.
　　I have but craved, accomplished my delight,
　　Then wished anew, and so with main and might
　　Stormed through my life; first grandly and with passion,
　　But now more wisely, in more prudent fashion.　　　11440
　　I know enough about the world of men,
　　The prospect yonder is beyond our ken;
　　A fool is he who that way blinks his eyes
　　And fancies kindred beings in the skies.
　　Let him stand firm here and here look around:
　　This world is not mute if the man is sound.
　　Why need he stray off to eternity!
　　What he knows here is certainty.

So let him walk along his earthly day:
If spirits haunt him, let him go his way,   11450
Find joy and torment in his forward stride,
And at each moment be unsatisfied.

CARE. One whom I can once possess
Finds the whole world profitless;
Eternal gloom descends and lies,
For him suns neither set nor rise;
With external senses whole,
Darkness dwells within his soul,
On the earth there is no treasure
He can grasp or own with pleasure,   11460
He starves in plenty, and for him
Weal and woe become mere whim;
Be it bliss or be it sorrow,
He postpones it till the morrow;
Living in the future ever,
He succeeds in no endeavor.

FAUST. Stop! You will not succeed with me!
I will not hear such folly. Hence!
Hearing this evil litany
Could addle wisest men's good sense.   11470

CARE. Whether he should go or stay,
His decision seeps away;
At broad highways' midmost he
Gropes by half-steps hesitantly.
He gets deep and deeper lost,
Sees all things as purpose-crossed,
Burdening himself and others,
Breathing deeply as he smothers,
Neither dead nor yet alive,
Succumb he can't, nor yet survive.   11480
Galling "O, I should!" combined
With his painful "Never mind . . . ,"
Liberated and suppressed,
Semi-sleeping with no rest,
He is fixed in place and groomed
For the hell to which he's doomed.

FAUST. Unholy specters! Thus you have betrayed
  The race of humans time and time again,
  And out of days of mere indifference made
  A filthy snarl and tangled net of pain.   11490
  From demons one can scarcely be quite free,
  Not to be broken are the spirit ties,
  And yet your power, great as it may be,
  O Care, I will not recognize.
CARE. Then feel it now, as I behind
  Me leave my curse and turn from you.
  Since human beings all their lives are blind,
  Now, Faustus, be you just so too!

  (*She breathes upon him. Exit.*)

FAUST (*blinded*). The night seems deep and deeper to be sinking,
  Bright light still shines within myself alone.   11500
  I hasten to enact what I am thinking;
  No will imposes save the master's own.
  Up, servers, from your couches, every man,
  And gladly see the boldness of my plan!
  Take up your tools, swing shovel now and spade!
  Bring instantly to flower the lands surveyed.
  Strict ordering and swift diligence
  Will yield the fairest recompense.
  In this great task one mind commands
  Sufficiently a thousand hands.   11510

Great Forecourt of the Palace

Torches.

MEPHISTOPHELES (*as Foreman leading the way*).
  This way! This way! Come on! Come on!
  You shambling lemur batches,[1]

---

1. Lemurs are the night-walking spirits of the unrighteous dead from classical mythology, not the nocturnal monkey-like mammals who inherited the

You semi-natures made of bone
And frazzled sinew patches.

LEMURS (*in chorus*). We come at call, we are on hand,
And as we heard by half,
There is, they say, a spacious land
That we're supposed to have.

Sharp-pointed stakes, here's your supply,
Here is the measuring chain;   11520
The summons was for us, but why,
Quite slips our minds again.

MEPHISTOPHELES. No fussing now for elegance,
Just go by your own measurements;
The tallest should lie down upon the ground,
The rest can lift the sod up all around.
Just sink the longish trench four-sided
With which our forebears were provided.
Out of the palace to the narrow home,
That is the sorry end to which we come.   11530

LEMURS (*digging and making droll gestures*).
When I was young and lived and loved,
Methought that was full sweet,
When frolic rang and mirth was loud
There I would stir my feet.

Now spiteful Age has struck at me
And hit me with his crutch;
I stumbled on a yawning grave—
Why must they open such! [2]

---

name. Wall paintings in an excavated grave at Cumae show them as skeletons with some bits of flesh and muscle still left on them. (See illustrations.)
In 1812 Goethe had written an article entitled *Der Tänzerin Grab* on the
subject of the Cumae tomb drawings.

2. The Lemurs' grave-digging song is imitated from an old English ditty
which Goethe found in Bishop Percy's *Reliques of Ancient English Poetry*
(1765) and of which Shakespeare had long before assigned a variant form
to the grave-diggers in *Hamlet*, Act V.

The English versions are as follows:

Percy	Shakespeare
I loth that I did love,	In youth when I did love, did love,
In youth that I thought swete,	me thought it was very sweete:

FAUST (*coming from the palace and groping his way by the doorposts*).

O how this clang of spades delights my soul!
These are the many who perform my toil   11540
And reconcile the earth with its own soil
And for the waves set up a goal
And gird tight limits round the sea.

MEPHISTOPHELES (*aside*). And yet all your activity
Serves us, with dam and dike creation;
For Neptune the great water devil
You are preparing one big revel.
You all are lost in every wise—
The elements are our allies,
And things head for annihilation.   11550

FAUST. Foreman!

MEPHISTOPHELES. Here!

FAUST.   By any means you may,
Get workmen here by throngs and hordes,
Incite with strictness and rewards,
Entice them, urge them, give them pay!
I want to have reports each day of how
The trench proceeds that we are starting now.

MEPHISTOPHELES (*half-aloud*).
They talked no trench when last they gave
Reports to me, but of a grave.[3]

FAUST. A swamp there by the mountain lies,
Infecting everything attained;   11560
If that foul pool could once be drained,

As time requires; for my behove
Methinks they are not mete.

For Age with steling steps
Hath clawde me with his crowch;
And lusty Youthe awaye he leapes,
As there had bene none such.

To contract O the time for a my behove,
O me thought there was nothing meete.

But Age with his stealing steps
  hath caught me in his clutch:
And hath shipped me intill the Land,
  as if I had never beene such.

3. A play on the two German words *Graben* ("trench") and *Grab* ("grave") allows Mephistopheles to clown the lines by claiming that *someone* has misheard directions.

The feat would outstrip every prize.
For many millions I shall open spaces
Where they, not safe but active-free, have dwelling places.
Verdant the fields and fruitful; man and beast
Alike upon that newest earth well pleased,
Shall settle soon the mighty strength of hill
Raised by a bold and busy people's will,
And here inside, a land like Paradise.
Then let the outer flood to dike's rim rise,   11570
And as it eats and seeks to crush by force,
The common will will rush to stem its course.
To this opinion I am given wholly
And this is wisdom's final say:
Freedom and life belong to that man solely
Who must reconquer them each day.
Thus child and man and old man will live here
Beset by peril year on busy year.
Such in their multitudes I hope to see
On free soil standing with a people free.   11580
Then to that moment I could say:
Linger on, you are so fair!
Nor can the traces of my earthly day
In many aeons pass away.—
Foresensing all the rapture of that dream,
This present moment gives me joy supreme.

(FAUST *sinks back; the* LEMURS *take hold of him and lay
him down on the ground.*)

MEPHISTOPHELES. No joy could sate him, no bliss could satisfy,
He chased his changeful vision to the last;
This final moment, paltry, void, and dry,
The poor wretch wants to hold it fast.   11590
Time masters him who could withstand
My power, the old man lies here on the sand.
The clock has stopped—
CHORUS.   Has stopped. As death-still
        as the midnight.

The clock hand falls.

MEPHISTOPHELES.   It falls. And "it is finished." [4]

CHORUS. And all is over.

MEPHISTOPHELES.   Over! Stupid word!
    Does it make sense?
    Over, and sheerest naught, total indifference!
    All this creating comes to what?
    To make things as if they were not.
    "A thing is over now!" What does that mean?   11600
    The same as if the thing had never been,
    Yet circles round and round as if it *were*.
    Eternal Emptiness I still prefer.

Burial

LEMUR (*solo*). O, who so badly built this house [5]
    With shovel and with spade?

LEMURS (*chorus*). For you, mute guest in hempen shroud,
    It's far too finely made.

LEMUR (*solo*). And who so badly decked the hall?
    Of tables, chairs, not any?

LEMURS (*chorus*). The lease was short-termed. After all,   11610
    Believers are so many.

MEPHISTOPHELES. Here lies the body; if the spirit strays,
    I'll soon confront it with that blood-signed scroll—
    They have so many methods nowadays
    To cheat the Devil of a soul.

---

4. John 19:30.
5. Again the Lemurs sing in imitation of the grave-diggers of *Hamlet*, V. The first quatrain here echoes Shakespeare's:

> A Pickhaxe and a Spade, a Spade,
>   for and a shrowding-Sheete:
> O a Pit of Clay for to be made,
>   for such a Guest is meete.

The rest is Goethe's own.

Our old way seems to give offense,[6]
Our new way they do not condone; [7]
Once I'd have done it all alone,
Where now I have to have assistants.
   We're badly off on every score.   11620
Old rights, time-honored ways of yore—
There's nothing left that you can trust.
Time was, a soul rode up the final gasp;
Then as with quickest mouse I'd make a thrust
And whoops! there she would be tight in my grasp.
Now they hang back, won't leave the dismal place,
Inside the filthy corpse they tarry late;
The elements in mutual hate
Expel them finally by sheer disgrace.
And if I fret for days and hours now,   11630
There still are questions of When? Where? and How?
Old Death has lost his rapid strength; about
The very Whether? there has long been doubt.
On dead-stiff limbs I've doted often, then
A false alarm and off they walked again.

(*Fantastic and imperious conjuring gestures.*)

Come on, then! On the double! All of you
Lords of the straight, lords of the crooked horn,
Chips off the ancient block, you devils born,
And bring the jaws of hell up with you too.[8]
For hell has many, many sets of jaws,   11640
By different ranks and standings it devours,
But we won't haggle over rules and laws
From now on in this final game of ours.

(*The hideous jaws of hell open on the left.*)

---

6. Violent murder in order to get the soul, as in the old *Faust Book*.
7. The "modern way" of patiently waiting for the decomposing body to release the soul.
8. From this point forward the scene adopts the stage uses of the medieval mystery plays: heaven is understood to be on the right and perhaps above; the earth is in the middle; on the left a huge head of beast or devil or whale represents hell by monstrously gaping jaws, fierce teeth, and a fire-belching gullet, down which sinners pass.

The eyeteeth gape; up from the vaulted pit
There seethes a tide of flame in raging flow,
And through the steam-clouds in the back of it
I see the fiery city all aglow.[9]
The red tide breaks in surges to the very teeth,
The damned swim, hoping rescue, up the bath;
But the hyena champs them back beneath   11650
And they retrace in pain their burning path.
There's much more off in nooks you may perceive,
The scariest things jammed in the tightest space!
It's good to scare the sinners: they believe
It's only an imaginary place.

(*to the* FAT DEVILS *with short, straight horns*)

You paunchy rascals with the cheeks that burn,
All fattened up on brimstone, how you glow!
Short dumpy things with necks that cannot turn,
Watch for a gleam of phosphor here below:
That will be Soul, or Psyche with the wings; [10]   11660
Once they're pulled off, she's just a nasty worm;
I'll set my seal on her, then off she slings
Down to the whirlwind and the fiery storm!
   Those nether regions [11] watch with care,
You lard-guts! Duty bids you so.
For if she deigns to dwell down there
We do not just exactly know.[12]
The navel's where she likes to hide—
Watch there, she might whisk past you to one side.

(*to the* LEAN DEVILS *with long, crooked horns*)

You fancy bucks, you giant fuglemen,   11670
Keep sawing air, don't stop from first to last.
With arms and sharp claws spread, be ready when

---

9. The infernal city of Dis, probably as conceived by Dante, who locates it
in the sixth circle of hell.
10. *Psyche*, the Greek word for "soul," represented as a butterfly.
11. I.e., of Faust's body.
12. It is possible that the soul inhabits below the waistline.

The fluttering thing on fleeing wing comes past.
She surely must find her old house a bore;
Then too, the "genius" also wants to soar.[13]

(*Glory from above, on the right.*)

THE HEAVENLY HOST. Follow, you envoys [14]
Of celestial joys
In unhurried flight:
Sinners forgiving,
Dust to make living;   11680
Down from above
Tokens of love [15]
To all creatures giving
In hovering flight.

MEPHISTOPHELES. Discords I hear and mawkish whimpering
Coming from topside with unwelcome light.
It's that half-boy-half-maiden simpering
In which a canting taste takes such delight.[16]
In our depravity, you know, we meant
And planned destruction for the human race;   11690
The most disgraceful thing we could invent
Would, in *their* worship, be in place.[17]
    Just see the minions mince and charm!
They've snitched a lot of souls in just this wise
By turning our own weapons to our harm;
They're devils too, though in disguise.
To lose out now would mean eternal shame;
Up to that grave, then, and cling fast to same!

---

13. *Genius*, the Latin word for the spirit that inhabits the human body.
14. "Envoys" (*Gesandte*) literally translates the Greek *aggeloi* ("angels," i.e., "messengers").
15. We translate Robert Petsch's gloss to this line which literally says: "Friendly traces" (*Freundliche Spuren*). All the angel choruses of this scene are elliptical to the point of incomprehensibility. Nor are they meant to be verbally transparent; rather, they must approximate the quality of rapturous music, clear to the heart but not to the mind.
16. Popular representations of angels, so mawkishly sweet as to make it impossible to decide whether they are male or female.
17. Such effeminate boys deserve to be raped, in Mephisto's opinion.

CHORUS OF ANGELS (*strewing roses*).

Refulgence of roses
Fragrance expending!   11700
Tremulous, swaying,
Life-force conveying,
Branchlet-bewisped
Buds now unclasped,
Bloom fullest and best.
   Springtime arise,
Crimson and green;
Bring Paradise
To him at his rest.

MEPHISTOPHELES (*to the* SATANS).

Why do you duck and wince? Is that hell's play?   11710
Stand firm and let them strew away.
Back to your stations, gawks, and stay!
They fancy they are going to snow
Hot devils under with their posy show.
Your breath will melt and shrivel that away.
Now blow, you puff-cheeks! [18] There! Enough! Enough!
You've bleached and blanched them with your huff and puff.—
Don't blow so lustily, shut snout and nose!
O, now you've overblown your blows.
You must learn when to stop! When will you learn!   11720
They're shriveled, but they're going to scorch and burn!
As bright and poisonous flames they're drifting near! [19]
Stand firm against them, crowd together here!
All courage vanishes, strength ebbs away.
The devils scent strange fires' caressing play.

ANGELS (*chorus*). Blossoms of joy,

Flames of high gladness,
Love they expend,

---

18. "Puff-cheeks" stands for the plural of untranslatable *Püsterich* (from *pusten*, "to blow, to puff"), the name of an ancient low-German folk divinity who blew out fires. The image is like those puff-cheeked heads representing the "winds" in the corner designs of old maps.

19. I.e., the roses, which are drifting through the air like snowflakes. The devils' poisonous breath has fanned them into flames.

Bliss they portend,
Heart as it may: 11730
Truth in their words,
Clear aetherwards
Eternal hordes,
Limitless day! [20]

MEPHISTOPHELES. O curses on this ninny band!
Upon their heads the Satans stand.
The louts turn cartwheels down the path
And plop ass-backwards into hell.
Take comfort from your well deserved hot bath!
I'm staying on here for a spell.—   11740

(*knocking aside the drifting roses*)

Will-o'-the-wisps, begone! Shine as you will,
Once caught, you're little turds of jelly still.
Why flutter so? Just go away! And quick!
Like pitch and sulphur to my neck they stick!

ANGELS (*chorus*). What you may not possess
You must abjure;
What gives your heart distress
You must not endure.
If it crowds in by force,
We must take valiant course.   11750
Love only lovers
Brings to the door.[21]

MEPHISTOPHELES. My head and liver burn, my heart is rent.

---

20. L. 11730: "according to the heart's desire" (Witkowski). Ll. 11731–34:
"The eternal hosts of Heaven shed about them limitless light ('day') with
the truth and with the 'aether'—the light, pure atmosphere which surrounds
them" (Witkowski); "Words of love shed light for all the heavenly hosts,
who dwell in the clear aether" (Robert Petsch). By "aether" Goethe meant
the "divine aither" of the Greeks, the "blazing element," the dazzling blue
of upper (Mediterranean) atmosphere where the gods dwell beyond the
reach of cloud and vapor. See W. K. C. Guthrie, *The Greeks and Their Gods*
(Boston: Beacon Press, 1955), pp. 207–8.

21. "When the element of love produces its effect, the moment for action
has arrived" (Witkowski). Each rose is an embodied "ardor of love" or
"flame of love," and once Mephisto feels *these*, he finds their sting more
painful than hell-fire.

A super-devilish element!
Worse stinging far than hell's own fire.—
That's why you lift laments so dire,
Unhappy lovers, who forever crane
Your necks to look at loved ones who disdain.
   Me too! But what makes my head that way tend?
Am I not sworn to fight them to the end?   11760
I used to find them such a hateful sight.
Has something alien pierced me through and through?
I love to have these darling boys in view.
What keeps me now from cursing them tonight?
If *I* am gulled at this late date,
Who will then as "the Fool" be styled?
These handsome rascals that I hate
Seem just too lovely, and I am beguiled.—
   Now pretty lads, come tell me true:
Are you too not of Lucifer's family?   11770
You're just so nice, I'd like a kiss from you,
I feel you're just the thing for me.
It comes so cozily, so naturally,
As if we'd met a thousand times before,
So kitten-sly and raffishly;
With every glance you charm me more and more.
Come closer, grant me just one glance!
ANGELS. But why do you fall back when we advance?
We move up closer; meet us if you can.

(*The* ANGELS, *moving about, come to occupy the entire
space.*)

MEPHISTOPHELES (*who is forced into the proscenium*).
You call *us* spirits damned, but you   11780
Are the real witch-masters tried and true,
For you seduce both maid and man.—
O cursed adventure! Do you claim
This is the element of love?
My entire body is aflame,
I hardly feel the burning from above.—
You hover to and fro; come down and stir

Your lovely limbs in ways a trifle worldlier.
Your seriousness is most becoming for a while,
But just for once I'd like to see you smile;   11790
That would give me a pleasure unsurpassed.
I mean the kind of looks that lovers cast.
A flicker of the lips, and there we'll have it.
I like you best, there, lad so slim and tall,
But clergy-looks don't go with you at all.
Give me a glance that's just the least bit avid.
Then, too, you could more decent-nakedly appear;
Those flowing robes are all too morals-emphasizing—
They turn their backs—a glimpse now from the rear!—
The little monkeys are so appetizing!   11800
CHORUS OF ANGELS. Turn, flames of love,
    Toward clarity;
Be the self-damned [22] saved
    By verity;
Self-redeemed be they
    From evil's sway,
Blessed to be
    In the totality.
MEPHISTOPHELES (*getting control of himself*).
    What is this!—I am raw with sores all round,
A very Job, shocked at the state he's in   11810
And yet triumphant as he looks within
Himself and trusts himself and his own kin;
My noble devil parts are safe and sound,
The love infection breaks out through the skin.
Now that the cursed flames are out, I call
Down curses, as you well deserve, on one and all!
CHORUS OF ANGELS. Sacred ardors!
    Whom you surround
    Has full life found
With the good, in bliss.   11820
    Ascend up allied
    And praises wreathe,

---

22. I.e., through lovelessness.

In air purified
The spirit may breathe!

(*They ascend, bearing with them* FAUST'S *immortal part.*)

MEPHISTOPHELES (*looking about*).
  What's this?—Now where can they have gone?
  You juveniles have caught me by surprise
  And off to heaven with the booty flown.
  So that's why they were nibbling at this grave!
  They've made off with my great and unique prize,
  The soul which he to me once pledged and gave,   11830
  They've smuggled it away, that's what they've done.
    To whom can I go for redress?
  Who will get me my well-earned right?
  You have been fooled in your old days. Confess,
  However, you deserve your sorry plight.
  I have outrageously mismanaged,
  A mighty outlay—shamefully!—is lost,
  Absurd amour and common lust have managed
  To catch the canny Devil to his cost.
  But if the one of wise experience got   11840
  Himself involved in that mad, childish game,
  Still, slight the folly was most surely not
  Which caught him at the last and overcame.

Mountain Gorges

Forest, cliff, wilderness.[1] *Holy anchorites,*[2]
*disposed up the mountainside, stationed in
the ravines.*

CHORUS AND ECHO. Woodlands, they falter toward it,
  Cliffsides, they weigh against it,

---

1. The scene designation applies properly only to the opening lines of the
"finale." Almost from the outset, and surely by l. 11890 and the indication

Root-snarls, they clutch into it,
Tree dense to tree up along it.
Waves in a foaming welter,
Nethermost cave yields shelter.
Lions in silence rove 11850
Friendly and tame around,
Reverencing holy ground,
Love's holy treasure-trove.

PATER ECSTATICUS [3] (*floating up and down*).
Ecstasy's ceaseless fire,
Love's bond of hot desire,
Seething heart of pain,
Foaming joy divine.
Arrows, transfix me!
Lances, enforce me!
Cudgels, batter me! 11860
Lightning bolts, shatter me! [4]
So the All may utterly
Abolish the Nullity,
Gleam the fixed star above,
Essence of endless love.

---

of "middle region," the "stage scenery" is in movement, causing the mountain gorges and the very earth to recede, and carrying both action and spectators upward in an ascension past the limits of earth into the upper atmosphere by l. 11997, and by l. 12032 into limitless vistas of blue sky.

The "it" of the opening lines is sky, viewed vertically upward from the depths of a mountain gorge, somewhat as a rapt viewer of a Baroque church ceiling might gaze into the perspectives of a vast painting of the Assumption of the Virgin until he feels lifted up out of the church and into the heavens themselves. (See last illustration.)

2. The holy anchorites are the hermits of the early Christian centuries who withdrew to the wilderness to devote their entire existences to the adoration of God. Goethe here makes them symbols of intense aspiration utterly possessed by love.

3. "Patres" is a general term for the early Fathers of the Christian Church; Goethe blends them poetically with the holy anchorites. "Pater ecstaticus" was an epithet historically bestowed upon Saint Anthony, Johann Ruysbroek, and Dionysius the Carthusian; flying (levitation) was a capacity attributed to Saint Francis Xavier, Peter of Mantua, and Filippo Neri. Goethe's Pater ecstaticus blends all these into a single type-figure of ecstasy and thirst for the infinite.

4. These four lines denote the ecstasy of martyrdom, rapturous welcome of torment in order to escape from mortality to the consummate bliss of heaven.

PATER PROFUNDUS [5] (*lower region*).

As rocky chasms here beneath
On deeper chasms base their thrusts,
As countless brooklets, shining, seethe
In downward leaps and foaming gusts,
As upward to the air above   11870
The tall tree in its power strains,
Just so, it is almighty Love
That forms all things and all sustains.

There is a roaring all around
As if woods were billows under gales,
And yet there falls with gracious sound
The wealth of waters to the vales,
As if bound to bring moisture there;
The lightning flash of flaming dart
That struck to purify the air   11880
And purge infection from its heart—
All are Love's messengers proclaiming
Creation's ceaseless workings multifold.
May my soul also know such flaming,
Where spirit, now perplexed and cold,
In gross net of the senses caught,
Is riveted in chains that smart.
O God! Assuage and calm my thought,
Illuminate my needy heart!

PATER SERAPHICUS [6] (*middle region*).

What cloud of dawning at this minute   11890
Parts the pine trees' floating hair?
Do I guess what lives within it?
Here is a youthful spirit choir.

CHORUS OF BLESSED BOYS. Tell us, Father, where we wander,

---

5. "Pater profundus," "the mystical Father," was an epithet applied to Saint Bernard of Clairvaux and to Thomas of Bradwardyne. Here the adjective "profundus" is taken literally, so that this Pater is placed in the "lower region." His lines, like some of the preceding lines, imply an underlying metaphor of "the cathedral of Nature" as conceived by the Supreme Architect who understands mass and strain and thrust. Love, he says, has the force of gravity and of heliotropism.

6. "Pater seraphicus" has been applied as an epithet to Saint Francis of Assisi.

Tell us, kind man, who we are.
Happy are we, and so tender
Is the life that we all bear.
PATER SERAPHICUS. Children, you were midnight-born,[7]
Sense and spirit half attained;
From your parents you were torn,   11900
For the angels you were gained.
One who loves, before your faces
You feel present; draw, then, near;
Rugged earthways left no traces
On you as you now appear.
Come you down, and with the loan
Of my earthly-bounded eyes,
Using them as if your own,
View the land that round you lies.

(*He takes them into himself.*) [8]

These are trees; these, cliffsides jutting;   11910
That, a waterfall that plunges,
By its awesome down-course cutting
Short the steep path as it lunges.
BLESSED BOYS (*from within*).
This is mighty to behold,
But a place in which to grieve,
Chills us with a terror cold.
Good man, kind man, let us leave.
PATER SERAPHICUS. Rise to higher spheres; mature
Unobserved by any eyes,
As, in ways forever pure,   11920
God's own presence fortifies.
For throughout free air above
Spirits taste no other food
Than revelation of eternal Love
Which nurtures to beatitude.

---

7. I.e., dead at birth.
8. The souls of the infant dead actually enter into the heart of the Pater seraphicus and speak from within.

CHORUS OF BLESSED BOYS (*circling about the highest peaks*).
    Gladly entwine
    Hands in a ring,
    With feelings divine
    Dance and sing.
    Trust in the lore   11930
    Divinely told,
    Him you adore
    You shall behold.

ANGELS (*soaring in the higher atmosphere, bearing the immortal
       part of* FAUST).
    Delivered is he now from ill,
    Whom we a spirit deemed:
    "Who strives forever with a will,
    By us can be redeemed." [9]
    And if in him the higher Love
    Has had a share, to meet him
    Will come the blessed host above   11940
    And warmly greet him.

THE YOUNGER ANGELS. Loving-holy penitents,
    By the roses that they rained,
    Helped us to the triumph gained
    In this task of eminence,
    Helped to win this treasured soul.
    Demons yielded from their goal,
    Devils at our onslaught fled.
    Spirits felt Love's pain instead
    Of their usual hellish anguish;   11950
    Bitter pangs could even vanquish
    The arch-Satan's self. Exult!
    Joyous is the high result!

---

9. The quotation marks do not indicate a quotation, but are Goethe's own punctuation to signify the particular importance he attached to the words so enclosed. Goethe told Eckermann, June 6, 1831: "In these verses is contained the key to Faust's redemption [*Rettung*]: within Faust himself an ever loftier and ever purer activity to the very end, and from above the eternal Love coming to his assistance. This is completely in accord with our religious concept, according to which we do not become blessed through our own strength merely, but through the additional divine grace."

THE MORE PERFECTED ANGELS. Earth remnants still arrest us,
 Hard to endure;
 Were he made of asbestos,[10]
 He is not pure.
 When once strong spirit force
 Subsumes man's elements,
 No angels can divorce   11960
 The quintessence
 Of dual self made one;
 The two parts allied
 Eternal Love alone
 Can then divide.[11]
THE YOUNGER ANGELS. Misted at rocky height
 Spirits appear
 Moving closer in sight
 As they haste along.
 The cloudlets grow more clear,   11970
 I see a lively throng
 Of blessed boys,
 From earth's oppression free,
 Joined in a ring,
 Glad with the joys
 Of spheres so beauteously
 Decked with new spring.
 With these let him begin,
 And, rising with them, win
 Perfection gradually.[12]   11980

---

10. "Asbestos," the "unburnable" material, considered as the closest approximation to the stuff of immortal spirits. Modern utilitarian use of the material has stripped the word of the semi-magical connotations it once had.

11. Not even the More Perfected Angels have yet attained the stage where their earthly components have been entirely blended with their spiritual components to form the single perfect "substance" of Love. (An analogy with chemistry seems to underlie the concept.) Once the synthesis has been accomplished, however, nothing can reverse the process except "Eternal Love alone."

12. The Younger Angels are less far advanced toward ultimate perfection than the More Perfected Angels, but further advanced than the Blessed Boys, those souls of infants born dead or dying in infancy. To this elementary group the spirit of Faust is now assigned to begin his curriculum of perfec-

THE BLESSED BOYS. With joy we receive
 Him in pupa stage;
 In him we achieve
 Angelic pledge.[13]
 Unravel the cocoon strands
 Around him rife.[14]
 Great he already stands
 With holy life.

DOCTOR MARIANUS [15] (*in the highest, purest cell*).
 The prospect here is free,
 The mind uplifting.   11990
 There ladies move past me
 Upward drifting.
 The Glorious One beneath
 Her starry wreath
 In splendor there is seen,
 All Heaven's Queen.

(*enraptured*)

 Highest mistress of the world,
 Admit me, in this blue
 Tent of heaven here unfurled,
 To thy mystery's view.   12000

---

tion. Just as Homunculus had to dissolve himself into the sea and recapitulate all stages of human evolution in order to achieve the supremely beautiful form of the human body, so Faust must shuffle off his mortal body, begin with the lowest spiritual forms, and recapitulate all stages of spiritual evolution in order to achieve supremely beautiful spiritual form. The afterlife is the spiritual counterpart of individual life and generic life on earth, a cosmic version of "ontogeny recapitulates phylogeny."

13. The pledge that they too will evolve into "angels" along with Faust.

14. As with Mephisto's reference at ll. 11659–61, the human body and human life are made parallel to the ugly caterpillar, and the human soul and life after death are made parallel to the splendid butterfly that develops out of the caterpillar and flies blessedly away. The present lines reverse Mephisto's use of the metaphor.

15. "Doctor," the medieval term meaning "learned teacher," is used rather than "pater," which suggests the early Christian era; "Marianus" means "pertaining to the Blessed Virgin Mary"; hence, teacher of the mysteries of the Virgin Mary.

What earnestly and tenderly
Stirs men's hearts, approve,
And all things they bring to thee
In holy joy of love.
  Courage fights invincibly
Till thou bidd'st it cease,
Ardor mellows suddenly
As thou givest peace.
Virgin pure in fairest sense,
Mother, of all honor worth,   12010
Queen in eminence,[16]
Of gods the peer by birth.
  Around her dense-
ly gather clouds,
Penitents
In gentle crowds
About her knees,
Bright aether breathing,
Mercy beseeching.
  To thee, inviolate,   12020
It is not denied
That the easily misled
Should in thee confide.
  In their weakness swept away,
Hard they are to save;
Who of his own power may
Wrest chains from lust's slave?
Whose foot will not fail him fast
On the slippery path?
Who is not deceived at last   12030
By a cozening breath?

(*The* MATER GLORIOSA *soars forth.*)

---

16. Just as the entire "finale" of *Faust* is inspired by the last pages of Dante's
Paradiso, so the figure of the Doctor Marianus recalls Saint Bernard, whose
enraptured prayer to the Virgin opens Canto XXXIII of the *Paradiso: Vergine
madre, figlia del tuo figlio* ("Virgin mother, daughter of thy Son," l. 1),
Donna ("Lady," l. 13), *Regina* ("Queen," l. 34).

CHORUS OF FEMALE PENITENTS.

Thou soarest on high
To eternal realms.
O hear our cry!
Peerless art thou,
Merciful art thou!

MAGNA PECCATRIX (St. Luke 7:36).[17]

By the love which at the feet
Of thy transfigured Son God-born
Shed tears as though of balsam sweet
Despite the Pharisee's high scorn;   12040
By the alabaster ointment box
Shedding fragrance down on Him,
By the hair and flowing locks
Which then dried each sacred limb—

MULIER SAMARITANA (St. John 4).[18]

By the well whereto were driven
Abram's herds, and by the well-dips
Whence a cooling drink was given
To the Saviour's thirsting lips;
By the spring of purity

---

17. In Luke 7:36–50 is told the story of an unnamed woman sinner ("peccatrix")—the word "magna" seems to be Goethe's addition—who came to the
house of a Pharisee where Jesus was having dinner, bringing with her an
alabaster box of ointment, ". . . and stood at his feet behind him weeping,
and began to wash his feet with tears, and did wipe them with the hairs of
her head, and kissed his feet, and anointed them with the ointment" (verse
38). The Pharisee thought to himself (verse 39): "This man, if he were a
prophet, would have known who and what manner of woman this is that
toucheth him: for she is a sinner." But Jesus tells him that she has done the
things which he, as host, had neglected to do, and adds (verse 47): ". . . her
sins, which are many, are forgiven, for she loved much: but to whom little
is forgiven, the same loveth little."

18. In John 4:1–26 Jesus stops at Jacob's well in the hostile territory of
Samaria and there asks a Samaritan woman ("mulier Samaritana") to draw
water for him to drink, saying that he could give her living water if she knew
the gift of God, and that such water once drunk will be "a well of water
springing up into everlasting life." This woman is also a great sinner, apparently, for Jesus tells her quite rightly that she has had five husbands "and
he whom thou now hast is not thy husband." Yet He converses graciously
with her and to her declares himself to be the Messiah.

Which from thence outpours and flows   12050
Ever clear and copiously
As through all the worlds it goes—
MARIA AEGYPTIACA (*Acta Sanctorum*).[19]
By the consecrated tomb
Where the Lord was laid of yore,
By the arm that beckoned doom,
Thrusting me back from the door;
By the forty-year repentance
That I lived in desert waste,
By the blessed farewell sentence
That upon the sand I traced—   12060
ALL THREE. Thou who never dost deny
Help to those whose sins are great,
And eternally on high
Dost repentance elevate,
Grant to this good soul as well,
Who did only once transgress,
Hardly knowing that she fell—
Grant remission limitless.[20]
UNA POENITENTIUM, ONCE NAMED GRETCHEN (*nestling close*).
Deign, O deign,
Amid thy reign   12070
In radiance,
To look in mercy on my joy.[21]
My once beloved,
No more troubled,

---

19. The legend of St. Mary of Egypt (Maria Aegyptiaca) is told in the *Acta Sanctorum* (*Acts of the Saints*) under the heading "April 2." She was a prostitute who on a visit to the Church of the Holy Sepulcher in Jerusalem felt herself thrust back from the church door by the force of an invisible hand. Conscience-stricken, she withdrew to a desert and spent forty-eight years in rigorous mortification of the flesh. In the moments before her death she wrote a message in the sand, asking the monk Socinius to bury her and to pray for her soul.
20. Accepting the poet Richard Dehmel's emendation of *ungemessen* ("limitless") rather than *angemessen* ("appropriate").
21. These lines echo Gretchen's prayer of ll. 3587 ff. more exactly than translation can convey, transforming them from grief to gladness.

Joins me in joy.

BLESSED BOYS (*drawing near in a circling movement*).

So soon he has outgrown us
In might of limb;
Reward will soon be shown us
For care of him.
Too little time we sojourned   12080
For life to reach us,
But those things he has learned,
And he will teach us.

A PENITENT, ONCE NAMED GRETCHEN.

Amid the noble choir of Heaven
He hardly knows that self of his,
He guesses not the new life given,
Yet of the holy host he is.
See how he wrests himself out free
Of his integument of earth,
How in ethereal raiment he   12090
Shows youthful vigor in new birth.
Vouchsafe to me to be his guide,
His eyes still dazzle with new day.

MATER GLORIOSA. Rise, and in higher spheres abide;
He will sense you and find the way.

DOCTOR MARIANUS (*prostrate on his face, in adoration*).

Gaze upward to that saving glance;
Toward beatitude,
Gentle penitents, advance,
Be changed with gratitude.
Let every better sense be keen   12100
To do thee service duly;
Virgin, Mother, and our Queen,
Goddess, help us truly.

CHORUS MYSTICUS.[22] All transitory
Things represent;
Inadequates here

---

22. Originally marked "Chorus in Excelsis," this "mystical chorus" is sung by all the choirs of heaven together. Its intricately meshed rhymes are only partially reproduced in translation.

Become event,
Ineffables here,
Accomplishment;
The Eternal-Feminine
Draws us onward.[23]   12111

FINIS

---

23. These lines can be interpreted as follows. All transitory things are—as in Plato's doctrine—imperfect reflections of divine realities. Man's utmost striving while on earth is necessary, but it requires the complement of heavenly assistance (see above, l. 11937*n*). Transition from earthly form into eternal form is accomplished, though no words are adequate to describe it. The Eternal-Feminine is the unfailing inspiration, the moving force giving impetus in earthly life as in the life hereafter to strive from lesser stages upward toward infinite perfection. That perfection is Love; in Dante's final line of the *Paradiso*, "the Love that moves the sun and the other stars."

The Library of Liberal Arts